India Higher Education Report 2020

India Higher Education Report 2020 critically analyzes the role played by the state, industries, and higher-education institutions in the employment and employability of educated youth in India. The book discusses a wide range of topics such as employability skill gaps of higher-education graduates; curriculum and skills training systems; formal and informal modes of skill formation; crisis of jobless growth in India; migration, education, and employment; dimensions of gender, caste, and education; general, technical, and professional education; vocationalization; qualifications framework, and skills certifications; curriculum and pedagogy in higher education for skill development; industry–academia linkages; entrepreneurship education and executive education; and sustainable employment.

The book focuses on theoretical insights, empirical evidence, and recent data on key issues and challenges of higher-education graduate employment in a knowledge economy driven by the unprecedented expansion of higher education and increasing digitization. It offers successful cases of institutional responses, examples of policy and practices as well as perspectives of different stakeholders such as employers, employees, teachers, and students in response to present trends in the changing landscape of higher education. Their attitudes about the future demands of the job market for the youth, who are new to the workforce across sectors, subject disciplines, and gender are also explored.

This volume will be an important resource for scholars, teachers, and researchers of higher education, public policy, political economy, political science, labour studies, economics, education, sociology in general as well as for policymakers, professional organizations and associations, civil society organizations and government bodies.

N.V. Varghese is Vice-Chancellor, National Institute of Educational Planning and Administration (NIEPA) and the founding director of the Centre for Policy Research in Higher Education at NIEPA, New Delhi, India.

Mona Khare is Professor and Head, Department of Educational Finance, Centre for Policy Research in Higher Education, National Institute of Educational Planning and Administration, New Delhi, India. She is associated with various government bodies and international education forums in research, consultancy, and advisory activities.

India Higher Education Report 2020

Employment and Employability of Higher Education Graduates in India

Edited by
N.V. Varghese and Mona Khare

Routledge
Taylor & Francis Group
LONDON AND NEW YORK

First published 2022
by Routledge
2 Park Square, Milton Park, Abingdon, Oxon OX14 4RN

and by Routledge
605 Third Avenue, New York, NY 10158

Routledge is an imprint of the Taylor & Francis Group, an informa business

British Library Cataloguing-in-Publication Data
A catalogue record for this book is available from the British Library

Library of Congress Cataloging-in-Publication Data
A catalog record for this book has been requested

ISBN: 978-0-367-71283-9 (hbk)
ISBN: 978-0-367-74530-1 (pbk)
ISBN: 978-1-003-15834-9 (ebk)

DOI: 10.4324/9781003158349

Typeset in Galliard
by Apex CoVantage, LLC

Contents

List of figures viii
List of tables x
Preface xiii
Acknowledgements xv
List of abbreviations xvii
List of contributors xxii

1 Employment and employability of higher-education graduates: an overview **1**
N.V. VARGHESE AND MONA KHARE

PART I
Economic growth and employment of the educated **23**

2 The crisis of jobless growth in India **25**
RAJAT KATHURIA AND UJJWAL KRISHNA

3 On the persistence of informal work and self-employment in India **37**
S. CHANDRASEKHAR AND VASAVI BHATT

4 Migration, education, and employment in India **51**
S. IRUDAYA RAJAN

5 Declining labour-force participation in India: does education and training help? **68**
S. MADHESWARAN AND J.K. PARIDA

6 **Trends in employment and unemployment in India: dimensions of gender, caste, and education** 89
RAJENDRA P. MAMGAIN AND KHALID KHAN

PART II
Graduate employability and skills mismatch 109

7 **Skills mismatch of higher-education graduates in India: factors determining employability quotient** 111
MONA KHARE

8 **General, technical, and professional education: employability skill gaps** 132
RITIKA SINHA

9 **Education, skills mismatch, and wage differentials** 153
SAHANA ROY CHOWDHURY, CATHERINE BROS, AND SAYOREE GOOPTU

PART III
Education and skill formation 167

10 **India's National Skills Qualifications Framework and employment: the promise and the reality** 169
SANTOSH MEHROTRA

11 **Curriculum and pedagogy in higher education for skill development** 196
NIKHIL AGARWAL AND APRANT AGARWAL

12 **Skilling India: vocational orientation to higher education** 207
PANKAJ MITTAL

13 **Skill universities in India** 219
S.K. SHUKLA AND KOMAL RAGHAV

14 **Informal modes of skill formation** 230
VINEETA SIROHI

PART IV
Education–industry relationship **247**

15 Industry–academia linkages in India's technical education sector 249
RAJ AGRAWAL AND ANUJA PANDEY

16 Refuelling entrepreneurship education in India: a case study 268
KAVITA SAXENA

17 Executive education and career advancement: sustainable employment 290
NEETU JAIN AND AJAY K. JAIN

Index 317

Figures

2.1 Gap between profits and workers' wages in net value added in industry 26
3.1 Scatter plot of share of household industry workers in a state and logarithm of per capita state domestic product 40
3.2 Share of top-ten states in all-India total number of household industry workers in 1991 and 2011 41
3.3 Distribution of workers by class in household industry (HHI) and non-household industry (NHHI) 42
3.4a Distribution of main workers in household industry (HHI) and non-household industry (NHHI) by age group in 2011 42
3.4b Distribution of marginal workers in household industry (HHI) and non-household industry (NHHI) by age group in 2011 42
3.5 Distribution of workers by education in manufacturing in household industry (HHI) and non-household industry (NHHI) 43
3.6 Distribution of workers by education in household industry (HHI) and non-household industry (NHHI) in 2011 43
4.1 Indian-origin students enrolled in institutions abroad, 2012–2017 63
5.1 Labour-force participation rate (LFPR) by sector and gender groups in India, 1983–2018 70
5.2 Open unemployment scenario (based on UPSS) in India, 2012–2018 83
5.3 Disheartened labour force (based on UPSS) in India, 2012–2018 84
6.1 Trends in WPRs 91
6.2 Trends in gender gap in WPRs 91
6.3 Trends in WPRs by social groups 92
6.4 Education-specific WPRs by gender: 2017–2018 93
6.5 Changes in nature of employment, 1983 to 2017–2018 95
6.6 Education-specific nature of employment, 2017–2018 96

6.7 Education-specific workers working as helpers in household enterprises 97
6.8 Structure of employment by social groups, 2017–2018 (%) 98
6.9 Trends in unemployment rate among graduate youths (15–29 years) 104
6.10 Trends in unemployment rate among diploma-holder youths (15–29 years) 105
7.1 Employer–employee gap in foresight on future job market 126
7.2 Employer responses on future importance of skills 127
8.1 Employability per cent across education domains 136
8.2 Trends in domain-wise employment opportunities 138
8.3 Industry expectations from higher-education institutions (academia) 141
9.1 Educational levels 157
9.2 Wage distribution per educational levels 158
9.3 Share of sectors in states' GDP 159
9.4 Share of industry in states' GDP and over-education 163
9.5 Share of manufacturing in states' GDP and over-education 163
11.1 India's education and skill development structure 199
11.2 CASECAC framework for innovative pedagogy 203
15.1 Specialization of universities 249
16.1 Key aspects of educating emerging entrepreneurs 274
16.2 Evolution of entrepreneurship education in India 275
16.3 Mentoring pool for entrepreneurship education 276
16.4 Key aspects of entrepreneurship curriculum 279
16.5 Experiential learning as a part of PGDM-E 282
16.6 Teaching pedagogy at EDII 283
16.7 Key programme takeaways for alumni 284
17.1 Competency framework for Indian civil service 294

Tables

1.1 Sectoral share of employment 5
1.2 Employed by gender and level of education, 2011–2012 7
1.3 Distribution of employed by caste and level of education, 2011–2012 7
1.4 Unemployment rates among social groups (rural and urban) 9
3.1 Distribution of men and women by usual status for each general educational level in 2017–18 45
4.1 Percentage distribution of lifetime migrants by type of migration, 1971–2011 54
4.2 Percentage distribution of lifetime migrants by stream of migration, 1971–2011 55
4.3 Percentage distribution of lifetime migrants by reasons for migration, 1981–2011 56
4.4 Intra-state, interstate migration for education in India, 1981–2011 57
4.5 Top-five education destination regions for major origin states, 2011 58
4.6 Top-five origin states of interstate student out-migration in India, 2011 59
4.7 Top-five destinations for interstate student in-migration in India, 2011 60
4.8 Net migration occurring among major migrant gaining and losing states, namely, student migration in 2001 and 2011 61
4.9 Top-ranking institutions at the top destinations in India, 2018 62
4.10 Top-ten destinations for Indian-origin students in 2017 63
5.1 Labour-force participation rate by sector, sex, and level of education in India, 1994–2018 72
5.2 Labour-force participation rate by sector, age groups, and level of education in India, 1994–2018 73
5.3 Employment in agriculture and allied sectors by level and type of education, 1983–2018 76

5.4 Employment in manufacturing sector by level and type of education, 1983–2018 78
5.5 Employment in non-manufacturing sector by level and type of education, 1983–2018 79
5.6 Employment in service sector by level and type of education, 1983–2018 81
5.7 Open unemployment by level and type of education, 1983–2018 83
5.8 Disheartened labour force by level and type of education, 1983–2018 85
6.1 Workforce participation rates (15 yrs+), by social group: 2017–2018 94
6.2 Quality of employment, 2017–2018 (row %) 95
6.3 Industrial structure of employment, 2017–2018 98
6.4 Workforce across their education and industry of employment, 2011–2012 and 2017–2018 99
6.5 Changing trends in occupational pattern 100
6.6 Occupational patterns among workers by their social groups, 2017–2018 (%) 101
6.7 Occupational patterns of graduate and illiterate workers, 2017–2018 101
6.8 Occupational patterns of graduate and illiterate workers, 2017–2018 102
6.9 Caste and gender-specific unemployment rate, 2017–2018 (%) (15+ Labour Force) 103
6.10 Unemployment rate among youth, 2017–2018 (%) (15–29 years) 104
7.1 Perception gap on skill importance from employer 114
7.2 Relative ranking of skill importance 115
7.3 Major areas of perception gap 116
7.4 Acquired skills gap 117
7.5 Regression results of factors influencing employee employability quotient 118
7.6 Employee campus experience for employability training 122
7.7 Employers' foresight on the job market 125
8.1 Trends in domain-wise employability 138
8.2 Employee perspective on skill importance 144
8.3 Self-rating of skills by employees from various educational backgrounds 146
8.4 Skill perception gap 147
8.5 Difference in college/university experience based on educational background 148
9.1 Eqn. (1) estimates: mining, quarrying, and manufacturing labourers 160
9.2 Estimates of equation (1): manufacturing labourers 161

9.3	Statewise extent of over-education	162
9.4	Conditional Estimates of equation (1): manufacturing labourers	164
13.1	Total number of students enrolled under B.Voc. programmes in universities and colleges in India from 2011–2012 to 2018–2019	220
13.2	List of skill universities in India	221
13.3	Courses and fee structure of skill universities in India	222
15.1	Enrolment at undergraduate level in major disciplines/ subjects (%)	250
15.2	A typology of industry–academia links, from higher to lower intensity	253
15.3	Priorities for university-industry partnerships at different stages of economic development along the three missions of universities	254
15.4	Recent industry–academia linkages initiated by IITs and IIMs	255
16.1	Interdependence of university, government, and industry in the triple helix model	271
16.2	Importance of entrepreneurial education	273
16.3	List of top-ten B-schools offering entrepreneurship programmes in India	277
16.4	Hard and soft skills of entrepreneurship education	278
16.5	Unique aspects of EDII's PGDM-BE	282
17.1	Demographic profile of the respondents	302
17.2	Mean score-wise ranking of competencies	303
17.3	Results of exploratory factor analysis of 28 competencies	303
17.4	Mean scores of training pedagogy and learning tools	305
17.5	Exploratory factor analysis for training pedagogy and learning tools	305
17.6	Correlation among three dimensions of competencies, career orientation, and training pedagogy	306
17.7	Multiple regression analysis for competencies categories as criterion and training pedagogical tools as the predictors	307

Preface

Higher education plays an important role in promoting economic growth, social progress, and human development. While higher education is an important source of economic growth, it can also be a source of economic and social inequalities if opportunities for higher education are not equally distributed. Recent decades showed an unprecedented expansion of higher education, both globally and in India. The emergence of the knowledge economy has elevated skill requirements and qualification levels for job entry. A post-secondary level education has become a necessary qualification in the job market. Similarly, the anti-poverty initiatives and EFA (Education for All) programmes have contributed to the massive expansion of education at the school level. These two factors, namely, elevated qualification requirements in the labour market and the expansion of school enrolments increased social demand for higher education.

India has experienced the highest rates of growth it has ever seen in higher education since the turn of this century. With more than 900 universities, 39,050 colleges, and 36.6 million students, India has the second largest higher-education system in the world. It can be expected that the expansion will continue, given the favourable demographic dividend and the largest youth population.

The present India Higher Education Report (IHER 2020) is sixth in the series initiated by the Centre for Policy Research in Higher Education (CPRHE) of the National Institute of Educational Planning and Administration. The series is envisaged to provide an in-depth analysis of some of the critical dimensions of higher education in India, with contributions from eminent scholars engaged in research, policy, and planning in the area of higher education. The first Report—IHER 2015—provided a comprehensive account of the higher-education situation in the country, focusing on various challenging issues facing the higher-education sector in India. Subsequent reports—IHER 2016, IHER 2017, and IHER 2018—focused on equity in higher education; quality and teaching-learning in higher education, and financing of higher education, respectively. The fifth IHER 2019 is on Governance in Higher Education.

IHER 2020 is devoted to the theme of employment and employability of higher-education graduates. The aspects covered in the volume include issues related to jobless growth and the employment and unemployment trends;

informal modes of skill formation; and the role of industry in skill building. We are grateful to the authors of the various chapters for their valuable contributions and for their continued support. I take this opportunity to place on record my deep appreciation for the efforts made by my colleague at CPRHE, NIEPA, Professor Mona Khare, Head of Department of Educational Finance, in bringing out this important volume.

N.V. Varghese
Professor and Vice-Chancellor
National Institute of Educational Planning and
Administration (NIEPA), New Delhi, India

Acknowledgements

The CPRHE published the first issue of the India Higher Education Report series (IHER) in 2015. We are happy to present the sixth volume IHER 2020, titled Employment and Employability of Higher Education Graduates in India. The IHER 2020 discusses various aspects of graduate employment and employability in India, focusing on employment trends, employability challenges, and skill building initiatives in Indian higher education. This volume, as the previous ones, is the outcome of support received from various intellectuals and institutions and the efforts put in by the CPRHE.

IHER 2015 was a comprehensive volume covering various issues and challenges facing higher education in the country. It was felt that the subsequent issues in the series should focus on specific themes. The theme considered for the current IHER is graduate employability. This proposal was discussed and approved in the Executive Committee (EC) meeting of the CPRHE in 2019. We would like to express our sincere thanks to members of the EC of the CPRHE.

The volume includes chapters by some of the leading academics and policymakers in higher education. They not only contributed their individual chapters but also contributed substantially to shape the current volume through their extensive comments on chapters by others. We gratefully acknowledge the valuable contribution of all the authors.

We are grateful to the registrar, NIEPA, Professor Kumar Suresh, and his team for their support in facilitating the publication process and procedures. We also thank Mr Pramod Rawat and his colleagues in the NIEPA publication department for their help at different stages.

We thank Ms Shoma Choudhury and her entire team at Routledge for their help in the processing of this manuscript for publication.

We are also grateful to all colleagues in CPRHE, namely, Dr Nidhi Sabharwal, Dr Garima Malik, Dr Anupam Pachauri, Dr Jinusha Panigrahi, Dr Malish CM, and Dr Sayantan Mandal for their continuous support and several rounds of comments.

Ms Anjali Arora, Monica Joshi, Mayank Rajput, Chetna Chawla, and Abbas Beg extended all logistics support to organize peer review meetings and contacting the authors. We gratefully acknowledge their support in preparing this volume.

N.V. Varghese and Mona Khare

Abbreviations

ADB	Asian Development Bank
AEC	ASSOCHAM Education Committee
AI	Artificial Intelligence
AICTE	All India Council of Technical Education
AISHE	All India Survey on Higher Education
AISU	Association of Indian Skills Universities
ASSOCHAM	Associated Chambers of Commerce and Industry of India
B.Arch.	Bachelor of Architecture
B.A.	Bachelor of Arts
B.B.A.	Bachelor of Business Administration
B.C.A.	Bachelor of Computer Applications
B.Com.	Bachelor of Commerce
B.Sc.	Bachelor of Science
B.Skill.	Bachelors of Skill
B.Voc.	Bachelors of Vocational Studies
BFSI	Banking, Financial Service and Insurance
BLA	Bachelor of Liberal Arts
BMET	Bureau of Manpower and Training
BPO	Business Process Outsourcing
BSNL	Bharat Sanchar Nigam Limited
CAGR	Compound Annual Growth Rate
CAM	Census Adjustment Multiplier
CBC	Competency Based Curriculum
CBSE	Central Board of Secondary Education
CC	Community Colleges
CDS	Current Daily Status
CEIS	Career Education in IBM Software
CEO	Chief Executive Director
CGPA	Cumulative Grade Point Average
CIE	Continuous Internal Evaluation
CMIE	Centre for Monitoring Indian Economy
COE	Centre of Excellence

CoP	Communities of practice
CPRHE	Centre for Policy Research in Higher Education
CSTARI	Central Staff Training and Research Institute
CV	Curriculum Vitae
CWS	Current Weekly Status
D.Voc.	Diploma of Vocation
DDU-GKY	DeenDayal Upadhyay-Grameen Kaushalya Yojana
DGET	Director-General of Employment and Training
DI	Dis-similarity Index
DIY	Do It Yourself
DMLT	Diploma in Medical Laboratory Technology
DNEP	Draft National Education Policy
DOPT	Department of Personnel and Training
DST	Department of Science and Technology
ED	Cell Entrepreneurship Development Cell
EDCs	Enterprise Development Centres
EDII	Entrepreneurship Development Institute of India
EFA	Exploratory Factor Analysis
EG	Economic Growth
EMBA	Executive MBA
EPFO	Employee Provident Fund Organization
EQ	Emotional Quotient
FGD	Focus Group Discussion
FPM	Fellow Programme in Management
FY	Fiscal Year
GDP	Gross Domestic Product
GEC	General Education Council
GEM	Global Entrepreneurship Monitor
GER	Gross Enrolment Ratios
GO	Graduation Outcomes
GoI	Government of India
GST	Good and Services Tax
HD	Human Development
HEIs	Higher Educational Institutes
HHI	Household Industry
HR	Human Resource
HRD	Human Resource Development
ICT	Information and Communications Technology
IIDEM	Industry Integrated Dual Education Model
IIM	Indian Institutes of Management
IIT	Indian Institute of Technology
ILD	Institute of Leadership Development
ILFS	Infrastructure Leasing and Finance Services
ILO	International Labour Organization

IoT	Internet of Things
IP	Intellectual Property
IQ	Intelligence Quotient
IRIFM	Indian Railways Institute of Financial Management
IT	Information Technology
ITES	IT-Enabled Services
ITI	Industrial Training Institute
KAUSHAL	Knowledge Acquisition and Upgradation of Skilled Human Abilities and Livelihood
KPO	Knowledge Process Outsourcing
KYC	Know Your Customer
LFPR	Labour Force Participation Rate
LMIS	Labour Market Information System
M.Voc.	Master of Vocation
MAYA	Movement for Alternatives and Youth Awareness
M.B.A.	Master of Business Administration
MC	Master Craftsperson
M.C.A.	Master of Computer Applications
MDPs	Management Development Programmes
MEA	Ministry of External Affairs
MGNREGA	Mahatma Gandhi National Rural Employment Guarantee Act
MHRD	Ministry of Human Resource Development
ML	Machine Learning
MNC	Multinational Corporation
MoL&E	Ministry of Labour and Employment
MOOC	Massive Open Online Course
MoU	Memorandum of Understanding
MSDE	Ministry of Skill Development and Entrepreneurship
MSME-DIs	Micro, Small and Medium Enterprises Development Institute Centres
MSMEs	Micro, Small and Medium Enterprises
NAAC	National Assessment and Accreditation Council
NAPS	National Apprenticeship Promotion Scheme
NBFC	Non-Banking Financial Company
NCERT	National Council of Educational Research and Training
NCEUS	National Commission for Enterprises in the Unorganized Sector
NCF	National Curriculum Framework
NEEM	National Employment Enhancement Mission
NGO	Non-Governmental Organization
NHEQF	National Higher Education Qualification Framework
NHHI	Non-Household Industry
NIELIT	National Institute of Electronics and Information Technology
NIEPA	National Institute of Educational Planning and Administration

NIIT	National Institute of Information Technology
NIMI	National Instructional Media Institute
NIOS	National Institute of Open Schooling
NIRF	National Institutional Ranking Framework
NITTTR	National Institutes of Technical Teacher Training and Research
NLET	Not in Labour Force Education and Training
NLMA	National Literacy Mission Authority
NOS	National Occupation Standards
NPTEL	National Programme on Technology Enhanced Learning
NSDC	National Skill Development Corporation
NSQF	National Skill Qualification Framework
NSS	National Sample Survey
NSSO	National Sample Survey Office
NSTEDB	National Science and Technology Entrepreneurship Development Board
NTVQF	National Technical and Vocational Qualifications Framework
NVEQF	National Vocational Education Qualifications Framework
NVQF	National Vocational Qualifications Framework
OAEs	Own-Account Enterprises
OBC	Other Backward Class
OBE	Open Basic Education
OC	Other Category
OECD	Organization for Economic Co-operation and Development
OJT	On-the-Job Training
OLPE	Open Learning Programme in Entrepreneurship
PGDM-BE	Post Graduate Diploma in Management-Business Entrepreneurship
PGP-CEM	Post Graduate Programme for Certificate in Entrepreneurship Management
Ph.D.	Doctor of Philosophy
PLFS	Periodic Labour Force Survey
PMEGP	Prime Minister Employment Generation Programme
PMKVY	Pradhan Mantri Kaushal Vikas Yojana
PMMY	Pradhan Mantri MUDRA Yojana
PPP	Public-Private Partnership
PSE	Public Sector Enterprise
PSSCIVE	Pandit Sundarlal Sharma Central Institute of Vocational Education
PSU	Public Sector Undertaking
QF	Qualification Frame
QPs	Qualification Packs
R&D	Research and Development
RNCP	Repertoire National des Certifications Professionnelles
RP	Research and Professional Practice

RPA	Robotic Process Automation
RPL	Recognition of Prior Learning
SANKALP	Skill Acquisition and Knowledge Awareness for Livelihood Promotion Programme
SC	Scheduled Class
SCI	Scotland's Colleges International
SDC	Skill Development Centres
SDGs	Sustainable Development Goals
SIDO	Small Industries Development Organization
SIF	Student Innovation Fund
SKPs	Skill Knowledge Partners
SMEs	Small and Medium Enterprises
SRI	Stack Route Immersive
SSCs	Sector Skill Councils
SSLC	Secondary School Leaving Certificate
ST	Scheduled Tribe
SWAYAM	Study Webs of Active-Learning for Young Aspiring Minds
TCS	Tata Consultancy Services
TDCs	Technology Development Centres
TiE	The IndUS Entrepreneurs
TISS	Tata Institute of Social Sciences
TISS-SVE	School of Vocational Education
TLR	Teaching, Learning & Resources
TVET	Technical and Vocational Education and Training
UGC	University Grants Commission
UKIERI	UK India Education and Research Initiative
UN	United Nations
UNDP	United Nations Development Programme
UNESCO	United Nations Educational, Scientific and Cultural Organization
UPSS	Usual Principal and Subsidiary Status
VA	Voluntary Agencies
VAS	Vocational Aptitude Systems
VET	Vocational Education and Training
VTPs	Vocational Training Providers
VUCA	Volatility, Uncertainty, Complexity and Ambiguity
WEF	World Economic Forum
WEP	World Employment Programme
WITP	Work Integrated Training Programme
WPR	Workforce Participation Rate
XLRI	Xavier School of Management

Contributors

Aprant Agarwal is a freelance researcher and a social scientist.

Nikhil Agarwal is an innovation and policy expert and currently CEO of IIT Kanpur Foundation for Innovation & Research in Science & Technology (FIRST), India. Also, he is Vice Chairman, Mahaashmita Livelihood Rural Accelerator Program (MILAP), Government of Maharashtra. He was former CEO of the Andhra Pradesh Innovation Society (APIS), Government of Andhra Pradesh.

Raj Agrawal is Director of All India Management Association (AIMA-CME), India. He was earlier Director of IILM Academy of Higher Learning, Greater Noida. "Visiting Research Professor" in Montana State University, Billings, Montana, USA. He is currently a consultant in UNCTAD and resource person in Globalisation of Service Project of William Davidson Institute at the University of Michigan, Ann Arbor, Michigan, USA.

Vasavi Bhatt is PhD Scholar at the Indira Gandhi Institute of Development Research, Mumbai, India.

Catherine Bros is Associate Professor of Economics at Université Gustave Eiffel, Paris, France, and an invited scholar at International Management Institute, Kolkata. She currently serves as an associate editor of the journal *Studies in Microeconomics.* Her research interests are provision of public goods, decentralization, and social fragmentation primarily focused on the Indian subcontinent.

S. Chandrasekhar is Professor at Indira Gandhi Institute of Development Research, Mumbai, India. He served as Advisor to the President of the Confederation of Indian Industry and Co-Chairman and Managing Director of Jubilant Bhartia Group. He is a recipient of the Fred H Bixby Fellowship awarded by Population Council, New York, as well as the Japanese Award for Outstanding Research on Development.

Sahana Roy Chowdhury is Associate Professor of Economics at International Management Institute, Kolkata, India. She has been consultant at NIPFP and

Fellow at ICRIER, Delhi. She is currently Editor-in-chief of the journal *Studies in Microeconomics.*

Sayoree Gooptu is a PhD scholar in the Department of Economics at Jadavpur University, India. She has qualified for UGC and NET-JRF, and her research revolves around the areas of economics of education.

Ajay K. Jain is Professor with the Management Development Institute, Gurgaon, India. Formerly, he worked in Aarhus University (triple crown accredited), Denmark as Visiting Professor. He is a visiting faculty to University of Free State (2009), South Africa, IULM University Milano, Italy (2013), Indian Institute of Management, Lucknow (2007–2009), and All Indian Management Association, New Delhi.

Neetu Jain is Associate Professor at the Behavioural Science Indian Institute of Public Administration, India. She has more than 19 years of teaching, training, research, and consultancy experience.

Rajat Kathuria is Director and Chief Executive at the Indian Council for Research on International Economic Relations (ICRIER), New Delhi, India. He has worked with the World Bank, Washington, DC, as a consultant and carried out research assignments for a number of international organizations, including ILO, UNCTAD, LirneAsia, the World Bank, and ADB. He is founder member of the Broadband Society for Universal Access and served on the Board of Delhi Management Association. He is on several government committees and on the research advisory council of State Bank of India.

Khalid Khan is Assistant Professor at the Indian Institute of Dalit Studies, India. His research interests are economics of education, labour economics, and ageing with a focus on marginalized groups and social exclusion.

Mona Khare is Professor and Head, Educational Finance, CPRHE/National Institute of Educational Planning and Administration, New Delhi, India, and member of the 15th Finance Commission for Education sector funds estimation, Govt. of India. She has been associated with UNESCO, the Asian Productivity Organisation, the British Council, Commonwealth, SAARC, World Bank, and government bodies in research and consultancy, is twice-recipient of 'Young Economist Award' by the Indian Economic Association and has been awarded by the Government of Madhya Pradesh for their Distance Education Programme (EDUSAT). She was a member of Commonwealth Education Ministers Conference Drafting Committee of the post-secondary forum for SDGs.

Ujjwal Krishna is a specialist doctoral research scholar at the Institute for Human Security and Social Change, La Trobe University, Melbourne, Australia.

S. Madheswaran is Professor and Head, Centre for Economics Studies and Policy, Institute for Social and Economic Change, Bangalore, India. Formerly, he was Advisor, Planning, Programme Monitoring and Statistics Department, Government of Karnataka and First Chief Evaluation Officer, Karnataka Evaluation Authority. He has coordinated and edited the Redesigned Economic survey of Government of Karnataka and New Evaluation and Monitoring Policy 2010, Youth Development Report, GOI, 2016–2017, in addition to several national and international research assignments.

Rajendra P. Mamgain is Chair Professor, S.R. Sankaran Chair (Rural Labour) at National Institute of Rural Development & Panchayati Raj, Hyderabad, India. With over 25 policy-oriented research studies to his credit, he has authored/co-authored many books and research papers in various national and internationals journals of repute.

Santosh Mehrotra is Professor of Economics at the Centre for Labour, Jawaharlal Nehru University, India. He spent 15 years with the UN, was head UNICEF's global research programme at Innocenti Research Centre, Florence, and was chief economist, Global Human Development Report New York. Formerly, he was Head, Development Policy Division of Planning Commission, Government of India. He was also the Director General (2009–14) of the National Institute of Labour Economics Research, Planning Commission.

Pankaj Mittal is Secretary General of the Association of Indian Universities (AIU) and has held senior positions with the University Grants Commission. He was former Vice-Chancellor of Bhagat Phool Singh Mahila Vishwavidyalaya, Haryana, and recipient of many awards and honours such as Fulbright Nehru Scholarship grant for educational administrators, the President of India Award in 2017 for Digital Initiatives in Higher Education, First Padma Shri Subhasini Devi Award 2018, and Qimpro Gold Standard Award for leadership in Education for 2018.

Anuja Pandey is Associate Professor, Marketing & Retail, All India Management Association, India. She is Managing Editor of AIMA's Journal of Management & Research and Head–AIMA India Case Research Centre (ICRC) and Program Director of AIMA's Post Graduate Management Certificate programmes.

J.K. Parida is Assistant Professor, Department of Economic Studies, Central University Punjab, India. He was former Deputy Director, National Institute of Labour Economics Research and Development, NITI Aayog, Government of India, and has published widely.

Komal Raghav is Post-Doctoral Fellow, Economics Department, Jiwaji University, Gwalior, India. She has qualified for UGC-NET and has eight years of teaching experience.

S. Irudaya Rajan is Professor at Centre for Development Studies, Kerala, India. He has coordinated seven major migration surveys in different states of India.

He was Chair Professor of research unit on international migration, Ministry of Overseas Indian Affairs. He is associated for research with the European Union, the International Labour Organization, the International Development Research Centre, the Canadian Institute of Health Research, the World Bank, the International Organization of Migration, the South Asian Network of Economic Institutes, the Rockefeller Foundation, UNESCO, among others.

Kavita Saxena is an educator in the area of marketing management and entrepreneurship with over 16 years of experience in academia and industry. She is involved in mentoring start-ups and teaches courses related to entrepreneurial marketing, small business promotion, design thinking, and digital marketing. She has handled several national and international projects and has published widely.

S.K. Shukla is Professor and Head, Economics Department, Jiwaji University, Gwalior, India. A D.Litt. and with more than 35 years of teaching experience, he has published in various national and international journals and has authored textbooks of repute. He was Past President of Madhya Pradesh Economic Association in 2009–2010. He has been associated with the UPSC and PSC of various states.

Ritika Sinha is Associate Professor at CBSMS (Post graduate department of Management Studies Bangalore Central University), India. She has over 19 years of postgraduate teaching and research experience in the field of finance & marketing in the MBA departments of reputed universities. She has authored books in the area of economics and business environment and has published widely.

Vineeta Sirohi is Professor in the Department of Educational Administration at the National Institute of Educational Planning and Administration (NIEPA), New Delhi, India. She is consulted by UNESCO, the World Bank, and ILO and is a National Awardee for Innovative Research Paper in a National Seminar by NCERT.

N.V. Varghese is Vice-Chancellor, National Institute of Educational Planning and Administration (NIEPA), India, and the founding director of the Centre for Policy Research in Higher Education (CPRHE) at NIEPA. Formerly, he was Head, Governance and Management of Education, International Institute of Educational Planning (IIEP/UNESCO), Paris.

Chapter 1

Employment and employability of higher-education graduates

An overview

N. V. Varghese and Mona Khare

The rate of economic growth determines the size of the national income, and the employment pattern determines the distribution of employment among nationals. Economists in the 1950s postulated a positive association between rates of economic growth and generation of employment. The employment elasticity of growth continued to be positive and high in many decades that followed. These trends have been changing in recent decades. It is observed in many economies that the growth in employment lagged behind the rates of economic growth, and it became close to zero, giving way to what is termed as jobless growth (ILO, 2014). Consequently, the global youth unemployment remained high and increased from 201 million in 2014 to 212 million by 2019. If new labour market entrants are taken into account, an additional 280 million jobs needed to be created by 2019 to close the global employment gap (ILO, 2015).

According to the NSSO Reports, India had a labour force of around 485 million in 2012. The huge youth population that India has currently is projected to increase to 350 million by 2022. The country is already experiencing the phenomenon of jobless growth. The situation of jobless growth may lead to explosive levels of unemployment in general and similar levels of unemployment of the educated, in particular. It seems India is already transiting from a situation of 'jobless growth' to 'job-loss growth' (Kannan & Raveendran, 2019), which will have serious implications for employment of the educated.

Being educated was considered to be security against unemployment. The level of education and the rate of unemployment were represented by an inverted 'U'-shaped curve (Blaug, 1973) which peaked at the secondary education level. The empirical evidence before the 1990s indicated that unemployment was mostly a problem of non-educated and less educated. Even among the educated, the problem of unemployment was mostly a problem of matriculates in the 1950s, the undergraduates in the 1970s, and the postgraduates of universities who joined the pool of unemployed in large numbers in later decades (Varghese, 1989). Today the curve representing the rate of unemployment and the level of education continues to move positively and, perhaps, endlessly. The rate of

DOI: 10.4324/9781003158349-1

unemployment seems to increase with increasing levels of education till the post-graduate levels of education.

The increasing rate of unemployment of the educated challenges the views on education as a guarantee against unemployment. The enrolment in higher education is increasing, and the number of graduates coming out of the universities is also on the rise. Most of them remain unemployed not only because of non-availability of jobs but also due to lack of 'job-readiness' among the graduates. The widening employability skill gaps add to the problem of unemployment of the higher-education graduates, in turn, which accentuates the problem of jobless growth.

Employability implies a good mix of skills, competencies, and attitudes to perform on the job, and it enjoys a high premium in the labour market. It has become a major concern globally and in India. The emphasis of the SDGs 2030 on job readiness and the United Nations (UN) on the employability as a priority area for youth development are indications of global commitment to employability skills. The education systems in many countries are being reformed to improve job readiness and to enhance employability skills among the youth. The qualification frameworks developed in many countries attempted to link the education and training systems with the demands of the production sectors. These frameworks are becoming the basis for curriculum reforms in many universities of the developed and developing countries.

Economic growth and employment

The models of economic growth in the first development decade helped improve output but not its distribution among the nationals. Therefore, the strategy of growth followed in the second development decade, focused on '*Redistribution with Growth*' (Chenery et al., 1974). To promote employment and better income distribution, the World Bank focused on agriculture and rural development, and the International Labour organization (ILO) introduced the World Employment Programme (WEP) in the 1970s. The agenda for global development centred mostly on 'employment-oriented strategy of rural development' (Mellor, 1975).

The changes in the employment patterns in the subsequent decades contributed to the widening of income inequalities, challenging the validity of the Kuznets curve linking growth and income inequality (Piketty, 2006). The employment trends from the 1980s indicated a decline in the share of industrial employment in some high-income economies such as the Republic of Korea, Singapore, Spain, and the United Kingdom, while it remained stable in developing countries and increased in some of the emerging markets. The machines replaced workers in many routine jobs, leading to increasing unemployment of the medium-skilled workers. A phenomenon noticed recently is that the advanced economies experience fast growth both in high-skill cognitive occupations and low-skill occupations, while jobs are shifting away from middle-skilled categories (World Bank, 2019).

The decline in medium-skilled jobs and a rise in the demand for jobs at the lower and upper ends of the skill hierarchy compelled educated medium-skilled workers to compete for lower-skilled occupations. This resulted in increasing wage and income inequalities between those who are employed in high-end jobs and others (ILO, 2015). This has become a continuing source of widening inequalities in employment and income. It is projected that the demand for high-level skills will grow, and many low- and medium-skilled jobs will become obsolete. The routine manual, non-routine manual, and routine cognitive jobs will decline, and jobs in the non-routine analytical domains will grow. The demand for skills and skilled people competent to work in jobs requiring expert thinking and complex communication grew steadily and consistently over the past decades (Salmi, 2017).

Technology is enhancing the skill requirements in the labour market. The premium is rising for skills that cannot be replaced by robots—general cognitive skills such as critical thinking and socio-behavioural skills such as managing and recognizing emotions that enhance teamwork. Workers with these skills are more adaptable in the changing context of the labour markets. The empirical reality is that the labour market for certain categories of the educated continue to enjoy better employability and higher wages. The high private returns to education, in general, and for the skilled and of the higher-educated in certain domains (increased to almost 15 per cent a year) reflect this change (World Bank, 2019).

Another trend is the informalization of employment. Although, the demand from international organizations and employees' unions is for good-quality productive employment, the empirical evidence shows a trend contrary to this. A noticeable trend is that employment has become more and more informal. It is no more a question of employment in the informal sector but also a trend of informalizing employment even in the formal sectors. The ILO estimates (ILO, 2014) that the informality rate in employment is as high as 90 per cent in some of the countries in South and South East Asia. It seems informal employment (in the informal and formal sectors) may remain the main stake for developing countries. The share of informal employment is more than 70 per cent in Sub-Saharan Africa, 60 per cent in South Asia, and remains at more than 50 per cent in Latin America. In India, the informal sector has remained at around 90 per cent. Jobs in the informal sector are characterized by low productivity and low wages, with the employees enjoying no social protection (World Bank, 2019).

The 'future of work will be determined by the battle between automation and innovation' (World Bank, 2019, p. 28). Automation reduces employment in the traditional sectors and especially those depending on routine work. The innovations, on the other hand, bring new tasks and jobs which require higher-order skills. In other words, it can be argued that the low- and middle-level skilled workers will benefit less from technological change because of higher susceptibility to automation. The technological change and innovations will benefit the more educated and that, too, in selected domains.

Jobless growth in India

The relationship between economic growth and employment has traditionally been positive in India. In the 1970s and 1980s, a 3–4 per cent growth in GDP contributed to around 2 per cent growth in employment. In this century, even 7 per cent growth in GDP could not contribute more than 1 per cent to employment growth (APU, 2018). In the 1980s an investment of one crore created around 90 jobs in the organized manufacturing sector, while the corresponding figure in 2010 had fallen to ten. Increasing capital intensity of production has been a feature of the manufacturing industry in India. As a result, the average annual employment elasticity of output in India has been declining, reaching 0.1 in 2016.

The Indian experience shows that high economic growth need not necessarily lead to high employment growth. It is not just the aggregate rate of economic growth but the pattern of that growth which is crucial. A moderate but sustainable rate of growth which involves employment generation and poverty reduction is preferable to a higher rate of growth that is based on greater income inequalities. Studies suggest that the virtuous circle of sustained Economic Growth–Human Development (EG/HD), as evidenced in literature where high growth leads to high per capita incomes and low unemployment, in turn leading to better quality employment and better education status leading to lesser inequalities and sustained equitable growth in a circular fashion reinforcing each other, eludes India (Khare, 2020a).

The growth in employment is experienced in the informal sector and the high-technology sectors. The informal or non-formal sector in India account for 50 per cent of the GDP and 92 per cent of the employment (Singh & Chhabra, 2017). As per the National Sample Survey 75th Round, 2019 informal employment also includes informal employment outside the informal sector, that is in formal sector enterprises and household sector (PLFS 2018–2019). Formal employment is only 8.0 per cent and is mostly in the public sector (60 per cent), occupied predominantly by males (79.5 per cent).

India experienced changes in the sectoral contribution to GDP and employment. Over a period of time the share of primary sector in GDP and employment declined and that of the manufacturing and service sectors increased. The sharp increase in the share of services in employment in India has occurred at a much lower level of per capita income than in the developed countries when they experienced a similar expansion (Ghosh & Chandrasekhar, 2007). Agriculture and allied activities still support 44 per cent of the labour force even though their share in GDP has fallen to 18.5 per cent. On the other hand, services account for more than 50 per cent of GDP but only 30 per cent of employment. While the share of the primary sector has been declining, that of the service sector is increasing (see Table 1.1).

According to the NSS surveys, the sector contributing the maximum to employment generation is construction. Between 2004 and 2011, the share of

Table 1.1 Sectoral share of employment

Sector	*2004–2005*	*2011–2012*	*2017–2018*
Agriculture	58.5%	48.9%	44.1%
Manufacturing	11.7%	12.6%	12.1%
Non-Manufacturing	6.4%	11.7%	12.7%
Service	23.4%	26.8%	31.0%

Source: Authors' computations based on NAS, CSO, GOI (various years).

manufacturing in total employment increased from 11.7 to 12.6 per cent, services from 23.4 to 26.8 per cent, and construction from 6.4 per cent to 11.7 per cent. Today, construction employs almost as many workers as the entire manufacturing sector—around 50 million. But unlike manufacturing, it affords seasonal and non-steady employment.

Another aspect of employment is its status. In 1987, 55.5 per cent of workers were self-employed. By 2015, this had fallen to 46.6 per cent. Correspondingly, the proportion of regular wage workers rose from 15.6 per cent to 20.6 per cent. The capital intensity in both labour- and capital-intensive industries has meant low elasticity of employment in general. As noted already, this trend is prone to produce jobless growth.

The most salient point to note, from an employment perspective, is that the manufacturing sector has failed to expand its employment share significantly over the past 25 years. Its share is remaining in the range of 10–13 per cent of the workforce. This is low when compared to other developing countries with similar levels of per capita income. NSS data reveal an 'infantilization' of the sector over time—that is, a process wherein smaller firms increase their share in the sector (Ghose, 2016). The share of own-account enterprises (OAEs) or single-worker firms in total firms went up from 32 per cent in 1994 to 59 per cent in 2015. This increase has come almost entirely at the cost of family-based enterprises, while the proportion of establishments (enterprises that hire at least one wage worker) has not changed over the entire period. Further, the share of contract work and other precarious forms of labour has grown since the early 2000s.

The inability of high rates of economic growth to promote increased employment growth characterized Indian economic growth. The NSS surveys of the 1990s and 2000s revealed a decline in the rate of employment generation in India. More importantly, the rate of growth in regular employment was close to zero. The wage employment, although increased during the initial periods of liberalization, declined in the later period. The significant increase was experienced in self-employment across sectors and rural and urban areas.

The rate of growth of employment declined since 2004–2005 when economic growth was high, indicating a significant decline in employment elasticity with respect to growth. In the decade of 2004–2014, the economy grew at an annual rate of around 8.0 per cent and jobs at a rate of below 1.0 per cent. The employment elasticity to output was close to zero in 2011–2012, reflecting a stage of jobless growth. Further, at present, India is moving from a jobless growth to job-loss growth—between the period 2011–2012 and 2017–2018, 6.18 million people lost jobs, and those who have lost jobs are all with low education—less than secondary level of education (Kannan & Raveendran, 2019). India experiences a high rate of open unemployment—over 5 per cent overall, and 16 per cent for youth. According to some estimates (Ghose, 2016), the economy still needs to generate 16 million new jobs annually to accommodate surplus workers. This consists of around eight million new entrants every year.

Education and employment in India

Labour force participation rates

According to NSSO, the labour force in 2012 was around 485 million. The labour force participation rate declined from 61.6 per cent in 1983 to 36.9 per cent in 2018. The overall participation rate declined primarily because of the sharp decline in the participation rates of females. While the male participation rates remained stable at around 55.0 per cent, the female labour force participation rates declined sharply from 30.0 per cent 1984 to 22.5 per cent in 2011–2012. It accounts for nearly a 25.0 per cent reduction in the participation rates of women. An even more disturbing figure is that of those who are not working, not looking for work, and not undergoing education or training, that is not in Labour Force, Education and Training (NLET). In India this accounts for 100.2 million young people. The open unemployment rate for youth population stands at a much higher rate of 17.8 in 2017–2018, a more than 10 per cent point jump from 2011 to 2012. Those not in education, employment, or training (NEET) too has increased and remains highest for the age group 20–29, the most desirable age for any person to be employed. This percentage for the youth population as a whole has not only remained high (around 30%) from 1990s onwards but has shown an increasing trend in the past decade or so (Khare, 2020b).

There are debates about the factors influencing a decline in the LFPR of females. The most common argument is centring on income and substitution effects. The substitution effect implies that educated women make a trade-off in favour of work between leisure and work. The income effect argument shows a tendency among women in families with higher incomes to withdraw from the labour force. The educated women, in general, tend to marry men with higher qualifications and higher incomes and it discourages women's participation in the labour market. In India the income effect seems to be especially strong. The fall in the female LFPR may also be due to their entry to pursue education as the enrolment ratios of girls have increased at all levels of education in India.

Employment by education level

The education levels of those employed indicate that less than 10 per cent had higher-education degrees. Of the labour force, 146 million (30 per cent) were illiterate; 201 million (40.6 per cent) were with education below the level of secondary; 57.2 million (11.8 per cent) had secondary level of education; 15 million (3 per cent) had technical education; and 7.2 had tertiary level education (see Table 1.2). More than half of the female workers and nearly one-fourth of the male workers are illiterate.

The employment by educational levels of the disadvantaged (see Table 1.3) indicates that illiterates account for a good share of the employed among the disadvantaged groups—46.2 per cent among the ST, and 38.8 per cent among SC categories. The disparities in the share of the educated among the disadvantaged

Table 1.2 Employed by gender and level of education, 2011–2012

Educational level	*Persons*	*Male*	*Female*
Illiterate	30.7	23.0	50.8
Literate and below primary	10.9	11.3	9.9
Primary	13.3	13.9	11.9
Middle	16.4	18.5	11.1
Secondary	11.8	13.9	6.4
Higher secondary	6.6	7.8	3.4
Diploma/certificate	1.4	1.6	0.8
Graduate and above	8.8	10.0	5.7
Total	100.0	100.0	100.0

Source: NSSO (2014) (68th round).

Table 1.3 Distribution of employed by caste and level of education, 2011–2012

Educational Categories	*ST*	*SC*	*OBC*	*Others*
Illiterate	46.2	38.8	31.5	17.9
Literate and below primary	13.0	12.2	11.3	8.6
Primary	13.3	15.2	13.1	12.3
Middle	14.0	15.7	17.3	16.5
Secondary	5.9	8.9	12.2	15.4
Higher secondary	3.7	4.4	6.2	9.8
Diploma/certificate	0.5	0.8	1.5	2.0
Graduate and above	3.2	4.0	6.9	17.4
Total	100	100	100	100

Source: NSSO (2014) (68th round).

and other groups widen at higher levels of education. For example, while the share of the middle-level educated in employment is comparable among the social groups, the disparities in their respective shares increase when one moves to secondary, higher secondary, and higher-education levels.

The share of the disadvantaged groups is higher in the casual labour category, while other groups have a higher share in the regular employment category. The shares of females, SC, ST, and OBC in casual employment are higher than that in other categories. These job categories are vulnerable jobs and informal in nature with no social protection. Nearly 50 per cent of the Muslim urban male workers and about 60 per cent of urban female workers were engaged in self-employment. Among Hindus in urban areas, about 44 per cent of male workers and about 40 per cent of female workers were engaged in regular wage-salaried employment, whereas the access to regular employment for Muslims are 29.8 and 21.9 per cent, which is very low when compared to other religious communities (Madheswaran & Singhari, 2017). Most illiterates are casual workers, while half of the workforce with secondary level of education are self-employed.

This shift can be explained by two facts: one, the rising graduate population in the country; and two, better quality of employment for those with higher-education degrees. According to the India Labour Report, about 46 per cent of the 'graduate and above' workers in India are regularly employed. Studies across the globe have proved that income elasticity of higher education is much higher than that of all other levels of education (Khare, 2014). The population of youth (age group of 15 to 29 years) in India is expected to increase steadily to approximately 350 million by 2022 (World Bank, 2006). Educational qualification levels of the people in the age group 15 to 29 are also expected to increase.

Unemployment of the educated

According to the 68th round of the NSSO, the unemployment rate increases consistently with increasing levels of education for both males and females in rural as well as in urban areas. There is a declining trend in the rate of unemployment at the postgraduate and above level. It seems that the peak in unemployment rates traditionally has been at the secondary level. In the 1980s and 1990s, the relationship between education levels and unemployment rate used to take an inverted 'U'-shaped curve, indicating increasing unemployment rates with educational levels, reaching a peak and declining thereafter. The peak used to be the secondary level of education (Varghese, 1996). However, the peak has shifted from secondary to university graduate level of education, indicating the gravity of the situation faced by the higher-education graduates. Surprisingly, the unemployment rates among those with diploma or certificate levels are also high, which raises questions about the quality and relevance of training programmes offered by our technical institutions.

Nearly one-third (30 per cent) of the total unemployed in the year 2011–2012 were having qualification levels of graduates and above. This share is not only high, but it has also been increasing—it increased from 21 per cent in 2004–2005 to 30 per cent in 2011–2012. Of those with graduate and above levels of education in 2011–2012, 22 per cent were graduates and 8 per cent were postgraduates. The unemployment rate among India's educated was 11.4 per cent in 2017–2018 (Periodic Labour Force Survey, 2019). According to the survey report, the unemployment rate for educated rural females was much higher. This figure, increased from 9.7 per cent to 15.2 per cent during 2004–2005 and 2011–2012 and further to 17.3 per cent in 2017–2018.

The trends in unemployment rates are similar among all social groups. The unemployment rates are consistently high by levels of education for all social groups. The unemployment rates in general and those among the graduates and above, in particular, are higher among females, disadvantaged groups, and among minorities. This pattern is consistent both in the urban and rural areas (see Table 1.4). For any given level of education above secondary level, unemployment rates are higher among the SC, OBC, and ST than among general categories.

A breakdown of graduate job seekers by streams of study reveals that the majority are from general academic disciplines with arts graduates topping the list comprising about 40 per cent of the graduate job seekers (Khare, 2017). Also, the last few years have hardly seen any change in their percentage shares by major disciplines. Only a marginal dip is observed in the percentage share of science, engineering, veterinary, and education graduate job seekers (Khare, 2016). This is indicative of the fact that it is comparatively easier for engineering and science graduates to get employed perhaps for the simple reason that industries and occupations related to engineering and science have been among the top-five occupations on employment indexes across major regions of the world (Khare, 2018).

There exists a positive association between levels of education of the employees and wage levels. The wage differentials between secondary school graduates and tertiary education graduates are the sharpest, and it is widening in this century (Varghese, 2019). In 2004–2005 and in 2011–2012, the wage levels of tertiary graduates were double that of the secondary school graduates. This also reflects the trends we discussed earlier that more educated people in higher-end job categories are beneficiaries of increases in wages than are those at the lower-end jobs.

Table 1.4 Unemployment rates among social groups (rural and urban)

Social group	*Not literate*	*Literate & up to primary*	*Middle*	*Secondary*	*Higher secondary*	*Diploma/ certificate*	*Graduate*	*Postgraduate & above*
ST	0.1	0.4	1.8	6.2	6.4	5.5	8.9	8.9
SC	0.3	1.6	2.5	2.6	5.0	12	10.5	13.1
OBC	0.4	0.8	2.1	2.7	4.0	10	8.2	8.3
Others	0.4	1.4	2	2.2	4.5	4.7	6.4	6.1
All	0.4	1.1	2	2.7	4.4	8.1	7.6	7.5

Source: Based on NSSO (2014) (NSS 68th round).

This pattern of concentration of less educated in lower-end jobs with their associated wage structure is a source of inequalities. In fact, the higher-educated occupy higher-paid jobs, and therefore employment opportunities are determined by educational levels. Strategies to increase enrolment and retention of the disadvantaged in higher education and providing technical and professional training could be effective means for enhancing their employability and for reducing income inequality.

Educational opportunities are unevenly distributed among regions and social groups. Educational inequalities are persisting in India and are noted to be much higher than those in most of the less-developed countries. More importantly, the less-developed states in India, such as Orissa, Madhya Pradesh, Bihar, and Uttar Pradesh, record higher educational inequality when compared to the developed states (Kundu, 2017). In other words, the states which have relatively higher concentration of the poor also have higher educational inequalities.

Not only the headcount number but also the percentage of educated job seekers to total job seekers has increased from 70.7 per cent in 2000 to 76.5 per cent in 2009 and further to 81.5 in 2010. Among the educated job seekers it is the percentage of graduates that has witnessed the greatest increase, from 17.85 in 2004 to 26.64 in 2008, registering an 8.79 per cent increase but then a decline in 2010. The percentage of school graduates seeking jobs has in fact gone up, indicating difficulty in finding jobs with lower qualifications. Still those with the grade 10 education comprise the major chunk of the educated jobseekers (Khare, 2014).

Unprecedented expansion of higher education

Higher education in India experienced an unprecedented expansion in this century. It transitioned from a slow-growing and low-enrolment elite sector to a stage of fast-growing massification in the past decade. Between 2000 and 2018, the growth rates accelerated to reach two digits, the gross enrolment ratios (GER) trebled to reach 26.2 per cent, the number of universities more than trebled to 903, the number of colleges more than quadrupled to 40,000, and student enrolment increased more than 4.5 times to a total of 36.8 million.

Till the 1980s, it was believed that expansion of higher education would lead to increased unemployment of the educated. Therefore, the focus of policy prescriptions in higher education was consolidation of the sector instead of expansion of the sector. The 1986 policy on education recommended delinking of degrees from jobs as a strategy to reduce social demand for higher education and eventually to reduce unemployment of the educated. However, the social demand continued to increase. When the government experienced financial constraints to satisfy the social demand for higher education, permission to own and operate private universities was granted.

The policy towards private institutions has played an important role in the expansion and diversification of higher education in India. While privatization through self-financing, capitation fee colleges were permitted, private universities were not granted permission. Most of these self-financing institutions offered study programmes and courses in the market-friendly subject areas of engineering, medicine, and management (Agarwal, 2007). Following the passage of the private universities Acts in several state legislatures, the private universities proliferated between 2002 and 2018.

The unprecedented expansion of higher education fuelled mainly by the private institutions combined with the jobless growth of the economy is leading to high levels of unemployment of the educated. This explosion in enrolment is the reason for an upward-moving curve replacing an inverted 'U'-shaped curve depicting rates of unemployment and levels of education. The major argument put forward by the employers is that Indian universities are producing unemployables. The demand for professional and technical courses in private colleges declined, and as a result many private colleges offering study programmes in engineering and management areas have closed down in recent years. Unfortunately, the rapid growth of higher-education enrolments added not only to the problem of joblessness but also to the problem of job readiness of the higher education graduates. Of the educated jobseekers in the country, less than 5 per cent of those registered with the employment exchange, are getting placed (Khare, 2016). Several reports point at lack of employability skills among a huge number of higher-education graduates in the country.

Employability skills

To understand the phenomenon of lack of employability skills among the graduates, it is important to notice the empirical reality of the negative association between the concentration of institutions of higher education and employability skills of their graduates. A correlation of 0.076 between the number of colleges and the per cent of employability is found in some of the states. 'The employability of Indian engineers continues to be painfully low with more than 80 per cent engineer's [sic] unemployable for any job in the knowledge economy' (Aspiring Minds, 2019). As noted earlier, labour markets in India are becoming more informal. Self-employment, informal wage work with no written contracts or protections, and low-productivity jobs are becoming the norm. Since many of these workers are outside the purview of the regulatory framework, they enjoy neither protection nor job security.

In the new and emerging knowledge sectors, the skill sets required in the labour market include professional and social skills of varying categories. India recently established a Ministry of Skill Development & Entrepreneurship (MSDE) and launched the Pradhan Mantri Kaushal Vikas Yojana (PMKVY) programme. This Skill India programme is an outcome-based skill training scheme for the youth to make them employable. Another important step taken in the recent past is to develop Qualification Frameworks (QF). India initially developed QFs in vocational education (NVEQF), which was replaced by National Skills Qualifications Framework (NSQF).

In pursuance of the decision of the Cabinet Committee on Skill Development, the Ministry of Finance notified the details of the National Skills Qualifications Framework (NSQF) on 27 December 2013 (MOF, 2013). The NSQF defines competence as proven ability to use acquired knowledge, skills, and personal and social abilities to do a job well. Learning outcomes represent what a learner knows, understands, and is able to do after completion of a learning process which will be expressed in terms of knowledge, skills, and competence.

The NSQF organizes qualifications according to a series of levels of knowledge, skills and aptitude. These levels are defined in terms of learning outcomes, regardless of the modes (formal or informal) of acquiring them. It is a nationally integrated education- and competency-based skills framework with provisions for multiple pathways, including mobility between technical and general education. It is expected that NSQF will provide principles for recognizing skill proficiency and competencies at different levels leading to international equivalency, multiple entry and exit, recognition of prior learning, and opportunities for lifelong learning.

The NSQF assures quality in higher education in terms of awarding credits and allowing transfer of credits. Re-routing the Indian education system with more flexibility in terms of entry and exit points, timeline mobility, and so on gives value to every form of education level and allows comparability among all qualifications—inter- as well as intra-country. Importantly, the transparency will help widen the horizon for employers to identify skills and for learners to choose from the category of work the qualification can serve.

The framework comprises ten levels—each level represents a distinct set of knowledge, complexity, and autonomy that is required to represent the competence of that particular level. Learning outcomes are the learning criteria set to each level. The NSQF levels are not related directly to years of study. Each level of the NSQF is associated with a set of descriptors made of outcome statements in five domains: (1) process, (2) professional knowledge, (3) professional skill, (4) core skill, and (5) responsibility.

The UGC is in the process of developing a National Higher Education Qualification Framework (NHEQF) whereby the levels of six and above (Varghese, 2018) will be brought under the post-secondary levels of education. The effort is to link the skills and higher-education curriculum and student assessment. The major question is how to link the skills indicated by the NSQF with the teaching-learning process in higher-education institutions.

It needs to be noted that the intention is not to envisage higher-education institutions solely as skill-imparting institutions. The higher-education institutions need to be focusing on research and education on the one hand and employable skills on the other. Based on the major functions, one may imagine a diversified institutional structure of higher education in India. The recently announced National Education Policy 2020 (NEP, 2020) emphasizes flexible pathways to higher learning and revised institutional structure. The pathways suggested for pursuing higher education include: (1) the three-year B.A./B.Sc. with liberal arts, (2) the four-year bachelor of liberal arts (BLA/BLE) with multiple exit options, (3) several options to pursue a one-year or two-year master's degree, (4) the M.Phil study programme will be discontinued, and (5) PhD or a doctoral degree can be pursued after a Master's degree or a four-year bachelor's degree with research.

It is also envisaged that a National Higher Education Qualifications Framework (NHEQF) outlining the learning outcomes associated with degree/diploma/certification to guide the curriculum development across all disciplines will be developed by the General Education Council (GEC) that will be created. To impart employability skills, the universities are expected to revise their curricula based on the National Higher Education Qualification Framework (NHEQF). To facilitate flexible pathways to higher learning, NEP 2020 envisages replacing the large number of small institutions with large multidisciplinary universities and colleges. There will be only three types of large-sized institutions—research universities, teaching universities, and autonomous colleges with a student strength of no less than 3,000. The vision of the NEP is 'to develop knowledge, skills, values, and dispositions that support responsible commitment to human rights, sustainable development and living, and global well-being, thereby reflecting a truly global citizen'. Highlighting the need for a holistic learning system, the policy envisages revitalizing and integrating vocational education. Among the important actionable points recommended are the following: (1) an innovative curricula of all HEIs with credit-based courses and projects in the areas of community engagement and service; (2) environmental education; (3) value-based education; (4) an identified set of skills and values to be incorporated at each stage of learning; (5) opportunities for internship with local industry, business, artists, crafts persons, and so on; and (6) research internships with faculty and researchers.

The current situation arising out of the COVID-19 pandemic is only going to add to the employment and employability challenges of the young graduates and add to that of the HEIs to deal with it. Not only has there been disruption in the learning process with delayed sessions, examinations, abrupt shifting to an online virtual mode of teaching, learning, and evaluation, for which neither the teachers nor the students were well equipped—but also future uncertainties loom large. The most common trend in higher education was closure of universities and hostels and transition to online transactions. Many universities in India do not have the technological infrastructure for the transition, and many students do not have technological devices to participate in the online courses. According to ILO (ILO Survey Report 2020), disruptions to education and training caused by COVID-19 will have profound additional impacts on young people's employability and employment which are likely to last for a long time. With economic growth dwindling to all-time low, job prospects are bleak. Various national and international agencies have projected negative growth and slow revival for India, as in many other countries. The International Monetary Fund (IMF) gives a projection of negative growth in real GDP (–4.5%) in 2020. The CARE Rating gives a forecast of negative (–6.4%) growth of the GDP in the FY 2020–2021. Similarly, the domestic rating agency, India Ratings and Research forecasts a lowest-ever GDP growth (at –11.8%) in the history of India's economic growth since the financial year 1951. The likeliest long-term scenario for advanced economies is one of low growth, low inflation, and high levels of debt. In India, worries primarily were loss of job, daily rations, and absence of a social security net. Such a scenario is only likely to aggravate the problem of joblessness. According to a World Economic Forum survey (conducted in September–October 2020), about 54 per cent of working adults fear losing their job in the aftermath of COVID-19. This figure was estimated at 57 per cent in India (Boyon, 2020). According to Centre for Monitoring Indian Economy, 27 million youth between 20 and 30 years of age in India lost their jobs in April 2020. The budgetary estimates by the Indian government reveal that there has been a deficit in the estimates of the number of jobs to be created compared to the actual jobs created over the years. While the organized sectors of employment in the country grew at nearly 29 per cent in financial year 2020, only 24 per cent of graduates were being hired. Already, companies have started large-scale layoffs and reduced internships and job offers. Many young graduates who were placed during campus recruitment drives are awaiting joining or have been placed on the bench by the hiring companies. Both the industrial and the higher-education sectors are struggling to adapt to the e-technology–enabled working mode of the new normal. According to the World Economic Forum (WEF), more than 1 billion jobs, almost one-third of all jobs worldwide, are likely to be transformed by technology in the next decade. Already 'industry 4.0' has intensified automation and digitization. The pandemic has forcefully increased its pace all of a sudden with hardly any time to adjust and adapt. As rightly pointed out by the WEF, it is skills and not college degrees that will outweigh the job space in future. A much greater emphasis on digital skills, community engagement, environmental awareness and protection skills, and above all creativity, innovation, and adaptability skills is foreseen. The pandemic has put both the employer community and the higher-education community under immense pressure, with learners (students) caught in this turmoil. According to the World Economic Forum, by 2022 at least more than one-half of all employees will need reskilling and upskilling to adapt to changing work requirements. Although it is beyond the scope of the current volume to discuss the impact of the COVID-19 pandemic on the higher-education sector and its implications for graduate employability in future, the book does provide deep insight into the skills mismatch situation of India's young graduates from varied vantage points. It can act as a good guiding point for future analysis and solutions to contain the deepening crisis of graduate employability.

India Higher-Education Report (IHER) 2020

Employment and employability of higher-education graduates

As discussed in the earlier sections, India at present seems to be experiencing job-loss growth, declining labour force participation rates, especially of women, despite increasing educational levels. Employability of educated youth continues to be an important concern despite the efforts made by public authorities. There have been efforts to link higher education with skills and jobs.

The Centre for Policy Research in Higher Education (CPRHE) at NIEPA conducted a study on 'employment and employability of higher-education graduates in India'. The study drew insights from both the industry sector by meeting employers and employees of selected companies and the higher-education sector by surveying the students, faculty, and administrative leaders in different types of higher-education institutions in order to understand the issue of graduate employability gaps and the expectations from the higher-education sector.

In its attempt to address contemporary issues in Indian higher education, the Centre for Policy Research in Higher Education (CPRHE) at NIEPA initiated an annual series of IHER on different identified themes. The first report was comprehensive in nature, covering all major aspects of Indian higher education. The IHER 2016 focused on equity in higher education. The IHER 2017 focused on teaching, learning, and quality in higher education, followed by the IHER 2018 on financing of higher education, and the IHER 2019 focusing on governance and management of higher education in India.

The current volume of the India Higher Education Report on the employment and employability of higher-education graduates comprises chapters that discuss at greater length and explore the issues discussed previously in this chapter. The volume is based on a compilation of papers from eminent academicians, policy experts and practitioners. These are organized under four themes (sections): (Part I) Economic Growth and Employment of the Educated, (Part II) Graduate Employability and Skills Mismatch, (Part III) Education and Skill Formation, and (Part IV) Education–Industry.

Economic growth and employment of the educated

Part I discusses the challenges faced by the educated youth due to jobless growth and the shifts towards informalization. The section has five chapters addressing the phenomena of falling LFPRs with rising levels of education and the comparative trends across regions, gender, and social groups.

Chapter 2, The crisis of jobless growth in India, is jointly written by Rajat Kathuria and Ujjwal Krishna. The authors discuss various dimensions of how growth in India has not resulted in productive job creation and reduction of inequality. They highlight the increasing wage profit gap in the net value added in the industry sector and question if the service sector alone can absorb the teeming millions and reduce the rising inequalities of physical as well as human capital. They argue whether skills training should be considered a public good.

Chapter 3, On the persistence of informal work and self-employment in India, by Vasavi Bhatt and S. Chandrasekhar, addresses the issue of persistence of employment in informal enterprises and self-employment in India. They analyze the trends and patterns of workers engaged in household enterprises and self-employment and trace the change in number of workers engaged in household and non-household industry at the subnational level. They also examine the educational attainment and earnings of those who are self-employed and take stock of the evidence on effectiveness of policies to increase productivity of informal enterprises in order to make them successful.

Chapter 4, Migration, education and employment in India, is by S. Irudaya Rajan. The author writes that the overall international mobility for education and employment has increased tremendously post-globalization, especially in the Global South. India's international student mobility, too, has been growing expansively, second only to China. As a growing amount of literature points to the interconnections between education and employability prospects globally, the author explores internal student migration in India and its consequent links with the work-study interconnections that exist worldwide. Consequently, while highlighting the dismal provision and limited accessibility of higher education for students from migrant-origin states (such as Uttar Pradesh and Bihar) that prompts their out-migration to several 'educational hubs' elsewhere, the chapter argues that in such a scenario, internationally comparable factors are at play even domestically in the context of migrant student aspirations as well as family decision-making.

Chapter 5, Declining labour-force participation in India: does education and training help?, by S. Madheswaran and J.K. Parida explores the trends and patterns of labour force participation by education, age, and gender groups in India. It also explores the sectoral employment patterns and outlines the process of recent growth of unemployment and disheartened labour force. They project that in the near future the LFPR of educated youth would increase massively following the "U" shaped hypothesis, unless measures are taken quickly on creating jobs by correcting the demand-side issues.

Chapter 6, Trends in employment and unemployment in India: dimensions of gender, caste, and education, by Rajendra P. Mamgain and Khalid Khan examines the trends in labour-force participation rates of population across different socio-religious groups. The gender and caste hierarchies in labour-force participation rates are also analyzed to draw meaningful insights on the nature and quality of employment available to the labour force belonging to different socio-religious groups. They emphasize that much of the slow development of labour force is increasingly being attributed to their poor quality of employment, low human capital base, and social exclusion and discrimination which they continue to face in their daily lives in various forms despite their comparatively higher labour-force participation rate (LFPR).

Graduate employability and skills mismatch

Part II comprises three chapters, each of which explore the issue of graduate employability and skills mismatch in India, a challenge possibly more complex than the one faced by other nations, given India's demographic bulge at the centre and massification of its higher-education sector in recent years. The three chapters assess the multidimensional nature of the problem of graduate employability explained by both supply and demand-side effects.

Chapter 7, Skills mismatch of higher-education graduates in India: factors determining employability quotient, by Mona Khare attempts to provide a comparative perspective of the major stakeholders: the employers, new employees, students, and teachers in understanding the issue of employability skill gaps among the higher-education graduates in India. Based on an extensive survey across different types of higher-education institutions and selected industries, this chapter highlights three types of gaps that are the cause for the existing challenge of educated youth not being able to seek and sustain themselves in the job market. The author also identifies the personal, household, and educational factors that may determine graduate employability.

Chapter 8, General, technical and professional education: employability skill gaps, by Ritika Sinha provides an insight into the skill gaps of employees across different educational domains, namely, general, technical, and professional education. Based on the evidence that discipline of one's study becomes very important in case of specialized/technical jobs but a large set of disciplines of study cuts across various industries, this chapter analyzes the domain-wise trends in graduate employment and employability as well as the difference in their employability skill gaps.

Chapter 9, Education, skills mismatch and wage differentials, by Sahana Roy Chowdhury, Catherine Bros, and Sayoree Gooptu explores the question of whether general education or vocational education fetches adequate return in the manufacturing and industrial sector of Indian labour market. Undertaking a statewise analysis, they examine whether the level of industrialization of any state can partially explain the extent of over-education in that region. They find that returns to formal vocational training are subject to the size of either the industrial or manufacturing sectors.

Education and skill formation

Countries across the world are reorienting their education systems towards skills training and vocational exposure. Part III has five chapters that provide an overview of this shift in India and discuss both formal and informal modes of skill delivery in higher education. The part also describes various initiatives taken up in India in recent times.

Chapter 10, India's National Skills Qualifications Framework and employment: the promise and the reality, by Santosh Mehrotra emphasizes the need for developing and implementing the National Vocational Qualifications Framework (NVQF), to streamline Technical and Vocational Education and Training (TVET) systems, and to enhance the value of TVET by providing training based on occupational standards as is being practiced in several countries across the world. This chapter is a critical assessment of the NSQF in India as well as the various tertiary level programmes of vocational education and training in India.

Chapter 11, Curriculum and pedagogy in higher education for skill development, by Nikhil Agarwal and Aprant Agarwal. This chapter discusses the importance of demand-based introduction of skill development courses in higher-education institutes and an innovative curriculum framework which tracks the progress of the workforce and accordingly helps them achieve an exponential growth. The chapter suggests a pedagogy approach, which not only views skill development courses in as methods of increasing employability, but also as generators of employment when these graduates/skilled workforce pursue individual and/or group-based entrepreneurship by converging education, skill, industry, and government initiatives.

Chapter 12, Skilling India: vocational orientation to higher education, by Pankaj Mittal highlights the impact of skilling on the economy of our country and underlines the role of entrepreneurship and the measures required for boosting it. Various international models of vocationalization adopted by different growing economies of the world are also studied while suggesting a model for India.

Chapter 13, Skill universities in India, by S.K. Shukla and Komal Raghav takes a look at the evolution of skill integration in Indian universities finally culminating into formation of specific skill universities. The chapter provides an overview of skill universities in India through a close examination of various aspects by way of case studies of five skill universities in India.

Chapter 14, Informal modes of skill formation, by Vineeta Sirohi underlines the trend of increasing numbers of graduates entering the informal sector and the fact that most informal-sector workers who possess skills have acquired them either through non-formal training or traditional education/informal training. Non-formal training is more structured as compared to informal learning in terms of learning objectives, learning time, or learning support. The latter typically does not lead to certification. The author discusses the concept of informal modes of skill formation by tracing its historical evolution, the theoretical premise for them, and the prevalent major forms of informal skill formation.

Education–industry relationship

No amount of skills training by the higher-education sector can be effective without the active role of the industry sector in assisting in preparing either future employees or future entrepreneurs. Part IV has three chapters, each dealing with a distinct aspect: industry–academia linkages in professional education, entrepreneurship education, and executive education. Each chapter provides a case study.

Chapter 15, Industry–academia linkages in India's technical education sector, by Raj Agarwal and Anuja Pandey investigates technical and higher education in India with a primary focus on industry–academia linkage and its outcomes. They argue that despite a huge network of technical and professional education in the country, the true potential of the industry–academia linkage is still insignificant. The authors also propose recommendations to stimulate industry–academia linkage.

Chapter 16, Refuelling entrepreneurship education in India: a case study, by Kavita Saxena proposes that due to the dearth of formal employment opportunities, promoting entrepreneurship as a career option among youth is desirable for individuals as well as for economic development. Discussing the growing importance and evolution of entrepreneurship education in India, the author highlights the existing gaps and challenges of this small sub-sector.

Chapter 17, Executive education and career advancement: sustainable employment, by Neetu Jain and Ajay K Jain highlights the significance of executive education for career planning and provides an overview of this sub-sector in India. Based on the training need analysis of select working executives in India, the chapter provides a critical evaluation of the implementation and efficacy of such programmes by way of a case study.

The IHER 2020 thus covers various dimensions related to work and work readiness of higher-education graduates in India. The report highlights the weak macroeconomic situation of jobless growth and the related gravity of graduate unemployment, which gets aggravated due to lack of employability skills among the educated youth. The rising concern towards the skills gap is seen to be getting translated into the skills integration and vocational orientation to higher education, as further emphasized in the National Education Policy (NEP) 2020.

Graduate employability has emerged as a global concern with the recent pandemic and technology integrated work processes further aggravating the situation. There are multiple dimensions to the whole challenge, with common and specific experiences across continents. While the degree and dimensions may differ between different groups of nations, the problem stands to disrupt the higher-education systems in economies of all sizes. National governments, international organizations such as UNESCO, the British Council, the World Bank, and regional associations such as the EU, SAARC, ASEAN and BRICS have come forward to launch schemes individually and collectively for skills training, innovations, and research. However, it was beyond the scope of this report to capture this diverse and ever-expanding landscape of graduate employability challenge, specifically with respect to India. The international comparisons within these regional associations, across public and private institutions, graduates from different disciplines, and the role of research and innovation as engines of future jobs offer scope for future research and many more series on the same topic.

References

Agarwal, P. (2007). *Private higher education in India: Status and prospects.* London: The Observatory on Borderless Higher Education.

APU (2018). *APU State of working in India 2018.* Centre for Sustainable Employment, Azim Premji University, Bangalore.

Aspiring Minds (2019). *National employability reports engineers 2019.* Aspiring Minds, Gurgaon.

Blaug, M. (1973). *Education and employment problems in developing countries.* Geneva: International Labour Office.

Boyon, N. (2020, October 19). Job loss is a concern for half of workers across the world. *Ipsos.* www.ipsos.com/en/workers-concerns-about-job-loss-and-access-new-skills-27-countries.

Chenery, H., Ahluwalia, M., Bell, C., Duloy, J., & Jolly, R. (1974). *Redistribution with growth.* London: Oxford University Press.

Ghose, A. K. (2016). *India employment report 2016: Challenges and the imperative of manufacturing-led growth.* New Delhi: Institute for Human Development and Oxford University Press.

Ghosh, J., & Chandrasekhar, C. P. (2007). *Economic growth and employment generation in India: Old problems and new paradoxes.* Paper presented at The IDEAs International conference on sustainable employment generation in developing countries: Current constraints and alternative strategies, Nairobi, Kenya: University of Nairobi.

ILO (2014). *Global employment trends 2014: Risk of a jobless recovery?* Geneva: International Labour Organization.

ILO (2015). *World employment and social outlook: Trends 2015.* Geneva: International Labor Office.

ILO Survey Report (2020). *Youth and COVID-19: Impacts on jobs, education, rights and mental well-being.* www.ilo.org/global/topics/youth-employment/publications/WCMS_753026/lang-en/index.htm.

Kannan, K. P., & Raveendran, G. (2019). From jobless to job-loss growth. *Economic and Political Weekly*, 54(44), 39.

Khare, M. (2014). Employment, employability and higher education in India: The missing links. *Higher Education for the Future*, 1(1), 39–62.

Khare, M. (2016). Taking the skills march forward in India: Transitioning to the world of work. In M. Pilz (Ed.), *India: Preparation for the world of work* (pp. 103–140). Wiesbaden: Springer VS.

Khare, M. (2017). Disparities in graduate employability skills. In N. V. Varghese, N. S. Sabharwal, & M. Malish (Eds.), *India higher education report 2016: Equity* (pp. 331–356). New Delhi: SAGE Publications.

Khare, M. (2018). Employability of graduates in India-hard realities. *International Higher Education*, 95, 29–31. USA: The Boston College Centre for International Higher Education.

Khare, M. (2020a). Exploring the relationship between economic growth, employment and education in Indian States. In G. Rangachar & M. Poornima (Eds.), *India's social sector and SDGs.* New York: Routledge.

Khare, M. (2020b, October). Graduate employment and sustainable employability skills in India. In N. V. Varghese & C. M. Malish (Eds.), *CPRHE Research Paper Series No 14.* New Delhi: CPRHE, NIEPA.

Kundu, A. (2017). Economic and educational inequalities in India within a global perspective: Focus on access and outcome indicators for different socio-religious groups. In N. V. Varghese, N. S. Sabharwal & C. M. Malish (Eds.), *Indian higher education report 2016: Equity*. New Delhi: SAGE Publications.

Madheswaran, S., & Singhari, S. (2017). Disparities in outcome: Graduate labour market in India. In N. V. Varghese, N. S. Sabarwal & C. M. Malish (Eds.), *India higher education report 2016: Equity* (pp. 301–330). New Delhi: SAGE Publications.

Mellor, J. W. (1975). Employment-oriented strategy of rural development. In R. Ephraim & L. J. Brainard (Eds.), *Problems of rural development: Case studies and multi-disciplinary perspectives* (pp. 131–139). Netherlands: Leiden, Brill.

MOF (2013, December 27). *National Skill Qualification Framework (NSQF)*. New Delhi: Department of Economic Affairs, Ministry of Finance.

NEP (2020). *National Education Policy 2020*. New Delhi: Ministry of Human Resource Development, GOI.

NSSO (2014). *Employment and unemployment situation in India (NSS 68th round)*. New Delhi: Ministry of Statistics and Programme Implementation.

Piketty, T. (2006). The Kuznets curve: Yesterday and tomorrow. In A. Banerjee, R. Bénabou, & D. Mookherjee (Eds.), *Understanding poverty*. Oxford Scholarship Online. DOI: 10.1093/0195305191.001.0001.

Periodic Labour Force Survey (2019, May). *Annual report of the periodic labour force survey 2017–2018*. NSSO, Ministry of Statistics and Programme Implementation, Government of India, New Delhi.

Salmi, J. (2017). *The tertiary education imperative: Knowledge, skills and values for development*. The Netherlands: SensePublishers-Rotterdam.

Singh, D., & Chhabra, N. (2017). The future of work: Issues for India. *Labour and Development*, 24(12), 1–20.

Varghese, N. V. (1989). *Education and labour market in India*. Research Report No. 67. International Institute for Educational Planning/UNESCO, Paris.

Varghese, N. V. (1996). Higher education and employment of the educated in India. *Productivity*, 37(3), 444–450.

Varghese, N. V. (2018). Qualification frameworks for improving quality and relevance of education. In N. V. Varghese, A. Pachauri & S. Mandal (Eds.), *India higher education report 2017: Teaching, learning and quality in higher education* (pp. 351–368). New Delhi: SAGE Publications.

Varghese, N. V. (2019). Knowledge, skills and sustainable development: The role of higher education. In R. Govinda & M. Poornima (Eds.), *India's social sector: Problems and prospects* (pp. 97–111). London: Routledge.

World Bank (2006). *India's employment challenge: Creating jobs, helping workers*. Chennai: Oxford University Press.

World Bank (2019). *World development report: The changing nature of work*. Washington, DC: The World Bank.

Part I

Economic growth and employment of the educated

Chapter 2

The crisis of jobless growth in India

Rajat Kathuria and Ujjwal Krishna

The catchphrase that the rich are getting richer while the poor are getting poorer is often invoked when describing the recent growth experience in several countries, including India. There is a widespread perception in India backed by empirical evidence that the benefits of faster GDP growth are being undermined by its pro-rich bias. In other words, growth has not resulted in productive job creation and inequality reduction in the country. The problem of jobless growth, at least in India, is not new. Other harmful spillovers of the current growth model—severe local air pollution and damage to health—also affect the poor disproportionately, exacerbating the vulnerabilities. Thus, even as India grapples with the problems of how to achieve rapid and sustainable economic growth, it must ensure that growth is more inclusive.

In 2013–2014, the average per capita income of the top quintile was almost 11 times that of the bottom quintile. Results of a recent survey reveal that almost 63 per cent of the top 10 per cent of rich Indians reside in urban India, whereas 85 per cent of the bottom-segment households reside in rural India. Over half of Indian households depend on agriculture as their principal means of livelihood, while it contributes just over 14 per cent to the GDP. India's population bulge has not coincided with a manufacturing boom; a similar population bulge in China caused an economic boom in that country. Also, most rich Indians live in locations with the highest level of urbanization, reinforcing spatial inequities. In addition, rural youth unwilling to work in the place of their birth are increasingly seeking non-farm employment elsewhere, thus further crowding the urban fringes and semi-urban areas. The daunting and growing calls by the relatively wealthy in two rich states of India—Gujarat and Haryana—by the Patels and Jats, respectively, to reserve places for their communities in educational institutions and public sector jobs, reflect the failure of the current growth model to absorb a million-odd young Indians joining the labour force every month. In practice, it is a reflection of inadequate job creation leading to social movements demanding favourable treatment and protection, with the attendant social and economic consequences, including eroding confidence in institutions. Through a discussion of the long-lasting disconnect between economic growth and employment, the chapter highlights the importance of skills training in the technology-integrated

DOI: 10.4324/9781003158349-3

service sector boom in the country in order for the demographic dividend to be realized. Arguing for skills training to be a 'public good' in light of 'market failure of skills delivery' in India, the chapter shows various initiatives currently being undertaken by the Indian government.

Growth and employment disconnect

India's structural transformation has not conformed to custom. The stage of industrialization in which a country experiences employment-intensive growth driven by manufacturing has been bypassed in favour of services-led growth. While the services sector did contribute enormously to growth in the last decade, its share in employment (25 per cent) is less than half of its share in GDP. From the perspective of inclusion, therefore, the shortcoming of India's sectoral composition of growth has been such that it has generated relatively fewer opportunities of productive employment for India's poor. The share of workers' wages in the net value added by industries has shown a secular decline in the 30 years since 1983, while the share of profits has climbed (see Figure 2.1). The cause does not lie in the failure of markets to reward labour adequately but in the nature of labour market rigidities that drive a wedge between GDP and employment growth.

Increasing informalization and contractualization of the workforce is an unintended consequence of labour regulations that seek to protect workers but end

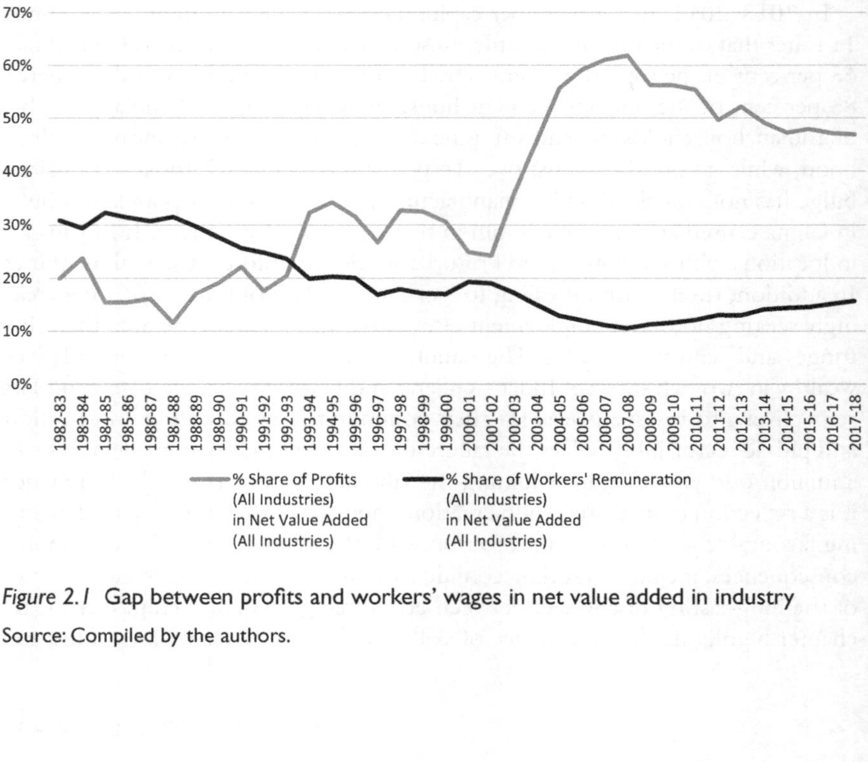

Figure 2.1 Gap between profits and workers' wages in net value added in industry

Source: Compiled by the authors.

up harming them. Two out of every three workers in the private organized sector in 2011–2012 were informal workers with no social security. Along with the growing capital intensity of manufacturing (Figure 2.1), it comes as no surprise that India's recent growth experience has been described as 'jobless'. Inequality has in fact risen since the early 1990s.

The jobs conundrum in the background of the structural transformation under way is a significant challenge for India, with both the manufacturing and services sectors of the Indian economy being affected adversely. This calls for an examination of the drivers of poor employment growth rates despite high economic growth and favourable demographics. India certainly needs to boost manufacturing growth to absorb more workers in order to realize the principal intent underlying the 'Make in India' initiative. Several recognized impediments—infrastructure bottlenecks, land acquisition, and environment clearances—need to be addressed, along with easing of labour regulations, to make manufacturing a jobs-escalator for India.

Of late, a segment of the economy—start-ups—is witnessing extraordinary dynamism. The resolution of growth and jobs will need multiple means at all ends of the spectrum—from informal to formal, from agriculture to manufacturing, from agriculture to services, from rigid to flexible, from full term to fixed, and from formal to gig.

Demographic dividend or disaster?

India is poised to become the youngest country in the world with an average age of 29 years by 2020 (UN Habitat, 2013) and will account for 28 per cent of the world's workforce (EY & FICCI, 2013). The demographic dividend is 'the economic growth potential that can result from shifts in a population's age structure, mainly when the share of the working-age population (15 to 64) is larger than the non-working-age share of the population (14 and younger and 65 and older)' (UNFPA, 2019). India, thus, stands at the cusp of a huge opportunity as never before. Unlike many countries that are struggling with ageing populations and rising dependency ratios, India boasts of a potential demographic dividend. Over 60 per cent of the population is in the working-age range of 15–59 years.

The advantage of the number of people in the workforce exceeding the number of dependents is that a significantly larger proportion of the population has the potential to be productive, by earning higher incomes and saving more, leading to a rise in savings as a proportion of gross domestic product (GDP). This corresponds with a rise in investment relative to GDP, according to the standard Harrod-Domar model. India's population pyramid is expected to 'bulge' in the aforementioned working-age bracket, leading to an increase in the working-age population from 761 million to 869 million between 2011 and 2020 (EY & FICCI, 2013). This phase of the demographic transition currently under way in India is expected to continue till around 2040 (World Bank, 2012). In the event that this growing workforce is not adequately skilled, the 'non-availability of skilled manpower may result in machines replacing labour on a large scale, (leading to) large numbers among the increasingly youthful labour force unemployed' (Mehrotra et al., 2013). While technological progress has been a recurring phenomenon globally, there are growing concerns over automation, spurred by exponential advances in Industry 4.0 technologies like machine learning, data mining, machine vision, computational statistics, artificial intelligence (AI), and 3D printing. 'Algorithms for big data are now rapidly entering domains reliant upon pattern recognition and can readily substitute for labour in a wide range of non-cognitive tasks' (Frey & Osborne, 2015). While automation has traditionally been viewed as replacing routine manual tasks, dramatically improved computational abilities have rendered the service sector uniquely vulnerable. Computerization is principally confined to low-skill occupations (Frey & Osborne, 2013). Frey and Osborne (2013), on the basis of World Bank data, estimate that 69 per cent of jobs in India are at a high risk of automation. Lee et al. (2017) indicate that there is a demand shift favouring skilled labour in India for the period 1994–2010. Therefore, a concerted effort to adapt to the changing nature of work needs to be made, where the availability of skilled manpower, equipped with skills that are increasingly adaptive and relevant, needs to be increased substantially to stem the tide of automation wiping away jobs *en masse*. A failure of the government to intervene adequately and incentivize markets to ramp up skills training efforts could result in a 'demographic disaster'. For a population with over 95 per cent of the population not formally skilled, India stands severely compromised to make a dent on its jobless growth.

Can service sector absorb the teeming millions?

India has a services-led economy where the service sector accounts for 54.77 per cent of the gross value added at current prices (Ministry of Statistics and Programme Implementation, Government of India, 2021), and the industrial sector accounts for only 27.48 per cent. Premature deindustrialization (Rodrik, 2016) is the trend in which peak manufacturing employment declines among emerging economies. The trajectory of shifting people from farms to high-paying factory jobs, as witnessed in the developed economies (the UK's peak manufacturing employment was at 45 per cent prior to the onset of the Second World War), will not be replicated by emerging economies like India and Brazil (where the same peak was no higher than 15%). This is due to the increasingly less labour-intensive nature of manufacturing processes in low- and middle-income countries given the intensified automation of such processes. Services-led growth in India is further exacerbated by the informality of the service sector. Informality is characterized by workers being engaged in economic activities that are less productive and that yield lesser income. Such workers are bound by less stable contracts and receive fewer social security benefits. Ninety-two per cent of India's workforce are informal, spanning both the organized and unorganized sectors (ILO, 2017), while 78 per cent of the workforce are in small enterprises employing fewer than ten workers in the time period of 2011–2012 (Mehrotra et al., 2013). Given that future growth could be even more jobless due to being service sector-driven, and owing to the changing nature and fabric of jobs, skilled labour will be substantially more valuable than it is today. To make sure that India realises its demographic dividend, reform and legislation aimed at making skills training more inclusive and accessible, with an improved quality of its delivery across classes, is critical to hedge against a future of immense technological unemployment.

Is technology a boon?

Technology offers both hope and challenges. Hope, because it allows expansion and better targeting of social welfare schemes. There is already evidence that MGNREGA payments through Aadhaar linked bank accounts have increased efficiency and reduced leakages.[1] The challenge is of course automation and job displacement. Can the role of technology fulfil its promise to resolve one of India's big challenges, namely, productive job creation? As of January 2016, there were 19,400 technology-enabled start-ups in India, of which 5,000 were seeded in 2015 alone. As of December 2015, eight Indian start-ups had graduated to the Unicorn club (valuations greater than $1 billion). This is a significant development and represents the dynamic role that liberated markets can play in an economy in driving innovation and growth. While growth has helped in reducing absolute poverty in India, it still persists.

Skill development in India: a classic story of market failure

Market failure, which is essentially 'a market's inability to deliver its theoretical benefits due to the existence of market imperfections' (Todaro & Smith, 2015), has frequently been deployed as the reason for governments to intervene and expand their role in developing countries with a view 'to alter the working of the free market' (Todaro & Smith, 2015). Some of these market imperfections include externalities, information asymmetries, principal-agent problems, and the lack of knowledge. All these characteristics seem to plague the Indian market and may be termed as some important reasons for skill asymmetry and deficiency among educated young people.

Is skills training a 'public good'?

While the provision of skills training has strong positive externalities like societal benefits such as better health, lower crime, and better-informed citizens as well as a 'higher possibility of a boost to the development and utilization of technology and innovation across the economy' (Keep, 2015), governmental intervention into the market for skill development is a contested issue. This can be viewed from the lens of the human capital theory and the public goods theory. In this respect, the human capital theory, which has arguably been more dominant, takes a more theoretical, free-market approach, in that it holds that a market failure doesn't occur at all in an economy since the incentive structure of the agents in the economy—the worker and the firm—is such that investing in skills training is desirable. Furthermore, the human capital theory argues against governmental intervention in the market for skill development since it holds that free markets can bring about sufficient investment in skills training. As such, the government's role should remain limited to ensuring the smooth functioning of the markets through the abolition of price controls and the promotion of competition and the circulation of market information. On the other hand, the public goods theory holds that there is likely to be an under-provisioning of training by firms given concerns related to poaching by other employers after training (Ra & Shim, 2009). Given that some of the employees 'would subsequently move to a different employer . . . the company that paid for the training course would reap only part of the return on its investment, (leading firms to be) tempted to under-invest in skills development' (Cunningham, 2011). However, there are very limited reliable data on the scale of poaching or its impact upon employers' training decisions (Keep, 2015). Nonetheless, skills training ought to be treated as a public good, since it will likely be under-provided if left entirely to markets. Therefore, governments ought to intervene by way of subsidies and incentives to firms and employees, in order to circumvent the problem of employers not finding it viable to bear the total costs of skills training (Ra & Shim, 2009).

A few other reasons that strengthen the case for public intervention may be identified as follows:

a. Self-investment in skills training

Bargaining externalities occur as workers are 'less likely to invest in their own training if employers have market power and are able to keep wages down' (Almeida et al., 2013). Coordination failures are possible in cases where the absence of skilled workers leads to a lack of high-productivity jobs being created or where the workers do not invest on their own skills in response to an absence of jobs. The failure of capital markets is pertinent, in that credit constraints prevent the supply of skills, since the ability of both firms and workers to finance skills training is compromised. The lack of information hampers the market for skills since the appropriate signals are not created for workers to make optimal decisions regarding investment in their skills and the choice of trade or specialization therein.

b. Firm size

Furthermore, the size of a firm is a determinant of the extent of its inclination to invest in skills training for its employees. Smaller firms face far greater challenges than larger firms in developing their human capital. 'While smaller firms train less, they are also less inclined to view an inadequately skilled workforce as a major constraint on their operations', effectively meaning that there exists a 'low-skills equilibrium' among smaller firms since they can sustain adequate productivity and ensure their survival in a market segment which doesn't require highly skilled workers (Vandenberg & Trinh, 2016). Given this size-induced market failure in skills training, the 'policy implications are not only that government can reduce the costs for firms to train but also that micro and small firms need to be sensitized to the benefits of skills upgrading'. Moreover, these subsidies need to also be directed at offering 'arrangements through local training providers that are easy to find, understand and administer' (ibid).

c. Government failure in skills provision

Government failure is, while also a risk, a comparatively lesser relevant factor when compared to market failure given that government failure in technical and vocational education and training (TVET) is limited to a failure to 'improve accountability and strengthen links with the private sector' (Almeida et al., 2013) and to when the government is unable to identify the changes of various skills demands (Shackleton, 1995). Bureaucratic failures of acting in self-interest, agency problems, and government efficiency are also possible sources of government failure in intervening in the market for skills (Ra & Shim, 2009). However, given the relatively weaker scope of self-regulation by markets in TVET compared to regulation by the government, it would be difficult to argue that this scenario represents a 'more inefficient allocation in the absence of the intervention', in order to qualify as government failure.

TVET had been largely private-sector-led, with limited government Industrial Training Institutes, until the Government of India introduced a chapter on skill challenges in the Eleventh Five-Year Plan document (Planning Commission, 2008), followed by the establishment of an institutional setup to address skills, which will be discussed in the next section. Government intervention necessarily needs to develop private-sector initiatives given governmental capacity constraints, as can be gauged from the annual formal government TVET capacity of 2.5 million and output of 1.5 million (Krishnan, 2017) vis-à-vis 12 million people being added every year to the workforce.

d. Limited involvement of industry sectors in skills training

In niche sectors of the Indian economy, which have experienced extremely high levels of growth with the opening up of the economy in the early 1990s, most notably information technology (IT) and IT-enabled services (ITeS), firms have taken the lead in investing in the improvement of industry-relevant skills training for their employees. Such investment has been fuelled by the strong demand for IT-ITeS. Such firms, of their own volition by and large, 'have stepped forward to create new training courses with more appropriate content, establish partnerships with academia and government, and apply explicit standards to assess and certify skills' (Almeida et al., 2013). Leading Indian IT firms like Tata Consultancy

Services (TCS), Infosys, and Wipro run their own large-scale technical and finishing schools. The fact that the Indian IT industry has developed an unparalleled skills-training infrastructure is attributable to its critical dependence on a highly skilled employee base as well as its immense revenues that allow for the space to make such investments. This is a set of conditions not easily found in other industries and sectors of the Indian economy. Moreover, the contribution of the IT sector to India's GDP stood at 8 per cent in 2020 (NASSCOM, 2021); therefore, the IT sector does not constitute a dominant proportion of the Indian economy. The Indian IT industry, while 'often represented as providing employment opportunities to a wider cross-section of society, (is however) more homogenous than is often supposed, in that the workforce is largely urban, middle class, and high/middle caste' (Upadhya, 2007). For these reasons, the IT-ITeS industry is not representative of either a substantial or a well-distributed employer-driven skills training infrastructure in India. Firm size, in addition to firm type, is also a barrier to investment in skills training, and therefore the micro, small, and medium enterprises (MSMEs) and the informal sector are relatively less inclined, in descending order, to match the skills training record of the IT-ITeS industry, which is characterized by large firms.

e. *Information asymmetry*

The market failure of skills in India is also due to an information asymmetry in the Indian labour market, where there is a large supply of skilled workers who are unable to find jobs, while industry and service establishments are unable to find skilled labour (Krishnan, 2017). This is due to inadequate signalling of skills by employees to employers, and hence a 'skill wage premium' is largely absent, creating a vicious cycle that further dissuades workers from investing in their own skills.

It can thus be seen that the market for skill development in India has failed due to the employers' lack of interest in investing in skills training for their employees and the deficit in the ability and willingness of employees to pay for getting skilled. These market failures are attributable by varying degrees to capital market failures, information asymmetries, poaching externalities, coordination failures, and firm size. Some policy responses to the market failure of skills include providing better information on the benefits of investing in skills, forming employer 'clubs' to overcome externalities and poaching by way of generating skills as a collective good, regulating and ensuring compliance through the imposition of statutory training levies, and assigning property rights for employers on their investment in skilling their employees to guard against poaching (Keep, 2015). Almeida et al. (2013) suggest identifying and addressing the market failure in skills by way of:

> increasing the bargaining power of workers, facilitating the diffusion of new technologies that will create demands for skilled labour, . . . opening credit lines for specific types of training, and providing information about labour market conditions and the quality of various training providers.

To combat the coordination failures and inappropriately structured incentives, Almeida et al. (2013) suggest that subsidies also need to be financed out of general revenues since the alternative route of payroll taxes (as in Brazil) would increase labour costs, leading to a decrease in the demand for labour. Thus, there may be several ways in which the government may intervene.

Capacity building through government intervention—a few initiatives

Efforts by the Government of India on skill development can be traced back to the Industrial Training Institutes (ITIs), the first of which was set up under the Ministry of Labour and Employment in 1969. However, they remained unable to keep pace with the changes in Indian industry's requirements and provided increasingly irrelevant skills training. The institutional landscape for skill development in India has evolved since 2008, when the National Skill Development Corporation (NSDC), a public-private partnership between the Government of India and private chambers of commerce and industry, was formed as the government's implementation arm, initially under the Ministry of Finance. NSDC funds private-sector initiatives in skill development and has delegated the task of determining the National Occupation Standards (NOS) as well as all other specificities of skills training as relevant to industry through, as of 2020, a network of 38 Sector Skill Councils (SSCs). To overcome the government's capacity constraints, NSDC supports 460 Training Partners (mostly for-profit organizations) and 8503 Training Centres through soft loans as a viability gap funding (NSDC, 2019). The National Skill Development Agency (NSDA), formed in 2013, was assigned to be an anchor for the National Skills Qualifications Framework and serve as the skills regulator. NSDA has been subsumed into the National Council for Vocational Education and Training (NCVET) as of 2019 to act as an overarching skills regulator. The Ministry of Skill Development and Entrepreneurship (MSDE) was established in 2014 and assumed administrative control of all of the agencies just mentioned. The Apprentices Act, 1961 was amended in 2014 to increase its attractiveness to industry, to cover the service sector, to link stipends to minimum wage, to abolish the trade-wise and unit-wise quota system where the government handed specific apprenticeship targets to industry, and to increase the flexibility of including new trades to keep pace with changes in technology (Krishna, 2017; Krishna, 2015). Further, 'penalties like imprisonment and other liabilities have been removed and industry has been allowed to self-regulate and electronically report its achievements' (Krishna, 2019). In 2015, the Skill India Mission was launched by the Prime Minister, and the National Policy of Skill Development and Entrepreneurship came into effect, superseding the National Skills Policy of 2009.

MSDE's flagship scheme, the Pradhan Mantri Kaushal Vikas Yojana (PMKVY), subsidizes the entire cost of skills training to ensure that socio-economically vulnerable young people are not denied access. NSDC, through its network of Training Partners, implements both the subsidized PMKVY skills training as well as the fee-based model, which has consistently demonstrated a markedly higher placement record when compared to the PMKVY, which can be attributed to the 'coefficient of seriousness' increasing manifold from the trainers and the students, given that students value the skills training programmes more if they or their families have saved and paid the fee (Krishna, 2017). This points toward subsidies as a solution to the market failure as an unsustainable long-term solution. The PMKVY includes Recognition of Prior Learning, which formally certifies the traditional and artisanal skills with incremental training like design and marketing, but its very short duration has been criticized as highly ineffective (Mehrotra, 2017).

The creation of a comprehensive Labour Market Information System (LMIS) is under way, which addresses the information needs of all stakeholders in the skills ecosystem (Vandenberg & Trinh, 2016) by way of 'correctly anticipating skills (that) will help reduce skills mismatch, (and) preparing people for technological change' (ILO, 2011). This mismatch can be reduced with improved skill gap studies, currently patchy and available only at the district headquarter level to solve information asymmetries and signalling and coordination problems. Since very few employers are engaged in enterprise-based skilling, private training providers, facilitated by government intervention to catalyze investments from industry by way of direct engagement of employers with private-sector training providers, are necessary to make vocational training demand-driven (as opposed to being supply-driven) (Mehrotra, 2017). Circumventing market failure also requires a functioning credit market with collateral guarantees for students and planned coordination with the private sector (Krishnan, 2017).

Some such initiatives are under way but need to be scaled up and monitored for quality and effective intervention.

Conclusion

The risk of jobless growth coinciding with India's demographic dividend threatens sustainable economic growth and human security in the long run. Reinventing the wheel is a tall order for any developing country that missed the bus to develop a labour-intensive manufacturing sector at the crucial juncture of its structural transformation. If India is to face the reality of service-sector-led growth, then in a world increasingly characterized by the redundancy of lower-order tasks, skill development is essential to make India's youth automation-resilient. A global scan of the literature on skill development and TVET reveals that skills training is prone to market failure in several countries and that concerted government intervention in the form of subsidies, levies, and information provision is needed to remove various types of externalities and information asymmetries. The case of India is largely similar to the global average; however, the challenges of skill development assume far more importance in the Indian paradigm due to the potential demographic dividend at this stage in the age structure of the population. Due to the extremely low governmental capacity to deliver skill straining directly, the Indian government's intervention needs to alter the incentive structure of firms and workers towards intensifying private-sector investment in skills.

Various initiatives currently being undertaken by the Indian government have been discussed, largely in line with the theoretical fixes to the factors underlying the market failure of skills, while their shortcomings were also flagged. On balance, it is fair to conclude that the market failure of skill development is a bigger risk than government failure, given the fact that a *laissez-faire* market for TVET cannot be self-regulated well. Avoiding creation of governmental regulation on the argument that inefficiencies may creep in is unwise due to the alternative being far riskier. The government's inability to accurately predict changes in skill demands has been partially addressed with private-sector-led SSCs being delegated the task. A purely market-led model for skills training would never be able to grow beyond its niche sectors, towards which efforts of private skills training would be skewed. As a result, structural inequalities would persist and the demographic dividend would be wasted, possibly with calamitous effects on social welfare and stability in a future world characterized by automated processes and more or less wiped out low-skilled jobs.

Note

1 The Mahatma Gandhi National Rural Employment Guarantee Act (MGNREGA) is a law whereby any adult who applies for employment in rural areas has to be given work on local public works within 15 days. If employment is not given, an unemployment allowance has to be paid. Accessed from www.mgnrega.co.in/.

References

Almeida, R., Behrman, J., & Robalino, D. (2013). *The right skills for the job? Rethinking training policies for workers.* Washington, DC: The International Bank for Reconstruction and Development, the World Bank.

Cunningham, S. (2011). *Understanding market failures in an economic development context* (1st ed.). Pretoria: Mesopartner Monograph 4.

EY & FICCI (2013). *Reaping India's promised demographic dividend: Industry in the driving seat.* EY and Federation of Indian Chambers of Commerce and Industry. India: Ernst & Young LLP.

Frey, C. B., & Osborne, M. (2013). *The future of employment: How susceptible are jobs to computerization?* Oxford: Oxford Martin School, University of Oxford.

Frey, C. B., & Osborne, M. (2015). *Technology at work: The future of innovation and employment.* Citi GPS: Global perspectives and solutions. Oxford: Oxford Martin School, University of Oxford.

ILO (2011). *Indian national workshop on skills data and LMIS.* New Delhi: International Labour Organization/Regional Skills Programme/Japan.

ILO (2017). *India labour market update.* New Delhi: International Labour Organization Country Office for India.

Keep, E. (2015). *Market failure in skills.* SSDA Catalyst Issue 1. Wath-upon-Dearne, England: Sector Skill Development Agency.
Krishna, J. (2015). Let industry embrace apprenticeship reforms. *Financial Express.* www.financialexpress.com/industry/let-industry-embrace-apprenticeship-reforms/156635/.
Krishna, J. (2017). National Apprenticeship Promotion Scheme (NAPS) opens a floodgate of opportunities for industry-driven apprenticeship programs. *National Skills Network.* www.nationalskillsnetwork.in/apprenticeships-naps/.
Krishna, J. (2019). *Apprenticeships could address most of India's skill development challenges.* Geneva: International Labour Organization (ILO). www.ilo.org/wcmsp5/groups/public/-ed_emp/-ifp_skills/documents/publication/wcms_660768.pdf.
Krishnan, K. P. (2017). *Skills development: Legacy, current challenges & planning for the future.* Singapore: Institute of South Asian Studies, National University of Singapore.
Lee, J., Mehrotra, S., Francisco, R., & Wie, D. (2017). *Human capital development in South Asia: Achievements, prospects and policy challenges.* Manila: Asian Development Bank.
Mehrotra, S. (2017). Why India needs to re-think the skilling system and re-align the roles of key stakeholders. *National Skills Network.* www.nationalskillsnetwork.in/santosh-mehrotra-skill-development/.
Mehrotra, S., Gandhi, A., & Sahoo, B. K. (2013). Estimating India's skill gap on a realistic basis. *Economic & Political Weekly*, 48(13), 102–111.
Ministry of Statistics and Programme Implementation (2021). *National accounts statistics 2021.* New Delhi: Government of India.
NASSCOM (2021). *Future of technology services: Winning in this decade.* New Delhi: National Association for Software and Services Companies.
NSDC (2019). *Training partner dashboard.* New Delhi: National Skill Development Corporation.
Planning Commission (2008). *Eleventh Five Year Plan.* New Delhi: Government of India.
Ra, Y., & Shim, K. W. (2009). *The Korean case study: Past experience and new trends in training policies.* Social Protection & Labour Discussion Paper 0931. Washington, DC: The World Bank.
Rodrik, D. (2016). Premature deindustrialization. *Journal of Economic Growth*, 21(1), 1–33.
Shackleton, J. R. (1995). *Training for employment in Western Europe and the United States.* Aldershot: Edwin Elgar.
Todaro, M., & Smith, S. C. (2015). *Economic development* (12th ed.). Harlow, England: Pearson Education Limited.
UNFPA (2019). *World population dashboard.* New York: United Nations Population Fund.
UN Habitat (2013). *State of the urban youth 2012–2013: Youth in the prosperity of cities.* Nairobi: United Nations Human Settlements Program.
Upadhya, C. (2007). Employment, exclusion and 'merit' in the Indian IT industry. *Economic & Political Weekly*, 42(20), 1863–1868.
Vandenberg, P., & Trinh, L. Q. (2016). *Is there a size-induced market failure in skills training?* ADBI Working Paper No. 598. Tokyo: Asian Development Bank Institute. www.adb.org/publications/there-size-induced-market-failure-skills-training/.
World Bank (2012). *More and better jobs in South Asia.* Washington, DC: The International Bank for Reconstruction and Development, the World Bank.

Chapter 3

On the persistence of informal work and self-employment in India

S. Chandrasekhar and Vasavi Bhatt

Recurring questions in the literature in the context of developing countries is whether self-employment is a choice or necessity and whether the self-employed can be classified as successfully employed (Gindling & Newhouse, 2014). These questions are relevant, since informal enterprises continue to account for nearly a third of the gross domestic product and 70 per cent of employment in developing countries (World Bank, 2019).

Today the pressing question in the Indian context is whether one would see a meaningful transformation of occupation patterns in the labour market. In 2017–2018, out of the estimated 372.6 million workers in India, 52.2 per cent reported being self-employed. The self-employed are not a homogenous group,[1] and as we will discuss later in this chapter their average earnings are not necessarily enough to eke out a meaningful livelihood. Informality and self-employment are viewed as a consequence of lack of alternative opportunities for those entering the workforce. An additional corroboration of extent of informality is the presence of a total of 63.39 million unincorporated non-agricultural enterprises (excluding construction), in 2015–2016, which while providing employment to 111 million people, were not productive (Government of India, 2018a). In these enterprises, either the owner is the sole employee, in which case they are called Own Account Enterprises (OAE) or the owner also hires workers, and these enterprises are called Establishments. The lack of dynamism is reflected by the absence of shift from predominance of OAE to Establishments, since only 16 per cent of these enterprises can be classified as establishments.

Taken together, four factors, namely, a labour market characterized by a large amount of informality, low productivity of unincorporated enterprises, near zero elasticity of employment,[2] and the shift towards automation of routine jobs,[3] do not augur well for Indians transitioning from school to work in the next decade. This is despite the fact that the incoming pool of workers will have a higher level of educational attainment than those currently working. Estimates from Periodic Labour-Force Survey 2017–2018 (PLFS) indeed confirm the upward trend in educational attainment of those aged 15–29 years.[4]

Over two decades after the ushering in of economic reforms, India continues to be a country of self-employed and characterized by a large number of

DOI: 10.4324/9781003158349-4

unincorporated enterprises. The conventional wisdom is that during the process of economic growth and development, one is expected to observe a redistribution of workers from low- to high-productivity sectors, a decline in the importance of informal, unorganized, or household enterprises, and a shift in the occupation structure from self-employment to regular wage-salaried. A reading of the lecture delivered in memory of Alfred Nobel by Kuznets would confirm the belief of economists that such a transformation would be a resultant of economic growth (Kuznets, 1971). Despite India's gross domestic product growing at 6.7 times, from $270 billion in 1991 to $1.8 trillion in 2011,[5] it is apparent that to a major extent the conventional wisdom of there being a transformation of labour market outcomes has not been fulfilled.[6] Irrespective of whether one views it from the lens of gross value added by unincorporated enterprises or the earnings of the self-employed, it is a story of inadequacy of earnings.

Today the overarching question is how to ensure that self-employment is a sustainable livelihood option and whether there are lessons from experience of other countries. India faces the daunting challenge of achieving Goal 8 of the Sustainable Development Goals on decent jobs, self-employment, and entrepreneurship.

It is against this backdrop that this chapter addresses the issue of persistence of employment in informal enterprises and self-employment in India. This chapter is structured as follows. In the section 'Data and definitions', we focus on definition of informal or unorganized sector and worker. In the sections 'Coexistence of formal and informal' and 'Recent patterns', which form the core of this chapter, we present the trends and patterns of workers engaged in household enterprises and self-employment. The data we analyze come from Census of India B-series tables[7] 1991–2011 and the PLFS 2017–2018.[8] The Census tables allow us to trace the change in number of workers engaged in household and non-household industry at the subnational level. The Census tables also have information on the class of workers, namely, employer, employee, family worker, and single worker. We also use data from the PLFS in order to examine the educational attainment and earnings of those who are self-employed. In the section 'From subsistence to success', we take stock of the evidence on effectiveness of policies to increase productivity of informal enterprises in order to make them successful. 'Conclusion' ends the chapter.

Data and definitions

The National Commission for Enterprises in the Unorganized Sector (NCEUS), which was established in 2004, defined the unorganized or informal sector as 'all unincorporated private enterprises owned by individuals or households engaged in the production and sale of goods and services and operated on a proprietary or a partnership basis and employing less than 10 persons'. The Commission defined unorganized workers to be 'those who are working in the Unorganized Sector and the workers in the formal sector without any employment security and social security[9] provided by the employer'. Based on the NCEUS definition, it is possible to arrive at an estimate of the number of unorganized workers using NSSO's survey of employment and unemployment. In the context of this chapter, the important characteristic of household industry is that it is not run on the scale of a registered factory and not more than 10 persons are engaged if the establishment uses power or not more than 20 persons if the establishment does not use power. Workers can be classified as employers, employees, single workers, or family workers. An employer is an individual who hires one or more workers to work such that he is not only responsible for his own work but also giving jobs to others. An employee on the other hand works under someone for salary or wages in cash or kind. Single workers work by themselves, neither working for anyone nor hiring anyone. A family worker is engaged in a family enterprise and does not receive any wage or salary either in cash or kind.[10]

It is possible to identify workers in household industry from NSSO's survey of employment and unemployment and the PLFS by triangulating information on enterprise type, use of electricity, number of workers in the enterprise, and availability of social security benefits. However, we do not use the PLFS to provide an estimate of the number of unorganized workers. Instead, we use the PLFS to focus on the educational attainment and earnings of the self-employed. In the NSSO data, an individual who is self-employed is an own-account worker or employer or unpaid family worker in the household enterprise.

Coexistence of formal and informal

In order to explain the coexistence of the formal and informal enterprises and persistence of self-employment, we draw upon two recent overviews, namely, entrepreneurship in the informal economy (Webb et al., 2013) and informality and development (La Porta & Shleifer, 2014). Webb et al. identify three theoretical frameworks, namely, institutional theory, motivation-related theories, and resource allocation theory, in order to understand the existence and persistence of informal enterprises. Of these, the resource allocation theory is probably the most relevant in the Indian context. They advance the following proposition: 'Leveraging family resources is positively related to opportunity exploitation in the informal economy and subsistence yet negatively related to long-term effectiveness' (p. 609). The idea behind this proposition is that in the absence of employment opportunities in the formal sector and lack of financial resources, an individual would pursue opportunities in the informal sector where family members provide unpaid labour. In general, such an activity barely covers subsistence needs and does not lead to long-run improvements in income and non-income dimensions of well-being. This explanation is consistent with the view that informality is a by-product of poverty and theories of duality—existence of a formal and informal sector with little overlap (La Porta & Shleifer, 2014).

While the consensus view is that, with economic growth, duality would disappear, the evidence is mixed, and the numbers open to interpretation. In the aggregate, the share of output from the informal sector in India's GDP is estimated to be around 50 per cent (Government of India, 2015).[11] This would imply that informality has not declined in a $2 trillion dollar economy. Ghani et al. (2013), after reviewing the growth of the unorganized sector in India, flag the reasons for its persistence as an open research question. However, one does find a negative correlation, albeit weak, between gross domestic product and share of informal workers at the subnational level. This is evident when we plot the logarithm of per capita gross state domestic product of Indian states against the share of household industry workers in total non-agricultural workers in each state (see Figure 3.1).

The share of workers in household industry in total workers increased from 2.4 per cent in 1991 to 3.8 per cent in 2011. In terms of absolute numbers, a total of 18.3 million workers were engaged in household industry in 2011. The top seven states, namely, Uttar Pradesh, West Bengal, Bihar, Andhra Pradesh, Tamil Nadu, Maharashtra, and Madhya Pradesh, accounted for 73.3 per cent of household industry workers. The aggregate share of the top-ten states in total household industry workers remained unchanged at 88 per cent over the period 1991–2011. However, the share of Uttar Pradesh, West Bengal, and Bihar increased (see Figure 3.2).

In 2011, we find that 57 per cent of household industry workers are engaged in Divisions 10–16 of National Industrial Classification.[12] The share of workers is highest in manufacture of food products (15.4 per cent), tobacco products

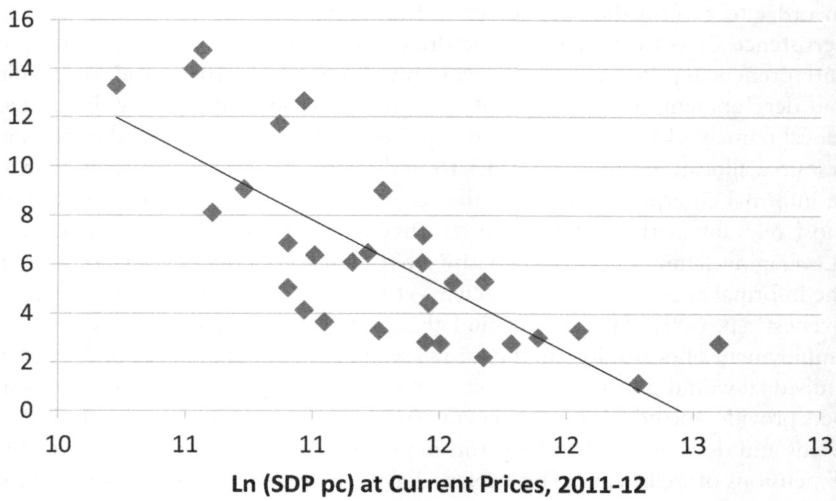

Figure 3.1 Scatter plot of share of household industry workers in a state and logarithm of per capita state domestic product

Source: Census of India 2011 Tables and Reserve Bank of India Database of Indian Economy (Online).

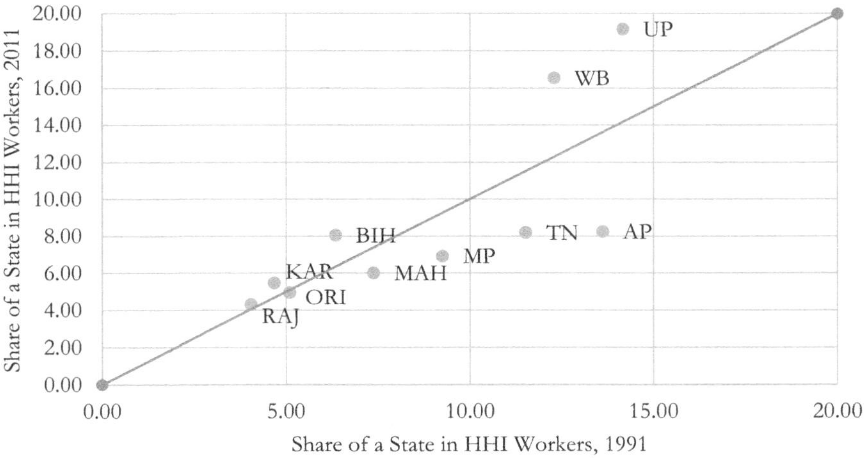

Figure 3.2 Share of top-ten states in all-India total number of household industry workers in 1991 and 2011

Source: Census of India 1991 and 2011 Tables.

(12.9 per cent), and textiles (15.9 per cent). In contrast, less than 8 per cent of non-household industry workers are engaged in these divisions. What is apparent is the clear segmentation of household and non-household workers by division of National Industrial Classification. In the empirical literature, the co-agglomeration of formal and informal is the focus of analysis by Mukim (2015). She identifies buyer–seller linkages as one of the important reasons for co-agglomeration. She finds evidence of co-agglomerations in apparel, furniture, and metal-making industries.

Among those engaged in household industry, the largest share is accounted for by family workers (see Figure 3.3). While both men and women are engaged as family workers, the share of women is higher than men. Employees account for the largest share of workers in non-household industry, followed by single workers.

One does not observe any stark differences by gender and age group in the distribution of main workers in household and non-household industry (see Figure 3.4a). On the other hand, when we compare Figure 3.4a with Figure 3.4b, we do find a difference across main and marginal workers. The inverted 'U'-shaped pattern evident in the case of main workers is not evident in the case of marginal workers. If one had access to panel data, then it would have been possible to understand whether there is a shift from cultivation or agriculture into other types work across age cohorts.

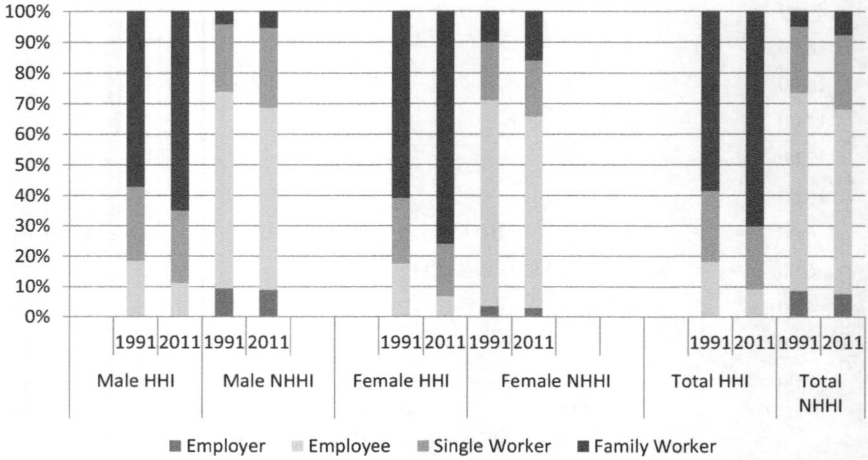

Figure 3.3 Distribution of workers by class in household industry (HHI) and non-household industry (NHHI)

Source: Census of India 1991 and 2011 Tables. https://censusindia.gov.in/DigitalLibrary/Archive_home.aspx.

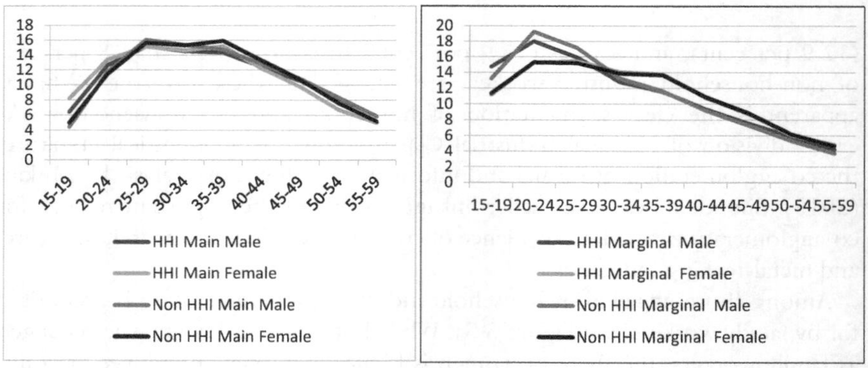

Figure 3.4a Distribution of main workers in household industry (HHI) and non-household industry (NHHI) by age group in 2011

Figure 3.4b Distribution of marginal workers in household industry (HHI) and non-household industry (NHHI) by age group in 2011

Source: Census of India 2011 Tables.

When we examine the educational attainment of workers engaged in manufacturing, we do find a decline in the share of not literates. This is not surprising, since the share of not literates has declined in the population as a whole. When we compare workers in household and non-household industry in 2011, we do not find stark differences in distribution of workers by educational attainment (see Figure 3.5). This is consistent with evidence from other countries that educational attainment of workers across the formal and informal sectors is not very different. When we consider non-agricultural workers in 2011, then there are indeed differences across sections of industry (see Figure 3.6).

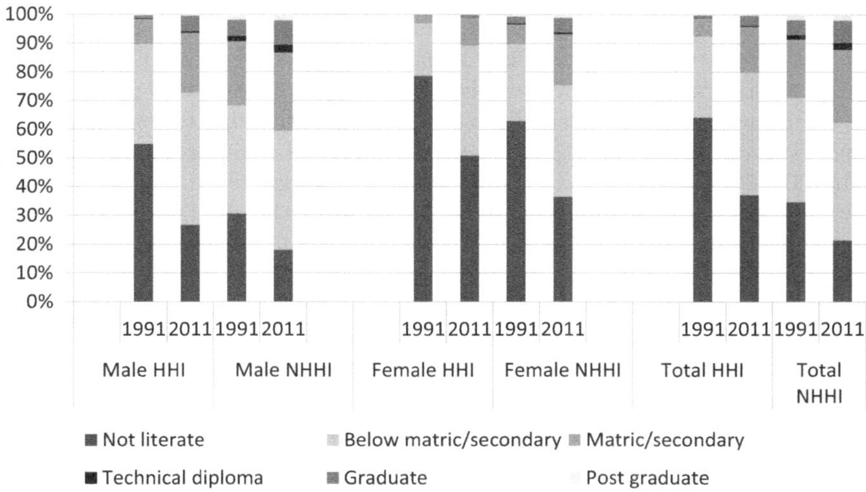

Figure 3.5 Distribution of workers by education in manufacturing in household industry (HHI) and non-household industry (NHHI)

Source: Census of India 1991 and 2011 Tables.

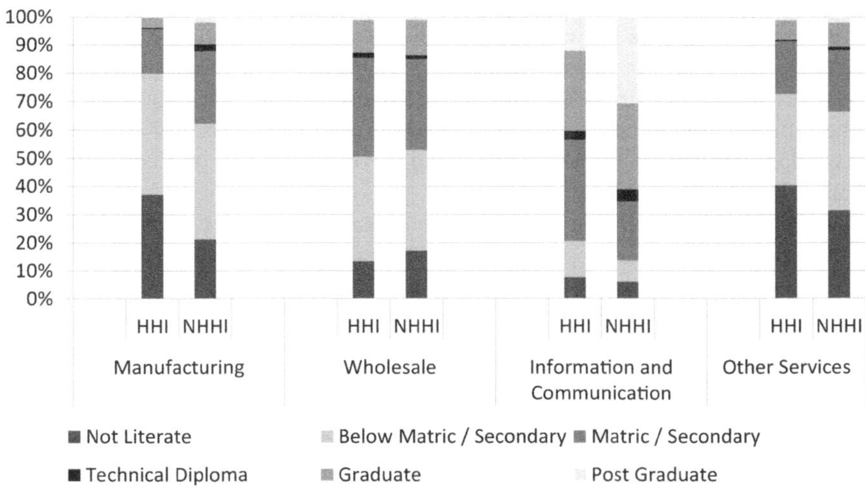

Figure 3.6 Distribution of workers by education in household industry (HHI) and non-household industry (NHHI) in 2011

Source: Census of India 2011 Tables.

Recent patterns

Having reviewed the patterns from the Census of India, we examine the patterns evident in the PLFS. Our focus is on the younger age cohort, namely, those in the age group 15–29 years. The labour force participation rate and work force participation rate among those aged 15–29 years is 38.2 per cent and 31.4 per cent, respectively.[13] The average number of years spent by this age cohort in formal education is greater than that for the whole workforce. In 2017–2018, the averages for men and women in this cohort are 9.8 years and 10 years, respectively (Government of India, 2019a). Estimates from earlier surveys conducted by NSSO did suggest an improvement in educational attainment in recent years. In 2007–2008, the age-specific attendance ratio among those aged 14–17 years was 64 per cent (Government of India, 2010a). In 2014, this ratio had increased to 76 per cent, and it is 32 per cent among those aged 18–23 years (Government of India, 2016).

When we focus on the usual status of those aged 15–29 years, we find that the patterns evident in Table 3.1 are in line with expectations. Men and women who have a graduate or postgraduate degree are more likely to be regular salaried. A disconcerting finding in the PLFS, which received a lot of attention, is the proportion of unemployed individuals among the educated. Individuals who are not literate or have not completed primary education are likely to be working as casual labour. We do find own-account workers and unpaid family workers in each education category. Even among men who are graduates we find that nearly 19 per cent are own-account or unpaid family workers. It is interesting that this ratio is lower for women, since they are either attending educational institutions or attending to domestic duties.

If the formal sector is unable to generate labour-intensive employment opportunities, then despite the entry of an educated labour force, one will not see a slowing down of rate of growth of informal sector. There is some evidence to support this conjecture. Over the five-year period 2010–2011 and 2015–2016, the number of workers in unincorporated enterprises increased by 6.7 per cent. Coupled with this is the worrying finding from PLFS that the unemployment rate is high among youth.[14]

It is in this context that one needs to make a distinction between educated workers and educated entrepreneurs, for it is the latter who will ensure that the newly formed enterprises are establishments and not OAE. The logical question pertains to the role of vocational education. It is estimated that among the 15–29 year old men and women, 2.7 per cent and 2.1 per cent, respectively, received formal vocational/technical training. The top three fields of training are electrical, power, and electronics (11.5 per cent), IT-ITeS (20.5 per cent), and textiles and handlooms, apparels (9.3 per cent). The proportion of individuals who reported receiving non-formal vocational training is higher at 9.1 per cent and 3.1 per cent for men and women, respectively.

Table 3.1 Distribution of men and women by usual status for each general educational level in 2017–18

Status	*Men (15–29 Years)*							
	Not Literate	*Literate & Upto Primary*	*Middle*	*Secondary*	*Higher Secondary*	*Diploma/ Certificate Course*	*Graduate*	*Post Graduate & Above*
Own Account Worker or Employer	17.1	15.2	10.9	7.8	7.3	7.7	10.3	7.8
Unpaid Family Worker	12.7	13.4	12.3	7.9	7.6	4.6	8.9	7.7
Regular Salaried/ Wage Employee	10.7	14.1	11.7	11.2	11.4	28.6	27.6	42.6
Casual Wage Labour	36.8	32.2	17.7	9.3	5.2	4.8	2	1.2
Unemployed	9.2	8.1	9	6.3	8	25.7	24.3	26.6
Attended Educational Institution	0.4	11.7	35.6	56.1	59.4	27.3	25.5	13.5
Other Categories	13	5.3	2.8	1.4	1.2	1.3	1.4	0.5
Total	100	100	100	100	100	100	100	100

Status	*Women (15–29 Years)*							
	Not Literate	*Literate & Upto Primary*	*Middle*	*Secondary*	*Higher Secondary*	*Diploma/ Certificate Course*	*Graduate*	*Post Graduate & Above*
Own Account Worker or Employer	2.7	3.5	2.3	1.8	1.7	2.5	2.6	2.7
Unpaid Family Worker	10.3	6.6	4.8	3	2.6	2.5	1.6	2.1
Regular Salaried/ Wage Employee	1.2	1.5	1.3	1.8	2.6	19.4	11.7	21.7
Casual Wage Labour	9.3	6.6	3.1	1.8	0.6	0.3	0.3	0.2
Unemployed	0.1	0.4	1	1.2	2.4	18.8	12.4	20.2
Attended Educational Institution	0.3	8.9	30.7	49.4	51.8	26.7	23.5	12.7
Attended Domestic Duties	72.6	71.3	56.1	40.4	37.9	28.7	47.3	40.2
Other Categories	3.4	1.2	0.6	0.6	0.4	1	0.6	0.1
Total	100	100	100	100	100	100	100	100

Source: Government of India (2019a).

The returns to vocational education is an under-researched area in India and moving forward, this issue merits attention. Furthermore, if there is a pivotal role for vocational education in creating a large pool of skilled entrepreneurs, then it is not backed by evidence.

From subsistence to success

If informal enterprises and self-employment are a consequence of lack of alternatives, then does it mean that these enterprises or individuals are less likely to be successful? Defining the metric for what constitutes success is very subjective. Gindling and Newhouse (2014) analyze data from a large cross section of countries in order to identify individuals who are self-employed and live in households with a per capita consumption of at least $2 a day. They classify these individuals as being successfully self-employed since they are above the poverty line of $2 a day. They estimate that 34 per cent of individuals who are self-employed can be deemed to be successful. One might indeed ask whether being above the poverty line constitutes being a successful entrepreneur. A better metric for success would be productivity or incomes.

Till recently, the conversation on poverty and well-being in India was anchored to a consumption norm and not income norm. That is also because the official statistical system was singularly focused on a survey of consumption expenditure. The only exception was the situation assessment of agricultural households which was last conducted in 2013. What this survey revealed is that the income of agricultural households with less than one hectare of a land was barely enough to meet their consumption expenditure. In a country where nearly three-quarters of the households possessed less than one hectare of land, this is an alarming finding. In short, those with less than one hectare of land and engaged in agriculture could be deemed unsuccessful. Hence, it did not come as a surprise that the government of India set itself the objective of creating an ecosystem that would facilitate doubling of income of farmer households by 2022.

Until the conduct of PLFS, there was no estimate of earnings of the self-employed available from the official surveys conducted by NSSO. Earlier surveys of employment and unemployment collected the wages of the regular-salaried and the casual labour. In rural India the ratio of average earnings of the regular wage-salaried is 1.47 times that of the self-employed, while in urban India this ratio is 1.17. The estimates from PLFS were startling for the differences in earnings across men and women. In rural areas, the monthly average gross earnings of self-employed men is between Rs. 8500–9700, but in the case of women it is significantly lower, at Rs. 3900–4300. In urban areas, it is around Rs. 16,000 for men and between Rs. 6500–7500 for women (Government of India, 2019a). When the only source of earnings for the household is from self-employment, the average monthly earnings is Rs. 9,600 in rural and Rs. 15,000 in urban areas.

The estimates of yearly gross value added of unincorporated enterprises also do not paint an encouraging picture. The low productivity of unincorporated enterprises is evident from the fact that in 2015–2016 the annual gross value added in rural and urban OAE is Rs 71,302 and Rs 126,445, respectively. These averages suggest at best a marginal existence of the self-employed and those who are part of an OAE.

In the past few decades, the Government of India has tried a slew of initiatives for supporting self-employment and fostering microenterprises. The objective of Prime Minister's Employment Generation Programme (PMEGP), which is a credit-linked subsidy programme, is to promote self-employment. Such programmes have been in existence in the past and were called Prime Minister's Rozgar Yojana and Rural Employment Generation Programme. However, evaluation studies[15] and reports suggest that this programme has been hampered by delays in sanctioning of loans and demand for collateral. Another ongoing scheme is the Pradhan Mantri MUDRA Yojana, popularly known as Mudra loans. Under this scheme, loans are given to non-corporate, non-farm small and micro enterprises. While no formal evaluation studies of this scheme have been published, back-of-the-envelope calculations suggest that Mudra loans have not led to job creation to the scale that was expected. Overall, there is no evidence to persuade one that either the PMEGP or the PMMY have made a significant difference as yet.

The lack of success echoes the experience of other developing countries. Based on a systematic review of the studies, Grimm and Paffhausen (2015) identify five direct interventions that have been attempted by governments: access to finance, entrepreneurship training, business development services, wage subsidies, and improvements to the business environment (e.g. registration procedures). They arrive at three important insights. The first is that it is unlikely that such enterprises will be able to increase the number of workers employed by them. This is true in the Indian context too. Even in 2015–2016, just over 62 per cent of unincorporated enterprises have only one individual worker, while the share of enterprises with 2, 3, and 4 workers is 24 per cent, 7 per cent, and 3 per cent, respectively. The second insight pertains to the importance of easing finance constraints. In India, nearly 61 per cent of enterprises report not facing any specific problem, and problems cited by others are erratic power supply (4 per cent), shortage of raw materials (2 per cent), shrinking demand (16.8 per cent), non-availability or high cost of credit (8.3 per cent), and non-recovery of financial dues (9.5 per cent). In spirit, Mudra loans are supposed to address such credit constraints. However, access to credit by itself cannot address the larger issues, since Grimm and Paffhausen argue that business development services are as important as finance in mitigating the problems of microenterprises. The third insight they provide is that there is no compelling evidence to suggest that interventions that have been attempted to date have led to an increase in employment at the enterprise level. The aggregate numbers suggest that this is true in India, too.

Conclusion

The focus of this descriptive chapter is on the persistence of workers engaged in household industry or unincorporated enterprises and workers who are self-employed. Despite India's GDP increasing by 6.7 times in the period 1991–2011, there has not been a discernible decrease in the level of informality or self-employment. Nor has there been a shift from OAE to establishments. The analysis reveals that informality exists in reasonably visible numbers across all educational levels. A long-standing concern is the low productivity of informal enterprises. Evidence from PLFS confirms the belief that the average earning of the self-employed is inadequate for a decent livelihood. The emerging challenge, we argued, is the absorption of those planning their transition from education to work.

A blind spot in India's labour surveys pertains to non-standard forms of employment. A job is considered non-standard if it differs from full-time employment where there is a contract between the employer and employee. Non-standard employment can be of various types, including temporary employment, part-time employment, multiparty employment, disguised employment, and dependent self-employment. While the idea of non-standard employment is not new, the gig worker has become more prominent in recent times not only in the service sector but also in traditional industries (International Labour Office, 2018). The preliminary draft Code on Social Security, 2019,[16] prepared by Ministry of Labour & Employment, defines a gig worker as a 'person who performs work or participates in a work arrangement and earns from such activities outside of traditional employer–employee relationship'. The Code is the first step towards ensuring that gig workers and platform workers are eligible for social security schemes. It is envisaged that unorganized workers will be eligible for welfare and social security schemes. This will allow these workers to emerge from the shadows of the formal economy, and their contributions to the overall economy can be accurately measured. In addition, there is not enough evidence to prove a positive impact of vocational education and training. However, increasing the share of graduates as self-employed has its own advantages if they are able to transit from OAE to establishments.

Notes

1 Within the self-employed, there are two major categories, viz an own account worker and unpaid helper. A self-employed person is an own account worker if he or she operated their enterprises on their own account or with one or a few partners but without hiring any labour. A self-employed person is a helper in a household enterprise if he or she is 'engaged in their household enterprises, working full or part time and did not receive any regular salary or wages in return for the work performed. They did not run the household enterprise on their own but assisted the concerned person living in the same household in running the household enterprise'. While 38.6 per cent of total workers are own-account workers and employer another 13.6 per cent are helpers in household enterprises (Government of India, 2019a).

2 See chapter 2.
3 Based on task content, each job can be classified into one of the following mutually exclusive categories: routine manual, routine cognitive, non-routine manual, and non-routine cognitive. Analysis of data from the survey of employment suggests that it is the share of non-routine cognitive jobs that increased in the Indian economy over the period 1993–1994 and 2011–12 (Ishwarya, 2016).
4 See Statement 6 Government of India (2019a).
5 *Source:* https://data.worldbank.org/country/india. Accessed September 10, 2019.
6 Data from the Census of India tables reveal that the share of workers engaged as cultivators and agricultural labourers remained high, at 24.6 and 30 per cent, respectively, in 2011 (Census of India, 2011 B Series Tables).
7 Detailed definitions are available as part of the Census of India documentation, which is available at www.censusindia.gov.in/2011census/HLO/Metadata_Census_2011.pdf.
8 For details on the PLFS, the reader can refer to the report published by NSSO (Government of India, 2019a).
9 In recent years there has been a conscious policy decision to increase the number of workers covered by the Employee Provident Fund Organization (EPFO). The metric that is tracked is from the payroll data of EPFO.
10 The definition of each type of worker is from the Census of India documentation.
11 The approach taken by the authors of Economic Survey 2017–18 is different from that of NCEUS. They defined formal firms in two ways: whether the firm provides any form of social security to workers and whether firms are part of the tax net. They triangulate data from NSSO's 2015–16 Survey on Unincorporated Non-Agricultural Enterprises (Excluding Construction) and Good and Services Tax (GST) data. They estimate that while 0.6 per cent of firms pay taxes and provide social security, 87 per cent of firms neither pay tax nor provide social security (Government of India, 2018b).
12 The divisions are as follows: 10: Manufacture of food products, 11: Manufacture of beverages, 12: Manufacture of tobacco products, 13: Manufacture of textiles, 14: Manufacture of wearing apparel, 15: Manufacture of leather and related products, 16: Manufacture of wood and products of wood and cork, except furniture.
13 The labour force comprises the employed and the unemployed, while the workforce is composed only of the employed. The labour force participation rate (LFPR) and workforce participation rate (WPR) are two important indicators summarizing the labour market. The LFPR is defined as the ratio of labour force to total population, while the WPR is the percentage of employed people in the population.
14 The share of the public sector in organized employment declined between 1991 and 2012 by 12.1 percentage points, to 59.2 per cent. The public sector employed 19.1 million workers in 1991 compared to only 17.3 million workers in 2012 (Table 3.1 Government of India, 2010b, Table 3.1; 2019b).
15 https://pib.gov.in/newsite/PrintRelease.aspx?relid=170900.
16 https://labour.gov.in/sites/default/files/THE_CODE_ON_SOCIAL_SECURITY%2C2019.pdf.

References

Ghani, E., Kerr, W. R., & O'Connell, S. D. (2013). *The exceptional persistence of India's unorganized sector*. Policy Research Working Paper No. 6454. World Bank, Washington, DC.

Gindling, T. H., & Newhouse, D. (2014). Self-employment in the developing world. *World Development*, 56(C), 313–331.
Government of India (2010a). *Education in India: 2007–08: Participation and expenditure*. NSSO Report 532. Ministry of Statistics and Programme Implementation, NSSO, New Delhi.
Government of India (2010b). *Economic survey 2009–10*. Union Minister for Finance and Corporate Affairs, Government of India, New Delhi.
Government of India (2015). *Report on employment in informal sector and conditions of informal employment*. Ministry of Labour & Employment, Labour Bureau, Government of India, Chandigarh.
Government of India (2016). *Education in India*. NSSO Report 575. Ministry of Statistics and Programme Implementation, NSSO, New Delhi.
Government of India (2018a). *Operational characteristics of unincorporated non-agricultural enterprises (Excluding construction) in India*. Report No. 581. Ministry of Statistics and Programme Implementation, NSSO, New Delhi.
Government of India (2018b). *Economic survey 2017–18, chapter 2*. Ministry of Finance, Government of India, New Delhi.
Government of India (2019a). *Annual report: Periodic labourforce survey 2017–18*. Ministry of Statistics and Programme Implementation, NSO, New Delhi.
Government of India (2019b). *Economic survey 2018–19*. Union Minister for Finance and Corporate Affairs, Government of India, New Delhi.
Grimm, M., & Paffhausen, A. L. (2015). Do interventions targeted at micro-entrepreneurs and small and medium-sized firms create jobs? A systematic review of the evidence for low and middle income countries. *Laboureconomics*, 32, 67–85.
International Labour Office (2018). *Digital labour platforms and the future of work: Towards decent work in the online world*. Geneva: International Labour Office.
Ishwarya, B. (2016). *Emerging patterns in tasks and skills: Implications for labour market outcomes in India* (Ph.D. Thesis). Indira Gandhi Institute of Development Research, Mumbai.
Kuznets, S. (1971, December 11). *Modern economic growth: Findings and reflections*. Lecture to the Memory of Alfred Nobel. The Nobel Prize, Stockholm. www.nobelprize.org/prizes/economic-sciences/1971/kuznets/lecture/.
La Porta, R., & Shleifer, A. (2014). Informality and development. *Journal of Economic Perspectives*, 28(3), 109–126.
Mukim, M. (2015). Coagglomeration of formal and informal industry: Evidence from India. *Journal of Economic Geography*, 15(2), 329–351.
Webb, J. W., Bruton, G. D., Tihanyi, L., & Ireland, R. D. (2013). Research on entrepreneurship in the informal economy: Framing a research agenda. *Journal of Business Venturing*, 28(5), 598–614.
World Bank (2019). *Growing in the shadow: Challenges of informality, chapter 3, global economic prospects January 2019*. Washington, DC: World Bank.

Chapter 4

Migration, education, and employment in India

S. Irudaya Rajan

Human mobility is a subject that has become a major part of development policy thinking since the early 21st century (UNDP, 2009). According to the United Nations, '[M]igration is an expression of the human aspiration for dignity, safety and a better future' (UN, 2013).

In terms of accessibility, it is defined as 'the ability of individuals to choose their place of residence, from where they can easily access better facilities' (UNDP, 2009). This is important since the inflow/outflow of persons has far-reaching socio-economic impacts, including the housing, health, and education for both states of origin and destination (De Haan & Rogaly, 2002; Skeldon, 2017). For instance, migration of people for work and education has been a phenomenon that accompanies the structural transformation of economies. It has paved the way for the release of 'surplus labour' from relatively low-productive agricultural activities to sectors enjoying higher productivity, with resulting remittance flows increasing the overall household spending in the receiving regions, ultimately leading to a furtherance of socio-economic development in the less-developed regions (Government of India, 2017).

Migration and its link to achieving several developmental outcomes is evidenced to positively contribute to the collective attainment of SDGs worldwide (Hagen-Zanker et al., 2017), especially SDG 10.7, which aims to 'facilitate orderly, safe, and responsible migration and mobility of people, including thorough implementation of planned and well-managed migration policies' (International Organisation for Migration, 2018). However, mainstream research on migration chiefly focuses on international migration; often at the costs of its organic linkage with internal migration (Deshingkar & Sandi, 2011; UNDP, 2009). Moreover, while the majority of the research on internal migration is primarily concerned with the impact of labour migration on origin and destination areas (Mishra, 2016), the internal movement of human capital in search of education is a relatively under-researched area of study (Chandrasekhar & Sharma, 2014; Dodd et al., 2017). The issue of internal migration is an understudied phenomenon even globally, despite its numbers being estimated at least three times more than its international counterparts (UNDP, 2009). This is despite the fact that internal migration has played an important role in the developmental process of every country

DOI: 10.4324/9781003158349-5

by means of population redistribution and equilibrium (Singh et al., 2011). This is especially the case in the context of India's educational sector, since provision and access of quality education across all levels remain highly skewed in favour of a few 'developed' regions at the cost of many others (ASER, 2018). For instance, access to quality education (especially at the higher levels) still remains a challenge for a majority of the students, primarily those belonging to migrant-origin states such as Bihar, Uttar Pradesh, Rajasthan, and Odisha (ASER, 2018; Government of India, 2013). They then migrate to 'better off' destination states in pursuit of better education and employability prospects (Chandrasekhar & Sharma, 2014). Significant evidence suggests that skilling India's youth by providing access to higher education has significant beneficial implications for the Indian economy (Kumar, 2015).

Additionally, as research on family migration now demonstrates, education and employability have unintended implications on migratory decision-making of not just individuals but families as a whole, too (Findlay et al., 2017; Ryan & Sales, 2013). Factors such as lack of better higher-education facilities and concentration of premier institutions in a few selected places influence students to migrate, similar to workers who opt for migration in order to access better employment opportunities. In addition, migration for education involves a variety of factors due to socio-economically dependent characteristics of the migrant (Chandrasekhar & Sharma, 2014) and their ability to access better opportunities becomes a potential indicator of existing empowerment as well as an opportunity for such migrants' transformation (Willis, 2010).

To this end, this chapter explores the dynamics of internal mobility in India in the context of education by focusing on the resultant impacts of interstate student migration for higher education in India. This is done primarily to explore the phenomenon of intra-nation 'brain drain and gain' extensively (in terms of the student labour force). In this context, the background is first laid down by providing an overview of migratory trends in India. It is followed by an outline of India's statewise internal migration patterns for education, followed by the analysis of given data with respect to statewise trade-offs that have occurred as a consequence of such migration and eventually culminating into a broader discussion of the underlying themes, including its link to international student migration from India. Finally, the chapter concludes with a brief summary of the policy implications of the said processes and the subsequent recommendations therein.

Migration trends within India

A home to a quarter of the world's population, South Asia is a witness to several historical as well as ongoing instances of migration-related repatriation: whether as a consequence of large-scale indentured labour migration that occurred during British times (to, for example, the Caribbean Islands or Fiji), by virtue of foreign trade (as in the cases of Malta and Uganda), or because of a 'border anxiety' (as an outcome of Indo-Pak partition, for example) (Sharma et al., 2015; Talbot,

2016). Thus, South Asian borders are some of the most securitized yet porous borders in the world today (LIDC Migration Leadership Team, 2018).

India experienced large-scale internal and international migration. Of the total global migration of 272 million in 2019, India accounted for the largest migrant population of 32 million, including non-resident Indians and Indian Diaspora (17.5 million) (UN, 2019) International migration from India is mostly to developed countries and Middle East countries. The internal migration in India can be rural to urban areas, rural to rural areas, or urban to urban areas. It is estimated that nearly 9 million Indian people migrated annually from one state (region) to another within the country during the period between 2011 and 2016 (UNESCO, 2018).

Spatial mobility in India has been an ancient enterprise—for reasons of trade, kinship, leisure, and the like (Roy, 2012). Today, freedom of residence and mobility across all parts of Indian Territory is enshrined as a fundamental right within the Indian constitution under Article 19 (Government of India, 2007), although Article 19 has been affecting India's diverse communities (subgroups) unevenly (Bhagat, 2010; Tumbe, 2018). Eventually, Article 19 became a source of generational empowerment for the economically wealthy and socially elite across traditional village strongholds (Dodd et al., 2017; Harriss et al., 2010). Resultantly, the census of India started collecting information on reasons for migration since the 1981 Census. Over the decades, there have been changes in the reasons for migration; for example, 'Business' as a reason for migration was not listed in the 1981 Census and information on 'moved after birth' has been collected since the 2001 Census (Table 4.3). The migration within or across administrative boundaries in the country is also available in the Census data.

As evidenced by data, there have been slight demographic shifts in terms of migration type (Table 4.1). While intra-district movement has slightly reduced, the percentage distribution of inter-district as well as inter-state migration has significantly increased, especially in terms of overall female participation. This could be majorly attributed to the 'feminisation of migration' (Neetha & Rajan, 2019), especially in India's rapidly growing informal workforce in the urban sector. This could be further explained by looking at stream-wise migration distribution of the population (Table 4.2). The increased rural to urban migration of the female workforce (from 10.2 per cent in 1971 to 13.98 per cent in 2011) has complemented a simultaneous fall in their rural-to-rural migration (from 76.8 per cent in 1971 to 57.73 per cent in 2011). This implies that apart from an overall growing urbanization trend acting as the 'pull' factor, there has been a near-parallel fall in agrarian productivity which is 'pushing' these people out from the countryside (Breman, 2012; Mishra, 2016).

Of the reasons for migration in India (Table 4.3), education comprises a small percentage, especially for females. It is only in 2011 that the proportion of female migration for education has seen a sharp increase from 2001. Still, migration for education in India is huge in absolute numbers and closely related to migration for work/employment.

Table 4.1 Percentage distribution of lifetime migrants by type of migration, 1971–2011

Type of migration	*1971*			*1981*			*1991*			*2001*			*2011*		
	Persons	*Male*	*Female*	*Persons*	*Male*	*Female*	*Persons*	*Male*	*Female*	*Persons*	*Male*	*Female*	*Persons*	*Male*	*Female*
Intra-district	**65.8**	53.3	71.4	**63.1**	51.1	68.1	**62.1**	50.4	66.5	**62.57**	52.2	66.9	**61.68**	57.82	63.49
Inter-district	**22.4**	27.2	20.3	**25.3**	29.9	23.3	**26.0**	30.2	24.5	**24.12**	26.7	23.0	**26.26**	25.55	26.59
Inter-State	**11.8**	19.5	8.3	**11.6**	19.0	8.6	**11.8**	19.4	9.0	**13.31**	21.1	10.1	**12.06**	16.64	9.92
Total	100	100	100	100	100	100	100	100	100	100	100	100	100	100	100.00

Source: Compiled by the author from various Censuses.

Table 4.2 Percentage distribution of lifetime migrants by stream of migration, 1971–2011

Stream of migration	*1971*			*1981*			*1991*			*2001*			*2011*		
	Persons	*Male*	*Female*	*Persons*	*Male*	*Female*	*Persons*	*Male*	*Female*	*Persons*	*Male*	*Female*	*Persons*	*Male*	*Female*
Rural to Rural	65.4	50.8	76.8	63.12	45.2	73.3	64.2	43.3	72	55.5	28.8	66.6	47.51	25.68	57.73
Rural to Urban	13.8	24.0	10.2	16.10	27.7	12.0	17.7	29.8	13.2	16.7	27	12.4	17.38	24.66	13.98
Urban to Rural	5.6	7.5	5.1	5.93	7.6	5.5	6.0	7.4	5.4	4.2	5.0	3.9	6.00	7.07	5.49
Urban to Urban	9.8	16.6	7.5	11.74	19.2	9.1	11.7	18.9	9.0	11.8	18.2	9.2	17.36	24.53	14.00

Source: Compiled by the author from various Censuses.

Table 4.3 Percentage distribution of lifetime migrants by reasons for migration, 1981–2011

Reason of migration	*1981*			*1991*			*2001*			*2011*		
	Persons	*Male*	*Female*	*Persons*	*Male*	*Female*	*Persons*	*Male*	*Female*	*Persons*	*Male*	*Female*
Work/Employment	10.67	30.98	1.93	8.8	27.8	1.8	9.5	28.1	1.7	10.2	27.7	2.4
Business	–	–	–	2.3	7.1	0.5	0.9	2.6	0.2	1.0	2.3	0.4
Education	2.23	5.36	0.89	2.0	5.0	0.8	1.1	2.5	0.4	1.8	3.4	1.0
Marriage	51.51	3.06	72.36	57.3	4.1	77.0	49.6	2.3	69.6	49.4	4.3	69.7
Moved after birth	–	–	–	–	–	–	5.0	9.9	2.9	10.6	20.2	6.2
Moved with household	19.23	30.23	14.49	15.0	26.5	10.7	13.7	19.4	11.3	15.4	22.3	12.3
Others	16.36	30.37	10.33	14.2	28.4	8.9	20.2	35.2	13.9	11.7	19.8	8.1

Source: Compiled by the author from various Censuses.

Migration for education in India

Most often, intra-national student flows are determined by motivations similar to those of international study, such as the desire to accumulate cultural capital (by means of education) based on the perceived 'goodness' of infrastructural availability (Findlay et al., 2017) as well as prospects of employability (Reimeingam, 2016) apart from the importance of place and proximity to the parental home (Holton, 2015). Despite this, there is a massive lack of data on the matter, as there has been less interest globally in understanding 'movement between as well as within regions of a state' (Wu & Wilkes, 2017).

Within India, education exists as a reason for migration since the beginning of the Indian census-collection process (Government of India, 2017). According to the 1981 Census (the year in which it was first measured), there were around 4.6 million students within India who changed their usual place of residence in order to access better education facilities (inter- as well as intra-state). Furthermore, within the following three decades, the number of internal migrants for education has increased from 4.6 million in 1981 to 5.4 million in 2011—by around 20 per cent (Table 4.4).

State level scenario of student migration

According to the latest Census data (2011), there were about 29.2 million students enrolled in higher-education institutions across India, of which around 7.4 lakh were interstate student migrants (based on their domicile status). The enrolment in higher education in India increased to 37.4 million in the academic year 2018–2019 (Government of India, 2013). In terms of gender, almost half of them (44.44 per cent) were women. Also, in terms of streams across educational levels, a majority of the students pursued social sciences, followed by pure sciences, management, engineering, medicine, and all other fields (All India Survey on Higher Education Report, 2017).

Table 4.4 Intra-state, interstate migration for education in India, 1981–2011

Year	*Total student migrants*	*Migrants (in numbers)*		*Migrants (in percentage)*		*Total*
		Within state	*Outside state*	*Within state*	*Outside state*	
1981	4,569,157	3,953,497	615,660	86.53	13.47	100
1991	4,420,018	3,841,961	578,057	86.92	13.08	100
2001	3,318,176	2,768,804	549,372	83.44	16.56	100
2011	5,402,238	4,658,223	744,015	86.23	13.77	100

Source: Compiled by the author from various Censuses.

Table 4.5 Top-five education destination regions for major origin states, 2011

Origin States	*Top-Five Destinations States for Education*				
Andhra Pradesh	Karnataka	Tamil Nadu	Maharashtra	Odisha	Kerala
Assam	Karnataka	Maharashtra	West Bengal	Delhi	Uttar Pradesh
Bihar	Delhi	Uttar Pradesh	Jharkhand	Maharashtra	Karnataka
Chhattisgarh	Madhya Pradesh	Maharashtra	Karnataka	Odisha	Andhra Pradesh
Gujarat	Maharashtra	Karnataka	Rajasthan	Tamil Nadu	Madhya Pradesh
Haryana	Delhi	Rajasthan	Chandigarh	Punjab	Uttar Pradesh
Jammu & Kashmir	Karnataka	Maharashtra	Delhi	Uttar Pradesh	Uttarakhand
Jharkhand	Odisha	Karnataka	Delhi	Maharashtra	West Bengal
Karnataka	Maharashtra	Tamil Nadu	Andhra Pradesh	Kerala	Goa
Kerala	Karnataka	Tamil Nadu	Maharashtra	Andhra Pradesh	Delhi
Madhya Pradesh	Maharashtra	Uttar Pradesh	Rajasthan	Chhattisgarh	Delhi
Maharashtra	Karnataka	Gujarat	Madhya Pradesh	Tamil Nadu	Andhra Pradesh
Odisha	Andhra Pradesh	Karnataka	Maharashtra	Delhi	West Bengal
Punjab	Chandigarh	Delhi	Haryana	Himachal Pradesh	Maharashtra
Rajasthan	Maharashtra	Delhi	Gujarat	Madhya Pradesh	Karnataka
Tamil Nadu	Karnataka	Puducherry	Andhra Pradesh	Kerala	Maharashtra
Uttar Pradesh	Delhi	Maharashtra	Madhya Pradesh	Uttarakhand	Rajasthan
West Bengal	Karnataka	Maharashtra	Uttar Pradesh	Delhi	Odisha

Source: Compiled by the author from Census Commissioner (2011).

Furthermore, nearly half of these students have migrated to just four 'urban centres' within the Indian states of Maharashtra (16.22 per cent to Pune-Mumbai cities and surrounding districts); Karnataka (13.79 per cent to Bangalore city-district); Delhi (12.99 per cent to the broader National Capital Region); and Tamil Nadu (7.95 per cent to Chennai city-district).

Also, as can be seen in Table 4.5, there are distinct 'educational hubs' across these destination states with colleges/institutions which attract a majority of this student inflow. For example, Maharashtra receives the largest number of migrant student stock across India, which is ably justified by the fact that three institutionally dense districts fall within it—namely, Pune (470), Nagpur (433), and Mumbai (358). The district of Bangalore, which has the highest number of colleges (924) in the country, falls within Karnataka state, which then rightly occupies the number two position among student migrant destination states in India. This is an extremely crucial result, given that education is a foremost tool of social mobility in the context of India (King & Sondhi, 2018), as much as it is in the developed world (Wielgoszewska, 2018). Another interesting thing to note here is that the migration just described is a two-level process: with simultaneous prospects of educational training and employability aspirations, as has often been the case with student migrants globally, demonstrated ably by King and Sondhi (2018).

Although, overall, the proportions of interstate student migrants are less, when compared to their intra-state counterparts in all censuses by virtue of being costlier due to several factors, interstate migration mostly takes place at the higher-education level owing to the lack of quality higher-education opportunities in many states such as Uttar Pradesh and Bihar (see Tables 4.6 and 4.7).

Table 4.6 Top-five origin states of interstate student out-migration in India, 2011

State	*Migrants (in numbers)*	*Migrants (in percentage)*
Uttar Pradesh	128,533	17.28
Bihar	118,237	15.89
Kerala	62,033	8.34
Andhra Pradesh	38,010	5.11
Rajasthan	33,471	4.50
Others	363,731	48.89
Total	744,015	100.00

Source: Compiled by the author from various Censuses.

Table 4.7 Top-five destinations for interstate student in-migration in India, 2011

State	*Migration (in numbers)*	*Migrants (in percentage)*
Maharashtra	120,712	16.22
Karnataka	102,587	13.78
NCT of Delhi	96,615	12.98
Tamil Nadu	59,162	7.95
Uttar Pradesh	49,484	6.65
Others	315,459	42.39
Total	744,015	100.00

Source: Compiled by the author from various Censuses.

Migration for education: gainers and losers

The answer to the question as to which states are gainers and which are losers in education migration can be sought by identifying the top destinations and origin states for out-migrant and in-migrant students (Tables 4.6 and 4.7). As can be observed, Delhi, Karnataka, and Maharashtra are the top destinations, whereas Bihar, Uttar Pradesh, and Kerala are the top origins. Moreover, the imbalances in the net migration (i.e. out-migration minus in-migration) indicate the movement of students for the purpose of education across major Indian states (Table 4.8). According to the data from Census Commissioner (2011), there are more than 1 lakh students who have migrated from Bihar to other Indian states in order to access better education facilities. This means that Bihar has lost out on about 1 lakh (potential) human resources due to sustained, periodic education out-migration to the rest of India. In other words, Bihar has lost out a significant number of what we call the 'future labour power' of its regional economy, which undoubtedly shall affect its socio-economic prospects in the long run. On the other hand, the state of Maharashtra gained about 94 thousand 'future labourers' from the rest of Indian states owing to large-scale in-migration around the same time (see Table 4.8).

Interestingly, states that are gainers in education migration are also gainers in overall migration, but some states that are gainers in education migration may be losers for workforce. For example, Uttarakhand is gaining students over 2001–2011, despite losing out on overall workforce. This may imply an improved educational perception among students. On the other hand, West Bengal is losing out on both the workforce as well as educational migrants over the same time period, implying a negative perception of migration-inducing factors, including educational provision. Tamil Nadu can be considered an outlier for massive improvement in terms of its net migration score across 2001 and 2011 (both in terms of students as well as overall). This can be attributed to an increasing

Table 4.8 Net migration occurring among major migrant gaining and losing states, namely, student migration in 2001 and 2011

States	*Net Migration (Overall)*			*Net Migration (for Education)*		
	2001	*2011*	*Gaining/ Losing*	*2001*	*2011*	*Gaining/ Losing*
Maharashtra	5167271	6019149	Gaining	90540	93983	Gaining
NCT of Delhi	4396459	4773757	Gaining	62683	74822	Gaining
Haryana	937361	1310403	Gaining	−1946	−3605	Losing
Gujarat	835924	2344213	Gaining	−9924	−5885	Losing
West Bengal	769472	−24477	Losing	2545	−5610	Gaining in 2001; Losing in 2011
Karnataka	212182	744704	Gaining	78677	78677	Gaining
Madhya Pradesh	157428	−235160	Losing	10652	1758	Gaining in 2001; Losing in 2011
Goa	137546	163493	Gaining	−1210	−161	Losing
Uttar Pradesh	−6430511	−8257659	Losing	−53028	−79049	Losing
Bihar	−3641628	−6341849	Losing	−67908	−112874	Losing
Tamil Nadu	−941028	−334386	Losing	−5	35431	Losing in 2001; Gaining in 2011
Rajasthan	−868144	−1152418	Losing	−8667	−1883	Losing
Kerala	−599148	−636902	Losing	−37213	−52080	Losing
Andhra Pradesh	−532015	−43811–4	Losing	−18702	−14059	Losing
Assam	−301233	−163995	Losing	−6548	−10305	Losing
Odisha	−274348	−416025	Losing	−3028	2302	Gaining

Source: Compiled by the author from various Censuses.

investment in its educational as well as social sectors (Centre for Policy Research, 2016). As stated before, this is primarily attributable to lack of quality educational infrastructure as well as service delivery in some states, particularly at the higher-education level (Chandrasekhar & Sharma, 2014).

Furthermore, according to the latest National Institutional Ranking Framework (NIRF) Report 2018, the top-four ranking institutions in India are IISc-Bangalore, IIT Madras, IIT Bombay, IIT Delhi, which are in the states of Karnataka, Tamil Nadu, Maharashtra, and NCT of Delhi respectively (see Table 4.9). Interestingly, these states are also the top destinations for the interstate student migrants as articulated above. Thus, as much like in the case of work migrants, 'urban centres' do play an important role in student migrant decision-making as well (Kundu & Sarangi, 2007).

Poor public funding for higher education is often quoted as the reason for poor higher-education facilities in the states. For instance, Jharkhand, which is a major educational migrant-sending state, invested as much as 70 per cent of its educational budget in its elementary schooling programmes in 2011–2012. Diminished funding at higher levels translates directly into diminished educational

Table 4.9 Top-ranking institutions at the top destinations in India, 2018

States/UTs	*Institution Name (All India Rank)*				
Maharashtra	IIT Bombay (3)	Savitribai Phule Pune University (16)	Indian Institute of Science Education & Research Pune (32)	TISS Mumbai (49)	Symbiosis International University (67)
Karnataka	IISc Bangalore (1)	Manipal Academy of Higher Education (18)	NIT Surathkal (57)	JSS Academy of Higher Education & Research (59)	University of Agricultural Sciences (85)
Tamil Nadu	IIT Madras (2)	Anna University (10)	Vellore Institute of Technology (24)	University of Madras (29)	NIT Tiruchirappalli (31)
NCT of Delhi	IIT Delhi (4)	JNU Delhi (6)	University of Delhi (14)	Jamia Millia Islamia (19)	Jamia Hamdard (37)

Source: National Institutional Ranking Framework, MHRD, Government of India (2018).

outcomes; prompting migration streams to the aforementioned 'educational hubs' across the country (Varghese & Malik, 2015). Decreased public funding of education has accompanied a simultaneous increase in private funding of it, bringing newer sets of challenges for the lower-income groups (Khan, 2014), eventually prompting large-scale educational migration to centrally funded institutions as a consequence.

The link between education and employment

In the context of India, education is seen as a foremost tool of social mobility, with education levels and employment prospects known to have a direct relationship in general.

After all, the aforesaid process of education-employment link involves two stages: combining the prospects of education and employment together; since, students who migrate for attaining better education ultimately do so in order to realise their employment aspirations as demonstrated by Remesh (2012) in the context of North Eastern migration to Delhi.

International student migration from India

India's outbound international student migration for the purposes of education is one of the highest in the world, second only to China in terms of scale and size (Pande & Yan, 2018). According to the OECD data, there are around 3 lakh students of Indian origin studying in various countries globally today. This has been a consistently growing trend, with the number of students having increased from 217,319 in 2012 to 299,427 in 2017, with a growth rate of around 40 per cent during this period (see Figure 4.1).

Moreover, as of 2017 (the latest year for which data are available), more than 90 per cent of international student migrants are traversing to only ten countries worldwide (see Table 4.10).

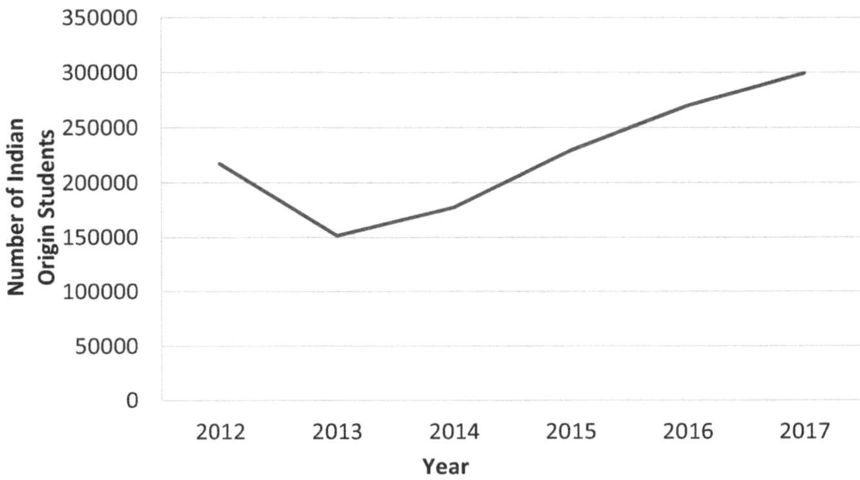

Figure 4.1 Indian-origin students enrolled in institutions abroad, 2012–2017

Source: Organization for Economic Co-operation and Development.

Table 4.10 Top-ten destinations for Indian-origin students in 2017

Country of destination	*Number of students*	*% share of students*
United States	142,618	47.63
Australia	51,976	17.36
Canada	32,616	10.89
United Kingdom	16,421	5.48
Germany	13,387	4.47
New Zealand	12,552	4.19
Italy	2,887	0.96
France	2,823	0.94
Poland	2,084	0.70
Netherlands	1,933	0.65
Total of top-10	**279,298**	**93.28**
Others	20,129	6.72
Total Number of students	299427	100.00

Source: OECD (2017).

Policy implications

The observations of this chapter indicate most education destination states also have one of the highest employment opportunities available, which attracts many workers, including students. The high employment opportunity also could be one of the reasons why students who migrate for educational purposes have an implicit employability incentive. Such an assertion, while currently unsubstantiated because of a lack of educational information specific to 'migrants' (last place of residence for education), could provide an interesting direction for future research by casually examining the correlations between migrant educational hubs and the distinct employment centres, respectively.

In recognition of the increasing importance of migration globally, the United Nations promulgated the *Global Compact for Safe, Orderly and Regular Migration (GCM)* in December 2020, a non-binding agreement adopted by all UN member states, including India, to better manage the diverse migratory processes globally (Akhil, 2019). Statistically, Indians make up the largest share of such a diaspora population globally, with around 31 million of them living outside India (Ministry of External Affairs, 2018). In such a context, it is crucial that migration of students be taken into the ambit of the UN's legislative purview with the intent of tracking it by nation, in alignment with best practices worldwide (such as having a national framework on internal migration management under GCIM guidelines). Such best practices especially include those that realistically take into account the interconnectedness of internal and international migration dynamics, specifically in the context of India and its long-standing community-wide diaspora network outside it. While India's Ministry of External Affairs (MEA) has recently tabled/devised the Draft Emigration Bill 2019 to address its distinct lacunae in terms of international migration management which even covers internationally out-migrating students under its ambit, what it essentially lacks is an overarching migration policy framework that takes into account the organic interconnectedness of internal and international migration trajectories within as well as outside India (Aggarwal et al, 2019). For instance, while the proposed bill is a useful advance in that direction, there still are at least 453.6 million internal migrants within India (Kundu & Mohanan, 2017; Rajan & Sumeetha, 2019), including students, who shall be completely outside the purview of such legislation. Consequently, in due recognition of such a reality, India must remodel the said bill along such lines, in order to take a long-sighted, concrete step in the progressive direction that India intends to go in by unprecedentedly signing an international compact of such a nature.

References

Aggarwal, V., Singh, P., & Mitra, R. (2019, August 26). Low interstate migration is hurting India's growth and states are to blame. *Business Standard*, pp. 1–7. www.business-standard.com/article/economy-policy/low-interstate-migration-is-hurting-india-s-growth-and-states-are-to-blame-119082600099_1.html.

Akhil, C. S. (2019). India and the global compact for migration. *Economic and Political Weekly*, 54(11), 10–13.

All India Survey on Higher Education Report (2017). *All India survey on higher education 2016–17*. Ministry of Human Resource Development, Government of India, New Delhi.

ASER (2018). *Annual status of education report (rural)*. ASER Centre, New Delhi. http://img.asercentre.org/docs/ASER2018/Release Material/aserreport2018.pdf.

Bhagat, R. B. (2010). Internal migration in India: Are the underprivileged migrating more? *Asia-Pacific Population Journal*, 25(1), 27–45.

Breman, J. (2012). *Outcast labour in Asia: Circulation and informalization of the work-force at the bottom of the economy* (2nd ed.). New Delhi: Oxford University Press.

Census Commissioner (2011). *D series, Migration tables. Registrar General of India*. New Delhi: Ministry of Home Affairs.

Centre for Policy Research (2016). *Tamil Nadu state report card 2016*. Accountability Initiative, Centre for Policy Research, New Delhi.

Chandrasekhar, S., & Sharma, A. (2014). *Internal migration for education and employment among youth in India* (No. 004). Indira Gandhi Institute of Development Research, Mumbai. www.igidr.ac.in/pdf/publication/WP-2014-004.pdf.

De Haan, A., & Rogaly, B. (2002). Introduction: Migrant workers and their role in rural change. *Journal of Development Studies*, 38(5), 1–14. https://doi.org/10.1080/00220380412331322481.

Deshingkar, P., & Sandi, M. (2011). *Migration and human development in India: New Challenges and Opportunities*. National Workshop on Internal Migration and Human Development in India, 2, 48–85. UNESCO-UNICEF, ICSSR, New Delhi.

Dodd, W., Humphries, S., Patel, K., Majowicz, S., & Dewey, C. (2017). The internal migration-development nexus: Evidence from southern India. *Asian and Pacific Migration Journal*, 26(1), 56–83. https://doi.org/10.1177/0117196816684349.

Findlay, A., Packwood, H., McCollum, D., Nightingale, G., & Tindal, S. (2017). Fees, flows and imaginaries: Exploring the destination choices arising from intra-national student mobility. *Globalisation, Societies and Education*, 16(2), 162–175. https://doi.org/10.1080/14767724.2017.1412822.

Findlay, A., Prazeres, L., McCollum, D., & Packwood, H. (2017). 'It was always the plan': International study as 'learning to migrate'. *Area*, 49(2), 192–199. https://doi.org/10.1111/area.12315.

Government of India (2007). *The constitution of India*. Ministry of Law and Justice, New Delhi.

Government of India (2013). *All India survey on higher education 2012–13*. Ministry of Human Resource Development, New Delhi.

Government of India (2017). India on the move and churning: New evidence. In *Economic Survey 2016–17* (pp. 264–284). New Delhi: Ministry of Finance.

Government of India (2018). *National Institutional Ranking Framework. Ministry of Human Resource Development*. New Delhi: Government of India.

Hagen-Zanker, J., Vidal, E. M., & Sturge, G. (2017). *Social protection, migration and the 2030 agenda for sustainable development*. London: ODI Briefing; SDC, FDFA. www.odi.org/sites/odi.org.uk/files/resource-documents/11583.pdf.

Harriss, J., Jeyaranjan, J., & Nagaraj, K. (2010). Land, labour and caste politics in rural Tamil Nadu in the 20th century: Iruvelpattu (1916–2008). *Economic and Political Weekly*, 45(31), 47–61.

Holton, M. (2015). Learning the rules of the 'student game': Transforming the 'student habitus' through (im) mobility. *Environment and Planning A*, 47(11), 1–16. https://doi.org/10.1177/0308518X15599293.
International Organisation for Migration (2018). *World migration report*. Geneva: United Nations Publications.
Khan, T. (2014). *Globalization and its impact on Indian higher education* (Doctoral Dissertation). Aligarh Muslim University, Aligarh.
King, R., & Sondhi, G. (2018). International student migration: A comparison of UK and Indian students' motivations for studying abroad. *Globalisation, Societies and Education*, 16(2), 176–191. https://doi.org/10.1080/14767724.2017.1405244.
Kumar, S. (2015). India's trade in higher education. *Higher Education*, 70(3), 441–467.
Kundu, A., & Mohanan, P. C. (2017, April 11). Internal migration in India: A very moving story. *The Economic Times*. https://economictimes.indiatimes.com/blogs/et-commentary/internal-migration-in-india-a-very-moving-story/.
Kundu, A., & Sarangi, N. (2007). Migration, employment status and poverty: An analysis across urban centres. *Economic and Political Weekly*, 42(4), 299–306.
LIDC Migration Leadership Team (2018, May 22–23). *Decentring the 'global': A South Asian migration research agenda*. Migration Leadership Team, Global Migration Conversation, New Delhi. www.soas.ac.uk/lidc-mlt/outputs/file133830.pdf.
Ministry of External Affairs (2018). *Population of overseas Indians* (p. 4). New Delhi: MEA, Government of India. https://mea.gov.in/images/attach/NRIs-and-PIOs_1.pdf.
Mishra, D. K. (Ed.) (2016). *Internal migration in contemporary India*. New Delhi: SAGE Publications.
Neetha, N., & Rajan, S. I. (2019). Migration and gender landscape: Labour demands, care work, and cultural pressures. In I. S. Rajan & N. Neetha (Eds.), *Migration, gender and care economy* (1st ed.). New York: Routledge.
Organization for Economic Co-operation and Development (OECD) (2017). *OECD handbook for internationally comparative education statistics: Concepts, standards, definitions and classifications*. Paris: OECD.
Pande, A., & Yan, Y. (2018). Migration of students from India and China: A comparative view. *South Asian Survey*, 23(1), 69–92. https://doi.org/10.1177/0971523118764971.
Rajan, S. I., & Sumeetha, M. (Eds.) (2019). *Handbook of internal migration in India*. Thousand Oaks, CA: Sage Publications.
Reimeingam, M. (2016). *Migration from North-Eastern region to Bangalore: Level and trend analysis*. Working Paper No. 371. The Institute for Social and Economic Change, Bangalore. www.isec.ac.in/WP371-Marchang Remeingam_2.pdf.
Remesh, B. P. (2012). Strangers in their own land migrants from the North-East in Delhi. *Economic and Political Weekly*, 47(22), 35–40.
Roy, T. (2012). *India in the world economy: From antiquity to the present*. Cambridge: Cambridge University Press. https://doi.org/10.1017/CBO9780511920516.
Ryan, L., & Sales, R. (2013). Family migration: The role of children and education in family decision-making strategies of polish migrants in London. *International Migration*, 51(2), 90–103. https://doi.org/10.1111/j.1468-2435.2010.00652.x.
Sharma, V., Saraswati, L. R., Susmita, D., & Sarna, A. (2015). *Migration in South Asia: A review*. New Delhi: Population Council. https://assets.publishing.service.gov.uk/media/57a08970ed915d3cfd000246/61263_Desk-review.pdf.

Singh, V. K., Kumar, A., Singh, R. D., & Yadava, K. N. S. (2011). Changing pattern of internal migration in India: Some evidences from census data. *International Journal of Current Research*, 3(4), 289–295.

Skeldon, R. (2017). *International migration, internal migration, mobility and urbanization: Towards more integrated approaches.* New York: Population Division, Department of Economic and Social Affairs.

Talbot, I. (2016). *A history of modern South Asia: Politics, states, diasporas.* New Haven: Yale University Press. https://doi.org/10.1017/S0021911818000815.

Tumbe, C. (2018). *India moving: A history of migration* (p. 304). New Delhi: Penguin Viking.

UN (2013). *Secretary-general's remarks to high-level dialogue on international migration and development.* United Nations. www.un.org/sg/en/content/sg/statement/2013-10-03/secretary-generals-remarks-high-level-dialogue-international.

UN (2019). *International migrant stock 2019.* Department of Economic and Social Affairs, Population Division, United Nations, New York.

UNDP (2009). *Human development report 2009, overcoming barriers: Human mobility and development.* United Nations Development Programme, New York. http://hdr.undp.org/sites/default/files/reports/269/hdr_2009_en_complete.pdf.

UNESCO (2018). *Global education monitoring report 2019: Migration, displacement and education: Building bridges, not walls.* Paris: Global Education Monitoring Report Team, United Nations Educational Scientific and Cultural Organization.

Varghese, N. V., & Malik, G. (Eds.) (2015). *India higher education report 2015* (pp. 1–12). New Delhi: Routledge.

Wielgoszewska, B. (2018). Onwards and upwards? migration and social mobility of the UK graduates. *Regional Studies, Regional Science*, 5(1), 402–411. https://doi.org/10.1080/21681376.2018.1552188.

Willis, K. (2010). Introduction: Mobility, migration and development. *International Development Planning Review*, 32(3–4), 1–14. https://doi.org/10.3828/idpr.2010.15.

Wu, C., & Wilkes, R. (2017). International students' post-graduation migration plans and the search for home. *Geoforum*, 80, 123–132. https://doi.org/10.1016/j.geoforum.2017.01.015.

Chapter 5

Declining labour-force participation in India

Does education and training help?

S. Madheswaran and J.K. Parida

The overall labour-force participation rate (LFPR) in India has been declining consistently since 1983. The falling overall LFPR and rising unemployment rate at a time when the Indian economy has been experiencing a structural transformation is a matter of serious concern. Because, a consistent fall of agricultural workforce without corresponding rise in non-farm employment (Mehrotra et al., 2014; Mehrotra & Parida, 2019) will have negative implications on growth and the process of socio-economic development in India.

Several studies have shown that the overall LFPR would tend to fall during the initial periods of economic development; it normally will reach the lowest point and then start rising as the country picks up growth (Durand, 1975; Bardhan, 1979; Mincer, 1985; Pampel & Tanaka, 1986; Psacharopoulos & Tzannatos, 1989; Schultz, 1990, 1991; Kottis, 1990; Goldin, 1994; Tansel, 2001; Mammen & Paxson, 2000; Fatima & Sultana, 2009; Luci, 2009; Tam, 2011; Klasen & Pieters, 2012; Chaudhary & Verick, 2014; Kapsos et al., 2014; Das et al., 2015; Mehrotra & Parida, 2017). In other words, the declining trends of LFPR are normally expected to happen during the initial stages of economic development. During these phases, the share of the traditional (mostly agriculture and allied sectors) sector in employment normally declines, with a corresponding rise in both industry and service sectors. People moving out of agriculture and allied sectors (of which females normally constitute a major share) to non-farm jobs tends to help improve their standard of living. This rise in standard of living has a likely negative effect on their labour-force participation in agriculture and low-paid allied activities. Moreover, the LFPR of children declines as the households start spending an increased proportion of their income on education. These factors are expected to be the principal determinants of declining LFPR in India. Furthermore, there is always an interplay of sociocultural factors which affect the labour-force participation behaviour of the individuals in India. In this context, this chapter intends to examine the broad trends, changing patterns, and determinants of labour-force participation behaviour of Indian population.

The rest of the chapter is organized into three sections. 'Data and methods' provides the sources of data and estimation methods. In 'Findings' we explain the broad trends and patterns of labour force participation, explore the sectoral

DOI: 10.4324/9781003158349-6

employment patterns by the level and types of education, and highlight the current scenario of rising unemployment and disheartened labour force in India. Finally, in 'Concluding remarks', we focus on concluding the chapter along with our policy suggestions.

Data and methods

This chapter is based on secondary data. The major sources of secondary data include National Sample Survey (NSS), the Periodic Labour-Force Survey (PLFS), and the Census of India. The unit level data collected during 1983, 1987–1988, 1993–1994, 1999–2000, 2004–2005, and 2011–2012 quinquennial employment and unemployment rounds and annual PLFS conducted during 2017–2018 are used. The labour market indicators (namely, Labour force, workforce, unemployment, and Not in Labour force Education and Training (NLET)) are calculated using both NSS and PLFS data. The Census population data for years 1981, 1991, 2001, and 2011 are used to adjust the NSS and PLFS estimates and to obtain the absolute numbers wherever required. Absolute number of workers, unemployed, and NLET population are estimated by multiplying the NSS and PLFS population estimates with the Census Adjustment Multiplier (CAM). CAM is just the ratio of Census Projected Population (for the relevant years of NSS/PLFS surveys) to the NSS/PLFS estimated population.

Findings

Trends in labour-force participation in India

The overall labour-force participation rate (LFPR) in India has declined from 61.6 per cent in 1983 to 36.9 per cent in 2018. The decline was perhaps steep in the rural areas where it declined from 63 per cent to 37 per cent, whereas it declined from 56.8 per cent to 36.8 per cent in the urban areas (see Figure 5.1, Panel A). The decline in overall LFPR in rural areas is due to the decline in LFPR of both men and women.

Although male LFPR in rural India had declined during 1983 and 1993–1994, since then it remained constant, at around 55 per cent (see Figure 5.1, Panel B). The female LFPR, on the other hand, has consistently been declining in rural India to reach a very low level (18.2 per cent) during 2018. In urban India, the male LFPR declined during 1983 and 1993–1994; but since then, it has been rising (although at a very slow rate) to reach 57 per cent during 2018. But it is important to note that the female LFPR in urban India remained constant, at around 16 per cent since 1993–1994.

According to some studies (Himanshu, 2011; Mehrotra et al., 2014), the rising mechanization in agriculture and growing enrolment of girls in higher education (Rangarajan et al., 2011; Kannan & Raveendran, 2012; Hirway, 2012; Parida, 2015) are among the major reasons for declining female LFPR in rural areas.

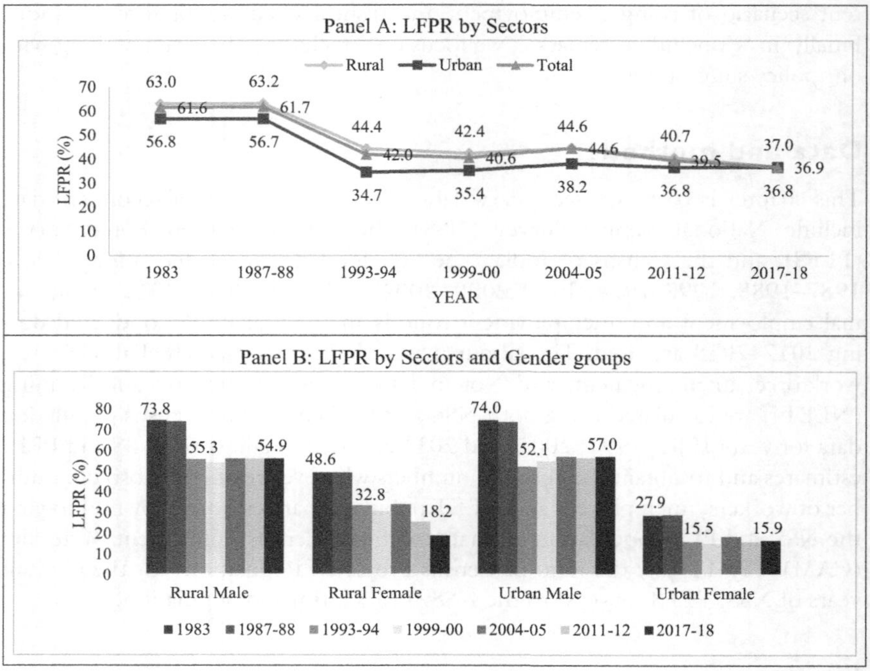

Figure 5.1 Labour-force participation rate (LFPR) by sector and gender groups in India, 1983–2018

Source: Authors' estimation and plot based on NSS and PLFS unit-level data.

Moreover, Mehrotra and Parida (2017) argued that the prevalence of social constraints and behavioural factors at the household level due to the recent improvement in the standard of living (negative income effect) also plays an important role in this process.

Thus, we would like to draw our attention to these two questions: (1) Why did LFPR of male in rural India and LFPR of female in urban India remained constant (almost) during 1993–1994 and 2017–2018? and (2) Which factors did cause the male LFPR to grow at a faster rate in urban India? To answer these questions, we examined the sectoral LFPR of both male and female by their levels of education.

Sector-wise labour force participation by level of education

The LFPR of rural males with either no education (illiterates) or up to the higher secondary education is showing a declining trend over the years, while the LFPR of rural males with graduate and above level of education has remained constant at around 82 per cent during 1993 and 2018 (see Table 5.1). It is the LFPR of males having either vocational qualification or a graduate level technical education degree that has been rising over the years. Based on this information, it could be argued that in the supply side, there is a skill constraint, which is restricting a large number of job seekers from participating in the labour market. This problem might also have emerged due to the demand-side constraint in rural areas. Those who lost their jobs in agriculture due to the recent growth of farm mechanization might not have obtained alternative jobs due to slow growth of non-farm-sector jobs in the rural areas (Parida, 2015; Mehrotra & Parida, 2019).

In urban areas, the female LFPR by the level of education and training reveals that there is a growing demand for relatively skilled female workers in urban India. Women with graduate and above level of general education, and with technical and vocational qualifications, have a relatively higher LFPR, when compared to their low-skilled counterparts. For the illiterate women, and women with up to the primary, secondary, and higher secondary level of education, declining trends of LFPR have been registered in the urban areas (Table 5.1). Hence, the female LFPR in urban areas could have increased because of increasing numbers of higher-educated women. Moreover, the promotion of the growth of modern service sectors which demand relatively skilled and higher educated workers is likely to boost the overall female LFPR in urban India.

Even though the LFPR of higher-educated (general), and technically and vocationally trained males is relatively higher, and it is on the rise in urban India; the LFPR of relatively lower-educated males has been declining constantly. The growth of service-sector jobs might have improved the LFPR of better-educated male, while the slow and negative growth of jobs in the urban manufacturing sector could be held responsible for the decline of male LFPR of relatively low-skilled men in urban India. The general conclusion that can be drawn is that LFPR of the higher-educated is increasing both for males and females, while LFPR of less-educated are declining for both sexes.

Labour-force participation by level of education and age groups

The overall LFPR of working-age population has been declining consistently in India. The rate of decline is higher in rural areas as compared to the urban areas. In rural areas, LFPR of working-age population declined about 14 percentage points (from 70.3 per cent to 53.6 per cent) during 1993–1994 and 2017–2018, whereas in urban areas, it declined marginally from 53.2 per cent to 51.6 per cent (about 2 percentage points) during the same periods (see Table 5.2).

The decline of overall LFPR in rural areas, is mainly due to falling of the LFPR of persons with a relatively lower level of education. The LFPR of illiterate persons declined from about 73 per cent to 64 per cent (9 percentage-point decline). For the persons with up to the primary level of education, it declined from 69.5 per cent to 63 per cent (13.5 percentage-point decline). For persons with secondary

Table 5.1 Labour-force participation rate by sector, sex, and level of education in India, 1994–2018

Level of Education	*Labour-Force Participation Rate by Sex Groups (%)*									
	Male					*Female*				
	1993–94	*1999–00*	*2004–05*	*2011–12*	*2017–18*	*1993–94*	*1999–00*	*2004–05*	*2011–12*	*2017–18*
Rural Areas										
Illiterate	53.6	51.4	51.0	53.7	49.3	37.8	35.7	39.3	31.5	22.3
Primary	53.1	35.6	52.7	50.5	51.4	21.8	15.3	24.2	19.1	13.9
Secondary	72.1	61.8	75.1	67.8	64.4	25.4	25.1	33.5	23.4	16.2
Higher Secondary	68.6	76.2	76.5	66.0	61.9	23.4	26.9	35.8	21.7	16.4
Graduate and above	82.0	91.2	90.7	84.1	82.1	35.1	44.3	47.4	36.5	31.7
Tech Below graduate	75.1	85.5	88.4	78.8	82.8	37.3	49.0	67.6	57.2	52.4
Tech Graduate and above			82.5	85.1	82.3			43.4	57.5	67.6
Vocational Trained			69.3	78.0	82.7			58.8	49.3	48.4
Rural Total	55.3	54.0	55.5	55.4	54.9	32.8	30.2	33.3	25.3	18.2
Urban Areas										
Illiterate	40.6	39.6	38.1	39.5	37.5	19.8	18.0	20.2	16.3	14.8
Primary	47.3	29.3	52.0	47.9	50.2	10.4	7.4	13.2	11.8	11.4
Secondary	67.0	58.6	70.0	66.2	65.7	13.1	11.2	14.1	11.7	11.8
Higher Secondary	60.7	68.3	68.8	63.2	60.4	14.7	14.2	21.5	14.3	14.4
Graduate and above	81.3	85.9	84.4	83.2	81.6	29.7	32.0	34.9	31.9	34.4
Tech Below graduate	80.4	83.5	85.3	79.7	83.8	46.8	47.3	57.7	47.1	54.4
Tech Graduate and above			82.6	82.0	83.9			50.0	53.0	62.3
Vocational Trained			63.9	81.4	84.1			44.0	45.9	48.5
Urban Total	52.1	54.2	57.0	56.4	57.0	15.5	14.8	17.8	15.5	15.9

Source: Authors' estimation based on NSS and PLFS unit-level data.

Note: Information on vocational qualification is collected since 2004–2005.

Table 5.2 Labour-force participation rate by sector, age groups, and level of education in India, 1994–2018

Level of Education	*Labour-Force Participation Rate by Sector and Age Groups (%)*									
	Rural Areas					*Urban Areas*				
	1993–94	*1999–00*	*2004–05*	*2011–12*	*2017–18*	*1993–94*	*1999–00*	*2004–05*	*2011–12*	*2017–18*
Age 15–59 years (Working-age population)										
Illiterate	72.7	70.8	73.5	64.1	55.1	53.8	52.0	54.4	50.9	48.0
Primary	69.5	73.7	70.1	63.0	56.0	54.0	60.0	57.6	55.7	53.4
Secondary	59.5	64.8	60.9	51.2	45.7	47.2	52.5	48.6	43.8	43.8
Higher Secondary	58.5	61.9	63.5	49.8	44.5	44.1	47.8	51.4	42.9	41.4
Graduate and above	74.9	81.7	80.6	69.6	65.4	65.2	68.2	67.5	65.8	64.7
Tech Below graduate	73.9	82.1	85.0	74.7	75.8	75.8	76.9	80.3	73.1	78.7
Tech Graduate and above			77.9	77.5	78.8			74.6	75.5	80.2
Vocationally Trained			65.1	68.2	69.8			56.0	67.8	68.5
Total Working Pop	70.3	68.7	70.6	60.9	53.6	53.2	53.8	56.2	52.7	51.6
Age 60 and more years (Elderly)										
Illiterate	43.0	38.3	40.0	38.2	27.2	24.3	21.0	20.9	18.9	18.7
Primary	62.7	53.6	57.3	53.3	44.2	32.3	25.6	25.1	24.8	25.8
Secondary	67.1	57.5	66.5	56.3	44.8	24.1	29.3	20.4	23.7	21.0
Higher Secondary	77.3	58.7	58.5	56.1	41.0	23.0	22.5	25.4	19.9	21.2
Graduate and above	70.2	61.2	60.4	54.4	29.5	26.4	25.1	24.2	21.7	18.2
Tech Below graduate	71.9	58.5	48.7	53.7	28.5	34.2	29.8	35.1	29.0	23.8
Tech Graduate and above			72.1	52.3	3.1			36.0	31.8	24.5
Vocational Trained										
Total Elderly	47.4	42.5	44.8	43.1	32.4	27.2	23.7	22.8	21.8	21.4

(Continued)

Table 5.2 (Continued)

Level of Education	*Labour-Force Participation Rate by Sector and Age Groups (%)*									
	Rural Areas					*Urban Areas*				
	1993–94	*1999–00*	*2004–05*	*2011–12*	*2017–18*	*1993–94*	*1999–00*	*2004–05*	*2011–12*	*2017–18*
Age 15–29 years (Youth)										
Illiterate	68.0	65.5	66.4	56.5	44.5	50.6	49.9	52.9	51.3	45.7
Primary	60.0	66.6	61.0	50.3	42.0	44.7	56.8	52.7	48.4	42.7
Secondary	46.1	55.1	48.1	35.0	27.6	31.2	45.3	35.3	29.1	27.9
Higher Secondary	44.5	49.8	49.9	35.5	30.4	27.0	33.4	34.7	26.3	26.4
Graduate and above	57.9	69.3	68.0	53.1	53.5	42.1	51.6	54.1	53.9	55.1
Tech Below graduate	56.4	74.5	76.5	64.3	67.6	55.9	64.0	69.1	56.8	68.2
Tech Graduate and above			65.1	59.2	71.9			60.1	61.2	69.8
Vocational Trained			65.1	55.7	59.5			56.0	51.3	57.0
Youth Total	61.3	59.3	60.2	46.4	38.1	40.7	43.2	46.6	40.5	38.5

Source: Authors' estimation based on NSS and PLFS unit-level data.

and higher secondary levels of education, it declined massively (about 14 percentage points). This result further supports the argument that due to increased enrolment in primary and secondary education, labour-force participation has declined in India (also see Rangarajan et al., 2011; Kannan & Raveendran, 2012; Hirway, 2012; Mehrotra et al., 2014; and Mehrotra & Parida, 2017).

Nevertheless, the LFPR of the persons with graduate and above level of general education, and with either technical or formal vocational education shows improvement. It implies two things: first, the young boys and girls in rural India are continuing their higher education and hence they opt to remain out of the labour market; secondly, after completion of their education they tend to join the labour force. This is also clear from the LFPR of youth in both rural and urban India (Table 5.2).

The main reason for an almost stagnant (or negligible decline) LFPR in urban India is the fact that the decline in the LFPR of less-educated persons is almost equally compensated by the rise in LFPR of higher (general) educated and technical and vocationally trained persons. Although youth LFPR did not decline much in urban India, its absolute value is still quite low when compared to other middle-income (in East and North West Asia and South America) and higher-income (North America and Europe) countries of the world. Since the Indian economy is currently passing through a phase of demographic dividend, an increasing youth LFPR is necessary to boost GDP growth over the long run.

The LFPR of the elderly population in both rural (15 percentage-point decline) and urban (6 percentage-point decline) India is showing declining trends (Table 5.2). While factors like mechanization in agriculture and improved standard of living in recent years (due to falling incidence of poverty) could be responsible for declining elderly LFPR in rural areas; improved standard of living and rising share and number of youth population together could have been responsible for declining elderly LFPR in urban India.

Education and changing employment trends in India

At the all-India level, structural transformation in employment had been taking place since 2004–2005, as the share and number of workers in agriculture and allied sector (traditional and low-productive sector) has been declining along with an increase in employment in non-farm sectors (relatively modern sectors).

Employment trends in agriculture and allied sectors

Total employment in agriculture and allied sectors was about 230 million in 1983, it increased to 269 million during 2004–2005, and later declined to 207 million during 2017–2018. Employment in agriculture and allied sectors has continued to increase at 3 million per annum until 2004–2005, but since then, it has been declining at the rate of 5 million per annum (see Table 5.3).

Table 5.3 Employment in agriculture and allied sectors by level and type of education, 1983–2018

Level and Type of Education	*1983*	*1987–88*	*1993–4*	*1999–00*	*2004–05*	*2011–12*	*2017–18*
Number of workers (in millions)							
Illiterate	157.2	157.2	149.0	141.5	138.0	97.3	79.7
Primary	65.4	71.9	86.6	96.6	118.3	118.0	86.0
Secondary	6.1	9.2	3.8	5.3	7.1	10.9	32.3
Graduate and above	1.0	1.6	2.0	3.0	3.5	4.8	6.3
Technical Education	0.6	0.8	0.9	1.2	1.6	0.9	1.1
Vocational Education	NA	NA	NA	NA	0.9	0.6	1.5
Total	230.2	240.7	242.3	247.6	269.4	232.4	206.8
Share of workers (in %)							
Illiterate	68.3	65.3	61.5	57.1	51.2	41.9	38.5
Primary	28.4	29.9	35.7	39.0	43.9	50.8	41.6
Secondary	2.7	3.8	1.6	2.1	2.6	4.7	15.6
Graduate and above	0.4	0.7	0.8	1.2	1.3	2.1	3.0
Technical Education	0.3	0.3	0.4	0.5	0.6	0.4	0.5
Vocational Education	NA	NA	NA	NA	0.3	0.2	0.7
Total	100	100	100	100	100	100	100

Source: Authors' estimation based on NSS and PLFS unit-level data.

The distribution of agriculture and allied sector workers by the level (general education) and types of education (general, vocational, and technical) shows that a major proportion of them were either illiterates or having up to the primary level of education. As the agricultural sector does not require many industrially skilled workers, the share of workers with secondary and above level of general education and with either technical or vocational qualification were quite low.

The number of illiterate workers in agriculture and allied sectors was 157 million during 1983 and it had consistently been declining to reach 78 million during 2017–2018. The share of illiterate workers also declined massively from about 68 per cent to only 38.5 per cent during 1983 and 2017–2018 (Table 5.3).

The number of workers with up to the primary level of education increased consistently from 65.5 million to about 118 million between 1983 and 2011–2012 but declined substantially later on to 86 million. This group of workers holds a dominant share of total agricultural employment. The share of workers having up to the primary level of general education continued to increase from about 28 per cent to about 51 per cent between 1983 and 2011–2012, and since then that share declined to 42 per cent (Table 5.3). This decline of share of workers was mainly due to the fall in absolute number of workers.

Most recently, both the number and share of workers having up to the secondary level of education increased substantially. The number of workers with secondary level of education in agriculture increased from 7 million during 2004–2005 to about 11 million during 2011–2012, and further to 32 million during 2017–2018. It is noteworthy that the share of workers with secondary level of education in agriculture had remained constant, at around 3 per cent, until 2004–2005. The share of workers increased to 4.8 during 2011–2012 and further to 15.6 per cent during 2017–2018 (Table 5.3).

While the absolute decline of the number of agriculture workers is an indication of the structural transformation process, those who lost jobs in agriculture were mostly illiterates or persons with up to the primary level of education. Most of them could be either landless casual workers or marginally self-employed farmers. Hence, for them, an alternative employment arrangement is necessary; otherwise, the incidence of poverty is likely to increase in India.

Due to the rising number and share of educated persons, it is expected that the process of mechanization and automation in agriculture will be enhanced further to speed up the structural transformation in India.

Employment trends in manufacturing sector

Total employment in manufacturing sectors was about 41 million during 1983, which increased to 58.4 million during 2017–2018. Manufacturing employment in India continued to increase at a slow rate (0.8 million per annum). But it is noted that during 2011–2012 and 2017 it declined by 2.5 million, which is of course an unprecedented trend (Table 5.4).

Table 5.4 Employment in manufacturing sector by level and type of education, 1983–2018

Level & Type of Education	*1983*	*1987–88*	*1993–4*	*1999–00*	*2004–05*	*2011–12*	*2017–18*
Number of workers (in million)							
Illiterate	15.0	15.9	13.4	13.0	14.4	13.1	9.4
Primary	19.4	21.3	21.9	24.7	32.4	36.2	25.9
Secondary	4.1	5.2	1.7	2.4	2.5	4.4	14.1
Graduate and above	1.2	1.8	1.9	2.6	2.3	3.2	4.7
Technical Education	1.3	1.6	1.6	1.7	2.3	2.9	2.4
Vocational Education	NA	NA	NA	NA	1.1	1.1	2.0
Total	40.9	45.7	40.5	44.4	54.9	60.8	58.4
Share of workers (in %)							
Illiterate	36.6	34.8	33.0	29.4	26.3	21.5	16.0
Primary	47.4	46.5	54.1	55.6	59.0	59.5	44.3
Secondary	9.9	11.4	4.2	5.4	4.5	7.2	24.1
Graduate and above	3.0	3.9	4.7	5.9	4.1	5.3	8.0
Technical Education	3.1	3.4	3.9	3.8	4.2	4.7	4.1
Vocational Education	NA	NA	NA	NA	1.9	1.7	3.4
Total	100	100	100	100	100	100	100

Source: Authors' estimation based on NSS and PLFS unit-level data.

The distribution of manufacturing-sector workers by their level (general education) and types of education (general, vocational, and technical) also shows that a major proportion of them were either illiterate or having up to the primary level of education. The share of workers with secondary and above level of general education and with either technical or vocational qualification is quite low in the Indian manufacturing sector.

The number of illiterate workers in the manufacturing sector was 15 million during 1983, which had declined marginally to 13 million in 2011–2012. But since then it declined massively to 9.4 million. The share of illiterate workers, on the other hand, declined massively from about 37 per cent to only 16 per cent between 1983 and 2017–2018.

The number of manufacturing-sector workers with up to the primary level of education, however, increased substantially from 19.4 million to about 26 million between 1983 and 2017–2018. Such workers hold a dominant share in total manufacturing employment. The share of workers having up to the primary level of general education continued to increase from about 47 per cent to about 59.5 per cent between 1983 and 2011–2012, and since then it declined to 44 per cent. It happened mainly because of the recent decline of its absolute number.

The number of manufacturing-sector workers with a secondary level of education, however, increased consistently from 4.1 million to about 14 million between

1983 and 2017–2018. The share of workers having a secondary level of general education also continued to increase from about 10 per cent to about 24 per cent between 1983 and 2017–2018 (see Table 5.4). Similarly, the number and share of workers with graduate and above level of education increased consistently in India.

Although the number and share of workers with technical education and with vocational training are increasing consistently, their share in total manufacturing employment is still quite low. Out of a total of 58 million manufacturing workers, only 2.4 million (4 per cent) were technically qualified, whereas only 2 million (about 3.5 per cent) were vocationally trained in India.

Employment trends in non-manufacturing sector

The non-manufacturing sector consists of construction, mining and quarrying, electricity, water and gas supply, and so on. But most of the employment in this sector is being generated in the construction sector only (Mehrotra & Parida, 2019). Total employment in non-manufacturing sectors was about 13 million during 1983, which increased hugely to 56 million during 2011–2012 and then to 60 million during 2017–2018 (see Table 5.5). The non-manufacturing sector (mostly the construction sector) which was creating about 4 million jobs per

Table 5.5 Employment in non-manufacturing sector by level and type of education, 1983–2018

Level & Type of Education	*1983*	*1987–88*	*1993–4*	*1999–00*	*2004–05*	*2011–12*	*2017–18*
Number of workers (in million)							
Illiterate	6.2	11.4	6.9	8.2	10.9	19.0	16.3
Primary	4.8	6.9	7.7	10.8	16.3	31.6	29.1
Secondary	1.0	1.5	0.5	0.7	0.8	2.2	10.1
Graduate and above	0.4	0.5	0.6	0.7	0.6	1.3	2.0
Technical Education	0.4	0.5	0.7	0.7	0.9	1.2	1.5
Vocational Education	NA	NA	NA	NA	0.3	0.4	0.9
Total	12.8	20.8	16.4	21.0	29.7	55.6	59.8
Share of workers (in %)							
Illiterate	48.2	54.9	42.1	38.8	36.6	34.1	27.2
Primary	37.8	33.4	46.9	51.3	54.8	56.7	48.7
Secondary	7.6	7.0	3.0	3.3	2.8	3.9	16.9
Graduate and above	2.9	2.3	3.9	3.3	2.0	2.4	3.3
Technical Education	3.4	2.4	4.1	3.3	2.9	2.2	2.5
Vocational Education	NA	NA	NA	NA	0.8	0.6	1.5
Total	100	100	100	100	100	100	100

Source: Authors' estimation based on NSS and PLFS unit-level data.

annum during 2004–2005 to 2011–2012, created only about 0.6 million per annum during 2011–2012 to 2017–2018. Slow growth of construction jobs has negative implications for low-skilled employment, real wages, and the incidence of poverty (Mehrotra & Parida, 2019).

The distribution of non-manufacturing-sector workers by their level (general education) and types of education (general, vocational, and technical) also shows that a major proportion of them were either illiterates or having up to the primary level of education. The share of workers with secondary and above level of general education and with either technical or vocational qualification were quite low (only 7 per cent) in the Indian non-manufacturing sector. This is as expected, as construction sector employment also does not demand highly educated workers. Hence, these 7 per cent (5 million) workers might have engaged in other subsectors of the non-manufacturing sector like mining and quarrying, electricity, water, gas supply, and so on.

The number of illiterate workers in the non-manufacturing sector was 6.2 million during 1983, which increased to 19 million in 2011–2012. But since then, it declined to 16.3 million. The share of illiterate workers in this sector also declined from about 48 per cent to only 27 per cent between 1983 and 2017–2018. The number of non-manufacturing-sector workers with up to the primary level of education, however, increased substantially, from 5 million to about 29 million between 1983 and 2017–2018. This group of workers holds a dominant share in the total non-manufacturing employment. The share of workers having up to the primary level of general education continued to increase from about 38 per cent to about 49 per cent between 1983 and 2017–2018.

Moreover, the number of non-manufacturing-sector workers with a secondary level of education also increased from 1 million to about 10 million between 1983 and 2017–2018. The share of workers with a secondary level of general education also increased from about 8 per cent to about 17 per cent between 1983 and 2017–2018 (see Table 5.5). Similarly, the number and share of workers with graduate and above level of education also increased from 0.4 million to 2 million during the same time.

Although the number and share of workers with technical education and with vocational training are also increasing consistently, but their share in total non-manufacturing employment is still quite low. Out of a total of 60 million non-manufacturing workers, only 1.5 million (2.5 per cent) were technically qualified, whereas only 1 million (about 1.5 per cent) were vocationally trained in India. This indicates that the share of non-construction jobs is only about 5 per cent of the total non-manufacturing jobs. Otherwise, this sector has lots of potential to create enough skilled jobs in India.

Employment trends in service sector

It is noted that the service sector is the only sector which sustained growth of non-farm jobs, and hence, it played an important role in the process of structural transformation in India. Total service-sector employment increased from 72 million to 153 million (more than doubled) between 1983 and 2017–2018. The number of illiterate workers in this sector is almost constant, at around 16 million over the years. But their share declined from 25 per cent to 10 per cent during the same period. The falling share of illiterate workers is compensated for by a rise in the number and share of workers with a primary level of education. Even though illiterates and workers with a primary level of education together hold a major share of service-sector employment (42 per cent during 2017–2018), the share of highly educated workers has consistently been rising.

The number of service-sector workers with secondary level of education increased from 14 million to about 39 million between 1983 and 2017–2018. This is really a massive rise. The share of workers with a secondary level of general education also increased from about 19 per cent to about 25 per cent between 1983 and 2017–2018 (see Table 5.6). Similarly, the number of workers with graduate and above level of education increased from 7.6 million (10.5 per cent) to 30 million (20 per cent) during the same time. It is expected that these workers are engaged in relatively skilled and high-paid jobs. The rise in the share of highly educated workers is a good sign, but it should continue to rise to sustain the process of structural transformation.

To sum up, it can be stated that education has yet to play an important role in driving employment growth in India. A major proportion of the Indian workforce is still having only up to the primary level of education. This is indeed very

Table 5.6 Employment in service sector by level and type of education, 1983–2018

Level and Type of Education	*1983*	*1987–88*	*1993–4*	*1999–00*	*2004–05*	*2011–12*	*2017–18*
Number of workers (in millions)							
Illiterate	17.9	19.9	17.6	17.8	18.6	16.2	15.7
Primary	28.1	33.1	42.7	49.1	55.9	63.1	48.4
Secondary	14.0	17.0	6.7	8.2	10.3	15.4	38.7
Graduate and above	7.6	9.5	10.7	14.6	14.6	23.7	30.2
Technical Education	4.8	4.9	4.6	5.4	7.8	8.8	11.4
Vocational Education	NA	NA	NA	NA	2.8	4.3	8.7
Total	72.4	84.5	82.3	95.1	110.0	131.6	153.1
Share of workers (in %)							
Illiterate	24.8	23.6	21.4	18.7	16.9	12.3	10.3
Primary	38.8	39.1	51.9	51.7	50.8	48.0	31.6
Secondary	19.3	20.2	8.1	8.6	9.4	11.7	25.3
Graduate and above	10.5	11.3	13.0	15.4	13.3	18.0	19.7
Technical Education	6.7	5.8	5.6	5.6	7.1	6.7	7.4
Vocational Education	NA	NA	NA	NA	2.5	3.3	5.7
Total	100	100	100	100	100	100	100

Source: Authors' estimation based on NSS and PLFS unit-level data.

bad news. Although the service sector is the only non-farm sector which holds a relatively higher share (about 40 per cent) of highly educated (i.e. workers with secondary and above level of education) workers, this is not enough when the number of educated youth job seekers is on the rise in India. Hence, unless policies are designed to create enough jobs in both manufacturing and non-manufacturing sectors along with formal jobs in the service sectors, the open unemployment among educated youth will continue to rise to an unprecedented level.

Rising unemployment and disheartened labour force in India

Although the overall unemployment rate is measured based on the either Current Daily Status (CDS) or Current Weekly Status (CWS) of employment, we have used the usual status in this context. Normally, the unemployment rate calculated based on usual status (usual principal and subsidiary status or UPSS) provides a lower unemployment estimate when compared to both CDS and CWS. However, it is important to note that the unemployment rate based on usual status shows the percentage of persons who searched/looked for jobs for long periods of time during the year (365 days) preceding the survey but could not get any employment.

Unemployment scenario in India

The overall open unemployment rate in India was almost constantly around 2 per cent until 2011–2012, but in 2011–2012 it increased to 6 per cent and thereafter to a massively high rate of 17.8 per cent (see Figure 5.2, Panel A and Panel B). This has happened for the first time in the history of India. As the Indian economy is passing through a phase of demographic dividend where the share of youth and working-age population is at the maximum, this rise is not surprising. But it is quite worrisome, as the economy seems to have failed to accommodate these unemployed persons in the labour market.

A look at the educational status of these unemployed persons during 2017–2018 revealed that about 1.5 million were illiterate, 8.6 million had up to the primary level of education, 8 million had secondary education, 12 million had a graduate and above level of education, about 4 million had technical educational qualification, and about 3 million were vocationally trained (see Table 5.7). It is also noted that with the rising level of education, the unemployment rate is also rising.

For each level of education, the unemployment rate increased during 2011–2012 and 2017–2018 (see Figure 5.2, Panel B). Among illiterates unemployment increased from 0.7 per cent to 7.1 per cent. For youth having up to a primary education, it increased from 3.7 per cent to 11.6 per cent. For secondary education, it increased from 6 per cent to 14.4 per cent; for higher secondary education, it increased from 11 per cent to about 24 per cent; and for youths having graduate and above level of education, it increased from 20 per cent to 36 per cent. Moreover, for youth having technical (37.3 per cent) and vocational (33 per cent) qualification, it is even higher. This is really a worrying fact.

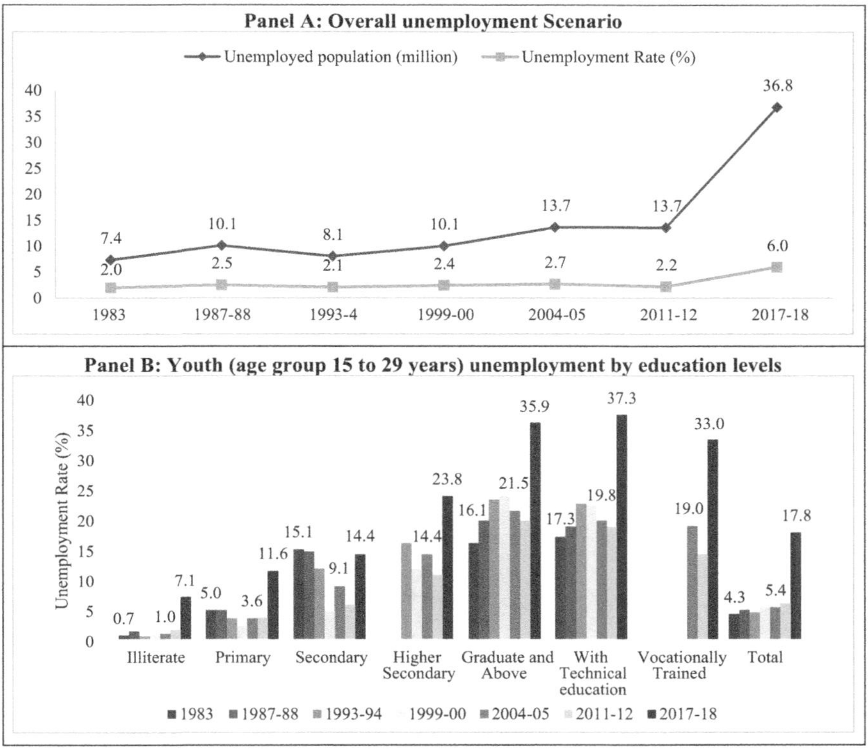

Figure 5.2 Open unemployment scenario (based on UPSS) in India, 2012–2018

Source: Authors' calculation and plot based on NSS and PLFS unit-level data.

Table 5.7 Open unemployment by level and type of education, 1983–2018

Level and Type of Education	*1983*	*1987–88*	*1993–4*	*1999–00*	*2004–05*	*2011–12*	*2017–18*
Open Unemployment (in millions)							
Illiterate	0.8	2.2	0.4	0.5	0.7	0.7	1.5
Primary	3.1	3.6	4.0	5.0	5.5	4.5	8.6
Secondary	2.1	2.6	1.2	1.4	2.2	2.1	7.9
Graduate and above	0.8	1.2	1.6	2.0	2.5	3.4	12.1
Technical Education	0.5	0.6	0.8	1.1	1.3	1.3	3.9
Vocational Education	NA	NA	NA	NA	1.5	1.7	2.8
Total Unemployed	7.4	10.1	8.1	10.1	13.7	13.7	36.8

(Continued)

Table 5.7 (Continued)

Level and Type of Education	*1983*	*1987–88*	*1993–4*	*1999–00*	*2004–05*	*2011–12*	*2017–18*
Unemployment Rate (%)							
Illiterate	0.4	1.1	0.2	0.3	0.4	0.5	1.2
Primary	2.6	2.6	2.5	2.7	2.4	1.8	4.4
Secondary	7.7	7.3	8.8	7.8	7.4	5.2	7.6
Graduate and above	7.1	8.0	9.3	8.9	8.7	7.5	16.9
Technical Education	6.8	7.4	9.6	10.7	9.7	8.9	19.4
Vocational Education	NA	NA	NA	NA	5.9	1.5	2.9
Overall UR	2.0	2.5	2.1	2.4	2.7	2.2	6.0

Source: Authors' estimation based on NSS and PLFS unit-level data.

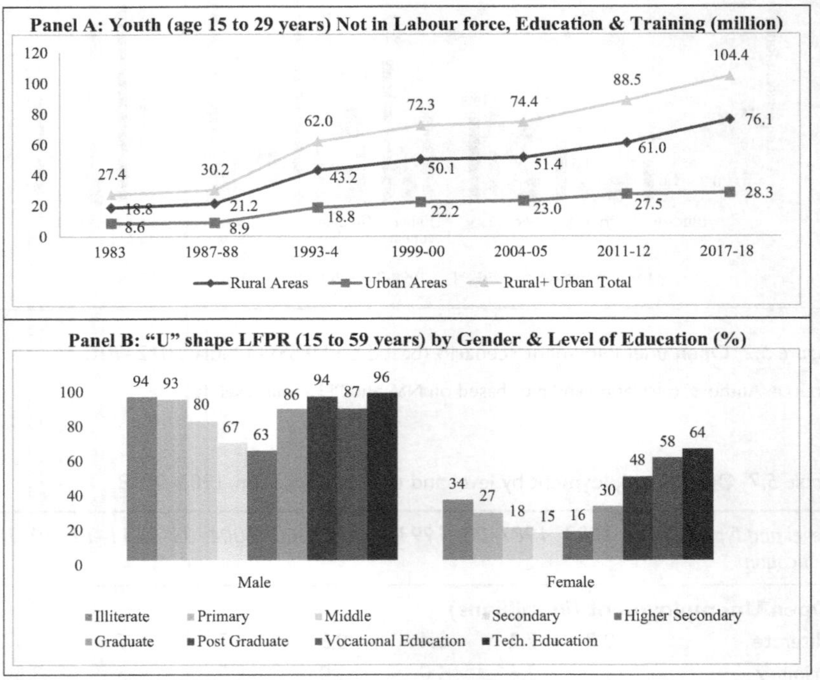

Figure 5.3 Disheartened labour force (based on UPSS) in India, 2012–2018

Source: Authors' calculation and plot based on NSS and PLFS unit-level data.

This increased unemployment among youth (currently about 25 million), particularly among educated and trained youth, is the main reason for declining overall LFPR to the lowest level in India. This is the reason for recent growth of the volume of disheartened labour force, which is otherwise defined as 'Neither in Labour Force nor in Education and Training (NLET)'.

Growth of disheartened labour force in India

The number of youths in the disheartened labour force was about 27 million during 1983. It increased to reach 74 million during 2004–2005. However, since then it is rising at an increasing rate. About 104.4 million (76 million in rural and 28 million in urban India) youth declared themselves as NLET during 2017–2018 (see Figure 5.3, Panel A).

In rural India the number of disheartened labour force increased from 19 million to 76 million between 1983 and 2017–2018, whereas in the urban areas it increased from 9 million to 28 million (see Table 5.8). Further, it is important to note that out of this disheartened labour force about 42 million were having a secondary and above level of education. The rise of educated disheartened youth (who did not search/look for jobs actively but were available for jobs) in both rural and urban India altogether has negative implications for growth and overall development of the society as a whole.

Table 5.8 Disheartened labour force by level and type of education, 1983–2018

Level and Type of Education	*1983*	*1987–88*	*1993–4*	*1999–00*	*2004–05*	*2011–12*	*2017–18*
Rural Areas (in millions)							
Illiterate	12.2	13.0	23.5	23.3	19.0	15.6	13.6
Primary	5.7	7.0	18.2	24.3	26.4	36.1	35.7
Secondary	0.7	1.1	0.9	1.6	2.1	4.8	18.9
Graduate and above	0.1	0.1	0.3	0.7	0.9	2.0	5.7
Technical Education	0.05	0.05	0.20	0.25	0.33	0.23	0.6
Vocational Education					2.7	2.3	1.7
Rural Total	18.8	21.2	43.2	50.1	51.4	61.0	76.1
Urban Areas (in millions)							
Illiterate	3.1	3.0	5.5	5.2	4.1	3.6	2.8
Primary	3.8	3.9	10.5	12.8	12.5	13.9	10.2
Secondary	1.2	1.5	1.2	1.9	2.1	3.8	8.0
Graduate and above	0.4	0.5	1.4	2.0	2.4	3.8	5.6
Technical Education	0.10	0.10	0.22	0.37	0.44	0.71	0.8
Vocational Education					1.6	1.6	1.1
Urban Total	8.6	8.9	18.8	22.2	23.0	27.5	28.3
Rural + Urban Areas (in millions)							
Illiterate	15.3	15.9	29.0	28.4	23.1	19.2	16.3
Primary	9.5	10.9	28.7	37.0	38.9	50.0	45.9
Secondary	1.9	2.6	2.1	3.5	4.1	8.7	26.9
Graduate and above	0.5	0.6	1.7	2.7	3.3	5.8	11.2
Technical Education	0.14	0.16	0.42	0.62	0.77	0.94	1.4
Vocational Education					4.2	3.9	2.8
Rural + Urban Total	27.4	30.2	62.0	72.3	74.4	88.5	104.4

Source: Authors' calculation and plot based on NSS and PLFS unit-level data.

In fact, the situation is alarming because more than 100 million youth are currently attending education and training (in addition to those currently unemployed or currently NLET). and hence currently out of the labour force. As LFPR normally increases with the increase in education levels following a 'U'-shaped pattern (see Figure 5.3, Panel B), after completing education/training they would either search for jobs or remain NLET. If they join the labour market, the unemployment rate would increase further. But if they prefer to remain NLET, it would increase the volume of the disheartened labour force or the so-called potential reserve army.

This huge army of NLET youth, along with the elderly population (which started growing),[1] would constitute the total demographic liability of the economy.

Concluding remarks

We find that labour-force participation rate has consistently been declining in India. This decline is mainly due to a sharp decline in the LFPR of women. Similarly, the LFPR is low at lower levels of education in farm, non-farm, and service sectors of the economy. The sectoral employment pattern reveals that still a higher share of workers in India are low skilled (either illiterate or with up to the primary level of general education). But, since the increasing levels of education have positive implications for overall LFPR (following the 'U'-shape hypothesis), it is highly desirable to promote higher education.

On the supply side, the open unemployment rate and the volume of disheartened labour force increased massively in India in recent years. Therefore, unless and otherwise measures are taken, at the earliest, to create jobs in the non-farm sectors, the Indian economy will fail to harness its demographic dividend. This dividend is likely to disappear after 2040.

Note

1 The share of elderly population in India increased from 8.6 per cent (Census, 2011) to 9.8 per cent (PLFS, 2017–2018) as per latest data.

References

Bardhan, P. K. (1979). Labour supply functions in a poor agrarian economy. *American Economic Review*, 69(1), 73–83.

Chaudhary, R., & Verick, S. (2014). *Female labour force participation in India and beyond*. Working Paper Series. ILO Asia-Pacific, DWT for South Asia and country office for India, New Delhi.

Das, S., Chandra, S. J., Kochhar, K., & Kumar, N. (2015). *Women workers in India: Why so few among so many?* IMF Working Paper No. WP/15/55. Asia and Pacific Department, International Monetary Fund, Washington, DC.

Durand, J. D. (1975). *The labor force in economic development*. Princeton, NJ: Princeton University Press.

Fatima, A., & Sultana, H. (2009). Tracing out the U-shape relationship between female labor force participation rate and economic development for Pakistan. *International Journal of Social Economics*, 36(1/2), 182–198.
Goldin, C. (1994). *The u-shaped female labor force function in economic development and economic history.* NBER Working Paper No. 4707. National Bureau of Economic Research, Cambridge.
Himanshu (2011). Employment trends in India: A re-examination. *Economic and Political Weekly*, 46(37), 43–59.
Hirway, I. (2012). Missing labour force: An explanation. *Economic and Political Weekly*, 47(37), 67–72.
Kannan, K. P., & Raveendran, G. (2012). Counting and profiling the missing labour force. *Economic and Political Weekly*, 47(6), 77–80.
Kapsos, S., Silberman, A., & Bourmpoula, E. (2014). *Why is female labour force participation declining so sharply in India?* ILO Research Paper No. 10. International Labour Office, Geneva.
Klasen, S., & Pieters, J. (2012). *Push or pull? Drivers of female labor force participation during India's economic boom.* IZA Discussion Paper Series Working Paper No. 6395. Institute for the Study of Labor, Bonn, Germany.
Kottis, A. P. (1990). Shifts over time and regional variation in women's labour force participation rates in a developing economy: The case of Greece. *Journal of Development Economics*, 33(1), 117–132.
Luci, A. (2009). Female labour market participation and economic growth. *International Journal of Innovation and Sustainable Development*, 4(2/3), 97–108.
Mammen, K., & Paxson, C. (2000). Women's work and economic development. *Journal of Economic Perspectives*, 14(4), 141–164.
Mehrotra, S., & Parida, J. K. (2017). Why is the labour force participation of women declining in India? *World Development*, 98(C), 360–380.
Mehrotra, S., & Parida, J. K. (2019). *India's employment crisis: Rising education levels and falling non-agricultural job growth.* CSE Working Paper No. 04. Centre for Sustainable Employment, Bengaluru.
Mehrotra, S., Parida, J. K., Sinha, S., & Gandhi, A. (2014). Explaining employment trends in the Indian economy: 1993–94 to 2011–12. *Economic and Political Weekly*, 49(32), 49–57.
Mincer, J. (1985). Inter country comparisons of labour force trends and of related developments: An overview. *Journal of Labour Economics*, 3(1), 1–32.
Pampel, F. C., & Tanaka, K. (1986). Economic development and female labour force participation: A reconsideration. *Social Forces*, 64(3), 599–619.
Parida, J. K. (2015). Growth and prospects of non-farm employment in India: Reflections from NSS data. *The Journal of Industrial Statistics*, 4(2), 154–168.
Psacharopoulos, G., & Tzannatos, Z. (1989). Female labor force participation: An international perspective. *The World Bank Research Observer*, 4(2), 187–201.
Rangarajan, C., Kaul, P. I., & Seema (2011). Where is the missing labour force? *Economic and Political Weekly*, 46(39), 68–72.
Schultz, T. P. (1990). Women's changing participation in the labour force: A world perspective. *Economic Development and Cultural Change*, 38(3), 457–488.
Schultz, T. P. (1991). *International differences in labour force participation in families and firms.* Economic Growth Center Working Paper No. 634. Yale University, Economic Growth Center, New Haven.

Tam, H. (2011). U-shaped female labor participation with economic development: Some panel data evidence. *Economic Letters*, 110(2), 140–142.
Tansel, A. (2001). *Economic development and female labor force participation in Turkey: Time-series evidence and cross-province estimates.* Economic Research Centre Working Paper No. 01/05. Middle East Technical University, Turkey.

Chapter 6

Trends in employment and unemployment in India

Dimensions of gender, caste, and education

Rajendra P. Mamgain and Khalid Khan

The question of employment has always remained at centre stage in the development discourse, particularly in developing countries like India since it has significant implications for widening socio-economic inequalities (IHD-ISLE, 2014). India experienced persistently slow growth in quality employment opportunities amidst a fairly long period of high economic growth since the economic reforms of the early 1990s (Mamgain & Tiwari, 2018; Mehrotra & Parida, 2019; Kannan & Raveendran, 2019). The slow growth in employment (or jobless growth) has become a political issue in the country in recent years. The expansion of education is also accompanied by increasing unemployment of the educated (Bairagya, 2018). The growing income inequalities are being attributed quite significantly to the growing inequalities in the labour market in terms of unequal opportunities for employment, rapid increase in the contractual and casual jobs devoid of any social security, growing wage inequality, faster penetration of technology leading to decreasing or stagnant demand for low-order repetitive jobs and high demand for high-end occupations, which are few in number (ILO, 2014; Nayyar, 2017). The socially marginalized sections of the population, such as Scheduled Tribes (STs) and Scheduled Castes (SCs) still remain at the bottom of the social hierarchy in terms of various socio-economic indicators of development, which is increasingly being attributed to their poor quality of employment, low human capital base, and social exclusion and discrimination which they continue to face in their daily lives in various forms despite their comparatively higher labour-force participation rate (IHD-ISLE, 2014; Thorat & Newman, 2010; Madheswaran, 2017). Though education remains a significant determinant in access to quality employment and earnings (Madheswaran, 2017; Tilak, 2005), the access to quality education is increasingly criticized for its deepening dualism in educational development in India. At the same time, social networks are re-emerging as important hiring practice in job even in formal employment in India in recent years (Mamgain, 2019).

Given this brief background, the chapter aims to critically examine the trends in the nature and quality of employment opportunities for persons with different levels of education. It argues that prospects of participation in work and the nature of work are significantly determined by education, gender, social belonging, and location of a household (i.e. rural-urban, or state). Apart from such endowment factors,

DOI: 10.4324/9781003158349-7

chances of getting employment are also affected by the prevalence of discrimination based on caste, gender, and ethnicity in the labour market to a significant extent. The focus of this chapter is on the latter aspect, highlighting social disparities. The section 'Changing contours of participation in work' of the chapter examines the trends in participation of population in economic activities or work across different social groups—that is, Scheduled Tribes (STs), Scheduled Castes (SCs), Other Backward Classes (OBCs), and Others (OCs). The gender and caste hierarchies in workforce participation rates (WPRs) are analyzed to draw meaningful insights. In the section 'Employment and its quality', the nature and quality of employment are analyzed. It shows how the quality of employment characterized in a 'decent work' framework has deteriorated over the years and that the access to such employment is comparatively reduced for SCs and STs when compared to OCs. The question of unemployment is analyzed in the section titled 'Unemployment'. It shows a steep rise in the incidence of unemployment in India in recent years due to slow growth of employment opportunities, which is a serious policy concern. The conclusion summarises the major features emerging from the analysis and also flags a few policy issues. The chapter is largely based on the NSSO unit-level data on employment and unemployment from its thick rounds and the recent Periodic Labour-Force Survey (PLFS) data of the National Statistical Office (NSO) for the year 2017–2018. We have used population of 15 years and above as the age for the analysis of employment and unemployment based on usual activity status (UPSS) during a reference period of 1983 to 2017–2018. However, we have focussed more on recent period—that is, 2004–2005 to 2017–2018 for a comparative analysis.

Changing contours of participation in work

An estimated 466.4 million of the Indian population were working in 2017–2018, constituting about 34.7 per cent of the total population in the country (Kannan & Raveendran, 2019). In the age group of 15 years and above, nearly 47 per cent of the population was in the workforce. With respect to gender, over 71 per cent of men and nearly 20 per cent of women were working in this age group in the country during 2017–2018. The patterns of workforce-population rates (WPRs) for men do not vary substantially across rural and urban areas in the country. These, however, significantly vary in the case of women. In urban areas, only 18 per cent of women are workers, while nearly 24 per cent in rural areas of India are workers.

The longer-term trends in WPRs of men and women in India broadly follow the declining pattern. However, the decline in WPRs has been more pronounced among the rural female population, particularly since 2004–2005—almost reaching 24 per cent by 2017–2018. The decline in male WPRs both in rural and urban areas has been relatively very slow but comparatively higher than in rural areas between 2004–2005 and 2017–2018 (see Figure 6.1).

Associated with the declining trend in WPRs, there has been a rapid increase in the gender gap, particularly in rural areas, since 2004–2005, areas which were otherwise characterized by a low gender gap when compared to urban areas.

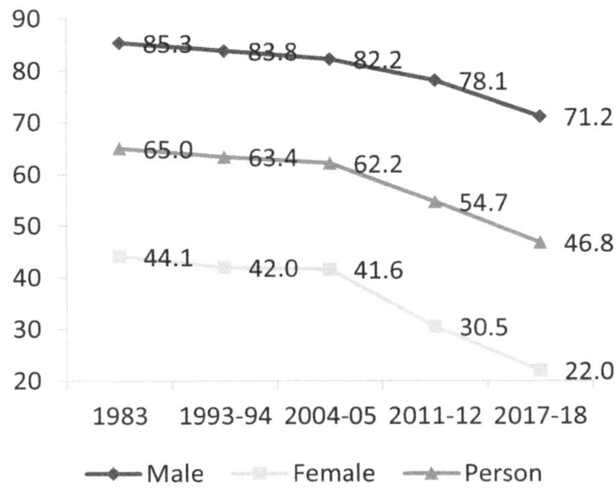

Figure 6.1 Trends in WPRs

Source: NSS (38th, 50th, 61st and 68th rounds) and PLFS (2017–2018).

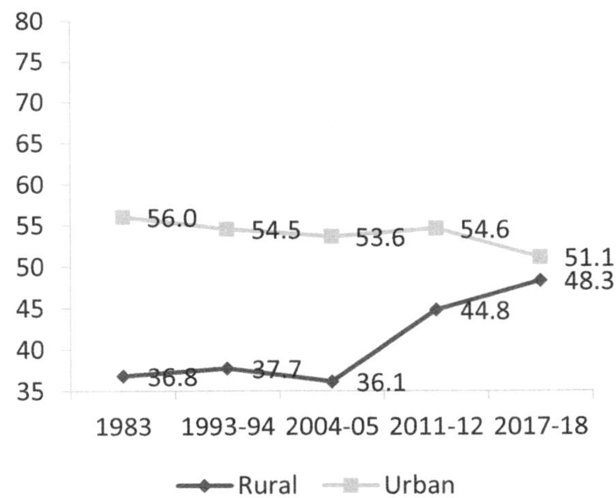

Figure 6.2 Trends in gender gap in WPRs

Source: NSS (38th, 50th, 61st and 68th rounds) and PLFS (2017–2018).

Urban areas, though, suffer with the highest gender gap in WPRs but tended to improve marginally in recent years (see Figure 6.2). Across the globe, such gender gaps tended to decline in developed countries alongside their development (ILO, 2019).

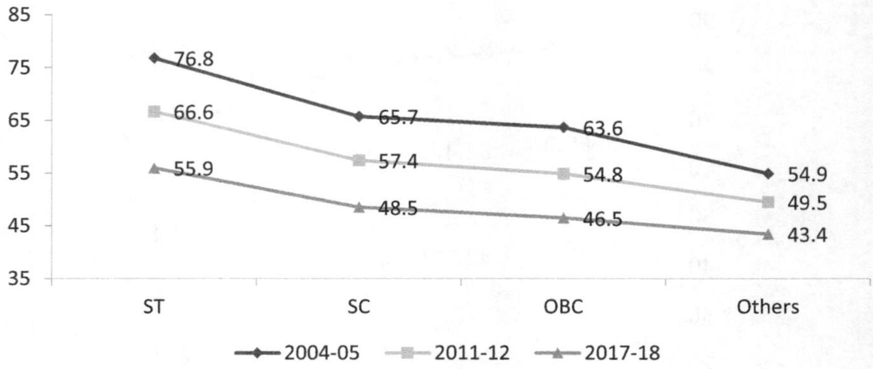

Figure 6.3 Trends in WPRs by social groups

Source: NSS (61st and 68th rounds) and PLFS (2017–2018).

WPRs of SC/STs are higher than those of OCs. The declining trend in WPRs among all social groups is observed. But it has been highest among ST who experienced a decline of about 20 percentage points in their WPRs since 2004–2005. The next highest decline of 17 percentage points is seen in the case of SC and OBC, followed by a relatively lower decline of nearly 12 percentage points among OCs (Figure 6.3).

Education and WPRs

The educational attainments of the workforce in India are much lower than those of the working population of many developing countries such as China, Brazil, and South Africa (ILO, 2019). Much of the labour market outcome in terms of employment and earnings depends on the quality of education, and its quality is a matter of concern and is being questioned in recent years (Blom & Saeki, 2011; FICCI, 2010). Ideally, education improves the chances of a person to participate in work (Schultz, 1961). However, there is a vaguely 'U'-shaped relationship between the educational levels and work-participation rates. WPRs are comparatively higher among persons with lower or no educational levels; they tend to decline among those having middle, secondary, and senior secondary education and then rise among those with a diploma or graduate level education. One of the reasons for lower WPRs among secondary and senior secondary graduates is their comparatively higher transition to higher studies after an initial drop out at elementary level education. However, the other possible reason—their low employability and associated high unemployment rate among them—does not hold true. The highest WPR among diploma graduates reconfirms the role of vocational and technical education in improving the chances of getting employment in the labour market (Mathur & Mamgain, 2004). This broad pattern in WPRs is more prominent among women in the population (see Figure 6.4).

The decline in WPRs has been experienced by populations with different levels of education. However, it has been sharper among illiterates, those with a primary-level education, and those with a diploma-level educations; it is even more pronounced in the case of women (Figure 6.4). This trend shows only that while overall employment opportunities are declining in the country, the most affected groups are less educated. The employment opportunities for diploma holders and graduates are also dwindling, resulting in a sizeable decline in their WPRs.

The WPRs among the illiterate population is highest among STs, followed by SCs, OBCs, and OCs. A similar pattern is observed from school education up to middle level, while the WPR is much different across social categories for secondary and senior secondary levels of education. In the case of graduate persons, WPR is similar among caste groups, but it is higher among STs. However, WPR among diploma holders is lower among SC/ST than OBC/OC. These patterns only reiterate the fact that SC/STs are compelled to join the workforce in school age probably due to their weaker socio-economic background (see Table 6.1).

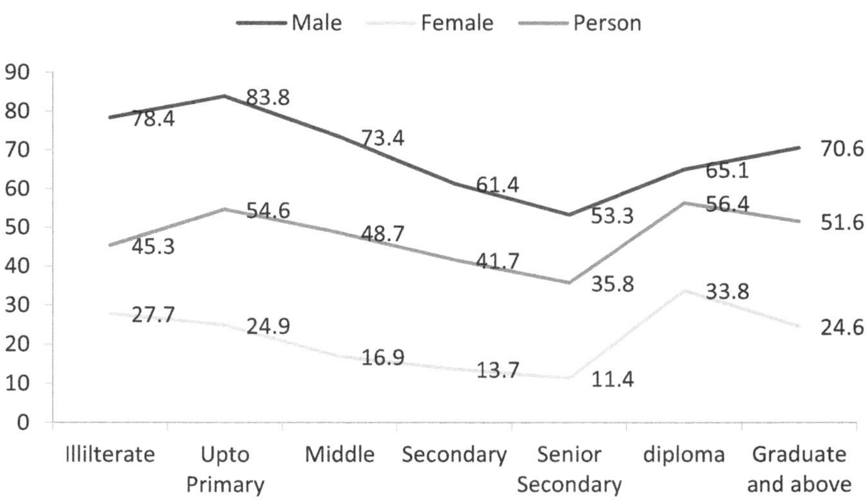

Figure 6.4 Education-specific WPRs by gender: 2017–2018

Source: PLFS (2017–2018).

Table 6.1 Workforce participation rates (15 yrs+), by social group: 2017–2018

	Illiterate	*Up to Primary*	*Middle*	*Secondary*	*Senior secondary*	*Diploma*	*Graduate and above*	*All*
STs	57.9	66.9	54.5	43.0	38.7	52.8	58.4	55.9
SCs	47.6	58.0	49.7	41.7	35.8	52.6	51.3	48.5
OBCs	44.0	54.0	49.8	42.1	35.4	57.1	51.1	46.5
Others	37.2	48.5	44.4	40.7	35.7	57.5	51.6	43.4
Total	45.3	54.6	48.7	41.7	35.8	56.4	51.6	46.8

Source: Periodic labour-force survey, 2017.

Employment and its quality

Nature and structure of employment

Casual employment is considered a most vulnerable form of employment, subject to uncertainty, and generally fetching a low income. Self-employment is a mixed bag of activities with a large number of workers engaged in low-paid activities that suffers with high incidence of underemployment. Regular employment is the most preferred mode of employment, though a majority of such workers have low income and do not get any social security benefits (Srivastava & Naik, 2017; Mamgain & Tiwari, 2018). Viewed from this perspective, about 52.0 per cent of the workforce in India was self-employed in various economic activities in 2017–2018. This also includes about 14 per cent of workers working as helpers in household enterprises. The proportion of such workers is comparatively much higher among women than men; one-third among them work as helpers in household enterprises. Less than 25 per cent of workers are engaged in casual wage work, while the remaining are in regular-salaried jobs (see Table 6.2).

Over the period, the share of self-employed among workers hovered between 57 and 52 per cent between 1983 and 2017–2018 since 1983. The proportion of casual-wage labour remained close to 30 per cent for a fairly long period, till 2011–2012 but tended to decline by about 5 percentage points thereafter by 2017–2018. Similarly, the proportion of workers working as helpers in household enterprises substantially declined from 24 per cent in 2004–05 to about 14 per cent in 2017–2018. The corresponding rise has been observed in the share of regular-salaried workers during the period 1993–1994 to 2017–18. Notably, the entire decline in the share of workers in household enterprises has been at the cost of the rise in the share of self-employed during the recent period 2011–12 to 2017–18, thereby suggesting a faster withdrawal from the workforce of those assisting household enterprises as helpers (see Figure 6.5). This has been largely valid in the case of female workers.

How this structure of employment differs among various social groups can be seen in Table 6.2. The highest share of working persons is in self-employed among

Table 6.2 Quality of employment, 2017–2018 (row %)

Social group	*Self-employment*			*Regular-salaried work*			*Casual-wage labour*		
	Male	*Female*	*Person*	*Male*	*Female*	*Person*	*Male*	*Female*	*Person*
ST	56.6	54.8	56.0	14.0	11.0	13.1	29.4	34.2	30.9
SC	39.3	37.7	38.9	19.6	20.5	19.8	41.1	41.8	41.2
OBC	55.6	56.1	55.7	22.1	19.3	21.4	22.4	24.6	22.9
OCs	55.2	55.2	55.2	31.1	31.6	31.2	13.7	13.2	13.6
Total	52.4	51.9	52.3	23.4	21.2	22.9	24.2	26.9	24.9

Source: Periodic labour-force survey, 2017.

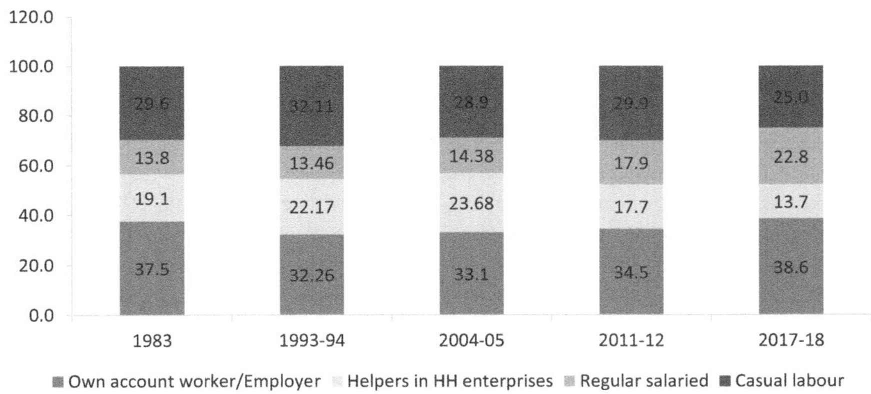

Figure 6.5 Changes in nature of employment, 1983 to 2017–2018

Source: NSS (38th, 50th, 61st and 68th rounds) and PLFS (2017–2018).

OBCs and STs, followed by OCs, and lowest among SCs (about 39 per cent). The share of casual worker is remarkably higher among SC (41 per cent) than the OCs (nearly 14 per cent). STs are also proportionately more concentrated in casual-wage employment than OBCs and OCs. The access to regular-salaried employment is far better among OC workers, as nearly 31 per cent among them are engaged in such work. The corresponding share is lowest among ST workers.

The interface between gender and caste can be seen in access to different types of employment. Proportionately the share of casual labour among SC female workers is almost three times higher than their counterparts belonging to OCs and nearly double that in the case of OBCs. Females are proportionately lower in self-employment when compared to their male counterparts. This is true across all social groups. It is also seen that a large majority of females reported as self-employed are working as helpers in their family enterprises. This also restricts their direct access to incomes or profit, economic empowerment, and household decision-making. In other words, most of the women, particularly belonging to SC and ST communities, have poor quality of employment, which is vulnerable to seasonality and fetches low incomes.

Education significantly determines the access to the quality employment (Schultz, 1961; Papola & Rodgers, 1992). While a majority of workers with lower levels of education, such as below secondary level, are working as self-employed, with a sizeable proportion as helpers in household enterprises and casual wage workers, the better-educated are predominantly in regular-salaried employment (see Figure 6.6). This pattern is observed over a long period as well and thus underscores the importance of education in improving access to regular employment opportunities (see Figure 6.7).

Mamgain and Tiwari (2017) show how after controlling factors such as gender, age, education, experience, and location, the likelihood of getting into regular-salaried jobs is significantly high among OCs when compared to SCs, STs, and OBCs. This pattern raises questions on the quality of education across different groups and unequal access to social networks in the labour market. The prevailing discrimination also works as an impediment in human capital formation among the underprivileged groups and hence their access to the labour market thereby significantly favouring OCs (Banerjee & Knight, 1985; Thorat & Newman, 2010; Mamgain, 2019). The existence of identity-based discrimination also impacts the choice of occupation in the labour market for households belonging to the marginalized groups (Attewal & Thorat, 2007; Neuman & Thorat, 2007).

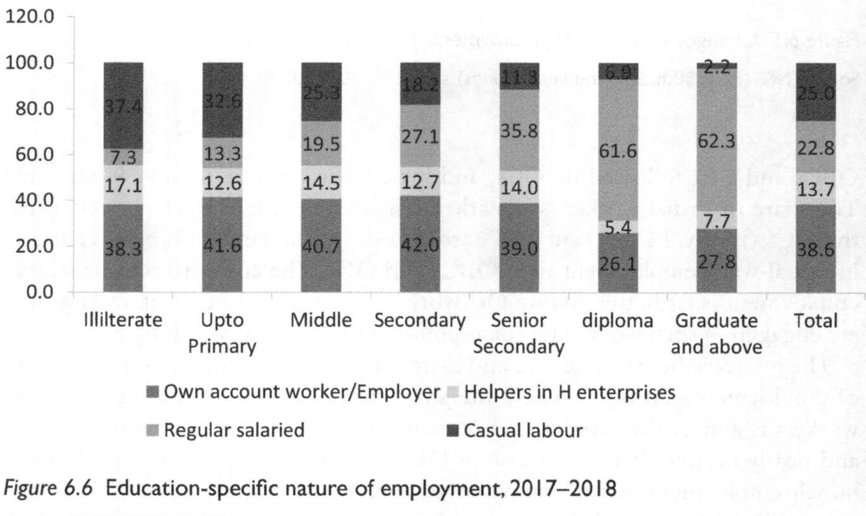

Figure 6.6 Education-specific nature of employment, 2017–2018

Source: PLFS (2017–2018).

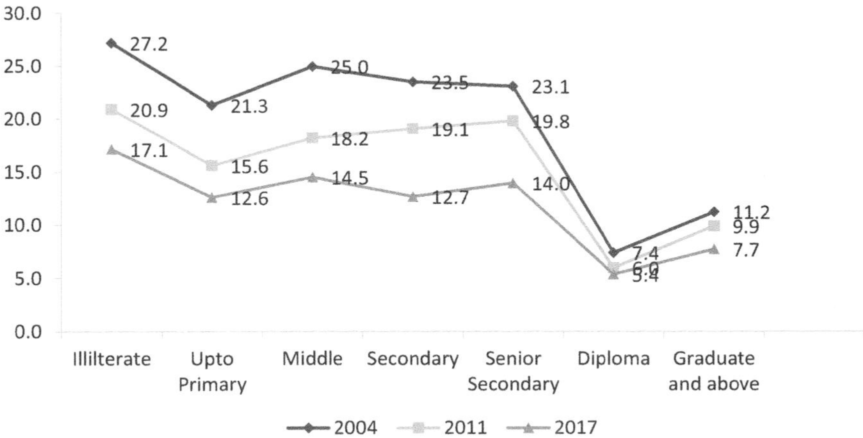

Figure 6.7 Education-specific workers working as helpers in household enterprises

Source: NSS (61st and 68th rounds) and PLFS (2017–2018).

Structural shifts in employment and social category

The slow pace of the shift of the workforce from agricultural to industrial and service sector has been one of the characteristics of growth of employment in India. The share of workers in agriculture and allied activities and mining though decreased substantively by nearly ten percentage points between 2004–2005 and 2011–2012, the shift has been comparatively much slow during the subsequent period, 2011–2012 and 2017–2018. An almost stagnant share of industrial sector in the later period also explains the slow growth of employment opportunities in manufacturing and construction enterprises, which were characterized either with relatively better employment elasticity when compared to service sector.

Agriculture yet remains the largest employer, with over 44 per cent of the Indian workforce in 2017–2018 working in agriculture. The next important sector in terms of employment is manufacturing (12.1 per cent), closely followed by construction (11.7 per cent), and trade (10.1 per cent). These four industry-groups together contribute nearly 78 per cent of total employment (see Table 6.3). With respect to gender, a majority of women workers are working in agriculture and allied activities. Other services and construction are next important sources of employment for women. The structure of women's employment is less diversified when compared to their male counterparts (Table 6.3).

Disparities in the structure of employment are seen among workers belonging to different social groups, with the highest, 69 per cent of STs, still working in the primary sector when compared to about 36 per cent in the case of OCs. A largest share of SCs in the secondary sector is mainly due to their relatively higher

Table 6.3 Industrial structure of employment, 2017–2018

Industry	*Male*	*Female*	*Person*
Agriculture	40.2	57.0	44.1
Mining	0.5	0.2	0.4
Manufacturing	12.0	12.4	12.1
Electricity and water	0.7	0.2	11.7
Construction	13.7	5.0	0.6
Trade, hotels, and restaurants	13.7	6.3	12.0
Transport, storage, and communication	7.4	1.1	5.9
Other services	11.8	17.8	13.2
Total	100	100	100

Source: Periodic labour-force survey (2017).

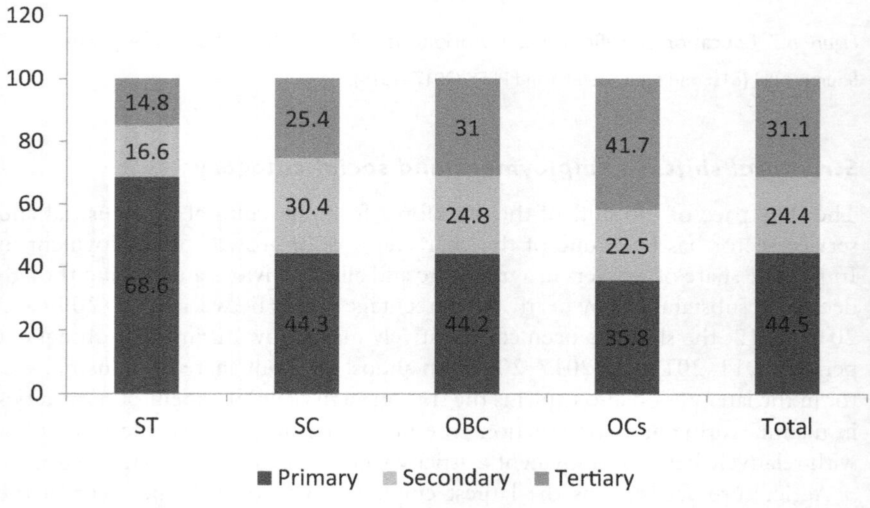

Figure 6.8 Structure of employment by social groups, 2017–2018 (%)
Source: PLFS (2017–2018).

share in the construction sector. OCs have proportionally higher share in the tertiary sector largely due to their higher share in the trade and education sectors (see Figure 6.8).

The varying structure of employment is largely associated with the endowments of workers, such as education, skill, gender, and place of residence. However, SC/ST and women still face discrimination in access to various types of better-paid employment. Social networks and their quality still continue to be the major source of job information and access to jobs in the formal labour market

Table 6.4 Workforce across their education and industry of employment, 2011–2012 and 2017–2018

Year/Industry	*Illiterate*	*Up to Primary*	*Middle*	*Secondary*	*Senior Secondary*	*Diploma*	*Graduate and above*	*Total*
2011–2012								
Primary	67.5	53.0	45.7	40.4	34.4	12.0	13.2	49.4
Secondary	21.4	27.8	27.5	23.3	19.6	36.2	14.8	23.7
Tertiary	11.2	19.3	26.8	36.3	46.0	51.8	72.0	27.0
2017–2018								
Primary	66.2	49.1	42.7	35.9	32.1	11.2	13.0	44.5
Secondary	20.7	29.0	28.5	26.8	22.3	36.7	14.9	24.4
Tertiary	13.0	21.9	28.9	37.3	45.7	52.1	72.1	31.1

Source: Periodic labour-force survey (2017).

Note: Primary sector consists of agriculture and allied activities; secondary sector is based on industrial activities and tertiary sector refers to the service sector.

(Mamgain, 2019). Due to weak social networks, a large proportion of SC/ST and women workers find difficulty in getting access to jobs in the labour market despite their better education and other attributes.

As is well known, workers with low educational levels are mainly working in agriculture and allied activities. On the other hand, over 72 per cent of graduate workers and 52.1 per cent of those with a diploma are employed in the service sector in 2017–18 (see Table 6.4). This pattern indicates the importance of education in getting access to services sector employment. This pattern holds true for both women and men belonging to different social groups. Over the years, a substantive proportion of workers with middle and secondary level of education has shifted from agriculture to other industry sectors, mainly construction. This is clearly visible in Table 6.5. Education thus definitely helps workers in moving away from primary to secondary and tertiary industry sectors.

Occupational structure and social category

With respect to the occupational hierarchies, legislators, senior officials, and managers are on the top and elementary occupations are on the bottom (see Table 6.5). Nearly 11.4 per cent of workers were in the top-two occupations in 2017–2018. If skilled agricultural workers and elementary occupations are combined together, a highest percentage of the workers across the occupation (56 per cent of workers) belong to these two occupational groups. The period between 2011 and 2017 has witnessed a marginal reduction in the share of most of the low-quality occupations, while the share of the top occupations has marginally increased.

Table 6.5 Changing trends in occupational pattern

Occupation-NCO-1 digit	*2011*	*2017*
Legislators and officials	6.8	7.3
Professionals	3.6	4.1
Technicians and associated professionals	3.1	3.9
Clerks	1.9	1.9
Service workers and shop and market sales workers	7.4	9
Skilled agricultural	31.8	30.7
Craft-related trade works	12.9	11.6
Plant and machine operation	4.7	5.6
Elementary occupation	27.8	25.9
Total	100	100

Source: National Sample survey of employment and unemployment, 2011 and periodic labour-force survey, 2017.

With respect to gender, over two-thirds of female and 54 per cent of male workers are engaged in elementary occupations. The corresponding ratio in top occupations is 9.4 per cent and 12 per cent, respectively, in 2017–2018.

Nearly 80 per cent of ST workers and two-thirds of SC workers are working in elementary and skilled agriculture and fishery occupations. The corresponding percentage of OCs in such occupations is far less when compared to ST/SC. Nearly one-fifth of OC workers work in the top-two occupations, whereas the corresponding share is much less in the case of SC and ST workers. In lower middle occupations such as crafts-related work and plant and machinery operation, the proportion of workers among each social group does not vary substantially (Table 6.6). Thus, a broad pattern of a proportionately low share of SC/ST workers in top-end occupations when compared to OCs and OBCs shows the concentration of SC/ST working in low-end occupations.

Table 6.7 shows the changes in occupational pattern of graduate and illiterate workers between 2011–2012 and 2017–2018. The data show a reduction in the share of top-two occupations but an increase in the share of low-quality occupations among the graduate workforce. This trend holds among educated workers also, thus indicating a slow growth in employment opportunities in top occupational categories and faster rise in unemployment for graduates in India. For example, the share of educated in elementary occupations has increased from 25.9 per cent to 27.8 per cent between 2011 and 2017, while the corresponding share increased from 2.4 per cent to 3.5 per cent among graduates and decreased from 40.6 per cent to 39.7 per cent among illiterates.

Education significantly determines the occupational level of workers irrespective of gender (Table 6.8). We have compared an occupational structure of graduate and illiterate workers for men and women separately. The majority of graduate workers irrespective of their gender are employed in the top-three

Table 6.6 Occupational patterns among workers by their social groups, 2017–2018 (%)

Occupation-NCO-1 digit	*STs*	*SCs*	*OBCs*	*OCs*	*Total*
Legislator, senior officials, and managers	2.5	4.4	7.4	11.3	7.3
Professionals	1.5	2.2	3.4	7.4	4.1
Technicians and associated professionals	2.5	2.8	3.5	5.7	3.9
Clerks	1.0	1.2	1.8	3.1	1.9
Service workers and shop and market sales workers	3.9	6.9	9.8	11.2	9.0
Skilled agricultural and fishery workers	45.6	23.5	31.9	28.2	30.7
Craft and related trade workers	5.3	13.4	12.9	10.8	11.6
Plant and machine operators and assemblers	2.9	5.3	5.8	6.7	5.6
Elementary occupation	34.9	40.3	23.5	15.6	25.9
Total	100	100	100	100	100

Source: Periodic labour-force survey, 2017.

Table 6.7 Occupational patterns of graduate and illiterate workers, 2017–2018

Occupation-NCO-1 digit	*2011*			*2017*		
	Graduate	*Illiterate*	*Total*	*Graduate*	*Illiterate*	*Total*
Legislator, senior officials, and managers	17.1	2.8	7.3	16.0	3.3	6.8
Professionals	25.2	0.36	4.1	23.1	0.43	3.6
Technicians and associated professionals	17.4	0.24	3.9	19.2	0.15	3.1
Clerks	10.3	0.06	1.9	8.8	0.04	1.9
Service workers and shop and market sales workers	9.9	3.2	9.0	10.4	4.6	7.4
Skilled agricultural and fishery workers	11.3	39.8	30.7	12.3	41.0	31.8
Craft and related trade workers	4.0	10.8	11.6	4.3	8.4	12.9
Plant and machine operators and assemblers	2.4	2.1	5.6	2.6	2.5	4.7
Elementary occupation	2.4	40.6	25.9	3.5	39.7	27.8

Source: National sample survey of employment and unemployment, 2011, and periodic labour-force survey, 2017.

occupational categories. The proportion is even much higher (74.4 per cent) in the case of graduate women workers. In contrast, an overwhelming majority of illiterate men and women workers are working in agriculture and other elementary occupations. The likelihood of graduate female workers getting into higher-end occupations is much higher compared to their male counterparts, provided employment opportunities grow in the economy. This underscores the need to improve the educational transition of women towards higher education for improving their prospects to move out of the traditional agriculture and allied activities.

Table 6.8 Occupational patterns of graduate and illiterate workers, 2017–2018

Occupation-NCO-1 digit	*Male*		*Female*	
	Graduate	*Illiterate*	*Graduate*	*Illiterate*
Legislators, senior officials, and managers	17.9	3.8	8.4	2.5
Professionals	20.52	0.46	33.6	0.37
Technicians and associated professionals	15.89	0.09	32.4	0.23
Clerks	8.52	0.04	9.7	0.04
Service workers and shop and market sales workers	11.4	4.5	6.3	4.7
Skilled agricultural and fishery workers	14.2	39.2	4.7	43.7
Craft and related trade workers	4.6	9.9	3.0	6.3
Plant and machine operators and assemblers	3.1	3.8	0.42	0.48
Elementary occupation	3.9	38.3	1.5	41.7

Source: Periodic labour-force survey, 2017.

Extent of occupational segregation

How different are the occupational patterns of women and men from each other or of one social group from another? With the help of Duncan's Dissimilarity Index (DI), Mamgain (2017) shows that at least 36 per cent of the female workforce has to shift their occupations to have identical occupational characteristics with the male workforce. With regards to the occupational segregation among social groups, the highest level of dissimilarity is observed in the occupations pursued by STs in comparison to those falling in the category of OCs with a DI value of 0.32 in 2011–2012. The next highest level of dissimilarity is observed in the occupations pursued by SCs with respect to OCs. He observed an increase in occupational dissimilarity among SCs and OCs during the pre-reform period (1983 to 1993–1994) and thereafter a decline during the post-reform period, but at a slower pace after 2004. In other words, the advent of economic reforms and the consequent high-growth regime not only led to higher employment growth among SCs but also enabled them to diversify into new occupations wherein their presence had earlier been almost negligible. This decreasing occupational dissimilarity has been largely accompanied by their growing number entering into poor-quality jobs as well as improvement in their share in high end jobs.

Unlike the declining value of DI for SCs with respect to workers falling in the category of OCs, the DI value for STs has increased continuously over different points of time since 1983. This clearly reconfirms our earlier finding of the lowest pace of occupational diversification among STs compared to OCs over the years.

Unemployment

By including all ages of 15 years and above, nearly 6 per cent of the Indian labour force, both men and women, reported themselves unemployed in 2017–2018 based on their usual status. The aggregate unemployment rate almost tripled between 2004 and 2017 among both men and women.

The unemployment rate increased significantly among those with higher education, while the reverse is true for the population with no literacy or school education. The unemployment rate for the graduate and above level of education has more than doubled between 2011 and 2017, although the earlier period, between 2004 and 2011, witnessed a slight reduction, from 8.7 per cent to 7.5 per cent. The unemployment rate among the illiterate population is lowest and remained at 1.2 per cent between 2011 and 2017. The unemployment rate between 2011 and 2017 has increased for senior-secondary and diploma-level education also, but it has decreased for those with school-level education.

The unemployment rate has been highest among OCs and lowest among STs. When looking at only women, the unemployment rate is highest among OC women at 8 per cent. The corresponding incidence has been almost three-times lower among ST women. SC and OBC women fall in between OCs and STs with respect to the incidence of unemployment (see Table 6.9).

This broad picture of unemployment, however, hides several important aspects of unemployment. Unemployment is predominantly a youth phenomenon. About 20.1 million youths in India are unemployed, representing 84.7 per cent of the entire unemployed population in the country in 2017–2018. The number of unemployed youths in the country swelled from 5.60 million in 1993–1994 to 7.9 million in 2004–2005, to 9.14 million in 2011–2012 and further to 20.1 million in 2017–2018. The number of unemployed youth thus more than doubled between 2011–2012 and 2017–2018, which has attracted huge public attention and concerns in recent months after the release of 2017–2018 PLFS data. This is indeed an alarming situation, where the unemployment rate in the country has been recorded at its highest level during last 45 years. The incidence of unemployment (with respect to population) is almost three times higher (6.8 per cent) among youths compared to all adults (2.2 per cent).

The incidence of unemployment among youth also varies among labour force belonging to various social groups—ranging from the highest unemployment rate of one-fifth among OC to the lowest unemployment rate of 12.2 per cent

Table 6.9 Caste and gender-specific unemployment rate, 2017–2018 (%) (15+ Labour Force)

Social group	*Male*	*Female*	*Person*
STs	4.9	2.5	4.1
SCs	6.6	4.9	6.2
OBCs	6.0	5.7	5.9
OCs	6.4	8.1	6.7
Total	6.1	5.6	6.0

Source: Periodic labour-force survey, 2017.

among ST across the social groups. About 18 per cent of OBCs and SCs youth reported themselves unemployed in 2017–2018. This pattern can be seen in the case of both men and women across their social groups. However, a within-group comparison of unemployment rates among male and female youth shows a divergent pattern—the unemployment rate among STs and SCs young women is lower than that of their male counterparts, whereas the opposite is the pattern in the case of those belonging to OBCs and OCs (see Table 6.10). An increasing participation of female youth among STs in work along with a decline in their LFPRs between 2011–2012 and 2017–2018 could be one of the reasons for a decline in unemployment rate among them. A steep rise in unemployment among youth has been widespread, irrespective of gender and caste, but it has been relatively higher among SCs, STs and OBCs (see Figure 6.9).

Educated youths generally suffer with higher incidence of unemployment, which they continued to suffer with a rapid rise during recent periods. The unemployment has been highest at 36 per cent for graduate labour force in 2017–2018,

Table 6.10 Unemployment rate among youth, 2017–2018 (%) (15–29 years)

Social group	*Male*	*Female*	*Person*
STs	14.1	7.6	12.2
SCs	18.1	16.7	17.9
OBCs	17.7	19.1	18.0
OCs	19.1	23.9	20.1
Total	17.8	17.9	17.8

Source: Periodic labour-force survey, 2017.

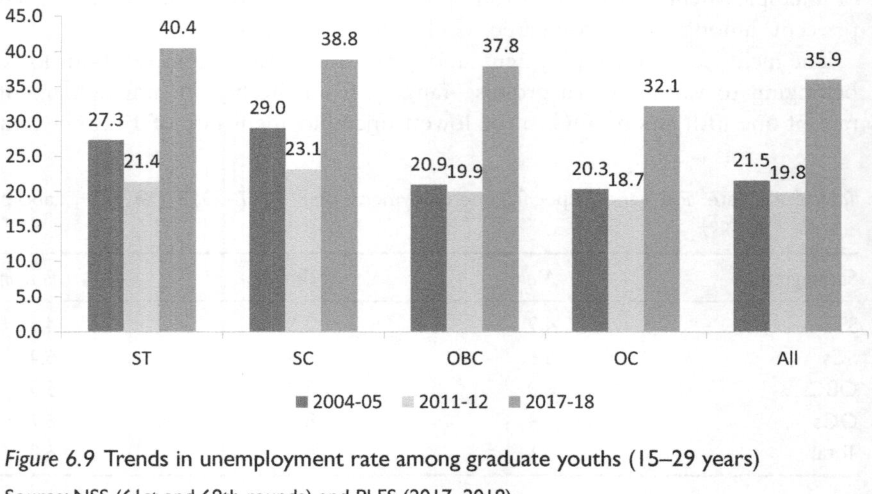

Figure 6.9 Trends in unemployment rate among graduate youths (15–29 years)

Source: NSS (61st and 68th rounds) and PLFS (2017–2018).

so far the period during 2004–2005 and 2017–2018 is concerned. However, the rise in the incidence of unemployment has been widespread, irrespective of the educational levels of youth.

It can be seen that ST, closely followed by SC and OBC youth graduates, face the highest rate of unemployment when compared to OCs. During the past, the unemployment rate tended to decline significantly, particularly among SC ST and SC graduates between 2004–2005 and 2011–2012, but it rose more sharply during the recent period, between 2011–2012 and 2017–2018 (see Figure 6.9). A steep rise in unemployment was observed between 2004–2005 and 2011–2012 for those youth with diploma-level education belonging to different social groups. Among diploma graduates, the unemployment rate is higher among SCs at 43.8 per cent (see Figure 6.10).

These patterns clearly show that while labour force with higher educational qualifications such as graduate and diploma-level education suffers with a very high rate of unemployment when compared to others, the rate of increase in the incidence of unemployment has been more worrying for those with comparatively lower levels of education. In this changing milieu, women, SCs, and STs are more adversely affected in finding jobs in the labour market.

In brief, a fast rise in an already high incidence of unemployment is a major issue confronting the youth population, irrespective of their gender and social group.

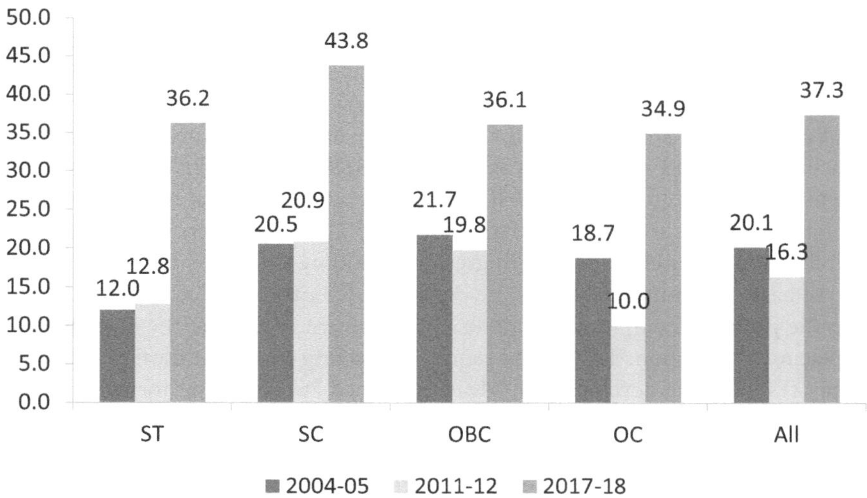

Figure 6.10 Trends in unemployment rate among diploma-holder youths (15–29 years)

Source: NSS (61st and 68th rounds) and PLFS (2017–2018).

Conclusion

The Indian economy is confronting a major challenge of creating employment opportunities for its rising population despite experiencing a reasonably high economic growth for a long period. This long period of 'jobless growth' has turned into 'job loss growth' with the steep rise in unemployment among youth both in rural and urban areas and the withdrawal of population, particularly rural females in large proportion from the labour force (Kannan & Raveendran, 2019). Dependence on self-employment particularly on agriculture is still very high, indicating a less-than-desired rate of growth in non-farm activities in the non-farm wage employment. The wage employment too suffers with a high degree of actualization and rapid informalization of available regular employment opportunities with deteriorating social security even within the formal sector in recent years. More than half of the regular employment is contributed by informal enterprises with almost zero social security. This process of informalization of employment opportunities has intensified in recent periods of high growth, thereby creating a deficit of 'decent employment' opportunities notably. More so, gender, caste, and ethnicity as social institution has played a significant role in determining the labour outcomes. A higher share of the women and STs have been employed in agriculture and household enterprises. The dependence of SCs is highest on casual wage employment, while the access of OCs, particularly men among them, is high on regular salaried employment. Thus, the major challenge is to create productive employment and decent work for all, which is also enshrined in the Sustainable Development Goal (SDG) 8 of the United Nations.

The role of education in improving the access to quality employment is also well known. However, the quality of education matters more. The policy interventions now should gear up improving access to quality education and training to all—but more to historically deprived sections of the society such as women, SCs and STs, and also economically weaker sections. Pre-labour market investments on human capital are important for building enhanced capabilities which have far-reaching inequality-reducing impact (UNDP-HDR, 2019). While there has been significant improvement in access to elementary education, a lot needs to be done to improve access to quality tertiary education. This would necessitate improved public budgets for education, with greater autonomy and accountability.

We have to seriously relook at the demand side bottlenecks which are hampering the growth of employment-intensive investment, including the rapid labour-replacing automation. This would require correcting trade and fiscal policies that support enterprise development. Measures aimed at promoting formality in the labour market and their effective monitoring are equally important for promoting social security of workers from disadvantaged sections in coming years.

Measures such as access to cheaper credit for enterprises and a plethora of government-funded self-and-wage employment programmes along with infrastructure development have helped in employment creation so far, but certainly the coverage of these supports is not on a desired scale which is evident from the sharp rise in unemployment among youth in recent years. These models of development need to be re-examined for their efficacy and preparedness to meet the rising challenge of unemployment. Past experience clearly shows how organizing workers, especially poor women, into collectives enables them to pool assets and skills to produce larger quantities of higher-quality goods, acquire new technology and skills, and enhance voice and agency, increasing their bargaining power and income and increasing political clout, as well. In brief, the challenge would be to ensure social justice along with the economic justice by encouraging the participation of women and socially marginalized groups in the labour market with remunerative income.

References

Attewal, P., & Thorat, S. (2007). The legacy of social exclusion. *Economic and Political Weekly*, 42(41), 4141–4145.

Bairagya, I. (2018). Why is unemployment higher among the educated? *Economic and Political Weekly*, 53(7), 43–51.

Banerjee, B., & Knight, J. B. (1985). Caste discrimination in the Indian urban labour market. *Journal of Development Economics*, 17(3), 277–307.

Blom, A., & Saeki, H. (2011). *Employability and skill set of newly graduated engineers in India*. Washington, D.C.: The World Bank. https://doi.org/10.1596/1813-9450-5640.

FICCI (2010). *The skill development landscape in India and implementing quality skills training*. New Delhi: Federation of Indian Chambers of Commerce and Industry.

IHD-ISLE (2014). *India: Labour and employment report 2014-workers in the era of globalization*. New Delhi: Academic Foundation, Institute for Human Development-Indian Society of Labour Economics.

ILO (2014). *World of work report 2014-developing with jobs*. Geneva: International Labour Organisation.

ILO (2019). *World employment and social outlook-trends 2019*. Geneva: International Labour Organisation.

Kannan, K. P., & Raveendran, G. (2019). From jobless to job-loss growth: Gainers and losers during 2012–18. *Economic and Political Weekly*, 54(44), 38–44.

Madheswaran, S. (2017). Is affirmative action policy for private sector necessary? In K. P. Kannan, R. P. Mamgain, & P. Rustagi (Eds.), *Labour and development: Essays in honour of Prof. T.S. Papola*. New Delhi: Academic Foundation.

Mamgain, R. P. (2017). Occupational diversification in India: Trends and determinants. In K. P. Kannan, R. P. Mamgain, & P. Rustagi (Eds.), *Labour and development: Essays in honour of Prof. T.S. Papola*. New Delhi: Academic Foundation.

Mamgain, R. P. (2019). *Formal labour market in urban India: Job search, hiring practices and discrimination*. New Delhi: SAGE Publications.

Mamgain, R. P., & Tiwari, S. (2017). Regular salaried employment opportunities in India: Nature, access and inclusiveness. *The Indian Journal of Labour Economics*, 60(3), 415–436.

Mamgain, R. P., & Tiwari, S. (2018). Regular salaried employment opportunities in India: Nature, access and inclusiveness. *The Indian Journal of Labour Economics*, 60(3), 415–436.

Mathur, A., & Mamgain, R. P. (2004). Human capital stocks, their level of utilization and economic development in India. *The Indian Journal of Labour Economics*, 47(4), 655–675.

Mehrotra, S., & Parida, J. K. (2019). *India's employment crisis: Rising education levels and falling non-agricultural job growth*. CSE Working Paper No. 2019–04. Centre for Sustainable Employment, Azim Premji University, Bangalore.

Nayyar, D. (2017). Economic liberalization in India: Then and now. *Economic and Political Weekly*, 52(2), 41–48.

Neuman, K. S., & Thorat, S. (2007). Caste and economic discrimination: Causes, consequences and remedies. *Economic and Political Weekly*, 42(41), 4121–4124.

Papola, T. S., & Rodgers, G. (1992). *Labour institutions and economic development in India*. Research Series No. 97. Geneva: International Institute for Labour Studies.

Periodic Labour Force Survey (2017). *Annual report: Periodic labour force survey 2017–18*. Ministry of Statistics and Programme Implementation, NSO, New Delhi.

Schultz, T. W. (1961). Investment in human capital. *The American Economic Review*, 51(1), 1–17.

Srivastava, R. S., & Naik, A. (2017). Growth and informality in the Indian economy. In K. P. Kannan, R. P. Mamgain & P. Rustagi (Eds.), *Labour and development: Essays in honour of Prof. T.S. Papola* (pp. 189–214). New Delhi: Academic Foundation.

Thorat, S., & Newman, K. S. (2010). *Blocked by caste: Economic discrimination in modern India*. New Delhi: Oxford University Press.

Tilak, J. B. G. (2005). *Post-elementary education, poverty and development in India*. Working Paper No. 6. Centre of African Studies, University of Edinburgh, Edinburgh. https://assets.publishing.service.gov.uk/media/57a08c5b40f0b64974001174/Tilak_India_PBET_WP6__final_.pdf.

UNDP-HDR (2019). *Human development report 2019-beyond income, beyond averages, beyond today: Inequalities in human development in 21st century*. New York: United Nations Development Programme.

Part II

Graduate employability and skills mismatch

Chapter 7

Skills mismatch of higher-education graduates in India

Factors determining employability quotient

Mona Khare

The turn of the century saw a rising consensus on the theories of 'education for better livelihood' and for shaping education to labour market needs. The early nineties saw a multipolar world with emerging economies of the Asian region witnessing high growth rates with widening employment opportunities. A distinct feature of this growth was it being led by manufacturing and export-base. As rightly pointed out by Woods (1994), the 'skill intensity of these exports was high', with increasing regional and international competition. In current times, growth is led by an information communication technology revolution resulting in 'knowledge driven' growth. This has further strengthened the link between education and economic prosperity with increasing demand for not just an educated but a highly educated and multiskilled labour force. Both the labour market and the higher-education system have become more segmented in recent years. While the labour market has become more flexible and limited (jobless growth), the higher-education systems have become more specialized and costly, thereby generating greater concerns over the 'value and returns to a University degree'.

The relative looseness in the relationship between higher education and the labour market of yesteryear has thus got ruptured, and new questions are being posed on the 'specific role of HE in regulating skilled labour, and the overall matching of the supply of graduates leaving HE to their actual economic demand and utility' (Bowers-Brown & Harvey, 2004). Today's universities are expected to educate; build expertise; participate in development of knowledge, and ensure that both the knowledge created and the experts educated are relevant to society. Graduates are to be globally competitive (Dearing Report, NCIHE, 1997), with high-level expertise on two fronts: one emphasizing discovery and the other focusing on exploiting the discoveries of others through market-related intelligence and the application of interpersonal skills Reich (1991, 2002). The globe is moving through the 4th industrial revolution, which is characterized by a fusion of technologies that is blurring the lines between the physical, digital, and biological spheres (mobile supercomputing, intelligent robots, self-driving cars, neuro-technological brain enhancements, genetic editing) at a pace never before seen (Klaus, 2016). The world is being led to an unprecedented 'skills revolution' (Manpower Group, 2012). It is from

DOI: 10.4324/9781003158349-9

here that the definition and understanding of the role of education took a new leap. The evolution can be traced from *'Education for the sake of Education'* to *'Education for better livelihood'* to *'Education for better living'*(Khare, 2016a). In this multifaceted requirement of graduate workforce, the new terminology that gained popularity with the world comprising of a set of both cognitive and non-cognitive attributes and skills in a knowledge framework is *'Employability Skills'*(UNESCO, 2001, 2012).

How to sustain oneself in the job market thus becomes the pivotal challenge, so much so that in this age of disruptive technologies the concept of 'employability skills' has shifted to sustainable employability skills which may be defined as an 'individual's preparedness for the world of work is complete. It means to be able to sustain oneself in the job market in the long run' marked by the ability to gain initial employment; to maintain employment and make 'transitions' within and outside the company, sector, region, or nation; remain employable throughout life (Khare, 2016b); lifelong learning (Scottish Executive, 2003); developing sustainable competencies (Watts, 2006) rise higher and higher in the employment ladder in gainful and rewarding employment. The framework for sustainable graduate employability that emerges is a maze of activities and institutional involvements providing mutual flexibility for the flow of students, teachers, industry personnel. It requires entry, exit, and re-entry between multiple stakeholders/agencies-HEIs, industries, training institutes, and community organizations (Khare, 2019).

Unfortunately, graduate employability is a challenge possibly more complex in India than other nations given its demographic dividend, its large and diverse student population, and a fast expanding higher-education sector. Based on secondary data sources and an extensive survey across different types of higher-education institutions and select industries, this chapter brings to the fore the status of educated youth in terms of their job preparedness on one hand and the comparative perspective of the major stakeholders—employers (senior level executives), neo-employees (with less than five years of work experience), students as well as faculty in HEIs on the other hand. Based on employee experiences, the chapter identifies certain determinants of graduate employability. It is found that three types of gaps, namely, awareness gaps, perception gaps, and skill gaps arise out of a differential understanding between the four major stakeholders, which calls for a multipronged approach to improve the sustainable employability of higher-education graduates in India.

Graduate employability challenges

Other than its 'demographic dividend', India distinctly faces a skewed job market growth with 60 per cent increments in jobs in the services sector (ASSOCHAM, 2012). With the number of higher-education job seekers rising rapidly, more than 70 per cent of college degree holders are currently engaged in the services sector where more than 50 per cent are in IT/ITES and Financial Services only (Khare, 2016a). There may be two reasons for this phenomenon. One is that industries and occupations related to engineering and science have been among the top five on employment indexes across major regions of the world during the period. The second reason is that comparatively this group of graduates is better equipped with 21st century skills because they come from better sociocultural, economic, and academic backgrounds. Thus, a huge mass of the graduate workforce finds it difficult to get jobs because of two things: a differently sized labour market for liberal vs professional graduates and a greater supply of higher-education graduates from general academic disciplines with Arts graduates topping the list (Khare, 2014). In addition, skill mismatches of graduates with a low level of work readiness is a constant complaint from the industry sector for both types of HEGs—those who come from professional and technical education or otherwise. This ubiquitous existence of skill mismatches can be explained by way of three kinds of gaps between the student, employee, teaching community and the employers.

Mismatches with employer community

Three types of gaps can be seen to be existing between those who are the suppliers of labour (students and employees); those who are major providers of learning and training (teachers), and those who are major agents of demand for labour (employers). These may be categorized as Awareness gap, Perception Gap, and Skills Gap (Khare, 2018).

Labour market awareness gap

The awareness regarding the new trades and sectors emerging in India and outside is extremely poor on part of students and teachers. While employers contend that the job market is likely to grow, with an increase in demand for professionally and technically qualified people at the graduate plus level and higher qualifications, for all jobs across occupational categories, students possess a pessimistic view. Although, both feel that the job market will be more competitive, their reasons for such a belief differ. Students give a rather simplistic reason of greater competition arising from a higher number of higher-education graduates and fewer jobs, but employers feel that the competition would be for the right kind of skill acquisition as 'jobs would be there' but it is only the 'nature of jobs that will change'. There is likely to be greater need for workers at high-end technically skilled jobs about which neither the students nor the teachers are aware or are competent enough to perform. This gap gets further highlighted by the fact that students, while choosing a particular course of study, assign greater importance to 'opportunity for better higher education and greater job opportunity' and lesser to 'better skill acquisition' from their choice of study.

Thus it can be seen that the disciplinary choices of students are largely guided more by past trends than future projections on the job front. Even today the preferred job sector and types by the students are limited to Finance, IT/ITES, with education, research, and training picking up slowly (Khare, 2014).

Perception gap on skills importance

Interestingly, the traits that are perceived to be more important by employers may not be perceived as important by other stakeholders. Of the 13 skill sets identified from an extensive review of the literature and a pilot survey, the relative importance assigned by employers reveals that personal skills followed by communication skills top the chart with 95 per cent and 92 per cent of employers rating it to be most important. On a five-point Likert scale, it is the foreign language skills that are rated the least important by employers. Not even a quarter of them consider language skills to be an important skill set. This possibly reflects the limited ability of employers to see into the future, where multilingualism, multiculturalism, foreign language expertise, and foreign cultural experience are likely to hold great importance. As the labour market becomes borderless with technological connectivity, and cross-border job experience is considered important in advanced countries and senior positions in MNCs, it is surprising that foreign language skills are so low on employers' importance scale.

Interestingly, the overall perception gap of all three—employees, students, and teachers —regarding the skills considered important by employers for sustainable employability is not very high, as revealed by high and significant correlation coefficients between their importance rating (see Table 7.1).

Table 7.1 Perception gap on skill importance from employer

Skills	*Employees*	*Students*	*Teachers*
Importance of academic excellence	0.03	−0.19	0.00
Technical skills	0.1	−0.07	0.42
Communication skills	0.09	0.10	0.33
Computer skills	0.08	−0.15	0.36
People-related activities	−0.02	−0.42	−0.49
Managerial skills	−0.07	−0.39	−0.23
Conceptualizing skills	−0.03	−0.49	−0.28
Personal skills	−0.08	−0.50	−0.28
Citizenship skills	0.63	0.30	0.24
Numeric skills	0.76	0.29	−0.15
Foreign language skills	1.13	0.76	0.99
Sector-specific skills	0.84	0.79	0.40
Ability to adapt	−0.06	−0.18	−0.08
Correlation	.947*	.784*	.771*

Source: Author's computations based on primary survey.

Note: The closer the value is to zero, the lesser the degree of the perception gap with respect to importance. Negative values reveal that the specified stakeholder group values the said skill less important than the employers, and positive mean they are perceived more important than to the employers.

While there is a very minor perception gap between employers and employees (r = 0.95), it keeps on increasing with students and teachers. The gap with teachers is highest, followed by the students. It can thus be said that overall the teachers are lesser updated. On the other hand, skills like sector-specific skills and foreign language skills have been overrated by students. Although the correlation coefficients between the mean scores on skill importance by the three stakeholders with that of employers does not reflect a very high level of disagreement on the degree of importance to individual skill type, the relative importance attached to the skill type differs as revealed by the relative rankings assigned by them (Table 7.2).

Further investigation reveals that while people-related, conceptualization, and personal skills are considered more important by the industry sector (both employers and employees), they are not considered as highly important by the higher-education sector (both students and teachers). Of the 13 skills that have been rated important by employers, students attach a lesser degree of importance to eight skills and employees to five of them (Table 7.1). What is also worth noting is the fact that there exists wide disparity in skill ranking between the industry sector and higher-education sector. Communication skills is the only skill that has the highest consensus, with employees, students, and teachers rating it to be topmost, although employers place it at only number three, which is still a high rank. Students and teachers assign much higher ranks to technical skills, academic excellence, and computer skills in comparison to employers. The major areas that are considered less important by all three stakeholders in comparison to employers are (see Table 7.3) five types of skills, namely, people-related, managerial, conceptualizing, personal, and adaptability. It can thus be seen that

Table 7.2 Relative ranking of skill importance

Skills	*Employers*	*Employees*	*Students*	*Teachers*
Academic excellence	9	8	5	5
Technical skills	6	4	2	2
Communication skills	3	1	1	1
Computer skills	7	5	4	3
People-related	5	6	9	9
Managerial skills	8	9	10	8
Conceptualization skills	2	2	8	7
Personal skills	1	3	7	6
Citizenship skills	11	12	12	12
Numeric skills	10	10	11	13
Foreign language skills	13	13	13	11
Sector-specific skills	12	11	6	10
Ability to adapt to and act in new situations	4	7	3	4

Source: Author's computations based on primary survey.

Table 7.3 Major areas of perception gap

Skills	*Employees*	*Students*	*Teachers*
People-related activities	−0.02	−0.42	−0.49
Managerial skills	−0.07	−0.39	−0.23
Conceptualizing skills	−0.03	−0.49	−0.28
Personal skills	−0.08	−0.5	−0.28
Ability to adapt	−0.06	−0.18	−0.08

Source: Khare, 2018. Author's computations based on primary survey.

the entire group of skills considered more important by employers are largely generic in nature and not technical or academic, while the opposite is the case with students and teachers. Such gaps in perception call for a critical look at the recruitment process by the industry sector and their claim on what it is that they consider important and the importance that the HE sector is attaching in preparing the young graduates. Students and teachers still consider academic excellence as one of the important—even a deciding factor—in job acquisition, which was supported in FGDs by the employees who opined that reasonably high marks in degree examinations are their gateway to the first round of selections for job recruitment. Other factors and skills come into consideration only if they score marks above the minimum threshold level. On student said, '[W]e are not even allowed to appear in campus placements if we do not have a high CGPA'.

Acquired skills gap (ASG)

The third gap that is more explicit is the skills gap or the skills deficit that is on the global agenda of education dialogue and youth concern. ASG reveals the extent to which employers are satisfied with their neo employees on the specified employability skills. In order to map these gaps, the difference in the mean scores of importance attached to these skill sets by employers and the satisfaction they derive from neo employees were calculated (see Table 7.4).

The table clearly reveals a high degree of skill gaps among the employees. The employers are dissatisfied with the neo employees on almost all skill sets. Although the perception gap regarding importance attached to these skills is not very high, with only five skills emerging as problematic areas, their numbers have increased in terms of acquired skill gaps. This means that neo-employees are aware of the kinds of skills that are considered important but are not able to embrace them up to the mark. Ironically, the three skills on which employers do not find employees to be much deficient are those that are lowest on their importance index for recruitment. On the other hand, the skill gaps are highest for the top-three skills ranked as important by employers (Table 7.2), namely, conceptualization skills, personal skills, and communication skills. Employees are also found to be lacking in managerial and technical skills. Personal skills are those that come to an individual

Table 7.4 Acquired skills gap

Employees		
Skills	*Skill Gap*	*Rank*
Conceptualization skills	−0.79	1
Personal skills	−0.76	2
Communication skills	−0.6	3
Managerial skills	−0.48	4
Technical skills	−0.42	5
People-related	−0.36	6
Ability to adapt	−0.33	7
Computer skills	−0.31	8
Citizenship skills	−0.23	9
Academic excellence	−0.17	10
Sector-specific skills	0.31	11
Numeric skills	0.32	12
Foreign language skills	1.27	13

Source: Author's computations based on primary survey.

Note: The closer the value to zero, the lesser the skill gap. Negative values reveal the skill gap.

naturally, by birth or through early childhood experience, such that they become part and parcel of an individual's personality, while technical skills are acquired during the course of education. However, both need to be honed and supplemented with managerial skills and a broad cross section of generic skills in the institutions of higher education in order to make the graduates employable for the long term. Thus, the role of household, higher education, and industry become important in determining an individual's employability quotient. Graduate employability quotient may thus be written to be a function of four types of capital:

$$\text{Graduate employability quotient} = f(\text{social capital, household capital, human capital, institutional capital}).$$

An individual's social capital may include factors such as gender, social category, residential status, family type, and so on. Household factors may range from family type, family size, household income, parental education, and the like. Human capital may be defined as factors related to an individual's education like nature/type/level of education, medium of study, examination results, and so on. The institutional capital may include various institution-specific factors such as on-campus teaching and learning facilities and career development activities.

In order to identify some such factors that may be important in defining individual employability, the following exercise on the employability quotient of graduate workers was undertaken.

Determinants of graduate employability

Based on the responses of the employees on their workplace and college/university campus experiences, an empirical exercise was attempted to understand the factors influencing the employability quotient (EyQ) of the employees. The EyQ was estimated for each individual as a weighted index of the self-rating of the individual employees on the 13 identified skill sets. An exploratory factor analysis was attempted to arrive at the relative weights assigned to the skill sets based on the first factor loadings. Thereafter, regression analysis was undertaken to identify the key determinants of graduate employability (Table 7.5). The independent variables used in the model are *socio-demographic factors* (such as gender, social group, household income, family background), *academic factors* (such as education, academic scores, medium of instruction) and *institutional factors* (such

Table 7.5 Regression results of factors influencing employee employability quotient

(Constant)	**3.74***
Ref: Male	
female	−0.06
Ref: Urban	
non_urban	−0.13*
Ref: Edu_mother_above_grad	
edu_mother_below_grad	0.13**
Ref: Technical and professional	
General_degree	−0.15*
Ref: Joint	
Nuclear_family	−0.08
median_monthly_HHincome	−0.11**
Ref: Yes_off campus support needed	
q59_NOoffcampus_support_needed	−0.08
Ref: Taken coaching yes	
q61_takencoaching_NO	−0.01
Ref: General	
nongeneral_socialcategory	−0.03
job satisfaction index	0.21*
Ref: Public institute	
nonpublic_institute	0.04
R square	0.211
N	429

Source: Author's computations based on primary survey.

Dependent variable: weighted average employability quotient
* 1 per cent level of significance,
** 5 per cent level of significance,
*** 10 per cent level of significance

as general facilities index, teaching-learning infrastructure, coaching and career development).

Factors that have been found to be significantly affecting the EyQ are place of residence (rural or urban), mother's education, type of degree, HH income, and job satisfaction index. Although the influence of factors like gender and social category on EyQ is not significant, but the negative beta coefficients show adverse impact which are warning signals. These may become important dampening factors for wages/employments or job quality in later years as did come out significantly during the focus group discussions with women employees of private sector organizations. It was very interesting to note from the qualitative data analysis that most companies follow equal opportunity employment policies and claim they do not differentiate on the basis of gender or different ethnic backgrounds if the candidates are equally good. However, the conditionality of being 'equally good' may put certain groups/communities in a comparatively disadvantageous situation. The regression results are contrary to this claim. It has been found that a dual combination of female employee belonging to the non-general caste group has a negative impact on the employee's employability quotient (though the coefficients are not statistically significant). A nationalized non-banking financial company (NBFC) emphasized that while they do not discriminate between male and female during recruitment, they observed females leaving jobs in mid-career due to family circumstances. This may at times become a deterrent in their career progression or skill upgradation opportunities for sustainable employability. These results find support in recent reports based on data from NSE, India according to which the female executives earned 45 per cent less than their male counterparts in 2019. Also, this gap is widening as gender bias hurts women's career growth. The inherent bias towards men in promotions becomes visible as they reach the middle-management level. In fact, according to the Monster India Wage Index Report 2018, the wage inequalities between men and women increase with increasing work experience and rising on the career ladder (The Economic Times, 2020).

Employees from non-urban locations have a 13 per cent lower employability quotient when compared to those who reside in urban locations. On the other hand, banking industry employers expressed that sincerity in work is higher in employees/students from families belonging to low-to-medium income, ethnic and disadvantageous sociocultural background as well as from smaller towns and cities. Also, their attrition rates and salary expectations are low. They are less demanding when it comes to promotions or salary revisions and hence are preferred for mass recruitment at junior levels. But a clear-cut bias towards many of the urban-centric characteristics such as 'well groomed', 'smart', 'English competency', 'general awareness', 'quick', 'confident', while recruiting is testament to the fact that those with an urban exposure are likely to have better EyQ, as is also proven by our regression results. Employers opine that rural students are difficult to be trained, as their soft skills are relatively poorer than those of the urban students. Even the teachers opine that the biggest challenge is to teach the basic skills to rural students who come to urban universities to pursue higher education.

> Industry expectation is that graduates must have proficient language skill, knowledge of current affairs and reasoning ability. A rural student, who has studied in a rural school, lacks these skills so that it is extremely challenging to groom them during the graduate courses.
>
> (FGD with Teachers in Government college of Delhi)

Language barrier has been highlighted by teachers to be a major deterrent, as most students in a college or state university are from the local area and adjoining hinterlands. So the teachers are, at times, forced to teach the subject in the regional language. As such, it hinders developing basic professional language skills among such students.

With respect to academic factors, the regression results show that the employees with general academic degree have a 15 per cent lower employability quotient. Though it is not significant, it comes to the fore that employees who have responded 'yes' to the need for taking off-campus support and coaching have a higher employability quotient. Also, the job satisfaction index and EyQ are positively and significantly associated with it. Those employees whose job satisfaction index is high are likely to have higher EyQ.

Although the relative importance of different factors differs across industrial sectors and industry types, by and large these organizations are on the same page when it comes to identifying factors that are considered important for sustainable employability of graduates. At times the considerations may be different for different job roles. One IT company has a positive bias towards women for managerial and customer care roles as opposed to hardcore IT roles. Interestingly, they considered women as better multitaskers. Another financial company shared that they also distinguish between female and male employees/students, as some of the jobs are male driven. The employers, however claimed that they believe in equality and diversity and promote students from rural/semi-rural areas and of any religion/caste during recruitment. Another finance company revealed that they hire graduate students only at operational level (Junior) from premier institutes offering accountancy and finance courses. The recruitment is extremely tough with several steps involved in short listing of the candidates. Functional and behavioural competencies and psychometric tools are some of the key elements tested and used in the recruitment process.

It can thus be seen that though recruitment policies promote inclusion and discourage discrimination on the basis of an individual's social capital and HH capital, in practice it is hard to achieve the stated policy. Institutional factors and human capital are significant determining factors of graduate employability that promote EyQ, while social and household factors may become discriminatory factors. In fact, a large body of literature points at increased stratification and differentiation in society arising out of class-cultural and academic profiles of graduates from different HEIs, along with different rates of graduate return (Archer et al., 2003; Scott, 2005; Little & Archer, 2010). Hence, it becomes even more of a responsibility of higher-education institutions to create an enabling environment to groom the students in generic, personal. and personality skills in addition to technical skills and academic knowledge so that their inherited disadvantages may be removed by improving their EyQ. Hence, campus experience by way of knowledge acquisition as well as skill acquisition is an important element of sustainable employability building.

Employee campus experience

In order to further understand the relative importance of institutional factors impacting EyQ, a simple regression model was used to test if academic scores or extracurricular activities impact the EyQ more. Employees' campus experience has been assessed by way of few input variables reflecting provision towards skill-building activities, and one output variable, marks obtained in their degree examinations. For the former, a Campus Facilities index was computed by averaging the Likert mean score values of the employee responses on their college/university campus experience associated with presentation/group discussion, industrial visit, mock interviews, aptitude building, vocational skill development activities, activities for developing personal skills, technical skills, CV writing, and quality of infrastructure.

Results from the campus experience of the employees bring some interesting observations to the fore as reflected from the regression equation shown here:

$$EyQ = 2.81 + 0.49^{*}\ CFI + 0.31^{*}\ AS$$

Where, EyQ: weighted average employability quotient based on Factor analysis
CFI: Campus Facilities index
AS: Academic scores (Marks in last degree exam)
* significant at 5% level of Significance

The results clearly highlight the important role played by higher-education institutions in providing an enriching environment with respect to nurturing skills for the workplace. Both academic performance and campus grooming have significant (both regression coefficients are positive and significant at 5 per cent) positive impact on the EyQ. A one per cent increase in campus facilities index for employees is likely to increase their employability quotient by 49 per cent. The funny thing is that the employers do not attach high importance to academic performance (Tables 7.1 and 7.2). This is contrary to the regression results as well as the employees feedback regarding academic performance as an important factor during campus placements. The employees stated that they are not even allowed to appear in campus placements if they do not have a certain threshold of marks in their degree examinations. Also, this threshold level varies from industry to industry and company to company and may range from 60 per cent to 80 per cent. However, they agree that academic performance is valued only at the entry level. There is a significant and positive relationship between marks and employability quotient also, but it is lesser than the impact of the campus facilities index on EyQ. One per cent increase in marks increases the employability quotient by 31 per cent. Thus, it may be said that although examination performance is important, other forms of career development exposure have greater importance in determining the EyQ of the higher-education graduates. These results are further supported by the fact that 56 per cent of the employees agreed that on-campus employability-enriching opportunities largely help the employees to find jobs that they aspire for. Similar sentiments were echoed during the FGDs with the employees. An employee of an IT company in Tier 3 city stated, 'I learnt communication skills through many debates, seminars, and interactive sessions in my college days which helped me to get over stage fear and to express my opinion in a much more efficient way'. A graduate employee from Delhi University opined that industry should play a crucial role in designing the curriculum so that tomorrow they do not complain that institutions/universities could not impart the required skills sets to students.

Unfortunately, a majority of employees feel that the efforts made by higher-education institutions towards employability building are deficient and not very effective, so they need to go for off-campus coaching (see Table 7.6). Fifty-five per cent of employees feel that off-campus coaching is needed to improve employability skills despite the fact that 67 per cent of them feel that their higher-education campus did provide them employability development opportunities, and 71 per cent also agree that teachers too provide such support during classroom interactions. However, a much higher percentage (79 per cent) expressed a mismatch between course curriculum and job requirements as a pressing challenge. It can thus be inferred that though higher-education institutions are making efforts to provide for employability building, the support mechanisms provided are inadequate, making the students rely on external support. The top reason for taking off-campus coaching as identified by the employees is that campus facilities are lacking in developing required employability skills and additional technical skills. A majority of students go for short/medium duration coaching in order

Table 7.6 Employee campus experience for employability training

Campus provided sufficient opportunities/enriching environment to enhance employability skills	67
Teacher provided job-related knowledge and aptitude-building support in classroom other than teaching the course curriculum	71
Mismatch between course curriculum and requirements of the job market	79
Off-campus support/coaching is needed to improve employability skills	55
Employee taken any off-campus coaching/training	56

Source: Author's computations based on primary survey.

to enhance employability skills (personality development/interview preparation/ communication skills). Unfortunately, it also came to the fore that willingness to improve on personality development is weak among youth, as very limited number of students proactively take part in the programmes/events organized by the colleges, particularly in smaller cities. However, the awareness and eagerness to actively engage in extracurricular activities to hone one's overall personality is high among the students in bigger cities. This once again reflects upon the quality of such activities provided in higher-education institutions. Greater involvement and exposure of teachers to guide the students and help arrange for creative and interesting activities may go a long way in encouraging students' participation in large numbers.

Some companies have also come forward to formally involve themselves with academia with the goal of training their potential employees. As was rightly emphasized by a senior company head:

> Employability is not the sole responsibility of companies or HEIs—all stakeholders should come forward to fill the gap and to incorporate new things in the curriculum. Inter-mobility should be there between academia and companies. In developed countries, academia and industry get together.
>
> (IT company HR Head)

In order to meet the expectation from students, a large-scale multinational IT company shared its 'campus engagement policy'. They organized an 'academic interface programme' in all the premier institutes across the country. This interface programme is planned to be quite broad-based, where they not only visit HEIs for campus recruitment but engage throughout the year with various activities/programmes such as Faculty Development programmes, Guest Lectures to students, and Kiosks in IT Fest for students. Employers also believe that it is important to collaborate and engage more with faculty in terms of designing the curriculum according to industry standards and refreshing the courses/syllabus according to technology changes. However, the senior management, even in this company that has a specific 'campus engagement policy', feels that it is not a company's responsibility to groom the students, which is a 'rather time-consuming job'. 'It is HEI's responsibility to teach students well, and faculty and infrastructure should be such that students learn from the institutions all that is required to move to the industry sector and we only have to polish a bit'.

Most employers feel it is a waste of time for them to engage with HEIs, as there are no perks, awards, or recognition attached with any such activity. Thus, they prefer to avoid participating actively in student engagement programmes. The companies are trying to encourage and incentivize their employees for campus-engagement drives. A large-scale multinational IT company has started giving 'star batches' (a small batch with a star mark to be pinned on their shirt) by way of recognition to those employees/employers who devote a certain proportion of their time in interacting with HEIs in a formal way. There are no monetary incentives nor any written code to consider such engagements for in-service promotions, but senior executives revealed that employee engagement in grooming of potential employees for the company is not completely overlooked at the time of career advancement. Also, the employees, while sharing their experience, said such activities give them a lot of happiness, satisfaction, and a sense of pride. They are also a good break from the regular routine of office work.

On the other hand, a nationalized finance company stated that the company does not have any organized process of placement from campuses or any systemic student-faculty-employer programmes. Some senior executives do interact with academia in their individual capacity and out of personal interest. This is mostly by participating in seminars, in conferences, or in delivering invited lectures in a sporadic manner, 'as and when I get an opportunity'.

Yet another nationalized finance company revealed that they only consider postgraduate students for placements, but they have a customized course for colleges that enrol postgraduates. It is named as 'Bank Young Bankers'. Through this customized course, the bank conducts training on soft skills, banking law practice, and internal software practice. The placement process allows the bank to assess the analytical, reasoning, and logical thinking skills through this short-term course for postgraduate students.

As the financial markets are becoming increasingly large and challenging as well as complex and dynamic, like other sectors today, an NBFC company responded to the need for knowledgeable and skilled market professionals by various stakes in the sector. Thus, they opened a more structured 'school of education', which is now engaged in imparting industry-specific skill building and knowledge advancement courses for young employees and graduate students. The courses designed and offered by them include full-time programmes targeting fresh graduates, summer schools, and internship programmes for students and other short-term joint programmes with companies/HEIs targeting fresh in-service people.

However, such structured academic endeavours of companies are limited to very few companies that are engaged in highly skilled product development or service delivery. Most large-sized companies are distinct in offering student mentoring, unlike small-scale companies. Smaller companies may sometimes offer short-duration internships on a case-to-case basis due to personal connections (friends and family) but lack any comprehensive plan for academic interaction. Some also use their CSR funds to randomly do some student-oriented activities.

Employees also suggested that as part of corporate social responsibility mandate, companies should adopt or own certain HEIs. They must engage with faculty, placement cells, in giving practical training to the students and investing in social capital.

It can thus be deduced that institutions need to develop two kinds of support activities for skill building of students. These may be categorized as follows:

Type I: This category of activities may be campus-based; should focus on the basic personality development and confidence building of students/

potential employees. Type one may include activities for soft skill building (presentations/discussions/aptitude building, etc.) and activities for improving other pre-preparatory job search requisites (CV writing/mock interviews, etc).

Type II: These types of activities may be categorized as off-campus-based, with formal involvement of the employer segment. These activities may focus on vocational and technical skill building exercises through real work place/life exposure and also awareness regarding future employment scenarios.

The role of the employer segment in both Type I and Type II activities is important. Only the relative role of the teaching community and the employer community for the two types is deemed to be different. Type I is more to be a responsibility of the teaching community and Type II more to be a responsibility of the employer community. The foundation of skilling the youth for sustainable employability rests on the employers—right from guiding for future needs to support the HEIs in preparing enabling environment for delivering those skills. It begins with how the employers foresee the job market.

Future vision of employers

An insight into the emerging labour market needs in future becomes the basic foundation for preparing students towards the workplace. In a market-driven knowledge system, the signals from employers assume great importance. As is evident from Table 7.7, employers feel that the job market is going to be more competitive in future but not equally rewarding, as the likelihood of big salary hikes and ease of getting regular employment is constrained.

Undergraduate degrees (UG) are considered not being sufficient in future, and thus there is greater value attached to higher and specialized qualifications along with short-term skills training. Senior employers from a surveyed company in the finance sector quoted actuarial sciences, big data analytics, audit and

Table 7.7 Employers' foresight on the job market

Factors	*More rewarding*	*More competitive*	*Easier regular employment*	*Fair and inclusive*	*UG degree sufficient*	*Higher and specialized qualifications valued more*	*Short skills training valued more*
Mean Score*	2.24	1.92	2.45	2.29	2.61	2.09	2.17
Ranks	4	1	6	5	7	2	3

Source: Author's computations based on primary survey.

*Mean score of employer responses on five-point Likert scale

accounting software, and financial analysis as some of the specialized areas that may be in future demand (see Figure 7.1).

Ironically, there exists a reasonably good amount of gap in between the assessment of the employers and the fresh employees in terms of assessing the future job scenario (Figure 7.1) The highest degree of gap emerged in assessing if the jobs are going to be more rewarding and whether UG degrees would be sufficient or short-term specialized skills trainings would be valued more. Thus, the role of the senior employer community in providing directions to the fresh employees as well as the HEIs becomes all the more imperative for sustainable employability skill building.

Employer responses on what kinds of skills and personality traits are going to assume greater importance in coming years brought to the fore some interesting observations (see Figure 7.2). It can be clearly seen that multitasking has been considered to be the most important future skill, with 89.1 per cent of employers supporting this view. This has been followed closely by the importance accorded to technical knowledge, wherein about 86 per cent of employers have responded in its favour. The third most important future skill has been identified as sensitivity and adaptability, with 65.1 per cent of employers being in agreement. 'Multitasking skills is the new mantra for a successful career in future times' is a statement made by a senior executive in an MNC. In the light of the industry 4.0 and the industry 5.0 revolution that has already made inroads in the industry sector, employers feel that technical know-how and expertise in

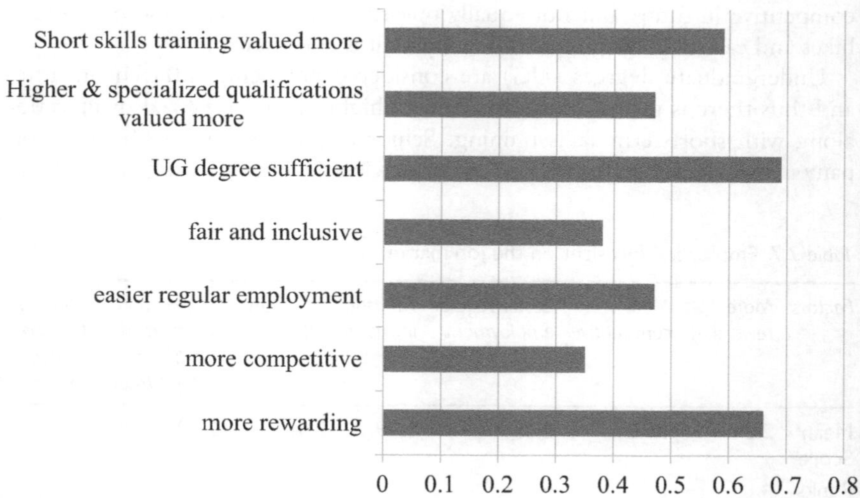

Figure 7.1 Employer–employee gap in foresight on future job market

Source: Author's calculations based on survey results.

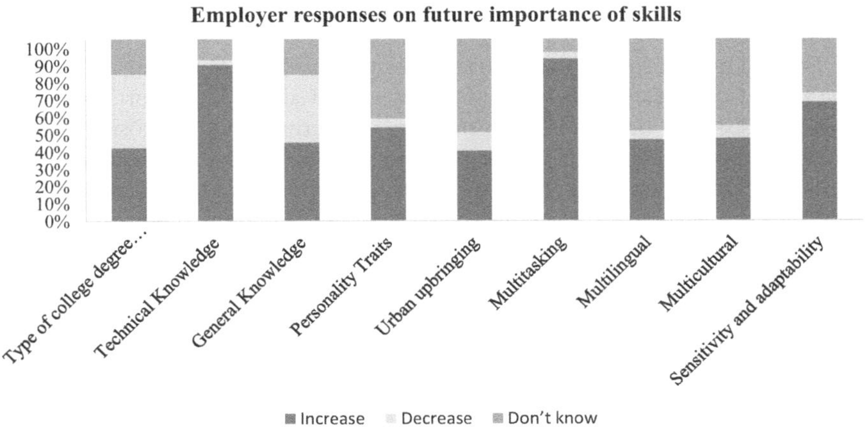

Figure 7.2 Employer responses on future importance of skills

Source: Author's calculations based on survey results.

automated, robotic, high-tech production processes is going to have an edge over general knowledge about work and business modus operandi. It is interesting to note here that the same employers who do not attach very high importance to technical skills currently (Tables 7.1 and 7.2) identify them as game changers for the future.

Employers agree that job growth in the past has been slow, but they are not pessimistic about the future even when technological revolution is likely to convert many man-run routine jobs into machine operated automated jobs. An employer in Tier 2 city feels that massive transformation is going in IT sector, and the pace of hiring has gone down in last decade due to automation of work. Also, banking sector executives have similar views that with automation and digitalization, the number of jobs in banks will reduce rapidly a few years later. But they foresee a very different set of skill sets to be emerging as new demands emerge from future industries.

As employees would be required to work in more diverse social groups, sensitivity and adaptability to new cultures, diverse work environments, and different social milieus also assume greater importance in the coming days.

Fewer employers feel that the type of college degree and urban upbringing (with only 40 and 38.5 per cent, respectively) will increase in importance in future. However, this is under the condition that the overall quality of higher education across all types of institutions all over the country improves and aligns itself to labour market needs. An infrastructure advisory and investment banking company in Mumbai specified that they do not necessarily always recruit students from premier institutes. They prefer to recruit employees from an average university, as they feel a student should be able to do multitasking irrespective of the type of educational institution that he or she has attended or its location (rural/semi-urban).

Though type of college degree has not been considered important, higher and specialized qualifications have been highly valued along with short training in specialized skills. Location (urban/rural) as a disparity factor may lose its current decree as more such institutions come up in smaller towns and cities. Employers also feel that technology can be an enabling factor in improving the access of youth to specialized trainings.

What thus matters more than the type of degree or college attended are their abilities and attitudes when handling multiple things and being ready to embrace every task that is thrown at them. That is what will help them stay employable in future. For large-scale mass level jobs multitasking is going to be a deciding factor, while for high-end jobs, specific technical and managerial skills would be the game changer.

It can thus be seen that the future job market is perceived to be slightly different from today's market in terms of the kinds of jobs that will be available. There is likely to be an increase in the importance attached to technical skills with increasing use of technology in day-to-day working, and not merely computer skills will suffice in future. There is likely to be a shift from generic to specific skill sets for high-end jobs as it is assumed by the employers that 'tomorrow's youth for such jobs would anyways be well groomed in generic skills'. These is a general observation by the employers that today's young employees are 'street smart', and they know well how to 'present themselves', so in a way some of the generic skills that we are talking about today may be an inherent part of their personalities in future.

However, they also are of the opinion that today's young employees are 'less sensitive', 'less patient', less attached', and that they look for 'quick success'. Such mechanized attributes may become their assets in a mechanized workplace in future but only for the short term and short gains. A high degree of dedication, focus, honesty, team spirit, and interpersonal sensibilities will be important for sustainable employment progression as production technologies become more and more complex and workplaces more and more diverse.

Conclusion and policy implications

The importance of employability skills and their types are in a way ubiquitously understood by all stakeholders. As far as knowledge and technical know-how are concerned, employers are reasonably satisfied with the fresh graduates. Functional skills that are relatively more industry-specific are taken care of by the industry sector as part of their in-house training and capacity building; however, it is the personal and soft skills that are found to be the major areas of concern. Expectation from the higher-education sector is thus to focus on imparting personal skills—skills that are inborn or acquired aptitude and attitude of an individual through lifelong experiences. Hence, it cannot be solely left to the higher-education sector to impart these traits through curricular teaching or extracurricular campus experience; rather it is the responsibility of major stakeholders of the education-employment ecosystem, including government, employers, parents, and society at large. If the challenge for the higher-education sector is to strengthen connectivity locally, nationally, and globally with industry/employers; academia/students; society and alumni, it is equally the responsibility of these stakeholders to be proactive and not just responsive to support the HEIs in effective delivery of the learning according to the new demand of the global economy. While HEIs are the pivot for preparing youth for the world of work, the industry sector is the spokes of the wheel for connecting the two and cannot just remain at the circumference. The employability quotient of the youth is more a function of the campus facilities for career counselling and grooming than their examination results, which may just be the threshold requirement in recruitment. The ability of HEIs to provide such campus facilities to students that can improve their employability quotient is largely dependent on the involvement of the industry sector.

Academic engagement of the employer segment with the HEIs differs from company to company depending upon the sector, the size of the company, its location, vision of the leadership, and voluntary initiatives of its employers. Very few companies have any policy for academic or non-academic engagement with HEIs, nor any budgetary provisions for the same. With no incentives—personal, professional or monetary—attached to employers' engagement with students and college activities, there is little enthusiasm among the employers to take active participation in the academic world. There cannot be a reactive engagement of the industry sector with the academia. What the future holds on the job front is best understood by the employers, and hence they must own the responsibility to communicate, cooperate, and collaborate with the higher-education sector.

Technical competencies of a cross-sectoral nature are likely to gain higher-order importance in future when compared to the generic skills of numeric ability, computer skills, or communication skills of today. Individual competencies of multitasking and specific high-tech skills would be the deciding factor for sustainable employability in future. The employer's role in making graduates ready for future work ranges from acting as guideposts for expected changes/shifts in future labour market demands and factors to proactively engage with academia in creating an enabling learning environment for their future/potential employees.

Hence strengthening of industry–academia linkages and employer-student interactions in various forms—formal, informal, long duration, short duration, on-campus, field-based—are imperative for graduates' sustainable skill development. There may be incentives from the government to encourage companies to have a proper well laid out 'academic campus connect policy' as well as in-house company level incentives to encourage employers to voluntarily and actively participate in their 'academic campus connect' activities. It may be helpful to have dedicated offices by way of 'campus connect offices' in both sectors, higher education and industry, with trained, experienced staff to institutionalize sustained linkages. Such offices may then be entrusted with the responsibility to enter into a mutual dialogue to develop long-term strategic as well as short-term action plans and facilitate their execution and implementation with mutual support. Two important areas of policy intervention may be ways and means to provide for greater industry interaction to the teaching faculty so that they may be able to bridge curricular gaps as well as understand the emerging needs of the employer segment and organize for appropriate skill development activities. Similarly, ways to involve senior leadership in both the higher-education sector and the industry sector to enter into long-term, systemically planned agreements for applied, technical, generic skill building, curriculum development, internships and campus placements need to be forged. It is not that the higher-education sector is not aware to the new expectations from it and is not making efforts at it, but such efforts are not much effective. Both capacities and competencies in the higher-education sector for effective skill building exercise are deficient, which can be changed only with active industry engagement. Work life exposure to both teachers and students is required. Tripartite arrangements between higher education, industry and skills training institutions to provide short duration futuristic high-tech skills that may be required in all domains may be explored. It is time that the ad hoc nature of industry–academia interaction ends as a policy prescription.

References

Archer, L., Hutchings, M., & Ross, A. (2003). *Higher education and social class: Issues of exclusion and inclusion.* New York: RoutledgeFalmer.

ASSOCHAM (2012, April 21). *ASSOCHAM report in financial services top job generator in tier II, III cities.* www.business-standard.com/article/companies/fin-services-top-job-generator-in-tier-ii-iii-cities-112042100037_1.html.

Bowers-Brown, T., & Harvey, L. (2004). Are there too many graduates in the UK? *Industry and Higher Education*, 18(4), 243–254.

Dearing, R. (1997). *Higher education in the learning society: Report of the national committee of inquiry into higher education.* London: HMSO. www.educationengland.org.uk/documents/dearing1997/dearing1997.html.

The Economic Times (2020, February 8). Pay gap between women & men CEOs doubles. New Delhi.

Khare, M. (2014). Employment, employability and higher education in India: The missing links. *Higher Education for the Future*, 1(1), 39–62.

Khare, M. (2016a). Higher education-university: Taking the skills march forward in India-transitioning to the world of work. In P. Matthias (Ed.), *India: Preparation for the world of work* (pp. 103–139). Wiesbaden: Springer VS.

Khare, M. (2016b). Disparities in graduate employability skills. In N. V. Varhgese, N. Sabarwal, & C. M. Malish (Eds.), *India higher education report 2016: Equity* (pp. 331–356). New Delhi: Routledge (Francis and Taylor), South Asia Edition.

Khare, M. (2018). Employability of graduates in India-hard realities. *International Higher Education*, 95, 29–31. USA: The Boston College Centre for International Higher Education.

Khare, M. (2019). *Employment and employability of higher education graduates in India-a multistakeholder perspective.* Paper presented in International Seminar on Employment and Employability of Higher education graduates organized by NIEPA and British Council, New Delhi, February 19–20.

Klaus, S. (2016, January 14). The fourth industrial revolution: What it means, how to respond. *World Economic Forum.* www.weforum.org/agenda/2016/01/the-fourth-industrial-revolution-what-it-means-and-how-to-respond/.

Little, B., & Archer, L. (2010). Less time to study, less well prepared for work, yet satisfied with higher education: A UK perspective on links between higher education and the labour market. *Journal of Education and Work,* 23(3), 275–296.

Manpower Group (2012). *Talent shortage survey: Research results.* https://candidate.manpower.com/wps/wcm/connect/be31f5804b6f7c07ada6ff4952b5bce9/2012_Talent_Shortage_Survey_Results_ManpowerGroup.pdf?MOD=AJPERES.

Reich, R. B. (1991). *The work of nations.* London: Simon and Schuster.

Reich, R. B. (2002). *The future of success.* London: Vintage Books.

Scott, P. (2005). Universities and the knowledge economy. *Minerva,* 43(3), 297–309.

Scottish Executive (2003). *Life through learning through life: The lifelong learning strategy for Scotland.* Scotland: Scottish Executive, corp creator. http://dera.ioe.ac.uk/id/eprint/8815.

UNESCO (2001). *Recommendations of the high level panel of the youth employment network.* United Nations, New York.

UNESCO (2012). *Education and skills for inclusive and sustainable development beyond 2015.* Thematic think piece for the UN task team on the post-2015 UN development agenda. UNESCO, Paris. www.un.org/millenniumgoals/pdf/Think%20Pieces/4_education.pdf.

Watts, A. G. (2006). *Career development learning and employability.* Learning and Employability Series Two. York: Higher Education Academy.

Wood, A. (1994). *North South trade, employment and inequality.* Oxford: Oxford University Press.

Chapter 8

General, technical, and professional education

Employability skill gaps

Ritika Sinha

Employability skill gaps have plagued Indian society and the whole world. This significant and multifaceted work is an attempt to bring forth the skill gaps that are prevalent among the employees from diverse educational backgrounds that form a part of this chapter. It also takes into account the perspective of the employers to identify and enumerate the important employability skills in order of relevance to industry. A number of reports issued by employers' associations and higher-education organizations have urged universities to make more concerted efforts towards cultivating the 'key', 'core', 'transferable', and/or 'generic' skills in institutions which are needed in many types of high-level occupations (Association of Graduate Recruiters, 1995; Universities UK, 2002; Confederation of British Industry, 1994, 2003). Employability of India's youth has remained stagnant for the past three years, lingering around 46 per cent for participants who are wishing to enter job market.

At undergraduate level, the highest number (35.9 per cent) of students are enrolled in arts/humanities/social sciences courses followed by science (16.5 per cent), engineering and technology (13.5 per cent), and commerce (14.1 per cent). Maximum student enrolments are for general education courses, followed by technical courses and then professional courses. Currently, 9.34 million students are pursuing B.A. programmes in India, making it the course with the highest enrolment pan-India, followed by B.Sc. (4.68 million) and B.Com. (4.03 million) (AISHE, 2019). Closely studying the industry trends, it can be noticed that e-commerce, BFSI, and BPO/KPO/ITeS are the industries that are expected to ramp up their hiring. Data reveal that more than 70 per cent of college degree holders are currently engaged in the services sector with IT/ITES and financial services leading, where their proportions are higher than 50 per cent (Khare, 2018). Watching this trend, it can be expected that significantly the employability of general education graduates in B.A., B.Sc., and B.Com. courses will serve as the human resource supply pool for these sectors.

'There is an improvement in the availability of employable talent at around 47 per cent in 2019, up from 33.9 per cent in 2014', (Wheebox founder and chief executive Nirmal Singh). However, there has been a decline in the employability

DOI: 10.4324/9781003158349-10

of people who took B.Tech., M.C.A., technical and computer-related courses. According to an estimate, not even a quarter of its engineering graduates and a mere 10 per cent of other graduates are employable.

A breakdown of graduate job seekers by streams of study reveals that the majority are from general academic disciplines, with arts graduates topping the list, comprising about 40 per cent of the graduate job seekers.

It may be comparatively easier for engineering and science graduates to get employed for the simple reason that industries and occupations related to engineering and science have been among the top five on employment indexes across major regions of the world.

There is a heavy congregation of industries like IT/ITES, health and community services, environment, architecture, biotech, life sciences, pharmacy, and agro-based and allied in the top growth group across all major regions of the world, all of which draw from the graduate pool of science and technology. In addition, these graduates are also employed in large numbers even in non-engineering occupations and industries (Khare, 2014). The education structures have not undergone much transformation to meet the current challenges and to match the drastic changes that have taken place in the industry.

The discipline of one's study becomes very important in the case of specialized/technical jobs, but a large set of disciplines of study cut across various industries. Thus, an insight into the skill gaps of the employees across different educational domains, namely, general, technical, and professional education, would be helpful in understanding the issue of graduate employability in a deeper way.

General education

These are courses that prepare graduates with basic generic skills, knowledge, literacy, art, and numeric abilities to perform a job role and are not designed specifically to meet professional needs or standards in a particular occupation or trade, and often this segment of educational qualification is pursued to prepare for advanced studies. In this study, we are considering arts, commerce, humanities, social science, and all other generic subjects under the category of general education. General education courses are rapidly gaining recognition in India and are the most sought after by the students. Universities offering general education courses provide multidisciplinary programmes which expose students to many different perspectives in and out of the classroom in collaboration with many other institutions. Programmes designed by the universities offer students a defining experience that blends academic rigour with a wide range of electives across disciplines. Universities providing general education courses have been trying to address the significant talent gap and prepare competent, motivated, socially committed graduates through a curriculum designed by various industry patrons, academicians, and other stakeholders.

The Government of India is also keen in taking actions for making the general education graduates more employable. It has embarked on a major initiative to boost the employability of the huge numbers of students passing out of general degree courses in the country, namely, B.A., B.Sc., and B.Com. courses, through a systematic integration of industry apprenticeship with education.

The Human Resource Development (HRD) ministry also during the discussion held in 'The Higher Education Policy Retreat 2018' in Mussoorie said that it is looking at ways to add up to a thousand hours of professional-oriented metrics to undergraduate courses. According to the initial discussions, it is proposed that up to 250 hours of soft-skills and another 250 hours of ICT will be added to the B.A., B.Sc., and B.Com. courses. The student can choose 500 hours of two separate and distinct job-oriented skills which are closely related and relevant to the discipline and which are directed towards supplementing the undergraduate level course.

The statistics presented in AISHE and India Skills Report (2020) talk positively about the general education courses. It clearly shows that the enrolment of general education graduates is highest and also that they have higher potential employment opportunities.

Technical education

These are educational programmes that provide specialized technical and practical knowledge in business/trade, applied sciences, and training in contemporary technologies. Here, a graduation in the field of engineering, polytechnic, and ITI is categorized under technical education for this chapter. Technical education emphasizes the understanding and practical application of basic principles of science and mathematics and prepares students for employment involving applied engineering and modern technology. Universities offering technical education place major emphasis upon the theories and understanding the principles of the subject matter in the areas of science and engineering. Universities have been continuing their efforts to enhance interaction with industry where working professionals would meet faculty to support curriculum design, competency development, and training requirements for the students. The industry has become more challenging due to ever-evolving technology and looks to hire technical graduates with relevant skills, but employability of technical graduates is low due to lack of cognitive and soft skills such as the ability to work in teams, readiness to learn, communication skills, managerial skills, and creativity. Some case study results showcase the importance of verbal and soft skills which appeared to be a strong predictor of technical knowledge.

The graduates are not only lacking cognitive and soft-skills but also lacking next-generation tech skills. Artificial intelligence is a very sought-after skill, and the very basis of new-age technology, but according to the Annual Employability survey, only 2.5 per cent of Indian engineering graduates have the relevant skills to make a career out of it. Machine learning and data science are very much sought after in the technology industry; these are things that are way beyond the vast majority of engineers. Only 1.5 per cent–4.5 per cent of engineers possess the necessary skills in data engineering, while only 2.8 per cent–5.3 per cent are qualified in wireless technologies. These figures pale compared to the percentage of engineers (5.5 per cent) that are qualified for basic programming. For data sciences, the number of the employable stands at 'only 50 per cent–60 per cent or 1.5 per cent of the total when we factor in other skills such as cognitive and language that are key for career success' (Annual Employability Survey 2019 by Aspiring Minds).

Professional education

Professional education consists of courses or advanced studies that would impart a skill set to build a career in a particular practice or a domain. This form of educational qualification is expected to remain as a source of livelihood throughout a person's life and facilitate advancing a profession as a lifelong career. For this study we have considered Master of Business Administration (MBA) and Master of Computer Applications (M.C.A.) as a degree under professional education. Universities offering professional education have to be relevant to the practicing managers, leaders, and policymakers in India as well as internationally. For that very reason, corporate connections and relationships with society across the world are being linked with research, teaching, and consultancy in such universities. External stakeholders need to participate in the activities conducted by the universities so that they can inculcate inclusive growth and contributions to the society. According to the India Skills Report 2020 released by Wheebox, an online assessment company, most employable candidates are MBA graduates, with 54 per cent of them found to be employable. The same study highlights the decline in the employability of other professional courses such as M.C.A. However, another study shows a different result. The study conducted by the Associated Chambers of Commerce and Industry of India (ASSOCHAM) Education Committee (AEC) found that only 7 per cent of management graduates are employable, except graduates from the elite institutions such as the Indian Institutes of Management (IIM). This chapter aims at prioritizing various dimensions of employability skills in order of perceived importance from the views of working professionals. It analyzes the nature and extent of employability skill gaps in employees from varied educational backgrounds. In order to engage in a multilateral discourse on employability skills among working professionals, the chapter considers the perceptions of employers and employees. The chapter also focuses on mapping if the skill gaps of employees differ across their educational background (general, technical, and professional), and identifies the differences in college experiences of employees across various educational backgrounds. It also studies the need for off-campus coaching/training for skill development based on educational background. It also highlights the initiatives taken by general, technical, and professional higher educational institutes in developing employability skills.

Domain-wise employment opportunities and employability

Initial employment chances immediately after graduation are likely to be heavily based on characteristics that are easily observable such as the level and field of the study programme. The findings of the India Skills Report (2020) reflect that among the percentage distribution of employment opportunities for general, professional, and technical education, it is the technical education that leads. Similar sentiments were captured from our survey, too. The majority of the employers (86 per cent) stressed the importance of hiring graduates with a technical background by ranking it first, while 88 per cent of the respondents gave a professional degree second rank.

One of the employers in the interview for the current research study also favoured a technical degree and said

> majority of the employees we hire are graduates who have a technical degree background. Out of more than 200 engineering and technical institutes, we have around 40 institutes on our list with whom we build a relationship from our company perspective, along with that we have around 7 or 8 B-schools also with which we have a collaboration.

Figure 8.1 demonstrates the employability of graduates from general, professional, and technical education, while Figure 8.2 illustrates the trends in domain-wise employment opportunities from 2014 to 2020. These two figures

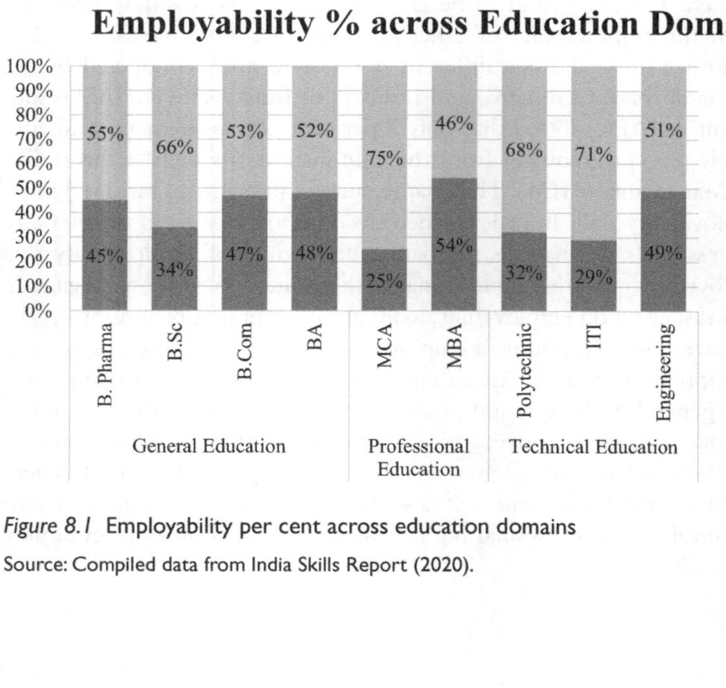

Figure 8.1 Employability per cent across education domains

Source: Compiled data from India Skills Report (2020).

capture education domain-wise data with their respective references to employability and employment opportunities. The India Skills Report (2020) mapped the employability and employment opportunities to identify the gap which is referred to as unemployment. Unemployment is caused due to insufficient job opportunities, but employability is a concern and due to low employability. These graduates either remain unemployed or go for professional courses to gain job-related skills. Professional graduates have fewer employment opportunities but higher employability. Management graduates have the highest employability score.

The engineering graduates, too, are highly unemployable (51 per cent) but much fewer than those with polytechnic or ITI degrees. According to the report, science graduates are found to be more unemployable (66 per cent) than the commerce and arts graduates. In the interview, a subject spoke along the same lines with regard to general education by expressing that 'graduates from general education backgrounds such as Sociology, Economics, Philosophy, History, etc. are hired for Business Process Services/Business Process Outsourcing'. This way the employment opportunities are better for the general education graduates. According to the industry trends, E-commerce, BFSI, and BPO/KPO/ITeS are booming. The general education graduates in B.A., B.Sc., and B.Com. courses (employability over 45 per cent individually for each course) will well serve as the resource supply pool for these sectors (India Skills Report, 2020).

Trends in domain-wise employment opportunities

Figure 8.2 illustrates the trends in domain-wise employment opportunities from 2014 to 2020. The most stable domain in providing employment opportunities has been the general education courses offering 30 per cent to 35 per cent of the employment opportunities. Peaks and valleys can be seen for the technical education course, while professional education courses' contribution to the employment opportunities seem to vary from 20 per cent to 30 per cent.

Trends in domain-wise employability

MBA-holders have taken over the slot of the highest employable cohort among the various course graduates with an employability score of 54 per cent. This position was previously held by engineers in earlier years. Employability of graduates with B.Pharm, B.Com., B.A., and Polytechnic degree has increased appreciably, at about 15 per cent (see Table 8.1).

According to the report, fresh graduates make up only for 15 per cent of the overall hiring in companies. Based on the educational qualifications in demand, engineers have been expected to be hired the most (31 per cent), closely followed by general education graduates (B.A/B.Com/B.Sc.) (25 per cent), which is in tandem with the hiring trends posted by BFSI, e-commerce, and BPO/KPO/ITeS.

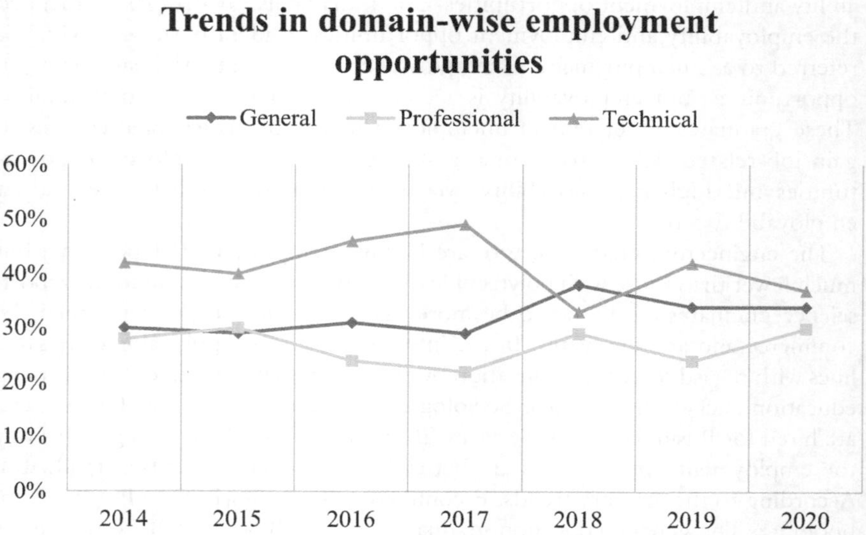

Figure 8.2 Trends in domain-wise employment opportunities

Source: Compiled data from India Skills Report (2020).

Table 8.1 Trends in domain-wise employability

		2014	*2015*	*2016*	*2017*	*2018*	*2019*	*2020*
General education	B.Pharm	54.65%	56%	40.62%	42.30%	47.78%	36.29%	45%
	B.Sc.	41.92%	38.41%	35.24%	31.76%	33.62%	47.37%	34%
	B.Com.	26.99%	26.45%	20.58%	37.98%	33.93%	30.06%	47%
	B.A.	19.10%	29.82%	27.11%	35.66%	37.39%	29.20%	48%
Professional education	M.C.A.	43.62%	45%	39.81%	31.36%	43.85%	43.19%	25%
	M.B.A.	41.02%	43.99%	44.56%	42.28%	39.40%	36.40%	54%
Technical education	B.E/B Tech	51.74%	54%	52.58%	50.69%	51.52%	57.09%	49%
	Polytechnic	11.53%	10.14%	15.89%	25.77%	32.67%	18.05%	32%
	ITI	46.92%	44%	40.90%	42.22%	29.46%	NA	NA

Source: India Skills Report (2020).

Employers' perception on employability skills by disciplines

The reason to bring in the employers' perspective is to provide an insight into the employers' needs and how the employers evaluate the higher-education graduates' employability skills based on the different educational backgrounds like general, technical, and professional education. The skills which employers specified to emphasize while screening candidates are domain knowledge, adaptability to the environment, learning agility, and positive attitude. The current status of employability among engineering and management graduates is quite worrisome and disheartening since only 2.5 per cent of them from the employable graduates are possessing modern technical skills such as artificial intelligence (AI), robotic process automation (RPA), machine learning (ML) and so on in the knowledge economy, as reported by the employability assessment company Aspiring Minds. Perceptions of the employers on graduates are a significant mechanism to provide a baseline for improvement. Employers' assessments are not only about graduates' personality and presentation but play a role in guiding for the relevant academic content and syllabus for the various courses. The information provided by employers can act as a reference for the university to understand the future needs or trends in the various fields of study, so that the university will be able to make appropriate changes in their academic programmes for the respective courses.

To gain an understanding about the employers' perspective, primary research was conducted. A survey of 121 employers using a structured questionnaire was conducted, and focus group discussions and in-depth interviews were held with some of the employers from two major IT organizations that have more than 500 employees in Bengaluru. The study on employers' perspectives on graduate employability based on the educational backgrounds has yielded interesting and useful results. It represents some key discussions concerning the cooperation and dialogue between higher education and the industry from employers' perspective.

Hiring patterns and satisfaction with the talent hired

Employers report that 50 per cent or more of their new hires hold either a bachelor's degree (technical) from a four-year college or a master's degree (technical/professional) from a two-year college. Employers indicate higher-education graduation in a technical/professional course to be essential and desirable key selection criteria for employment. Upon analysis of the demand outlook posted by various industries, it has been noted that engineers are preferred over a wide range of industries—automotive (auto and auto components), manufacturing, core sector, IT, and telecom forming more than 50 per cent of demand pool. Engineers are expected to be hired the most (31 per cent), closely followed by general graduates such as B.C.A., B.B.A., B.Com., B.Sc. (25 per cent). The overall demand for engineers has increased from last year by around 10 per cent. Additionally, this year, there is an increase in demand for MBA and postgraduate students compared to the previous year (India Skills Report, 2020).

The employers were divided in their opinion of agreement and disagreement with the skills of the graduates that their company had hired in the past three to five years. While more than one-fourth of the respondents (26.4 per cent)

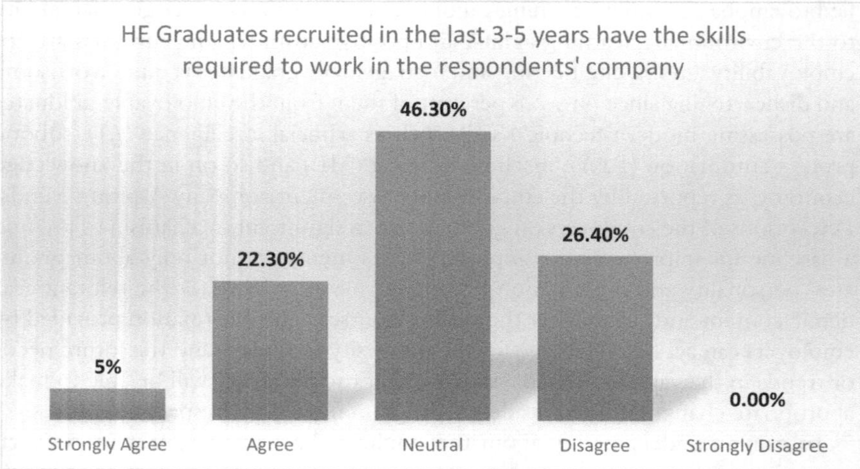

Image 8.1 **Higher education graduates recruited in the last three to five years have the skills required to work in the respondents' company**

disagreed that the graduates demonstrated the necessary skills needed in their company, 22.3 per cent had agreed to the statement. Only 5 per cent strongly agreed that the graduates met the skill requirements of their company.

The focus group discussions held with the employers helped in analyzing the expectations of the employers from higher-education institutions and the government. Employers point to a variety of types of knowledge and skills as important considerations when hiring graduates, placing greatest priority on adaptability, communication skills, continuous learning, and critical thinking irrespective of the field of study. The list of skills is given in Figure 8.3.

The chart in Figure 8.3 may be categorized into two factors—common skills and domain specific skills for the purpose of further analysis.

Common skills expected

Under the category of common skills, employers expect all the graduates from the higher-education institutions to hone up the common skills before completing their graduation. Common skills form the basic crux for the employer's expectation. Employers recognize capacities that cut across various fields of study as critical to a candidate's potential for career success, and they view these common skills as more important than a student's choice of course. In the focus group discussion, the employers recognized that having both 'field-specific knowledge and skills' and a 'broad range of common skills and knowledge' is most important for recent college graduates to achieve long-term career success irrespective of their

Common Skills Expected from Graduates (Essential Skills for Graduates being expected by Industry)		
Communication Skills	Positive Attitude	Adaptability Skills
Domain Knowledge	Teamwork	Critical Thinking
Interpersonal Skills	Computer & Digital Skills	Presentation Skills
Integrity and ethical conduct	Time Management	Continuous Learning
Leadership Skills	Emotional Intelligence	Citizenship Skills

Domain Specific Skills expected from Graduates

General Education	Technical Education	Professional Education
Conceptualizing skills	Technical Writing	Core Competency
Civic Literacy	Tech Proficiency (Artificial Intelligence & Machine Learning	Research Acumen
Agility Skills	Project Management	Analytical Thinking
Academic excellence	Risk Management	Personal effectiveness
Cross Cultural Awareness	Data Engineering	Creativity & Innovation

Figure 8.3 Industry expectations from higher-education institutions (academia)

Source: Drawn from the focus group discussion conducted by the researcher.

field of study. While one may think that choosing the 'right' course is key to getting a good job, the long-term professional success of a candidate will depend far more on acquiring the right skills for a rapidly changing workplace impacted by a competitive global marketplace where global supply chains link manufacturers and consumers everywhere and anytime in the universe.

A candidate's demonstrated capacity to be adaptable, have a positive attitude, communicate clearly, apply domain knowledge, and think critically are some common skills that are more important than their type of degree. Employers search for robust communication skills, trustworthiness, and integrity when they evaluate potential new hires. Each year for the past five years, employers have placed the ability to communicate effectively at the top of their demand list. They also award job applicants who show experience in teamwork and collaboration, who have interpersonal skills, who seem motivated, show resourcefulness, and take initiative. And they want new hires with a strong work ethic (deSilva, 2015).

Domain-wise specific skills expected

Domain specific skills are further divided for the three domains—general education, technical, and professional. The skills under theses domains are specialized skills, according to their required field of study as expected by the employers.

General education graduates

In this category, employers expect the general education graduates to hone up the diverse skills under the common skills category so that they can effectively utilize their academic knowledge to participate in the organizational development and society's development. Since the general education primarily has an undergraduate three-year course curriculum, the key responsibility expected of the educational institutions is to impart generic skills such as communication, adaptability, positive attitude, ethical reasoning, critical thinking, and listening skills. Also included are agility, cross-cultural awareness and the domain specific skills, including conceptualizing and civic literacy. In the employers' opinion, the generic skills that are not covered in their syllabus are more important for a fresh graduate than their core specialization.

Technical education skills

In the technical education category, employers expect the technical graduates to be well versed on the newest technical skills along with the common skills where they can minimize the training period of graduates. There is a gradual increase in the application of new technologies such as digitalization, artificial intelligence, machine learning, cloud computing, robotics, virtual reality, and augmented reality. Garnering a higher level of skill in the areas of these disruptive technologies will continue to be in high demand. The industries hiring technical education graduates desperately need the candidates to upskill on future technology. Technical writing, STEM and technical proficiency, project management, risk management and data analysis are some important skills expected by the employers to be imparted for technical education graduates during their course of study.

Tulsi and Poonia (2015) stressed the importance of technical graduates familiarizing themselves with concepts, tools; techniques, regular participation of graduates in workshops, and training programmes under the supervision of teachers and technicians; and training under skilled personnel/craftsmen. The authors also stressed the importance of having industry–academia exchange platforms to learn from skilled personnel and inviting professionals to deliver expert lectures and seminars on contemporary practices. Institutions should promote multidisciplinary research culture for collaborative research projects among graduates from various disciplines in engineering.

Yusofee et al. (2012) highlighted the present employment scenario and condition of the technical labour market. To be competitive it is imperative for job aspirants to have the required employability skills such as interpersonal skills, lifelong learning, self-management skills, and a good understanding of social and ethical responsibilities which are quite essential in order to be desirable to the employers.

Professional education skills

In the professional education skills category, employers expect professional graduates to hone up their specialized skills along with the common skills where they can completely manage their responsibilities by using their specialized skills. A definitive point of designing professional educational programmes is to deliver experts who can give specialized solutions for the societal needs (Hassan et al., 2007). The employability skills are those that help a professional student to accomplish this objective.

Today's highly technical and sophisticated jobs demand professional education graduates who can increase productivity and thereby add more value to an organization. Presently, 'employability' doesn't just mean getting jobs; it centres around manageability where the candidate with professional education can give solutions through innovation and best practices for various problems. Leadership skills, research acumen, analytical thinking, personal effectiveness, and creativity and innovation are some of the key skills expected by the employers to be possessed by professional education graduates.

Employees' job preparedness based on educational background

It's important to understand how well the employees from these various fields of study who have recently entered the job market fare on the required employability skills. Based on a survey of 319 employees from various domains of study, a self-rating index on 13 sets of skills was developed. From the perspective and experience of formerly being students, employees can provide feedback to help evaluate how the content and delivery of the curriculum in various disciplines of study can be improved. Recently entering employment means the employees can communicate what aspects have been the most important during the transition from university to employment, helping to identify gaps between the skills graduates have on graduation and the skills needed to function effectively in the working world.

Skills perceived as important by employees from various educational backgrounds

(General/Technical/Professional)

From Table 8.2 we can see how the employees perceive the 13 employability skills as important in order of relevance to seeking employability.

General Education: Employees with general academic qualification find that conceptualizing skills, communication skills, managerial skills are considered to be most significant followed by technical skills and personal skills. It is evident that employees seem to give less importance to numeric skills, sector-specific skills, and foreign language skills.

Table 8.2 Employee perspective on skill importance

Mean scores of the skills and competencies perceived as important by employees

*IMPe						
Importance rank	*Employability skills*	*General* G	*Employability skills*	*Technical* T	*Employability skills*	*Professional* P
1	Conceptualizing	1.37	Technical skills	1.34	Academic excellence	1.32
2	Communication skills	1.46	Academic excellence	1.43	Personal skills	1.5
3	Managerial skills	1.46	Communication skills	1.51	Technical skills	1.57
4	Technical skills	1.54	Computer skills	1.52	Conceptualizing	1.65
5	Personal skills	1.63	Conceptualizing	1.57	Communication skills	1.76
6	Adaptability	1.66	Personal skills	1.63	Computer skills	1.78
7	People-related	1.71	People-related	1.68	People-related	1.79
8	Academic excellence	1.77	Adaptability	1.77	Managerial skills	1.79
9	Computer skills	1.83	Managerial skills	1.86	Adaptability	1.84
10	Citizenship skills	1.91	Citizenship skills	1.92	Sector-specific skills	1.96
11	Numeric skills	2.2	Numeric skills	1.92	Citizenship skills	2
12	Sector-specific skills	2.34	Sector-specific skills	1.94	Numeric skills	2.06
13	Foreign language skills	3.11	Foreign language skills	2.67	Foreign language skills	2.45

Source: Primary research conducted by the researcher.

Technical Education: Employees with technical educational qualification find that technical skills, academic excellence, and communication skills are perceived to be the most important followed by computer skills and conceptual skills. Among the other skills, technical education graduates, like the general education graduates, seem to attach less prominence to numeric skills, sector-specific skills, and foreign language skills.

Professional Education: Employees with professional academic qualification rate academic excellence, personal skills, and technical skills with highest significance followed by conceptualizing skills and communication skills. The employees find that numeric skills and foreign language skills to be least important, which is similar to what general education and technical education graduates have perceived.

Self-rating of skills by employees from various educational backgrounds

From Table 8.3, we can infer employee self-rating on the skills and competencies possessed by the general, technical, and professional background graduates.

General Education: Employees with general education have rated that they have proficiency on the academic excellence, technical skills, communication skills, and adaptability followed by numeric skills, personal, and sector-specific skills. It is evident that employees find themselves less adept on citizenship skills, conceptualizing, and foreign language skills.

Technical Education: Employees with technical education have rated that they have proficiency on the technical skills, academic excellence, personal skills, and computer skills followed by communication skills, conceptualizing, and adaptability skills. It is evident that employees rate themselves lacking in numeric skills, foreign language skills, and sector-specific skills.

Professional Education: Employees with professional education have rated that they have proficiency on academic excellence, technical skills, conceptualizing, and numeric skills followed by sector-specific skills, citizenship skills, and managerial skills. They however, rate themselves lower on foreign language skills, computer skills, and personal skills.

Skill perception gap

From Table 8.4 it is evident that general education graduates have a larger skills gap, followed by technical graduates and professional education graduates. It can also be noticed that technical graduates have a negative skill gap for all skills except adaptability skills. Negative skill preparedness gap indicates that the employees do not fare well in their preparedness in demonstrating the required employability skills. Their perception of importance of the skills is higher, but they perceive not to be well prepared to demonstrate those skills. The technical graduates lack in most of the skills that are expected to be possessed by a graduate to be employable.

Table 8.3 Self-rating of skills by employees from various educational backgrounds

Mean scores of the self-rating of skills and competencies by employees

***SRe*

Importance Rank	*Employability skills*	*General* G	*Employability skills*	*Technical* T	*Employability skills*	*Professional* P
1	Academic excellence	1.43	Technical skills	1.68	Academic excellence	1.12
2	Technical skills	1.6	Personal skills	1.7	Technical skills	1.46
3	Communication skills	1.86	Academic excellence	1.74	Conceptualizing	1.54
4	Personal skills	1.97	Computer skills	1.75	Numeric skills	1.6
5	Adaptability	2.03	Communication skills	1.77	Sector-specific skills	1.65
6	Numeric skills	2.09	Conceptualizing	1.77	Adaptability	1.65
7	Sector-specific skills	2.11	Adaptability	1.77	Citizenship skills	1.71
8	Computer skills	2.14	People-related	1.8	Managerial skills	1.94
9	People-related	2.14	Citizenship skills	1.94	People-related	1.98
10	Managerial skills	2.14	Managerial skills	1.96	Communication skills	2.02
11	Citizenship skills	2.2	Numeric skills	1.97	Personal skills	2.04
12	Conceptualizing	2.26	Sector-specific skills	1.98	Computer skills	2.06
13	Foreign language skills	3.54	Foreign language skills	3.48	Foreign language skills	3.1

Source: Primary research conducted by the researcher.

Table 8.4 Skill perception gap

Skill Perception Gap						
Emp Skill Gap Ranking (Negative to Positive)	*(IMPe-SRe)*					
	Employability skills	*General*	*Employability skills*	*Technical*	*Employability skills*	*Professional*
1	Conceptualizing	−0.89	Foreign language skills	−0.81	Foreign language skills	−0.65
2	Managerial skills	−0.68	Technical skills	−0.34	Personal skills	−0.54
3	People-related	−0.43	Academic excellence	−0.31	Computer skills	−0.28
4	Foreign Language skills	−0.43	Communication skills	−0.26	Communication skills	−0.26
5	Communication skills	−0.4	Computer skills	−0.23	People-related	−0.19
6	Adaptability	−0.37	Conceptualizing	−0.2	Managerial skills	−0.15
7	Personal skills	−0.34	People-related	−0.12	Technical skills	0.11
8	Computer skills	−0.31	Managerial skills	−0.1	Conceptualizing	0.11
9	Citizenship skills	−0.29	Personal skills	−0.07	Adaptability	0.19
10	Technical skills	−0.06	Numeric skills	−0.05	Academic Excellence	0.2
11	Numeric skills	0.11	Sector-specific skills	−0.04	Citizenship skills	0.29
12	Sector-specific skills	0.23	Citizenship skills	−0.02	Sector-specific skills	0.31
13	Academic Excellence	0.34	Adaptability	0	Numeric skills	0.46

Source: Primary research conducted by the researcher.

The general education graduates have a large skill gap for conceptualizing skills, followed by managerial skills, while technical education graduates seem to lack primarily in foreign language skills followed by technical skills, and for the professional education graduates, the skill gap is evidently reflected in foreign language skills followed by personal skills. The negative differences for other skills among professional education graduates are negligibly lesser. General education graduates and professional education graduates fare well in academic excellence.

College/university experience of employees with respect to employability skill development

HEIs provide activities such as aptitude building, career guidance on technical skills, and personal grooming on personal skills for students to acquire job-ready skills. These activities contribute to forming college/university experience. The primary study helped in identifying the differences in college/university experience of employees from various educational backgrounds.

The college/university experience in the study covered the perspective of graduates related to the following types of skill development programmes/activities conducted during their graduation. They are presentation/group discussion, industrial visit, mock interview, vocational skills development, aptitude building, CV writing, and so on. From Table 8.5, it can be noticed that the college/university experience derived from the general education course is different from the experience in the technical/professional course. However, the technical and professional courses offer similar college/university experience. Only 15 per cent were either highly satisfied or satisfied with the skill/career development activities.

Table 8.5 Difference in college/university experience based on educational background

Dependent variable: college/university experience index			
Tukey HSD			
Nature of degree (I)	*Nature of degree (J)*	*Mean difference (I-J)*	*Sig.*
General	Technical	−0.01826	0.021
	Professional	0.20467	0.038
Technical	General	0.01826	0.021
	Professional	0.22293	0.071
Professional	General	−0.20467	0.038
	Technical	−0.22293	0.071

Source: Primary research conducted by the researcher.

*The mean difference is significant at the 0.05 level.

Employability skill development initiatives by general, technical, and professional education institutions

The employability skills initiatives of the three streams of higher-education institutes bring awareness about the skill development initiatives and programmes that augment employability of graduates in these institutions.

Internships and apprenticeships have been initiated as part of courses/programmes and can become enablers for job seekers to get employment in industry. These programmes, however, should be designed and implemented in partnership with the public- and private-sector institutions to help address future workforce needs.

Industry–academia linkages and exchange programmes have been initiated to improve professional knowledge, competence, skill, and effectiveness in a particular domain that needs expertise in order to effectively deliver the teaching/learning course curriculum. Also, industrialists and technocrats are now often seen in meetings with academia and part of curricula development in universities.

Universities and institutions are increasingly focusing on enhancing behavioural and social skills irrespective of academic discipline such as general, technical, and professional graduates, by upgrading their curricula. Industrial visits are being organized on a regular basis for the students to get more exposure towards technology and professional experience. SWAYAM, NPTEL, and other MOOCs have been initiated to bring about quality, access, and equity in higher education.

The initiatives taken by institutions to reduce the skill disparities and bridge the skill-gap among the general, technical, and professional education institutes are given as follows:

Initiatives taken by general education institutes

- The professional development and placement centres in institutions are an enabling platform providing opportunities of value-addition to classroom curriculum through workshops, lectures, hands-on training programmes, and interactive sessions.
- Business conclaves and international seminars are being conducted so that students are apprised of the experience of entrepreneurs and start-ups, including their ideas and motivation to start something on their own.
- National colloquiums are conducted as an interface between industry, academic experts, and the student community for deliberating contemporary national and international issues. Top leaders from industry and governance are invited to share their insights on the theme of the colloquium followed by technical sessions where speakers from different fields share their experiences and present the contemporary scenario.
- Diversified curriculum has brought over many organizations to recruit students for internships and placement offers where funding organization,

corporate social responsibility, corporate organizations, training institutes, schools, and NGOs are the most sought domains among the students.
- National level and inter-college/university cultural fests which include events such as dance, drama, music, and academically driven contests like quizzes.

Initiatives taken by technical education institutions

- Extensive infrastructure is built with state-of-the-art technology, expansive laboratory facilities, and valuable affiliations, and recognitions, networked partner industries, and R&D labs are provided in eminent institutions.
- Institutions give an equal emphasis on theory, practical/laboratory, and workshops.
- An innovation and entrepreneurship wing is created where institutions foster entrepreneurship and administer business incubators which provide support for technology-based entrepreneurship and facilitates the conversion of research activity into entrepreneurial ventures.
- Exclusive apprenticeships, internships, major projects, and minor projects are also included in the curricula. Industry sectors such as engineering and technology, data analytics, consulting firms, financial services, research and development, and IT/software are the most sought industry sectors among technical graduates. Internships for graduates are offered in sectors such as IT/telecom, automotive, engineering and technology, data analytics, biotechnology, construction, Add-on courses related to data analytics, artificial intelligence, machine learning etc.
- Institutions' emphasis is also given for flipped classroom, self-study, and experiential learning.
- Many interdisciplinary courses and open or global electives are also offered, and a student can choose from these according to his or her interest.
- All students have to undergo a Continuous Internal Evaluation (CIE) and formative assessment which include tests, quizzes, experiential learning, assignments, and seminars.

Initiatives taken by professional education institutes

- Business communication training helps overcome the mother tongue influence and develops language proficiency which helps to build confidence among students, thus increasing their employability.
- Outbound learning—Management students get trained at premier training academies and institutes to gain knowledge on time management, leadership, and team building.

- Training on Microsoft Excel, Microsoft PowerPoint, and other software builds technical competencies and also makes them proficient enough to become corporate trainers and ensures they are job-ready.
- Aptitude and soft skills training—The aim of having this programme is to ensure the students have the prerequisites of the placements. This programme will enhance their communication skills and group discussion and interview skills, which will yield overall development of students and placements.
- Business incubator provides support for entrepreneurship and facilitates the conversion of research activity into entrepreneurial ventures.
- Exclusive internship programmes offered in sectors such as consulting domain, business analytics, e-commerce, financial services, operations, IT products, real estate; training programmes related to communication, personality development, experts talks, workshops, faculty exchange programmes with industries.
- Skill development programmes–Professionals from different industries explain the necessary attributes required to build a career in their industries.

The industry-oriented curriculum has brought over various industry sectors to recruit students for internship and placement offers. Business analytics, e-commerce, financial services, operations, IT products, sales and marketing are the most sought after domains that are preferred by students enrolled in professional course education. Although, several initiatives have been taken by institutes, employees still find themselves lacking in satisfying their employers. Thus there is need to make these activities more effective.

Concluding observations

One of the biggest challenges higher-education institutions face today is in terms of enhancing employability of graduates irrespective of the nature of their degree. It is critical for the curriculum to keep pace with the fast-changing job marketplace with technological advancement and globalization. The industry has classified the employability skills into generic skills and domain-specific specialized skills. The employers' view that though both generic and domain-specific skills are necessary to be imparted to the graduates by the educational institutions, the need is to focus on the generic/common skills which give an edge to the graduates in becoming more employable. They emphasize that the common skills which are transferrable across various domains and jobs are more in demand.

There are a number of ways in which the institutions aim to enhance employability skills. Technical institutes offer programmes such as internships, sponsored lab/facility, sponsored/ consultancy project, and strong alumni association. Professional institutes focus more on having group discussion in classes, student presentations, teamwork assignments, analytical and practical problem-solving exercises, research programmes, and apprenticeship are also offered. The technical and professional institutes are already to a greater extent making use of the skill development approaches, but the general education courses focus more on blending academic rigor with a wide range of electives across disciplines. They should also make greater use of a structured approach to career development activities and workplace learning opportunities for their graduates. Employers recommend institutions in having an MoU with relevant industries (according to the nature of the degree) to have an option of 'Earn while you Learn'. There should exist sustainable and fruitful partnerships between the HEIs and industry.

References

AISHE (2019). *All India survey on higher education 2018–19.* Ministry of Human Resource Development, Department of Higher Education, Government of India, New Delhi.

Aspiring Minds (2019). *National employability reports engineers 2019.* Aspiring Minds, Gurgaon.

Association of Graduate Recruiters (1995). *Skills for graduates in the 21st century.* Association of Graduate Recruiters, Cambridge.

Confederation of British Industry (1994). *Quality assured-the CBI review of NVQs and SVQs.* CBI, London.

Confederation of British Industry (2003). *The UK as a place to do business: Is transport holding the UK back?* CBI Research Report. CBI Publication, London.

deSilva, D. (2015). Management education and employability skills: Business' looking for more than a quality major in graduates: Can academe get-with-it? Yes*! *Sri Lankan Journal of Human Resource Management*, 5(1).

Hassan, B., Mohd Zaidi, O., Zainal, M., Abang Abdullah, A. A., Badrulhisham, A. A., Abdul Hamid, H., Nik Abdullah, N. M., Azmi, H., & Zaidi, M. R. (2007). *The future of engineering education in Malaysia.* Malaysia: Department of Institutions of Higher Education Management, Ministry of Higher Education.

India Skills Report 2020 (2019). *India skills report 2020.* Taggd by PeopleStrong. https://wheebox.com/assets/pdf/ISR_Report_2020.pdf.

Khare, M. (2014). Employment, employability and higher education in India: The missing links. *Higher Education for the Future*, 1(1), 39–62.

Khare, M. (2018). Employability of graduates in India-hard realities. *International Higher Education*, 95, 29–31. USA: The Boston College Centre for International Higher Education.

Tulsi, P. K., & Poonia, M. P. (2015). Expectations of industry from technical graduates: Implications for curriculum and instructional processes. *Journal of Engineering Education Transformations*, 28(4), 42–49.

Universities UK (2002). *Higher education in facts and figures.* London: Universities UK.

Yusofee, M. D. Y., Zaharm, A., Omar, Mohd, Z., Mohamed, A., Mohamed, N., & Mustapha, R. (2012). Engineering employability skills for Malaysian industry: Framework development. *Technology Innovations in Education*, 36–47.

Chapter 9

Education, skills mismatch, and wage differentials

Sahana Roy Chowdhury, Catherine Bros, and Sayoree Gooptu

There are growing concerns over misallocation of skills in the labour market across the globe, irrespective of the stages of economic development. Skill shortage results in divergence of actual productivity from the frontier (or the potential) and lack of employability that often leads to labour substitution and mechanization resulting in potential job losses. This again has major policy implications for vocational education and skills training, such as the role of skill development initiatives and the upgradation and broadening of the ITI network. On the other hand, over-education/underemployment, as the literature defines, has major economic impacts. Over-education/underemployment are said to be the result of lack of absorptive capacity of the organized sector as the demand side factor, and lack of employability of the 'educated' labour pool as the supply side factor. If we assume that education acquisition leads to skill acquisition, then the efficiency of subsidizing education lies in its capacity to enable the educated pool to make productive contributions in the labour market. If the returns to education for the skilled are not 'adequate', then they cannot be productively engaged in the labour market. If the educated pool does not get adequate return from the labour market, they join the jobs down the job ladder, substituting the less-educated and contributing to either rising wage inequality or unemployment among uneducated/less educated or both. This is known as the 'bumping down' effect. Such a decision of acquiring higher education is also to give a signal to the employers and thereby enter the labour queue at the highest possible rank (Thurow, 1975). This scenario is not specific about the developing world, where prevalence of unemployment is quite rampant but also in many developed EU countries (Borghans & De Grip, 2000).

In most of the related studies, the motivation behind estimating skill mismatches comes from anecdotal evidence or casual empiricism that shows simultaneous prevalence of 'unabsorbed skill' or increasing unemployment among the educated pool while at the same time skill shortages in certain sectors of the labour market. However, quantifying the extent of skill mismatch is a challenging task; the problem lies in getting a convincing definition of 'mismatch' and finding the correspondence between 'skill' and 'education', as perceived by the market. We will first discuss how the literature defines 'mismatch', which basically relates

DOI: 10.4324/9781003158349-11

to the discrepancy between the education requirement of any job/occupation and the educational attainment of a worker employed in that job/occupation.

McGuinness et al., (IZA, 2017) provide a brief review of the literature on the measurements of skill mismatches. It says that skill mismatch can be a vertical mismatch (often measured in terms of over-education/under-education/over-skilling/under-skilling), skill gaps, skill shortages (measured in terms of unfilled vacancies), horizontal mismatch (workers are employed in jobs that are not relevant to the skills and knowledge accumulated by them in formal education), and skill obsolescence. These concepts are very different in how they manifest themselves, their determinants, and how their consequences are felt. Some relate to mismatches experienced by employees, while others relate to employers and firm-level difficulties. Some skill mismatch concepts are measured subjectively while others are derived from existing data. Skill gaps describe the situation whereby the employer believes that workers do not possess the adequate competencies to successfully discharge their current role; whereas skill shortages relate to a situation whereby employers are unable to fill key vacant posts due to a lack of suitably qualified candidates. Most of the literature focuses on measuring over-education and under-education (McGuinness, 2006; Quintini, 2011; Cedefop, 2010, 2015a, 2015b, 2015c).

As McGuinness et al. (IZA, 2017) describe, there are three approaches to measuring over-education and under-education: ***subjective method, empirical method, and job evaluation method***. The first two are most commonly used. The subjective method is based on worker self-assessment of the level of qualifications required 'to get' or 'to do' the job. This is then compared to the education actually acquired by the worker in the job, accordingly he is defined as overeducated, matched, or undereducated. The empirical method estimates the educational requirement of an occupation by assessing the mean or modal level of education within a given occupation, deeming workers with acquired education above (below) the average level as overeducated (undereducated). Also prevalent was the measure of over-education or under-education when compared to whether the worker is one standard deviation above (below) the chosen average, but this was highly criticized due to the arbitrary cut-off used. Another approach is the job evaluation method which is based on the assessments of professional job analysts who are tasked with measuring the educational requirements of occupations for the purpose of constructing occupational dictionaries; this is then compared with the actual education of the worker and he or she is defined as over-skilled or under-skilled.

We will follow here the empirical method (EM) to estimate the number of people who have excess (less) skill when compared to the 'required' education level, as perceived by the market. Unlike the methods described earlier, we will define a level of education as the 'required level of education' for a particular occupation, only if the 'returns to that education' is positive and 'high enough' when compared to the mean returns paid to the workers engaged in that occupation.[1] Under the EM method, what is typically used in the literature is that a worker is defined as overeducated (undereducated) when his education level is above (below) the mean level of education of all the workers employed in that occupation, irrespective of the returns in that occupation (mean-EM method). This method is likely to underestimate skill mismatch. Suppose a region has a large supply of educated (skill). It may be because of lesser cost of education acquisition or some other extra-economic (traditional or cultural) factor, in comparison with the industry absorption rate (demand) of the skilled in that region. In that case, if we count the overeducated by the mean-EM method, the mean might be driven to be higher. Workers engaged in the same occupations with much lesser education levels in some other regions, where industry demand for skills is high might appear to be undereducated. And this is in spite of the fact that the returns to education in the former region is low. This might imply that the industry does not (does) value skill in the former (latter) region. By the mean-EM method, workers engaged in the latter region will be counted as undereducated, but if we go by the 'returns to skill' method, they may not appear to be so. On the contrary, in regions where average skilled stock (education level) is high and also demand for skilled stock is high, these workers might not appear to be overeducated by the 'returns to skill' method. This is in contrast to the mean-EM method where they will definitely appear to be so. Thus, in a country with diverse supply-demand factors in labour market there may be underestimation of skill mismatch if one goes by the EM method. Mehta et al. (2012) follows the 'returns to skill' channel in defining over-education, making a comparison across a set of developing countries, including India. They have primarily estimated how many workers in the 'unskilled' jobs category, those that offer low returns 7 per cent, are there with respect to that of the secondary and tertiary schooling (who have obtained secondary or tertiary education). However, the cut-off of 7 per cent has been an arbitrary choice, not backed by any econometric rationale.

In our analysis we have used the unit-level data of the NSS 68th round. In order to estimate returns to education, we estimate the following Mincer equations for individuals employed in 'Elementary occupations'—manufacturing and industry as a whole. However, we wish to investigate how these returns to education relate to states' structure depicted by state's GDP, whether industrialized/manufacture-led or not; the reason being that returns to general and vocational education has a strong demand side relation. We define a worker to be overeducated if he or she is possessing skill in excess of the skill that gives positive (statistically significant) returns in the respective labour market. Given that the industry sector has a broader definition than the selected sample (e.g. labourers employed in the utility sector are not included in the sample), controlling by the percentage of states' GDP derived from the industry may appear as a loose control. Moreover, employment in mining and quarrying is likely to be closely tied with states' geographical characteristics such as the presence of natural resources. Therefore, we will focus on an even more restricted sample: labourers employed in the manufacturing sector.

Following our definition, we find the proportion of overeducated individuals in the manufacturing sector to be 66 per cent. Scatterplots indicate that there seems to be a positive relationship between the share of the industry (or manufacturing) in states' GDP and the extent of over-education. The caveat is that the education returns are national averages, which hide regional disparities; as the manufacturing sector grows, so does the returns; but if one takes the national average there will be overestimation of over-education for the industrialized states. As prima facie evidence that returns on education may vary depending on the size of the sector and that returns to education may be heterogeneous across regions, we try to assess whether formal vocational training appears as a good alternative to general education and could reduce over-education.

This can hardly be done if the skill mismatch estimates do not add a regional dimension; any combined country-specific estimate will have limited policy takeaways. Especially for India, with its diverse states—some rich in skilled/human capital stock but poor degree of industrial development/manufacturing activity/base, while some having high manufacturing activity but poor HC. Finding the root cause of skill mismatch will be difficult if region-specific study is not done. It is therefore crucial to delve deep and understand the region-specific demand-supply interactions and then frame suitable policies to intervene. So far, such sub-national studies are not done with regard to Indian labour market. We attempt to estimate over-education adding a regional dimension to it.

Data and estimation strategy

Our data are drawn from the National Sample Survey (NSS) carried out between June 2011 and July 2012 over the whole territory of the Indian Union. It contains information on education, employment, occupation, and weekly wages for 71,273 individuals. Given our interest in over-education, we focus on what the dataset refers to as 'Elementary occupations'. However, as we wish to investigate how these returns to education relate to states' structure of GDP, we focus on labourers in mining and construction and manufacturing, who account for respectively 75 per cent and 13 per cent of the sample.

In order to estimate returns to education, we estimate the following Mincer equations for individual i employed in sector j

$$ln\left(Wage_{i,j}\right) = \alpha + \sum\nolimits_{g\in[1;11]} \beta_g D_{g,i} + \delta VT_i + \gamma_1 Experience_i + \gamma_2 Experience_i^2 + \rho Sector_j + \chi X_{ik} + \varepsilon_{i,j} \quad (1)$$

where $Wage_{i,j}$ is the amount of weekly wage, $D_{g,i}$ is a binary variable equal to one if individual i has completed grade g so that for grade g, β_g is the return on that particular year/level of education. VT_i is a binary variable that indicates whether individual i received any formal vocational training. The proportion of individual who actually underwent vocational training is 0.8 per cent in the selected sample which is low in absolute terms but also in comparison with the whole NSS sample for which the figure stands at 5.7 per cent. X_{ik} represent additional individual controls such as age and social group, given that in the Indian context, it has been shown that the latter matters as far as wages are concerned. It is worth emphasizing that the sample has been restricted to males in order to partly alleviate concerns related to selection bias, given that female labour market participation rate stands at about 27 per cent.[2]

Given the unskilled nature of the considered occupations, not surprisingly, 32 per cent of the samples individuals are not literate or literate without schooling. Over the whole NSS sample, this figure was at 15.6 per cent while the 2011 Census of India estimates the National literacy rate at 74 per cent. Figure 9.1 provides a comparison between the distribution of educational level in the selected sample and in the whole NSS sample that gathers all types of occupations.

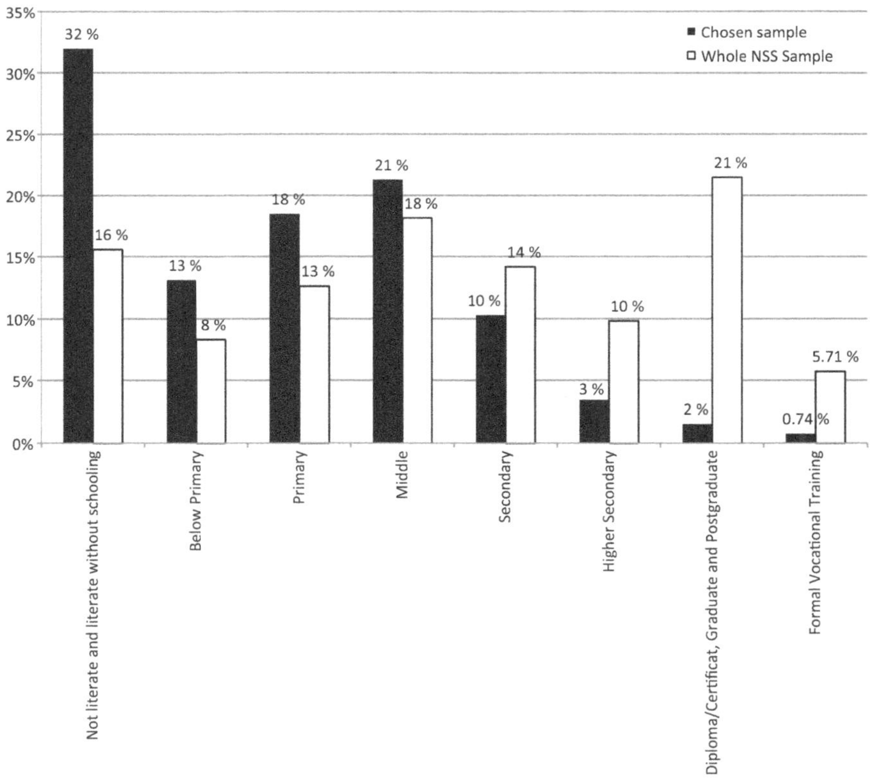

Figure 9.1 Educational levels

Source: Authors' calculations based on the 68th round of the National Sample Survey (NSS).

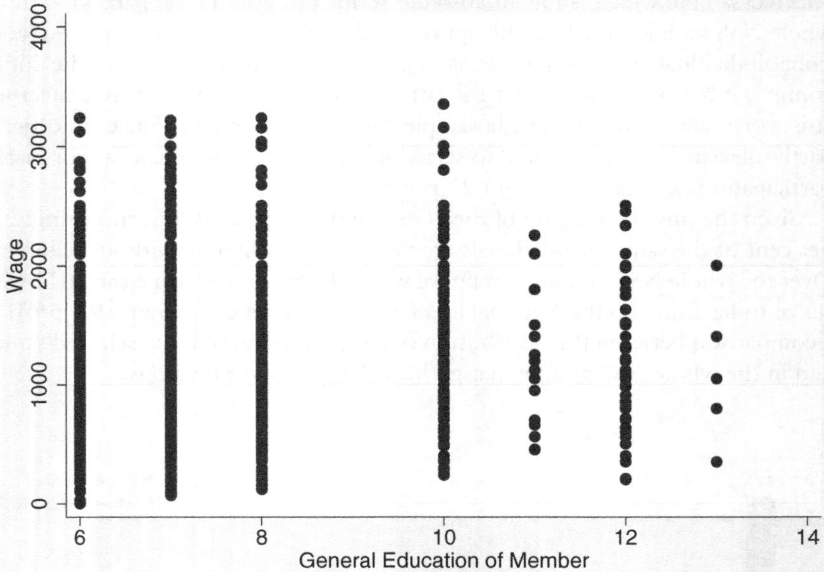

Figure 9.2 Wage distribution per educational levels

Source: Authors' calculations based on the 68th round of the National Sample Survey (NSS).

Figure 9.2 displays the wage distribution per educational level.[3] No significant pattern emerges as there does not seem to be any significant correlation between wages and educational level.

Results

Column 1 of Table 9.1 presents the estimates for equation 1. The reference category as far as education is concerned is not literate or literate without formal schooling. Results from column (1) show that attending primary school only provides a return that is significantly different from 0 and estimated at 7 per cent which is low compared to the cost of schooling. Other levels of education do not generate returns statistically different from 0. The absence of a correlation between education and wage is what was observed in Figure 9.2. However, having received formal vocational training does provide a substantial return that is significantly different from 0 at a 1 per cent level of significance and estimated at 37 per cent.

The lack of return for any level of schooling could mean that any individual who passed primary school and received additional education can be deemed overeducated, as the acquired education does not yield any return. By this yardstick, we could estimate that at the national level, 55 per cent of the considered labourers are either overeducated or underemployed. However, formal vocational training appears as a good alternative to general education as it provides substantial returns. Yet vocational training probably requires a minimum level of education. Indeed, 54.7 per cent of the individuals who received formal vocational training completed either middle or secondary school, while only 17 per cent did not go beyond primary school. The productivity of education may therefore be conditional on having received formal vocational training. Column (2) of Table 9.1 displays the estimate when having received formal vocational training is interacted with the educational level. It is clear from the results that formal vocational training does provide similar kinds of returns for those who have had a basic level of education and those who achieved higher secondary. The extent of over-education is therefore, as far as the considered labourers are concerned, 55 per cent.

As mentioned earlier, we wish to investigate the extent of over-education with respect to the sectoral structure of states' GDP. Indeed, the results presented in Columns (1) and (2) are national averages that may hide regional disparities. Figure 9.3 displays the sectoral composition of states' GDP.

Column (3) of Table 9.1 estimates equation 1 adding the share of states' GDP accounted for by the industrial sector as a control, and clustering standard errors at the state level. It should, however, be emphasized that, on the one hand, the industrial sector encompasses four subsectors that are mining and quarrying,

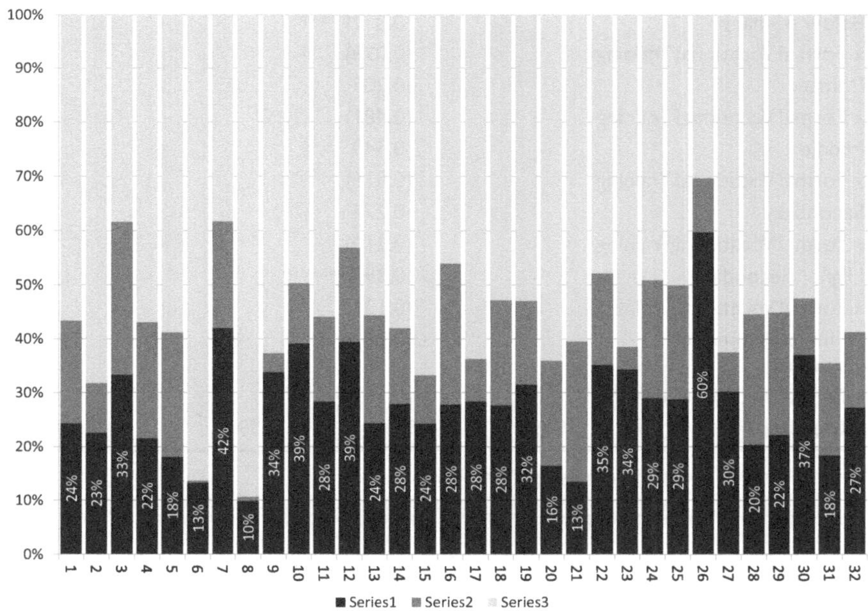

Figure 9.3 Share of sectors in states' GDP

Source: Authors' calculations based on data from the Ministry of Statistics and Programme Implementation (MOSPI).

Table 9.1 Eqn. (1) estimates: mining, quarrying, and manufacturing labourers

	(1)	*(2)*	*(3)*	*(4)*
	lnwage	*lnwage*	*lnwage*	*lnwage*
Below primary	0.0701^****	0.0699^**	0.0649	0.0379
	(0.036)	(0.036)	(0.048)	(0.032)
Primary	−0.00249	0.00197	−0.00107	−0.201
	(0.262)	(0.267)	(0.204)	(0.156)
Middle	0.0732	0.0759	0.0800	−0.152
	(0.261)	(0.266)	(0.213)	(0.160)
Secondary	0.144	0.151	0.150	−0.0683
	(0.262)	(0.267)	(0.217)	(0.173)
Higher secondary	0.0126	0.00998	0.0191	−0.0910
	(0.178)	(0.182)	(0.147)	(0.127)
At least diploma or	0.102	0.109	0.0959	−0.126
certificate (General)	(0.282)	(0.286)	(0.265)	(0.230)
At least diploma or	−0.173	−0.175	−0.179	−0.266^**
certificate (Technical)	(0.160)	(0.168)	(0.160)	(0.153)
Formal Vocational Training	0.368^******		0.365^******	0.0318
	(0.083)		(0.113)	(0.023)
Below primary		0.372^******		
x Formal Vocational Training		(0.038)		
Primary		−0.203		
x Formal Vocational Training		(0.481)		
Middle		0.340		
x Formal Vocational Training		(0.516)		
Secondary		−0.274		
x Formal Vocational Training		(0.210)		
Higher Secondary		0.393^******		
x Formal Vocational Training		(0.101)		
At least diploma or certificate		−0.247		
x Formal Vocational Training		(0.162)		
Observations	5939	5939	5939	5939

Source: All tables in this chapter are by the authors.

Standard errors (SE) in parentheses.

***, **, and * denote respectively significance at the 1 per cent, 5 per cent, and 10 per cent levels. Controls (not shown) include Age, Social Groups (SC, ST, OBC or other castes), level of experience and the sector (s)he is employed in. Column 3 includes the states share of GDP in the industrial sector. Column 4 includes state fixed effects. SEs in columns 3 and 4 are clustered at the state level.

manufacturing, construction, and utilities. On the other hand, we only consider in our restricted sample labourers employed in the first three subsectors. Results are little affected by this inclusion except that returns on the lowest level of education loses significance. In order to account for a wider set of states' characteristics, column (4) of Table 9.1 estimates equation 1 but adds state Fixed Effects and clustered standard errors at the state level. Returns from vocational training are not statistically different from 0 once state characteristics are accounted for.

Given that the industry sector has a broader definition than the selected sample (e.g. labourers employed in the utility sector are not included in the sample), controlling by the percentage of states' GDP derived from the industry may appear as a loose control. Moreover, employment in mining and quarrying is likely to be closely tied with states geographical characteristics such as the presence of natural resources. Therefore, we will focus on an even more restricted sample: labourers employed in the manufacturing sector. Table 9.2 reproduces Table 9.1 in the manufacturing sector only. The lack of variance prevented us

Table 9.2 Estimates of equation (1): manufacturing labourers

	(1)	*(2)*	*(3)*
	lnwage	*lnwage*	*lnwage*
Below primary	0.0614	0.0606	0.0467
	(0.082)	(0.081)	(0.067)
Primary	−0.267	−0.260	−0.246
	(0.469)	(0.280)	(0.256)
Middle	−0.256	−0.239	−0.277
	(0.465)	(0.271)	(0.236)
Secondary	−0.140	−0.128	−0.107
	(0.466)	(0.288)	(0.227)
Higher secondary	−0.241	−0.230	−0.257
	(0.324)	(0.199)	(0.212)
At least diploma or	−0.0501	−0.0422	0.0253
certificate (General)	(0.450)	(0.303)	(0.251)
At least diploma or	−0.328	−0.324	−0.325^**
certificate (Technical)	(0.254)	(0.210)	(0.184)
Formal Vocational Training	0.375^******	0.378^******	0.245^******
	(0.135)	(0.128)	(0.083)
Observations	813	813	813

Standard errors in parentheses.

***, **, and * denote respectively significance at the 1 per cent, 5 per cent, and 10 per cent levels. Controls are not shown. They include Age of the individual, Social Group (i.e. whether from a Scheduled Tribe, Scheduled Caste, OBC or other castes), his/her level of experience and the sector (s)he is employed in. Column 2 includes the states' share of GDP coming from the manufacturing sector. Column 3 includes state fixed effects. Standard errors in columns 2 and 3 are clustered at the state level.

from estimating returns of vocational training conditional on educational level. Thus column (2) of Table 9.2 is to be compared with column (3) of Table 9.1.

Results are similar to those obtained previously. Education beyond primary school does not generate any return, but vocational training does substantially, even after having accounted for states' share of GDP coming from manufacturing activities—column (2)— or state fixed effects. Given that any individual who received education beyond primary school, does not receive any return on it, he can be said to be overeducated, unless he was formally trained while in the labour market. Among labourers in the manufacturing sector, and following this definition, the proportion of overeducated individuals in the manufacturing sector is 66 per cent.

Table 9.3 displays the extent of over-education for 27 states and UTs as far as the mining, construction and manufacturing sectors are concerned (Column [1]) and for the sole manufacturing sector (column [2]).

Table 9.3 Statewise extent of over-education

% of sample overeducated		
State	*Industry*	*Manufacturing*
A and N Islands	11.1%	50.0%
Orissa	20.9%	
WB	21.5%	62.5%
Chandigarh	28.6%	
Bihar	34.5%	50.0%
Andhra Pradesh	34.8%	61.5%
Madhya Pradesh	39.1%	66.7%
J and K	42.0%	35.0%
Tamil Nadu	43.9%	71.7%
Gujarata	44.2%	74.5%
UP	44.6%	57.2%
Rajasthan	46.8%	53.4%
Karnataka	48.0%	61.8%
Delhi	48.8%	77.3%
Punjab	49.8%	60.6%
Tripura	53.1%	50.0%
Maharashtra	54.4%	77.3%
Haryana	56.9%	78.4%
Assam	57.1%	61.4%
Chattisgarh	57.3%	61.8%
Pondicherry	57.7%	85.7%
Kerala	60.9%	70.4%
Goa	63.3%	60.0%
Arunachal Pradesh	63.6%	75.0%
Uttaranchal	69.7%	
Meghalaya	79.6%	
Manipur	84.1%	60.0%

Scatterplots in Figures 9.4 and 9.5 indicate that there seems to be a positive relationship between the share of the industry (or manufacturing) in states' GDP and the extent of over-education. Indeed, the correlation is found to be 0.57 and 0.52 for the industry and manufacturing sectors, respectively. It should be emphasized that the extent of over-education that has been presented so far is based on national averages. This may hide wide regional disparities. Indeed if there is a relationship between the education level of labourers and the size of

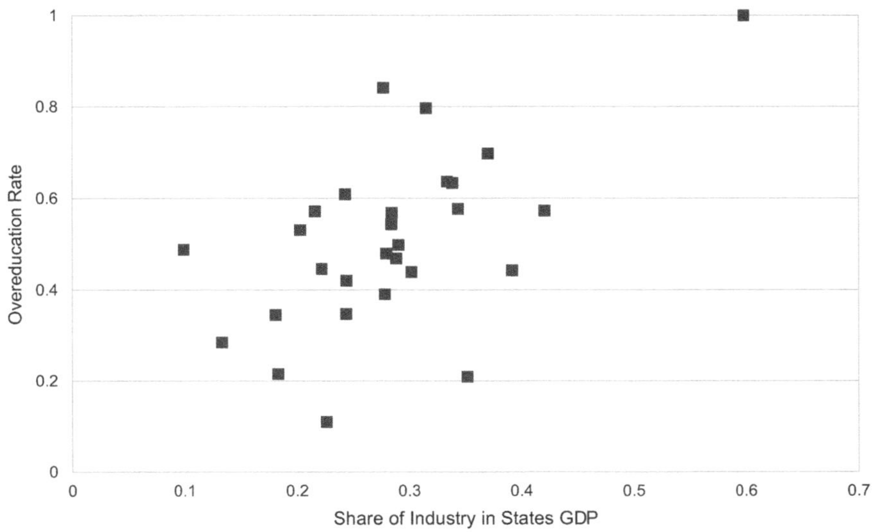

Figure 9.4 Share of industry in states' GDP and over-education

Source: Authors' calculations based on the 68th round of the National Sample Survey (NSS).

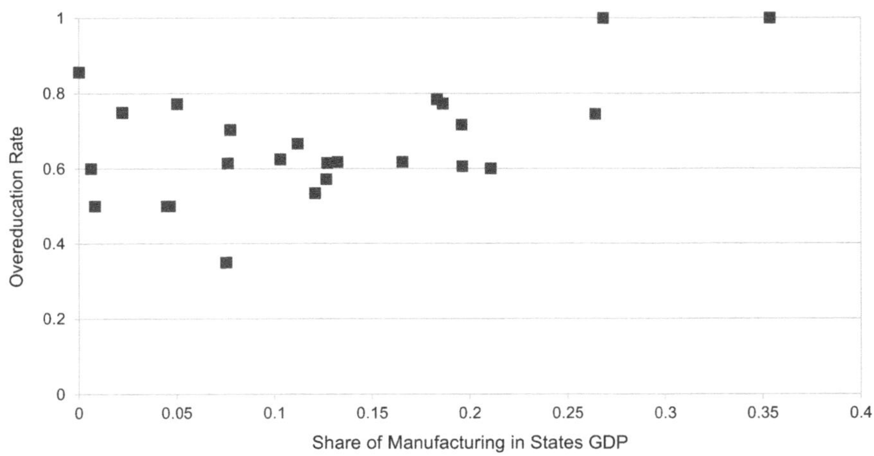

Figure 9.5 Share of manufacturing in states' GDP and over-education

Source: Authors' calculations based on the 68th round of the National Sample Survey (NSS).

the sectors they are employed in, as suggested by Figures 9.4 and 9.5, such a relationship may come from the fact that as the size of a sector grows, so do the returns on education. Thus, we would have had overestimated the extent of over-education. As prima facie evidence that returns on education may vary depending on the size of the sector, Table 9.4 shows the result when the effect of vocational training is made conditional on the size of the sector.

Results from Table 9.4 confirm that the high returns provided by vocational training are mainly found when the size of either the industrial or manufacturing sectors is not too large with respect to agriculture and services. Formal vocational training appears as a good alternative to general education and could reduce over-education. The difference between industrialized and non-industrialized

Table 9.4 Conditional Estimates of equation (1): manufacturing labourers

	(1)	*(2)*
	lnwage	*lnwage*
Below primary	0.0655	0.0607
	(0.048)	(0.081)
Primary	−0.0261	−0.306
	(0.197)	(0.278)
Middle	0.0565	−0.284
	(0.201)	(0.268)
Secondary	0.125	−0.173
	(0.215)	(0.287)
Higher secondary	0.00236	−0.260
	(0.142)	(0.209)
At least diploma	0.0730	−0.0902
or certificate (General)	(0.259)	(0.303)
At least diploma	−0.166	−0.329
or certificate (Technical)	(0.163)	(0.210)
Formal Vocational Training	1.772^******	0.924^******
	(0.434)	(0.208)
Formal Vocational Training	−5.196^******	
x % Industry	(1.571)	
	(1.058)	
Formal Vocational Training		−3.431^******
x % Manufacturing		(1.070)
Observations	5939	813

Standard errors in parentheses.

***, **, and * denote respectively significance at the 1 per cent, 5 per cent, and 10 per cent levels. Controls are not shown. They include age of the individual, social group (i.e. whether from a Scheduled Tribe, Scheduled Caste, OBC or other castes), his/her level of experience and the sector (s)he is employed in.

states that the chapter wants to highlight is that in the former, general education does provide a return, as individuals can learn from those who already have technical skills (spillovers), while when the industry is still developing, firms need technical skills as apriority.

Conclusion

As and when an economy matures, it needs to reshape its skill set by suitably identifying the skill types (education) that yield maximum returns to the society, the skills that help the economy to grow faster and channelize fiscal resources in the desired direction. Also, it is interesting to link the evolvement of the pattern of 'required skill sets' (e.g. vocational training vis-à-vis general education) along with the changing phases of economic growth, as reflected in the structural variations in the GDP across Indian States (68th round of NSS quinquennial survey on employment and unemployment in India). In contrast to the existing literature on estimating over-education, we use the 'returns to education' approach and define over-education as the proportion of labourers possessing education in excess of the education level that yields positive returns. In this chapter, we prove that the level of industrialization in a region has relation to the extent of over-education in that region. We show that the workers do not get any additional returns to education in general education beyond primary level but (formal) vocational training is found to yield strong returns in general for the nation. Not surprisingly, such returns are found to be higher for workers with higher levels of (general) education. While formal vocational training appears to be highly remunerative, high returns are mainly found when the size of either the industrial or manufacturing sectors is not too large. On the other hand, general education starts paying off in heavily industrialized states, while formal vocational training is not significantly correlated with higher wages. The policy implication might be that formal vocational training appears as a good alternative to general education and could reduce over-education in states that are less industrialized and are in transition. We find that the estimates of skill mismatch are huge. This has mainly two-pronged policy implications: to look through the labour market policies at the sub-national level, which comprises skill development initiatives, and to provide a big-push to states' industrialization pace. Since education policy is in the concurrent list taking cue from their skill-mismatch levels, states need to step-in to suitably shape their education policy. Given that vocational training gives a positive return in states with low level of industrialization, whereas it is the general education that yields better returns for the industrialized peers, aligning educational investments in sync with the industry demand will make it more productive.

A couple of caveats should be added. First, over-education has been estimated based on educational returns computed at the national level. However, the fact that returns to vocational training may be conditional on the size of the sector indicates that returns to education may be heterogeneous across regions. Second, the effect of the size of either the manufacturing or the industrial sectors may stem from the fact that these regions have been industrialized for some time, concomitantly to a limited supply of educated workers. Therefore, returns to education are particularly low in these areas, dragging the overall returns down. This calls for an analysis of the cohorts.

Notes

1 We assume wages correspond to marginal productivity. Hence, if an additional year of education is not remunerated it is assumed not to be productive with respect to the job. Second, if an individual settled for a job that does not provide a return to his education, it is because he was not able to get a job more appropriate to his level of education. In both cases he is overqualified. Mehta et al. (2012, *Economics of Education Review*) follows a similar approach.
2 The exclusion of females reduces the sample by 15.3 per cent. It is worth emphasizing the fact that the average level of education for women is significantly different from that of men by 1, 64 years.
3 The initial distribution contained 118 outliers out of 6,691 observations. These outliers lay more than 4.5 standard deviations away from the mean. They have been taken out from the sample.

References

Borghans, L., & de Grip, A. (Eds.) (2000). *The overeducated worker? The economics of skill utilization*. Cheltenham: Edward Elgar.
Cedefop (2010). *The skill matching challenge: Analysing skill mismatch and policy implications*. Publications Office of the European Union, Luxembourg.
Cedefop (2015a). *Skills, qualifications and jobs in the EU: The making of a perfect match?: Evidence from Cedefop's European skills and jobs survey*. Cedefop Reference Series 3072. Publications Office of the European Union, Luxembourg.
Cedefop (2015b). *Skill shortages and gaps in European enterprises*. Cedefop Reference Series 3071. Publications Office of the European Union, Luxembourg.
Cedefop (2015c). *Tackling unemployment while addressing skill mismatch: Lessons from policy and practice in EU countries*. Cedefop Research Papers No. 5546. Publications Office of the European Union, Luxembourg.
McGuinness, S. (2006). Overeducation in the labour market. *Journal of Economic Surveys*, 20(3), 387–418.
McGuinness, S., Pouliakas, K., & Redmond, P. (2017). *How useful is the concept of skill mismatch?* IZA Discussion Paper Series No. 10786. Institute of Labour Economics (IZA), Bonn.
Mehta, A., Felipeb, J., Quisingb, P., & Camingueb, S. (2012). Overeducation in developing economies: How can we test for it, and what does it mean? *Economics of Education Review*, 30(6), 1334–1347.
Quintini, G. (2011). *Over-qualified or under-skilled: A review of existing literature*. OECD Social, Employment and Migration Working Papers No. 121. OECD Publishing, France.
Thurow, L. C. (1975). *Generating inequality*. New York: Basic Books.

Part III

Education and skill formation

Chapter 10

India's National Skills Qualifications Framework and employment

The promise and the reality

Santosh Mehrotra[1]

Some 100 countries are either developing or implementing a National Vocational Qualifications Framework (NVQF) to streamline Technical and Vocational Education and Training (TVET) systems and to enhance the value of TVET by providing training based on occupational standards. India is one of those countries, which began its journey to develop the National Vocational Education Qualifications Framework in 2011, when the MHRD constituted a task force to draft the framework.[2]

NVQFs are an Anglo-Saxon phenomenon, programmes largely focusing on industry's or the employer's need for skilled manpower rather than preparing people for specific occupations. The latter programmes were explicitly shunned in the other major global model for TVET systems—the Germanic model—which is of much older vintage and is also proven to have been very successful in transforming Germany into a manufacturing superpower over a 150-year period. The Anglo-Saxon model is of much younger vintage, barely going back around four decades. The other big difference between the two was that while the German model evolved over the period of the first, second, and third industrial revolutions quite organically, the Anglo-Saxon was 'constructed'. We in India decided (in 2011) to adopt the Anglo-Saxon one, given the fashion that was emerging around the developing world. The Anglo-Saxon conception of TVET has also influenced the TVET policy of the European Union.

The literature around the NVQFs is elaborate, particularly on the issues around the adoption of the framework in a highly formalized workforce, such as in the United Kingdom, where it had taken decades, after much tweaking, to come to a level of maturity and acceptance. India, on the other hand, is a unique case due to the following reasons: (1) India's GDP growth rate had increased sharply in the new millennium, and employers were facing significant shortages of skills;[3] and (2) India's TVET system was in its infancy, extremely narrowly based, and seriously failing to deliver the vocational skills that met the requirements of the second-fastest-growing economy in the world. Implementing a vocational qualifications framework, hence, was not going to be easy in the circumstances. Around 2010, there were only industrial training institutes (ITIs) of the 1950s that were offering any TVET—under 4,000 of them (with private- and

DOI: 10.4324/9781003158349-13

public-sector ITIs accounting for equal proportions). Other than these, there were plenty of small, unregistered, private and unregulated skill providers spread across the urban landscape but offering very poor-quality training through short duration courses. To make matters worse, India had barely managed to achieve 74 per cent literacy by 2011, so a quarter of the workforce was illiterate and another half barely had a primary education. Worse still, there was little consensus among the policymakers on how the narrowly based TVET provision was to evolve, how it would grow in terms of quantity, and how provision of quality was to be ensured to the beneficiaries. An NVQF seemed to be the answer to these questions, at least to the extent that it would focus the attention of all those who were concerned with the situation just described. The National Skill Development Policy 2009 had mentioned the need for creating a qualification framework for India. There was a need for bringing all the key stakeholders on the same platform, so that there would be common understanding among stakeholders about what could be a way forward for expanding the TVET provision with quality. The NVQF could serve as one such platform.

The Ministry of Human Resource Development of the Union government took the lead and came up with National Vocational Education Qualifications Framework (NVEQF), which was formally launched in a few schools of Haryana in 2012. However, not to be deterred, the Ministry of Labour and Employment (which felt that this was their domain)[4] prepared its own NVQF. After two years of dialogue, mediated by the Planning Commission, the two ministries came to an agreement that both the NVEQF and NVQF will be subsumed in the National Skills Qualifications Framework (NSQF), which was officially notified as government policy in December 2013.[5] It is another matter that, as we argue in this chapter, how it was implemented changed its character dramatically from what was proposed by the MHRD Task Force. The sharp divergence between the promise and the reality is the subject of this chapter.

India's TVET system, by international standards, is at a very rudimentary level of development at the beginning of the third decade of the new century. TVET was a relatively neglected subject in India's educational planning, at least until the beginning of the 11th Five Year Plan (2007–2012) (Planning Commission, 2008). The rapid growth rate of the economy in the years since economic reforms resulted in a growing demand for better-skilled workers. India's planning apparatus had to respond. There was relatively limited access to TVET, mainly through approximately 4,000 industrial training institutes (roughly equally divided between the public and private sectors), and some other ministries offering some short-term courses (Planning Commission, 2013). The unorganized sector merely offered unpaid and unstructured apprenticeships of poor quality, which were unregulated. Of the private organized sector, which in any case accounts for a minuscule proportion of all non-agricultural enterprises in the economy, only 16 per cent in 2009 offered in-firm, enterprise-based training. There was practically no VET being offered in schools, and at the tertiary level there were a few thousand polytechnics and colleges. Apart from that, there were the technical institutes offering courses in pharmacy, hotel management, engineering, or management—supposedly regulated by the All India Council of Technical Education (AICTE). In addition, there was a multitude of small private skills providers, totally unregulated and offering courses of varying lengths, with no quality control or uniformity in course content or duration.

In other words, TVET provision in the country conformed to no particular model or vision. Only 2.3 per cent of the workforce had formally acquired any VET, according to the National Sample Survey Office (NSSO) in 2004–2005, a number which did not change when the NSSO did the same exercise in 2011–2012. This was the situation at the beginning of the second decade of the new millennium. (Unfortunately, the situation has not changed much in 2017–2018, as PLFS reports, with 2.4 per cent of the workforce having achieved formal VET.)

In response to the new and emerging demands of skilled manpower, the Government of India began investing in TVET, and the ecosystem has evolved and grown. The most important changes are the following. First, the National Skill Development Corporation (NSDC) was set up with two purposes: (1) to incubate private Vocational Training Providers (VTPs) offering short-term courses (of no more than 3–4 months); and (2) to incubate Sector Skills Councils, as industry-employer representatives of the private sector (in much the same way as other Anglo-Saxon countries have Sector Skill Councils). Second, the number of private ITIs has expanded: they grew from under 2,000 in 2007 to 11,000 or more by 2017. The expansion of public ITIs was very limited: from 1,896 to about 2,500 in 2017. Third, other than the Ministry of Labour and Employment (which oversaw ITIs) and the Ministry of Human Resource Development (which oversaw vocational education programmes in a few thousand senior secondary schools), very few ministries had offered VET courses through the schemes or programmes. There was limited activity by the Ministry of Rural Development and the Ministry of Micro, Small, Medium Enterprises for promoting VET. What transpired since 2007 is that a total of 20 or more ministries have initiated some small-scale training of short-duration nature. This further fragmented the total TVET provision in the country. Fourth, after the NSQF initiative, the MHRD introduced vocational subjects along with the general education subjects in Classes 9 to 12. This was recommended in the NVEQF document that vocational education should start earlier than class 11 (which was hitherto the case). These vocational subjects are aligned to the job roles classified in the NSQF from levels 1 to 4. Fifth, the in-house enterprise-based training expanded somewhat in the organized sector; a World Bank survey of enterprises in 2014 reported that 36 per cent of all registered enterprises were conducting in-house training. However, the majority of these enterprises were large corporations, while the Small and Medium Enterprises (SMEs) tended to ignore such in-house training. So these were the five pillars of the TVET 'system' by 2014, if one can call it that. This was the ecosystem to which the NSQF was meant to be applied.

This chapter has four sections. In the first section, we spell out what the goals of the National Skills Qualifications Framework (NSQF) are intended to be, both at the secondary, as well as the tertiary level. In the following section we examine the reality of what the NSQF has turned out to be as it got implemented, for any level of education or training. The next section examines the international evidence with Vocational Qualification Frameworks, both in rich as well as emerging market economies, where we discuss the literature to see if NVQFs have made any contribution to the evolution of education or skill systems. In the final section, we review briefly efforts of the government in respect of expanding TVET at the tertiary level, and the role of NSQF in it. More importantly, we present a case study of a new degree, a bachelor in vocational education (which University Grants Commission has promoted widely) at the tertiary level, but we focus on a case where it is working successfully and has gone to scale. However, we note that the contribution of the NSQF in this case appears limited, if it exists at all.

TVET challenges that NSQF could have addressed

Given the level of fragmentation of TVET (even within the public sector), it was not surprising that it was felt that a NSQF might focus the attention of policymakers on the subject of TVET. It was felt that TVET in India faced many challenges, which could perhaps be addressed within the ambit of NSQF, even though many of these problems were long-standing ones and could possibly have been addressed even without NSQF.

Lack of uniformity in qualifications across institutions

In general academic education, despite the common National Curriculum Framework (NCF), 2005 for schools, designed at the national level by National Council of Educational Research and Training (NCERT), there are reasonable variations in the level and standard of courses and programmes offered by various examination boards and educational institutions. However, the general academic curriculum at the secondary level is not at issue here. The issue is the variations in introduction of vocational subjects as compulsory or elective or in the secondary or higher secondary stage. The Central Board of Secondary Education (CBSE) and some State Boards are still running the vocational courses at the higher secondary stage (classes 11 and 12), introduced under the erstwhile centrally sponsored scheme of vocationalization of secondary education 1988. In some states, outdated two-year vocational courses are still being implemented and in most of these courses the enrolment is too low to justify their existence and benefits to the stakeholders. There is now some uniformity in place across programmes, at least within the secondary or higher secondary school system, which could possibly be attributed to the introduction of the NSQF since 2013. Vocational subjects aligned to the job roles pegged at NSQF levels 1–4 are being offered in Classes 9–12. However, it is uncertain if the same uniformity could not have been achieved in the absence of the NSQF. As we discuss later, China has uniformity across the nation without any NVQF.

In the absence of a national level approach to TVET planning, the courses and programmes in TVET a decade ago lacked uniformity in terms of duration, entry requirements for the course/programme, and nomenclature of qualification across institutions. For example, in the plumbing sector, the duration for the 'Certificate' course in Plumbing/ Sanitary Hardware Fitter/Plumber through the face-to-face mode in different institutions is two years, one year, six months, and four months, and the entry requirement also differed and could range from senior secondary certificate fail to Class 10th pass. There is not much difference on the ground even now, since the NSQF came into existence in December 2013.

In addition, the private-sector training institutions were offering VET according to their own curriculum. The main change that has come about is that NSDC, started to incubate private vocational training providers (VTPs), which began offering short-term courses in accordance with the requirements of the NSQF. However, the vast majority of private VTPs remain nearly as unregulated, as we noted in the introduction of this chapter (see Expert Group, 2017).[6] As a result, there are wide variations in the quality of training imparted through these institutions. This lack of uniformity is not good for the credibility of the VTPs or for the potential employers, since the latter cannot make out what competencies the certificate holder brings to the job.

The contrast with course curriculum design in China across the entire country is worth noting. After completing nine years of compulsory general academic education, nearly half the children enter senior secondary vocational schools in China's government system, the remaining half going into the general academic senior secondary stream. The course curriculum in the vocational senior secondary schools is split as follows: one third consists of general academic subjects common across the country; another third consists of a national common curriculum for the vocational subjects; the remaining third also relates to the vocational subject, but is determined locally in accordance with local needs and demand. Thus, there is need for uniformity across the country, with some space for local variations to suit the local needs of the region (Mehrotra et al., 2015). In addition, competencies must be defined for each level, so that a level actually specifies the ability to perform a job role. It does not appear that we have managed to achieve improvement in this regard.

Lack of clear recognized pathways of learning

The National Policy on Education 1986 envisaged vocational courses at the tertiary level for facilitating vertical mobility of students of the senior secondary level. However, with the introduction of the centrally sponsored scheme of vocationalization of secondary education in 1988, the vocational education programme in schools became terminal in nature, as they were designed to impart skills without any provision for vertical mobility and therefore they became dead ends. One of the factors responsible for the low demand for vocational education in schools was the lack of opportunities for vocational students for professional growth and educational advancement, as they were not studying the general education subjects. Provision for vertical mobility of the students was not available for the majority of vocational courses at the senior secondary level, although some states, like Kerala, made provision for general education subjects along with the vocational subjects to provide vertical mobility to vocational students.

Vertical mobility has been made possible since the implementation of the vocational education programme in schools under Samagra Shiksha. After the completion of senior secondary, a vocational student can enter the bachelor of vocational studies (B. Voc.) programme at the tertiary level, provided that the student has cleared the NSQF level 4. But there is still no vertical mobility for the vocational students of ITIs, even though some provision has been made for clearing general education subjects through open and distance learning system. Third, from the short-term courses (of 3–4 months) offered by institutions under various ministries or NSDC-funded private VTPs there is no scope for vertical mobility.

Lack of credibility among stakeholders

TVET, unlike general education, is supposed to lead to a certain level of competence to perform tasks in an occupation. Although a notion of competency has been introduced in the school vocational education programmes, introduced since 2014 in a few thousand secondary and higher secondary schools in India, that does not mean there is any means of testing actual competency, let alone employability.

One of the problems that TVET currently faces is that it suffers from low esteem. The vocational education system in secondary schools has very little credibility among employers, students, and parents because the quality of instruction is poor, there is lack of sufficient industry based internship, lack of industry participation in curriculum development and implementation, and in most of the vocational courses, industry is not involved in the process of certification of competencies. Low esteem of vocational education is a global phenomenon. However, that does not prevent half of all Chinese youth at age 15 (after completing the compulsory nine years of general academic education) from entering the vocational stream at the senior secondary level (Mehrotra et al., 2015). That is primarily because the employability of such vocational education students is high. If the vocational education is of good quality and involves the private sector in its design, the prospects of getting a job with a handsome salary would increase and it will make vocational education aspirational (quite unlike India).

In India, there is rather little evidence to suggest that VET has resulted in a wage premium (or a wage advantage) when compared to those who did not undergo VET, although in recent years there has been a substantial increase in the wages of the middle-level skilled manpower, but only because of the shortage of such manpower (Roy, 2008). However, Ranjan (2021) finds that in wage employment, as opposed to self-employment, there is indeed a wage premium of formal vocational education/training. In any case, the NSQF's potential contribution to this possible development still remains unclear.

Lack of horizontal mobility

There should also be the possibility of horizontal mobility so that the students from the vocational stream are able to enter the general education stream, if they so desire. The challenge, therefore, is to create a new system of secondary and higher secondary education where all students gets an opportunity to develop vocational skills along with academic skills. Vocational education in the schools should, therefore, be offered as a compulsory vocational subject.

The NSQF, which was piloted in a small number of schools in Haryana, is being generalized.[7] However, there is no transition possible in the way the school or tertiary education system has evolved since the introduction of the NSQF. It is not a suggestion that this kind of transition is easy to organize in any educational system. To do it in as rigid and rule-bound a system as India's has proved to be impossible, not that it has been attempted. Most importantly, it will require both the general and vocational education systems in secondary schools to shift to a credit-based semester system, as opposed to the current prevailing system of one-year courses, with an end-of-year examination. In addition, the assessment and evaluation system needs to be drastically modified to suit the requirements of competency-based assessment and certification in vocational education. It will also be useful in designing and implementing skill-training programmes if employers were seriously involved in this task, so that the competencies required to perform on the job are clearly specified. The employers would know the competencies possessed by the candidates applying for the job and can also suitably place them on the job. However, such employer engagement has not materialized under the SSC-based system (see Expert Group to the MSDE, 2017).

We noted earlier that there are five pillars of the TVET ecosystem in India. Among them, only the ITIs have succeeded in 2014 to introduce a semester system (Mehrotra et al., 2014). The credit-based system has several unique features: (1) ability to match students' scholastic needs and aspirations; (2) inter-institution transferability of students (following the completion of a semester); (3) part-completion of an academic programme in the institution of enrolment and part-completion in a specialized (and recognized) institution; (4) flexibility for working students to complete the programme over an extended period of time; and (5) standardization and comparability of educational programmes across the country. Very importantly, the credit-based semester will allow students unable to continue in the education system to exit, join the labour market, and later return to resume his or her course if he or she so wishes. This is the meaning of multi-entry and multi-exit that NSQF was supposed to enable.

Unfortunately, no credit-based teaching has evolved in schools (or any of the other pillars of skills ecosystem, since they only offer short-term courses). So the principle of modularity (and a credit-based system, which we had proposed in 2011), and thus the potential for multi-entry and exit has fallen by the wayside.

No formal recognition of informal (prior) learning

India has had a long history of informal apprenticeships in the presence of a craftsmen or a senior technician. However, the problem has been that there is no certification (recognition) for such learning, which disadvantages the worker in the labour market and constrains labour mobility between jobs. The Indian education system so far has been planned and organized primarily to cater to the needs of the organized sector, which employs only 22 per cent of the workforce (Mehrotra et al., 2014). A majority of workers in the unorganized sector have low levels of literacy, as they have left school at early stages of education. They face difficulty in returning to schools or training institutions to improve their skills, as the education or TVET system does not facilitate them to do so. Being adults, such skilled but older youth may feel stigmatized if they return to a regular school. That is why in China's TVET system, there are Adult Schools, which accommodate them. India may well consider using the infrastructure of existing secondary schools for adults, after normal school hours in a second shift, so that such adults have access to Recognition of Prior Learning (RPL) through such courses.

In 2011, Mehrotra et al. (2012) had written: 'The NSQF can facilitate the recognition of informal learning. For example, skills acquired at the workplace could be formally certified through an awarding body. The NSQF can provide opportunities to the people working in the unorganized sector to gain recognition of their competencies for national and international mobility or join the formal education and training system. This will be one of the most important contributions to inclusiveness in Indian society that the NSQF can make'.

The importance of RPL was recognized for the first time in National Skills Policy 2015. It noted that 400 million workers were to be trained between 2015 and 2022, of which 300 mn were to be provided RPL. There was no particular strategy laid out to extend RPL to these 300 million who were already in the workforce. The result has been that RPL has been provided as part of Pradhan Mantri Kaushal Vikas Yojana (PMKVY), but all that is done is to certify the informal worker in a matter of a day in most cases. In some cases, RPL takes a little longer. But there is no clear thinking with regard to how RPL should be imparted.[8]

Input-based traditional education system that promotes rote learning

Input based or traditional education is all about what resources have been placed at the disposal of the students. Classes in schools and colleges have grown, but the educational materials and delivery systems have changed only slightly. The major learning modes in schools and universities are lectures and textbooks; as a result, there is lot of emphasis on rote learning rather than experiential learning. The explicit assumption (see NSQF Notification of December 2013) was that such input-based learning, at least in TVET, would be replaced by a Competency Based Curriculum (CBCs).

For NSQF to succeed, new curricula would have had to be developed by the Pandit Sundarlal Sharma Central Institute of Vocational Education (PSS-CIVE), Bhopal, National Institutes of Technical Teacher Training and Research (NITTTR), CBSE, and State Boards would have to evolve towards competency-based curriculum and assessment. Similarly, Central Staff Training and Research Institute (CSTARI), Kolkata, and National Instructional Media Institute (NIMI) (the curriculum development institutions for ITI) would have been expected to create CBCs for the ITIs. Similarly, University Grants Commission (UGC) and universities would have to redesign their curriculum to develop CBCs.

A critical prerequisite for the success of NSQF would be the participation of industry representatives in the design and development of the curricula. Without this element, students graduating from vocational courses in schools will find no employment, which is the current problem with the TVET system. The NSDC funded Sector Skill Councils were supposed to provide this industry engagement, including participation in the curriculum development and implementation.

Unfortunately, instead of the focus being on developing CBCs associated with industry-required competencies being developed, what we got was the evolution of so-called National Occupation Standards (NOSs), four or five of which were combined together into Qualification Packs (QPs) corresponding to job roles. The preparation of these documents were supported by the newly created Ministry of Skill Development and Entrepreneurship (MSDE). Funds for preparing these NOS and QPs were transferred by MSDE to NSDC, which in turn were meant to transfer them to NSDC-funded SSCs. As Mehrotra et al. (2012) had noted, the NOSs were supposed to assist in achieving the following: Emphasis on learning outcomes, as opposed to inputs in qualifications descriptors:

> Every NOS will, therefore, be accompanied by a set of performance criteria which defines the outcomes of that NOS. This performance criteria define the curriculum, pedagogy, assessment and certification norms for achieving a particular NOS. NOS will be reviewed and updated in a 2–3 year cycle, therefore, it can assist in improving the quality of education and training programmes.
>
> (Mehrotra et al., p. 29–30)

Notice we do not even mention QPs. Notice also we specifically noted the need to define 'outcomes' by 'defining the curriculum, pedagogy, assessment and certification norms'. We even go so far as to specify the need to review and update NOSs. However, unfortunately none of what we had specified actually happened in reality between 2012 and 2020. How the NSQF actually got operationalized is discussed in the next section.

Operationalization of NSQF

The way the NVEQF got operationalized was as follows. There was an attempt to make levels in the VET system comparable to the grades (classes) of the general education system. There were to be levels in the VET system, starting with NVEQF level 1 at class 9 in school. The qualifications framework was to be implemented in the following manner:

> *Stage One:* NVEQ levels 1–4 will be implemented in schools/ITIs/Vocational Training Institutes (VTIs).
> *Stage Two:* NVEQ levels 5–7 were to be implemented in Polytechnics, Community Colleges, Colleges and Universities.

However, development of guidelines, in our original blueprint document (cited earlier as Mehrotra et al., 2012, which was written in May 2011 for the Ministry of Human Resource Development as the National Vocational Educational Qualification Framework), did not even mention bunching 4–5 NOSs into Qualification Packs. What it did discuss was development of competency-based curriculum (CBC) and training packages to be done simultaneously for all levels.

Subsequently, the NSQF was launched in December 2013, subsuming the NVEQF. The implementation schedule of the NSQF, as mentioned in the government notification, is as follows:

- Immediately on notification of NSQF

  All other Frameworks (NVEQF by MHRD in 2012 and NVQF by MoL&E in 2013) would be superseded by NSQF. NSQF compliant courses will receive government funding on preferential basis.
- After the 3rd anniversary date of NSQF notification (27th Dec 2016), government funding was only to be for NSQF compliant courses. All government funded training and educational institutions shall define eligibility criteria for admission to various courses in terms of NSQF levels. Recruitment rules of the GoI and PSUs of the Central government shall define eligibility criteria for all positions in terms of NSQF levels. State Government shall be encouraged to amend recruitment rules as well as those of their PSUs to define eligibility criteria for all positions in terms of NSQF levels.
- After the 5th anniversary date of the notification of the NSQF (27th Dec 2018), all training/educational programmes/courses to be NSQF-compliant. All training & educational institutions were to define eligibility criteria for admission to various courses in terms of NSQF levels.

The reality is that after three years (i.e. Dec 2016), most of the government-funded training institutions, which were to define eligibility criteria for admission in accordance with NSQF levels, did not manage to do so. Even the recruitment rules of most of the government or public undertakings were not modified to suit the eligibility for the various positions in accordance with NSQF levels. Not surprisingly, the December 2018 deadline for all training/education programmes being NSQF-compliant was not met. The date has been extended (with an indefinite terminal date).

The process of preparing the NOS/QP is seriously problematic. According to the information (provided to Expert Group report to MSDE, 2017, of which this author was a member and part-drafted its report) the following process is undertaken in making QP/NOS:

> Stage 1: The SSC (or Sector Skill Council) Governing Council appoints NOS Sub-Committee and issues request for proposal for contractors/consultants and by technical and financial bids appoints the contractor (usually an international consultancy like Price Waterhouse Coopers, McKinsey, Deloitte, Ernst & Young). The NOS Sub-committee undertakes stakeholder analysis and planning and appoints a sector expert group to advise on content.
>
> Stage 2: The contractor prepares industry occupational map. The NOS subcommittee agrees on priority areas. The contractor then undertakes functional analysis.
>
> Stage 3: The contractor then prepares first draft along with sector expert group. The contractor and the SSC get industry validation through industry networks. The SSC then notifies the drafts for comment on SSC website. The contractor analyses feedback and prepares final draft. The NOS Sub-committee follows the SSC quality assurance process.
>
> Stage 4: The NOS Sub-committee prepares case for approval and submits to NSDC (National Skill Development Corporation). The NSDC QRC (Quality Review Committee) secretariat undertakes quality control process and convenes Qualification Registration Committee. They then make QP and NOSs available for final comment on the website. The QPs and NOSs are thereafter entered in the National Qualification Register'.

It should be obvious that the development of standards is not underpinned by any in-depth research and adequate consultation; this is also evident from the rather limited use of these standards by industry. Nor are they seen as being very useful by tertiary level institutions (as we shall see in later parts of this chapter). The present pattern of consultation with industry, which basically involves seeking their inputs or reactions to a document presented to them, does not make for an intensive involvement. However, the problem with the approach in India is the following. There is no real substitute for industry being directly involved in framing standards, where industry experts, along with domain experts in training and education, sit together and develop standards. This is the process that is being followed, for instance, in Bangladesh, where, not surprisingly, the process takes a long time, and the country has managed to produce a very small number of NOSs (Mehrotra, 2019). The standards so developed are likely to have greater acceptance and buy-in by the industry and will also be pedagogically on a sound basis.

Teachers and trainers

Mehrotra et al. (2012) discussed the nature of radical reform needed in TVET in order to revive the sector. One of the major reforms in the TVET sector is that the vocational teachers and trainers will have to prepare their students for the new realities of the workplace and labour market by ensuring that competencies imparted to them are attuned to labour market requirements.

> Currently there is a severe shortage of teachers and trainers in TVET. There are several colleges and universities, which conduct teacher education programmes, both in the government and private sector, but very few of them have included vocational education as one of the component of the in-service syllabus. However, there are no competency standards for training teachers, trainers and instructors. A completely new approach is needed for pre-service and in-service vocational education or teacher development, which should be linked to the concept of mechanism of recognition of competencies rather than just the qualifications. Teacher education curricula and programmes will have to be redesigned to respond adequately to the demands for new teachers and trainers for transaction of competency units for the various skill qualifications. A shift must take place in training programmes to make the teaching-learning process more student-centric through participatory workshop experiences, project work and assignments.
>
> (Mehrotra et al., 2012)

Mehrotra et al. (2012) had also noted:

> Three different types of teachers and trainers would be needed for effective transaction of competency units: (a) teachers and trainers for general, cultural or scientific subjects (for example, language, environmental education, information and communication technology, health science, entrepreneurship development, sustainable development, rural development, etc.); (b) teachers and trainers for specialized theory (for explaining scientific principles, facts and figures, etc.); and (c) instructors for vocational practice (for example, operation of tools, equipment, machines, safety aspects, etc.).

We have no evidence to suggest that such requirements were met.

Teachers must be required to spend time in industry, doing practical training, on a regular basis as in China (Mehrotra et al., 2015). In senior secondary vocational schools (as also at tertiary levels of vocational education), teachers in China require at least two months every two years in practical training in an industry.

This in-service regular training is in addition to the fact that each teacher in senior secondary vocational schools must also be a graduate in a discipline he or she teaches apart from having a pedagogic qualification. This situation is superior to the one prevailing in India, where senior vocational secondary school teachers often lack basic qualifications, are not in regular positions (but in ad hoc or contractual posts), and certainly in ITIs have often received their training in ITIs themselves (see Mehrotra, 2014 for details). Such teachers simply lack the capability to teach effectively and impart practical-level competency to their students/ trainees. We have little evidence to suggest that any such radical reforms in teacher training have been put into place. In other words, an essential prerequisite of TVET reform was never really met in the six years since NSQF was implemented.

Implementation of vocational qualifications frameworks internationally: what does the evidence reveal?

In reality, there is no evidence from international experience to suggest that NVQF can be formulated quickly, let alone rolled out across the whole TVET system speedily. It is also not evident that the NVQF in any country has proven to be a means for creating what is called a flexible, open, accessible, and responsive workforce development system.

Policymakers and donors continue to support national qualifications frameworks and competence-based training systems, with the hope that they will improve the ways in which education and training programmes prepare people for work, help them to obtain jobs, and enable them to perform well at work. At least 142 countries are developing a framework and six major world regions are developing regional qualifications frameworks, with a view to supporting labour market mobility (ETF et al., 2013). A report from UNESCO (Keevy & Chakroun, 2015) proposes the development of world reference levels for qualifications, with similar aims. For example, the Bangladesh National Skill Development Policy 2011 seems to have had many expectations of the National Technical and Vocational Qualifications Framework (NTVQF), which began to be conceptualized in 2011. For instance, 'The NTVQF will expand the number of qualifications available in the country to better reflect the growing and changing occupational and skill profiles in both domestic and international labour markets' (Clause 5.2 of NSDP 2011).

The question is: Has this expansion happened? If so, how much? When we raised this question in Bangladesh, we learnt that a small number of standards under the NTVQF have been agreed upon among the stakeholders (Mehrotra, 2019). What is heartening is that the process of arriving at these standards is rigorous, and hence it has also been rightly time-consuming. The result is that only a small number of standards have been approved and implemented. However, the matter does not end there. We also learnt at the Bureau of Manpower and Training (BMET) that only 500 certified trainers exist as of late 2018, a good seven years since the implementation of the NTVQF began. It is understood that Bangladesh (a country that has one-seventh the population and workforce of India) needs 1,800 such trainers just for the current NTVQF courses. As the number of such courses grows, the number of qualified trainers will grow further. As it is, there is a serious shortage of properly qualified trainers for non-NTVQF courses (the same problem that besets India's TVET). The issues with implementation of the NTVQF do not end there. International experience from South Africa, Australia, and India suggests strongly that it has taken years for acceptance among industry employers of such standards for any trade for any particular level.

India and Bangladesh and most developing countries are characterized by a highly informalized economy. The only countries in the world that have seriously attempted the implementation of a NVQF are now industrialized countries; all highly formalized economies and most enterprises are formal sector ones, and almost all workers have formal conditions of work. So is India's NSQF going to be implemented only for the formal sector of the workforce, which accounts for a minuscule proportion of the total workforce? If it is going to extend to the unorganized sector enterprises, how will their views be taken on board? Unorganized enterprises which are registered with the government account for 97% of all enterprises in the non-farm sector.

Moreover, there is a plethora of international evidence that suggests that the benefits of NVQFs have been overstated, that their implementation in developing countries leaves very much to be desired, and that in the best of cases, their implementation is a work in progress (Allais, 2010; Pilcher et al., 2015).[9] Drawing from this evidence, we present the major findings of an international study that investigates the labour market outcomes of qualifications frameworks in six countries—Belize, France, Ireland, Jamaica, Sri Lanka, and Tunisia, as well as the regional framework in the Caribbean. The study finds limited evidence of success. Allais (2017) argues that the French framework, where labour markets are highly formalized, the most regulated, and collective bargaining had the widest reach, had the clearest relationships between qualifications and work. However, the qualifications framework did not seem to be the cause, but rather the effect of such relationships.

We will reflect on why policymakers and international organizations continue to push this policy that continues not to work. Raffe (2012), in a recent overview, argues that the evidence, while still inconclusive, shows that the impacts of qualifications frameworks have been less than expected, have often taken many years to appear, and have been negative as well as positive. A 16-country study commissioned by the International Labour Organisation (ILO) argued that qualifications frameworks have not provided quick-fix or simple solutions to the complex problems facing countries in relation to education, skills development, and employment (Allais, 2010).

The disconnect between empirical evidence and policymaker aspiration could partly be the result of the nebulous nature of frameworks; as a paper by Pilcher et al. (2015) argues, it is almost impossible to evaluate them because there is no way of developing a clear yardstick for measurement. It is well known that there is an enormous amount of consultancy opportunities around the development and implementation of such frameworks, especially given that much of the positive documentation comes from organizations involved in their development (for example, Cedefop 2013, 2015; European Training Foundation et al., 2013).

Research with a positive take tends to describe the QF rather than evaluate. What the literature rarely does is examine the alternative model to the Anglo-Saxon one in the world for TVET: The Germanic one (practiced not only in Germany, but also Austria and Switzerland). From a developing country policymaker's perspective, both emanate from now-industrialized countries, making both of them directly much less applicable to highly informalized economies in the developing world. However, the interesting point of relevance for developing countries is that Germany has built the most successful TVET system in the world, underpinning its manufacturing superpower status for 175 years, without any qualifications framework. Similarly, China has one of the most successful TVET systems operating for at least three decades since the economic reforms, and it has underpinned China's industrial strategy; however, it does not rely on an explicit qualifications framework.[10] The Chinese state regulates a vast network of institutions, essentially with the Township and County governments (or the rural and urban local bodies, which finance the TVET system), that has met the requirements of industry and agriculture with a fair degree of success. But it has not felt the need for a qualifications framework. Nevertheless, there continues to be strong donor support as well as support from international organizations[11] for the building and implementation of qualifications frameworks (Allais, 2017).

The international studies corroborate the argument in Allais (2010) that where occupations are not regulated in terms of licence to practice or similar requirements, policymakers try to improve education/work relationships by involving employers in developing competence statements for qualifications in the hope that the qualifications thus developed can be used to reform curricula and to reform the delivery of education. In other words, the implicit idea is that getting employers to specify competences will lead to a policy mechanism which plays a similar role to a framework of regulated occupations. But in reality this often is not the case. We have already seen in the previous section how poorly NOSs and QPs have been prepared, and how little industry engagement of a serious kind has occurred in India in the six years since implementation of NSQF began in January 2014.

One problem seen from the international evidence in all the cases is that in the absence of occupational regulation, employers tend not to be involved in qualifications frameworks, or to be involved sporadically or inconsistently. Occupational regulation is a situation where most employers are formal enterprises, with hierarchical levels of positions. Such formal enterprises are governed also by laws, which govern different aspects of minimum wages to be paid, benefits to be given, occupational health and safety concerns met, social insurance provided, pollution standards met, industrial relations are also governed, and so on. Entry into the occupation itself for the enterprise is governed by certain requirements, legal or otherwise. In a highly informalized economy, none of these conditions would apply in informal units; the majority of workers are self-employed (and have no employer as such), and even formal firms may only be registered under some Act of Parliament but are not regulated or inspected or monitored for most activities.

But more fundamentally, the idea of a NVQF is flawed: if the entrance to occupations is not regulated through licences to practice, even where employers do specify competences they are unlikely to value such qualifications in practice as they tend to be low level and narrow; this is aggravated by the ways in which competence-based systems cause problems for providers, as has been well documented elsewhere (Allais, 2007; Wheelahan, 2008; Wolf, 1995, 2002; Young, 2011).We have ourselves argued that the Qualification Packs developed for the job roles in various sectors under the NSQF have narrow NOSs (Mehrotra & Singh, 2017; Expert Group report to MSDE, 2017).

The framework in France is the only example of an occupational framework in the international studies where qualification levels are linked to levels of work and pay. However, the qualifications framework did not seem to be the cause but instead the effect or codification of such relationships (Allais, 2007). A regulated occupational labour market and strong collective bargaining has historically enabled the French system to relate qualification levels explicitly to levels in the workforce. What is now recognized as a qualifications framework, the National Register for Professional Certifications (Repertoire National des Certifications Professionnelles, or RNCP) is largely the same qualifications system that has been in place in France for further education and training since the early 1970s. In 1969, a grid of 'training levels' was adopted, with the explicit aim of linking education to the workplace. While duration of education was important, the levels were anchored against definitions of staff in work situations, which were then linked to qualifications. This, as Bouder and Kirsch (2007) point out, was circular. What this means is that unless you have levels of work (a hierarchy of levels of positions or posts at work), a QF cannot specify what qualification matches with which level of post.

For the Qualifications Framework, we have the additional problem that levels of qualifications for different occupations are difficult, if not impossible, to equate. On what basis would 500 hours of training as a motor mechanic be equated with 500 hours of training as a hair salon specialist? By assigning a level in a QF to each of those 500 hours, you would be equating what is conceptually impossible to equate. On top of that, if the QF attempts to equate that number of hours of training to some equivalent level of schooling at higher secondary or tertiary level of general education, what would be the basis for the QF to assign a level?

One abiding problem with NVQFs is that occupational standards should always be linked to occupational fields as opposed to specific jobs, but in NVQFs they tend towards specifying standards for specific jobs. This is particularly the case with the Indian NSQF—which makes it an inappropriate instrument to achieving quality skilling. However, the idea behind quality skill development is not to create a narrow description of the tasks undertaken by a novice but to identify the wider professional domain, taking into account processes of adaptation to the job and professional integration.

The fact that qualifications are a weak proxy for skill is widely acknowledged (for example, Guile, 2010), and it seems increasingly apparent that rising education attainment, rising youth unemployment, and the changing nature of work are creating challenges for transitions from education to work in many countries, but especially in India (which in 2018 had a 45-year high rate of unemployment of 6.1 per cent, and youth unemployment of 18 per cent) There is still little evidence to support qualifications frameworks as a way of improving these transitions. If the concern in developing countries is that it is not enough to pass a conventional examination, since 'competency' in performing a task is not demonstrated by doing so, then the answer is to ensure quality training of adequate duration, and not just a few hundred hours, with a well-structured curriculum that has been arrived at in consultation with employers/industry. In addition, the training should be imparted by trainers themselves aware of what employers expect, with training incorporating theory, practical workshop experience, and on-the-job internship or apprenticeship. Then competency will be an inevitable outcome, especially if the assessment is itself conducted by industry experts.

Qualification frameworks seem to continue to derive popularity from the way they promise to offer simple solutions to these very real and complex problems. Unregulated labour markets (which are typical to developing countries, including India), the diversity of provision particularly within TVET systems, and qualification inflation all aggravate the ways in which there are weak relationships between educational provision and labour markets. There is no evidence so far in the six-year experience with NSQF in India that there is an improvement in the weak relationship.

Qualifications frameworks which have either succeeded in creating some buy-in and understanding of the national system of qualifications as a whole (such as in Scotland and France) are invoked as proof that qualifications frameworks can perform this role; qualifications frameworks which codify relationships between training levels and employment levels are invoked as proof that qualifications frameworks can improve relationships between education provision and the labour market (Allais, 2017). But the main mechanism which is offered to developing countries in order to create a qualification framework is employer-led competency statements. This mechanism leads to complexity—undermining the aim of improving understandings of the qualification system—and does not lead to improved labour market outcomes.

There seem to be two options for policymakers: Accept that improving the description of your qualification system is a useful although very minor intervention; do it, but do not make extravagant claims about improving labour market relationships, or focus on occupational regulation and licence to practice—to prevent any further informalization of work and enterprises—in order to have clear relationships between education and work. Raffe (2015), reflecting on the reform of vocational qualifications in the UK, suggests that the best line of action may be to stop focusing on qualifications. Attempts to improve labour market outcomes through employer specification of learning outcomes cannot substitute for broadly supported relationships between training levels and employment levels.

Tertiary-level programmes of vocational education and training in India

We have already discussed in the initial sections of this chapter about the issues with the Indian NSQF. What is noticeable in the Indian case of the qualifications framework is that the focus has been on pre-tertiary level of education and training (for those aged less than 18 years). In other words, the focus has been on the so-called NSQF levels 1–4. To date, there has been limited focus on the so-called levels NSQF 5–7, which are supposed to cover the tertiary level. These levels are supposed to be approved and regulated by AICTE for technical tertiary institutions and UGC for universities. The latter two institutions have attempted to implement tertiary level courses in vocational education. There are three such institutional arrangements, whereby these tertiary skill-related programmes are being imparted. These three institutions are as follows: (1) Community Colleges; (2) Colleges and Universities offering B.Voc. degree programmes; and (3) Deen Dayal Upadhyay KAUSHAL (Knowledge Acquisition and Upgradation of Skilled Human Abilities and Livelihood) Centres.[12] The B.Voc. degree programme was to expand the scope of vocational education and provide vertical mobility to the students. These are credit-based modular programmes, wherein banking of credits for skill and general education components is permitted so as to enable multiple exit and entry. This will also provide the learner an opportunity for vertical mobility to the third year of B.Voc. degree programme after one-year diploma and a two-year advanced diploma. This is the only evidence of multi-entry and multi-exit in the whole NSQF, applicable only to tertiary education.

Model of vocational education at tertiary level: a case study of VET programme at Tata Institute of Social Sciences, Mumbai

The Tata Institute of Social Sciences (TISS), Mumbai, is a well-known institution of higher learning. In 2011, it started a School of Vocational Education. The VET programme at TISS has been a remarkable success. Today TISS-SVE (School of Vocational Education) imparts vocational education to thousands. It has expanded steadily and currently offers courses in 19 different verticals, across 90 locations spread over 22 states. In the process, it has catered to nearly 20,000 students, including the students currently enrolled. The list of 19 verticals includes agriculture, automotive, electronics, healthcare, media and entertainment, pharmaceuticals, printing and packaging, and renewable energy, in addition to the more popular, BFSI (Banking, Financial Services, and Insurance).[13]

Model of VET adopted by TISS

The B.Voc. programmes at TISS-SVE comply with all the guidelines laid down by the UGC. The courses are designed to match the requirements of levels 5, 6, and 7, respectively, of the National Skills Qualifications Framework (NSQF). However, what is noticeable is that the TISS-SVE model has in fact rather little to do with the NSQF, although the model appears to mention the 'required' NSQF, perhaps for no other reason than that the institution (TISS) that has initiated this programme is a deemed-to-be university and receives some limited funds from the University Grants Commission. Yet in this case study of VE provision at the tertiary level, we show it is possible to build a model that works for industry looking for young workers and for students in search of employability skills. It is essentially a demand-led model, which is ensuring high levels of placement for B.Voc. trainees.

The time spent by students in getting practical training is 60 per cent relative to coursework, which covers the remaining 40 per cent. Students are evaluated using a credit system in which each theory credit and each practical credit corresponds to 15 hours and 30 hours of work, respectively. Students must take six credits in vocational theory, 12 credits in general courses, and 12 credits in practical work in each semester, making a total of 30 credits spanning 630 hours, of which 360 hours are spent in receiving practical training. If a student exits after either the first or the second year, he or she can always rejoin at a later date for progression to the next level. This is precisely the kind of multi-entry and multi-exit that we had envisaged in the design of NSQF.

The training is based on the Work Integrated Training Programme (WITP), where students learn the skill by engaging in on-the-job training at a real shop floor of the industry/company. For effective delivery of this model, TISS-SVE leverages the expertise of a partner (which is the Hub) that will provide classroom-based training and will be known as a Hub in a Hub-and-Spokes model of training delivery to the trainee. Furthermore, there is an execution partner who provides on-the-job training to the trainee. They are called Skill Knowledge Partners (SKPs, which are the Spokes) and could include hospitals/industries/companies. Hence, in the Hub and Spoke model, students are placed in the SKPs for on-the-job training while classroom theoretical training is given to the trainee by the Hub Partner. The practical skills training component is delivered through partnerships with SKPs-who provide paid internships in most cases and paid employment in some cases, to students. This model of work-integrated training or On-the-Job Training (OJT) is a variation on the very successful Dual Model used in Germany and other countries. Students spend their days doing their respective jobs and then go to the nearest Hub Partner of TISS-SVE in the evenings or during the weekends to learn the theory associated with their fields as well as other generic courses.

Hub Partners are the 'learning hubs' that perform some of the most important tasks in this work-integrated learning model, and they are given 70 per cent of the revenue from student fees. They mobilize and select students, provide theoretical training in classrooms, identify and register SKPs, and even assess students by hosting written and oral examinations. Hubs deliver the content created by TISS-SVE for general education and the vocational theory component.

SKPs facilitate practical OJT by employing trainees full-time or on internship-basis and offering a stipend. SKPs also assess students on the vocational training component and provide internal assessment marks to TISS-SVE for inclusion in the final marksheet. SKPs are identified by hubs, but their appointment is done by TISS-SVE post due diligence. The Skills Training Providers provide the hands-on training that is the crux of vocational education. Students work with them full-time while they are getting trained and have three years of work experience at the end of their B.Voc. programme.

TISS-SVE performs the role of an anchor, monitoring all aspects of the activity, while also taking charge of assessment and certification. It collects a Performance Guarantee Fee from all partners.

Curriculum and pedagogy

The curriculum for the general education courses is prepared by TISS-SVE themselves and is common across all B.Voc. programmes. There are currently 15 general education courses in place, including courses in English, basic communication skills, financial literacy, digital literacy, and even a finishing school course. Facilitator guides contain lesson plans, which are self-explanatory and are therefore very helpful for the concerned trainers. Each B.Voc. programme consists of 12–14 vocational theory courses, besides 12 general education courses, adding up to a total of approximately 400 courses for which content has been created at TISS-SVE so far.

Assessment

The UGC guidelines for B.Voc. programmes suggest designing the examination and assessment strategy in association with the Sector Skills Councils (SSCs) or using SSC designated assessors to assess the skills component of the B.Voc. programmes. However, this is not really feasible if costs of the programmes are to be kept low. The charges levied by the SSCs are high, (Rs 1,500 per student for each examination) and this would increase the cost of the B.Voc. programme considerably. So in this model the SSCs have been bypassed. TISS, which is a deemed university, conducts its own examination and provides certification to students. TISS-SVE has created a Board of Examination and Evaluation that has standardized the processes of assessment. The theory and practical components are each examined in two parts—internal assessment and external examinations. This helps ensure fairness in the evaluation of students.

Monitoring for quality

In order to understand the efficacy of this entire arrangement and to ensure that students have a seamless experience, approximately 15–20 per cent of the students at each Hub are interviewed each month by TISS-SVE staff for feedback through telephonic interactions. This helps TISS-SVE to assess the health of all moving parts in this model, which ultimately serves the interests of the students. Another way of getting first-hand information from the students is through the counsellors empanelled by TISS-SVE at most cities/towns.

A professional company is paid to check the credentials of not just Vertical Anchors (who create curriculum, alongside TISS, where TISS does not have in-house expertise), Hub Partners, and SKPs (those getting into a legal contract with TISS) but also individual trainers, assessors, COE members, other empanelled partners, and even students (verification of certificates). Right from the first day of TISS's starting a vocational programme, the school has had a Vocational Aptitude Systems (VAS) department to develop a customized test for students to help them choose an appropriate vertical or trade for either work or educational purposes. Its main objective is to aid students who are mostly confused about their selection of a trade, either for work or study.

Sustainable funding model

In terms of financial viability of the educational institution itself, TISS-SVE has been able to become self-reliant despite keeping only 20 per cent of the revenue from fees and despite picking up all additional costs relating to improving quality, because they run a mix of B.Voc. and short-term courses, particularly customized courses for the corporate sector that brings in much more funds than the standard training imparted in the Hub-Spokes model. This approach of providing a mixed bag of courses to different stakeholders, for financial viability, is also worth emulating by other educational institutions.

TISS-SVE has succeeded largely in achieving its goal of keeping vocational education at a relatively low cost and, therefore, affordable. The fees for the courses are capped at a figure between Rs 1500 per month and Rs 4000 a month depending on the type of the course. Given that students receive stipends and salaries in some cases, and TISS-SVE negotiates with SKPs to provide them with a reasonable sum as stipend, most students are able to cover their fees from their own stipends. The revenue generated from the student fees, which is collected exclusively on behalf of TISS-SVE, is shared with all the partners.

Clearly, this case study offers multiple lessons for the way forward on VE at the tertiary level in India. First, the autonomy enjoyed by TISS was crucial for its success. The School of Vocational Education was granted considerable operational autonomy by TISS. This was important to enable the speed and agility with which TISS-SVE worked to touch the lives of almost 20,000 students in just six years. Other academic institutions must have similar autonomy if they are to succeed. They must have flexibility regarding faculty qualification and sole discretion on hiring staff. The usual UGC requirements of faculty qualifications are not relevant for vocational education, where competence and experience of the vocational teachers or trainers matters more than their qualifications.

Second, TISS-SVE took the decision very early on to sign up partners along the length and breadth of the country, because its mandate, as stated in its MoU with AICTE, was to incubate a National Vocational University using a hubs and spokes. TISS-SVE therefore signed up partners wherever SKPs (spokes) could be found, helping them achieve scale and spread quickly. It is only in February 2018 that TISS received its status as Category 1 institution of the UGC, one that frees it formally from jurisdictional constraints and allows it to have a national footprint. State-run educational institutions have regional constraints and also constraints on signing up students from other states. Given that the need to scale out quality vocational education is so severe and urgent, state governments must consider reviewing these constraints.

Thirdly, the seed funding provided by AICTE was critical in giving TISS the confidence to venture into creating the SVE and exploring opportunities without worrying about failures. Similar seed funding must be made available to all higher-educational institutions that are willing to explore vocational education. That the financial support TISS needed was so modest is extremely encouraging.

Since 2014, the model of VET adopted by TISS has emerged as a model of provision of VE at the tertiary level in India that genuinely offers hope. However, what is noticeable is that it has rather little to do with the NSQF, although it appears to mention the 'required' NSQF perhaps for no other reason other than that the institution that has initiated this programme is a deemed-to-be university and receives some limited funds from the University Grants Commission. However, as we explained, in this case study of VET provision at the tertiary level, it is possible to build a model that works for industry looking for young workers and for students in search of employability skills. It is essentially a demand-led model, which is ensuring high levels of placement for B.Voc. trainees.

One point that may be considered is the credibility of assessment. It may be mentioned that since TISS had a fantastic social impact imprint and past credibility. It was well positioned to leverage it. The same can be done by credible institutions in the country. Overall, this may provide more credibility and improve esteem of vocational education in the general populace.

Concluding remarks

We have seen in this chapter that while NSQF was introduced in India, after much discussion within the government of India (mainly between the Ministry of Human Resource Development and the Ministry of Labour and Employment), its implementation trajectory has left much to be desired. The promise and the reality have turned out to be rather different. This is not surprising. The fact is that the NSQF was not really rolled out in India in the way that the original blueprint had outlined. In addition, it appears that those entrusted with implementing the task perhaps never really understood the risks associated with rolling out a vocational qualifications framework in a developing country with (1) a highly informalized economy and workforce; and (2) low-quality general academic education accessed by the majority of young; and (3) a highly fragmented and extremely narrowly based skills ecosystem. The NSQF itself did not focus on building on competency-based curriculum (but rather on creating NOS and QPs, which were never accepted by industry, since they hardly contributed to it). Those implementing the NSQF did not recognize, it seems, the problems that vocational qualifications frameworks have faced even in Anglo-Saxon countries or the even-greater problems in emerging market economies. In fact, the skills ecosystem was facing a plethora of other problems (shortage of teachers, very limited serious industry engagement, a supply-driven as opposed to a demand-driven system), for which NSQF had no answers. That the promise and reality has turned out to be rather far apart is not inconsistent with the international evidence. However, in this chapter, we have presented a case study of a well-known national institution evolving a model to deliver VET at the tertiary level that potentially offers a way forward. Therefore, we summarize the lessons emerging for the whole TVET system in India, including for VET at the tertiary level.

We have argued elsewhere that government-managed TVET are rarely successful in achieving their goals of ensuring employability for youth and a potential ready pool of workers for industry (Mehrotra, 2014). Only an industry-driven TVET system will avoid the temptation of being supply-driven. India is in urgent need of radical reform to ensure a demand-driven TVET system emerges. On industry–academia collaboration for review of standards, the TISS-SVE experience, has thrown light on some of the inadequacies in the NSQF that require review. Similarly, the government has been promoting Skills Universities in India. However, the TISS-SVE model has provided a new starting point for many other institutions to discover their own models for vocational education. Evidently, the TISS-SVE model is very different from conventional universities, and this is one of the main takeaway messages. It is apparent that the need of the hour is not new vocational/skills universities but a more bottom-up approach in which educational institutions experiment the way TISS-SVE has done and find their own models.

TISS-SVE has had three groups of graduates (2017, 2018, and 2019). The average placement after three groups is 85 per cent, which shows how a demand-led programme can become successful. Meanwhile, UGC is attempting to expand B.Voc. courses in other universities, and state governments are attempting to set up vocational and skills universities. Similarly, private universities (e.g. Symbiosis University, Pune) are spending much more funds, where the per student cost can be quite high. UGC needs to learn the appropriate lessons from the case studies, since successful examples are few and far between in the Indian TVET ecosystem.

Finally, there is a case for review of government spending on short-term skilling courses. Short-term certificate courses that are presently the predominant method of providing skills training to youth in government programmes, such as PMKVY, can only be a starting point. Young people need holistic education, and short-term courses cannot compare with the value addition that students receive during the three years of the B.Voc. programme or even a one-year diploma programme. It is imperative that the government looks to similar industry–academia partnerships to convert all skills training efforts for youth into a more holistic education. The short-term courses will always remain as an important avenue for skill enhancement and lifelong learning, but they cannot remain the driving force of the TVET ecosystem.

Notes

1 I am grateful to Ashutosh Singh, Harshil Sharma, Sapna Poti, and Vinay Mehrotra for comments on an earlier draft. The usual disclaimers apply.

2 I was asked to chair the task force, which resulted in the National Vocational Education Qualification Framework (see Mehrotra et al., 2012). The other members were Dr. Vinay Mehrotra, Professor at the Central Institute of Vocational Education, and Basab Banerjee (National Skills Development Corporation).

3 For the first time in the history of India's planning, the 11th Five Year Plan (2007–2012) included a chapter on Skill Development, as did the 12th Plan (2012–2017) (Mehrotra & Guichard, 2020). I had the privilege of leading the team that wrote the 12th Plan chapter.

4 The Ministry of Labour & Employment prepared, and the Cabinet approved on 23 February 2009, a National Skills Development Policy, which included the following: 'National Vocational Qualifications Framework which will inter alia include opportunities for horizontal and vertical mobility between general and technical education, recognition, and certification of competencies irrespective of mode of learning'.

5 This term was adopted as a compromise term, since neither Ministry was likely to find the other Ministry's term acceptable. Since I was leading the team that wrote the 12th Plan chapter on skill development, I proposed to the Planning Commission that the term, NSQF, would be neutral, and hence likely to be acceptable to both the Ministries. So the term that we introduced in the 12th Plan chapter, NSQF, stuck, and became part of the national policy narrative.

6 The Expert Group report (2017) had identified large scale instances of fraud and poor quality training. The Comptroller and Auditor General of India, in a report to Parliament, identified the dysfunctionality and misuse of funds through the NSDC and its funded VTPs, including in the behemoth Infrastructure Leasing and Finance Services (ILFS), which had emerged as a major skill provider across the country. Its corruption then by 2018 led to its collapse as corporation.

7 It had been introduced in 2,000 secondary government schools across 22 states by early 2015. The number had reached 10,000 plus schools by 2019.

8 Instead of RPL, what we have had is the current program on adult education via NGOs and Jan Shikshan Sansthan, which has not done well. To promote Adult Education, particularly in the 15–35 age group, through the voluntary sector, the Department of School Education and Literacy, Ministry of Human Resource Development, has been providing support to Voluntary Agencies (VA) through two separate schemes, namely (1) Assistance to Voluntary Agencies in the field of

Adult Education; and (2) Jan Shikshan Sansthans. The former is conceptualized as an overarching programme to encourage innovation and creativity in literacy and continuing education. It includes establishment of State Resource Centers for technical and academic support to adult education. Jan Shikshan Sansthans, on the other hand, provides vocational education skill development training to those having no or a rudimentary level of education. The Government have now decided to merge both the schemes and rename the modified scheme as 'Scheme of Support to Voluntary Agencies for Adult Education and Skill Development' and continue to support the Voluntary Agencies on a project-to-project basis. Thus the new scheme subsumes the erstwhile NGO-based schemes of the National Literacy Mission. Besides revised parameters, enhanced financial assistance has been provided under some of the components of the revised scheme. The scheme will be administered through a new set of guidelines and terms and conditions, as specified by the Government from time to time.

9 It is rather ironic that ILO's own research globally had already warned that VQFs have had an extremely chequered history even in industrialized countries, where they began (the Anglo-Saxon ones). However, in Bangladesh, Lythe (2018), a consultant from New Zealand (another Anglo-Saxon country) tried to advocate strongly for the NTVQF, in the face of strong international evidence and also Bangladesh evidence that the QFs are somewhat peripheral to the structural problems that the SD ecosystem faces in these countries.

10 The entire Chinese SD ecosystem is to use five levels of certification: Primary Worker Certificate; Intermediate Worker Certificate; Advanced Worker Certificate; Technician Certificate; Senior Technician Certificate.

11 This statement does not apply at least to the Asian Development Bank's work in either Bangladesh or even other Asian economies, despite ADB's growing role in Asian countries in SD, especially in Bangladesh. It is perhaps not surprising that the ADB is witness to many fast-growing economies that have become manufacturing nations of global standing, with very strong TVET systems. But none of them adopted NVQFs at an early stage of development of their system.

12 The KAUSHAL scheme is described here: www.ugc.ac.in/skill/pdf/DDU%20KAUSHAL%20Centers%20XII%20Plan.pdf

13 *Vocational Education: A Case Study of TISS-S* Leena Chandran, Wadia Antara, Sengupta Sanchayan Bhattacharjee, Observer Research Foundation.

References

Allais, S. (2007). *The rise and fall of the NQF: A critical analysis of the South African national qualifications framework* (Doctoral Thesis). University of the Witwatersrand, South Africa.

Allais, S. (2010). *The implementation and impact of qualifications frameworks: Report of a study in 16 countries.* Geneva: International Labour Office.

Allais, S. (2017). Labour market outcomes of national qualifications frameworks in six countries. *Journal of Education and Work*, 30(5), 457–470.

Bouder, A., & Kirsch, J. L. (2007). The French vocational education and training system: Like an unrecognized prototype? *European Journal of Education*, 42(4), 503–522.

Cedefop (2013). *Analysis and overview of NQF developments in European countries, annual report 2012.* Cedefop Working Paper No. 17. Publications Office, Luxembourg.

Cedefop (2015). *National qualifications framework developments in Europe-anniversary edition.* Publications office of the European Union, Luxembourg.

ETF, Cedefop, & UNESCO Institute for Lifelong Learning (2013). *Global national qualifications framework inventory*. Report prepared for ASEM Education Ministers Conference, May 13–14. ETF, Cedefop, and UNESCO Institute for Lifelong Learning, Kuala Lumpur.

Expert Group (2017). *Report of the committee for rationalization and optimization of the functioning of the sector skill councils*. Ministry of Skill Development & Entrepreneurship, Government of India, New Delhi.

Guile, D. (2010). *The learning challenge of the knowledge economy* (Vol. 3). Rotterdam: Sense Publishers.

Keevy, J., & Chakroun, B. (2015). *Leveling and recognizing learning outcomes: The use of level descriptors in the twenty-first century*. Paris: UNESCO.

Lythe, D. (2018). *Assessment of the National technical and vocational qualifications framework and roadmap for development of the Bangladesh qualification framework*. ILO, Dhaka.

Mehrotra, S. (2014). *India's skills challenge: Reforming vocational education and training to harness the demographic dividend*. New Delhi: Oxford University Press.

Mehrotra, S. (2019). *Towards a new national skills development policy for Bangladesh*. Dhaka: ILO.

Mehrotra, S., & Guichard, S. (Eds.) (2020). *Planning in the 20th century & beyond: India, the planning commission and NITI aayog*. New Delhi: Cambridge University Press.

Mehrotra, S., Kamaladevi, A., & Gandhi, A. (2015). China's vocational education and training system: Lessons for India. *Economic and Political Weekly*, 50(28).

Mehrotra, S., Mehrotra, V. S., & Banerjee, B. (2012). *A national vocational education qualification framework for India*. IAMR Working Paper No. 4. National Institute of Labour Economics Research, New Delhi.

Mehrotra, S., Raman, R., Kumra, N., Kalaiyarasan, A., & Röß, D. (2014). *Vocational education and training reform in India: Business needs in India and lessons to be learned from Germany*. Working Paper. Bertelsmann Stiftung, Gütersloh.

Mehrotra, S., & Singh, A. P. (2017). Industry engagement in India's TVET: No skin in the game. In *International Handbook of Vocational Education*. New York: Springer.

Pilcher, N., Scott, F., & Smith, K. (2015). The impact of national qualifications frameworks: By which yardstick do we measure dreams? *Journal of Education and Work*, 30(1), 1–12. DOI: 10.1080/13639080.2015.1122178.

Planning Commission (2008). *11th Five year plan: Towards faster and more inclusive growth*. New Delhi: Oxford University Press.

Planning Commission (2013). *12th Five year plan: Towards faster, more inclusive and sustainable growth*. New Delhi: SAGE Publications.

Raffe, D. (2012). What is the evidence for the impact of national qualifications frameworks? *Comparative Education*, 49(2), 143–162. DOI: 10.1080/03050068.2012.686260.

Raffe, D. (2015). First count to five: Some principles for the reform of vocational qualifications in England. *Journal of Education and Work*, 28(2), 147–164. http://doi.org/10.1080/13639080.2014.1001334.

Ranjan, R. (2021) *Dynamics of youth employment, skill development and technology interface in India since 1991*, PhD thesis, unpublished, Centre for Informal Sector and Labour Studies, Jawaharlal Nehru University, New Delhi.

Roy, S. (2008). Skill premium: What caused the 'mismatch'? *Indian Journal of Labour Economics*, 51(4), 789–802. https://mpra.ub.uni-muenchen.de/18010/.

Wheelahan, L. (2008, April). *Can learning outcomes be divorced from processes of learning? or why training packages make very bad curriculum.* Presented at the 11th Annual Australian Vocational Education and Training Research Association Conference, VET in Practice, Adelaide.

Wolf, A. (1995). *Competence-based assessment.* Edited by H. Torrance. Buckingham: Open University Press.

Wolf, A. (2002). *Does education matter? Myths about education and economic growth.* London: Penguin.

Young, M. (2011). National vocational qualifications in the United Kingdom: Their origins and legacy. *Journal of Education and Work*, 24(3–4), 259–282.

Chapter 11

Curriculum and pedagogy in higher education for skill development

Nikhil Agarwal and Aprant Agarwal

Higher education in India has faced daunting tasks for many decades, such as issues related to curricula, faculty, funding, and skills education. From the very beginning, the notion of learning and culture is inherent in human life. With the rise of communities, societies, and civilizations, the organization of teaching and learning in the family environment becomes more formal instead of being informal. Learning-by-doing was prevalent in earlier times where individuals participated in various activities with respect to their community and families. Although learning is done through interactive processes rather than cultures and communities, sociologists have characterized socialization processes between family and community agencies, which academics see as an informal learning process. We can argue that the current system is highly dependent on class-based learning and rote learning which have their pros and cons.

The majority of the developed countries have taken adequate measures to establish education systems with extensive coverage to meet their challenging social and economic needs. Developing countries, on the other hand, are focused on basic literacy and primary education. Therefore, developing countries have not been able to simultaneously reduce the increasing gaps in the quality and coverage of education at higher levels.

Targeted quality content and targeted inclusion of less privileged groups and groups with special needs is imperative to strengthen people's economic participation, and a national education system must provide quality services to all sections of society. In order to be entirely achievable, the conditions and strategies of different countries must be identified and contextualized according to the targeted country. For the successful development of educational initiatives, active participation of the private sector and social participation of the local community is critical (Harman & Bich, 2010).

The objective of the chapter is to propose an emerging framework to support transformative curriculum and pedagogy in higher-education institutions in India for skill development. In this chapter, we have examined the existing concepts of skill development in higher education in detail. Further, the importance and influence of digital techniques such as e-learning and online assessment are considered in bridging the gap that affects skill development. We raise some of the

DOI: 10.4324/9781003158349-14

pressing issues and questions that help us to evaluate the current skill development curriculum holistically. What is the current format and status of the curriculum pertaining to skill development? What bodies/entities are involved in the development and implementation of the curriculum? What are the reasons for the non-convergence of various curricula and why is there a gap between the industry and academia?

4th industrial revolution: opportunities and challenges

The first industrial revolution was the transition to new manufacturing processes. The Second Industrial Revolution, also known as the Technological Revolution, was a phase of rapid industrialization. The third industrial revolution is characterized by a fusion of technologies that is blurring the lines between physical, digital, and biological spheres. Now it is time for the 4th industrial revolution. The World Economic Forum (WEF) articulates the 4th industrial revolution this way:

> We stand on the brink of a technological revolution that will fundamentally alter the way we live, work, and relate to one another. In its scale, scope, and complexity, the transformation will be unlike anything humankind has experienced before. We do not yet know just how it will unfold, but one thing is clear: the response to it must be integrated and comprehensive, involving all stakeholders of the global polity, from the public and private sectors to academia and civil society.
>
> (Klaus, 2016)

We certainly need to prepare ourselves for the new phase of human and societal development. India is the youngest country in the world, with 65 per cent of the population below the age of 35, India must take up the opportunities and challenges of the 4th industrial revolution with positive energy.

Skills needed in the 4th industrial revolution

It is predicted that there will be a massive skill shortage during the 4th industrial revolution. Since the contours of the 4th industrial revolution are still unfolding, organizations are a bit unclear about the skills needs. Experts have an opinion that there will be less dependence on human beings for routine jobs; however, they will never be made entirely obsolete. According to the World Economic Forum, '[T]the skill sets required in both old and new occupations will change in most industries and transform how and where people work'. Top skills needed to navigate through the 4th industrial revolution are:

- Complex problem solving
- Critical thinking

- Creativity
- People management
- Coordinating with others
- Emotional intelligence
- Judgement and decision making
- Service orientation
- Negotiation
- Cognitive Flexibility

These skills will become more critical once technology becomes more entrenched in our daily lives. The higher-education system in developing countries such as India should be more agile, futuristic, pragmatic, and endowed with essential resources. The higher-education institutions should embrace the changes and design the curriculum that can train the new India for years to come.

Skill development scenario in India

The skill development ecology in India is complex, broad, and diverse, providing different levels of expertise among a diverse population. The National Skill Development Mission (NSDM) was permitted by the Union Cabinet on 1 July 2015. The mission is designed to unite sectors and states in the field of vocational training activities. Furthermore, to realize the vision of 'efficient India', initially, seven sub-missions were proposed to serve as a primary component to achieve the mission's overall goals: (1) infrastructure, (2) institutional training, (3) trainers, (4) transformation, (5) employment abroad, (6) Leveraging Public Infrastructure, and (7) Sustainable livelihoods. Figure 11.1 presents the potential pathways for the learner.

The Ministry of Skill Development is mandated for skill development in India. At the central level, the Nodal Institute for Vocational Training is the Director-General of Employment and Training (DGET) of the Ministry of Labour and Employment. The DGET is responsible for policy development, standardization, approval, provision of professional tests and certifications, and the provision of vocational training and employment services. Along with that, the National Council for Skill Development (NSDC), presently part of the newly developed Ministry of Skills Development and Entrepreneurship, has been created to minimize the gap in creativity and promote private skill development initiatives.

Other than that, the primary, secondary, and higher education are managed under the aegis of the Ministry of Education (earlier known as MHRD). Along with that, higher education and universities provide all college education (science, arts, commerce, management). Polytechnic education and engineering education are covered by technical education. The University Grants Commission (UGC) is the leading body for teaching, testing, and research in the universities. All India Council for Technical Education (AICTE) is responsible for

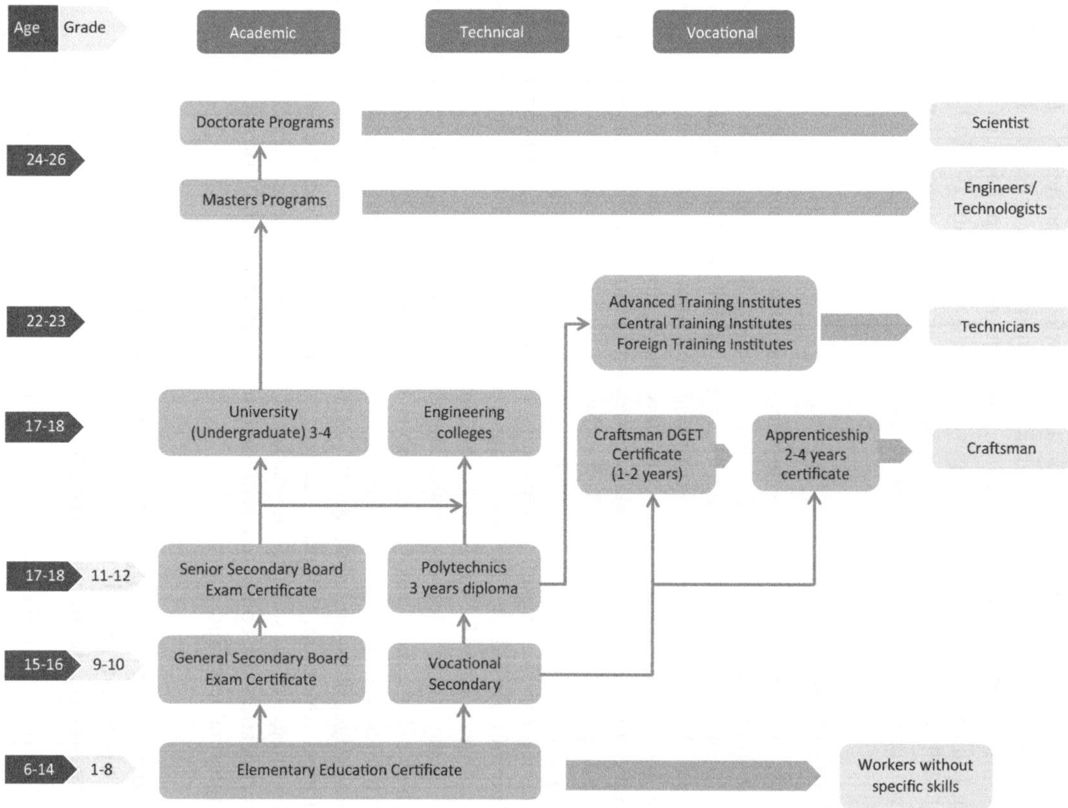

Figure 11.1 India's education and skill development structure

Source: Deen Dayal Upadhyaya Grameen Kaushalya Yojana (DDU-GKY).

management, vocational, and technical education in the country for the colleges that are not part of a public or private universities.

The government has identified over 40 crores people in the country in need of skill upgradation by 2022. The government has invested ₹ 4000 crores in the launch of SANKALP (Skill Acquisition and Knowledge Awareness for Livelihood Promotion Programme), another significant initiative under the Skill India Mission. Through this, it aims at providing market-relevant training to 35 crores young Indians. Apart from this, the government is setting up 100 India International Skills Centres that will conduct advanced courses in foreign languages to help youngsters prepare for overseas jobs.

Skill universities

In 2018, the Ministry of Skill Development and Entrepreneurship (MSDE) had laid the guidelines for setting up skill universities. To bring uniformity in the nomenclature, skill universities offer bachelors of skill (B.Skill.) and bachelors of vocation (B.Voc.). Similarly, masters of skills and masters of vocation are offered at the master's level. Skill universities have the option to set up industry labs, training centres, and specialized skill centres with industry collaboration to bring cutting-edge technology and skills for the candidates. The skill universities are offering sector-level degrees, certificates, and diplomas directly related to the job requirements in the market. These courses are ranked higher than conventional programmes offered by ITI/Polytechnics and also different from conventional programmes such as B.Sc (IT) or B.Sc (Computers).

To make these degrees/qualifications-compatible, the government has launched a National Skills Qualifications Framework (NSQF), a competency-based framework that organizes all qualifications according to a series of the level of knowledge, skills, and aptitude. By 2020, all the qualifications in the country (vocational education, skill training, general education, and technical education) will be integrated to suit the job market. Under NSQF, the learner can acquire the certification for competency needed at any level through formal, non-formal/informal learning.

The pedagogical approach towards skill development curriculum: developing a learner-centric environment

In the modern education system, the students are smart enough to access any relevant information encoded digitally. As a teacher, it is not necessary to over-indulge in their daily educative aspects. As an alternative, it is essential to guide them all along the path of these digitized forms of education. The job of an instructor is to encourage students and to bring out their creative abilities.

One of the distinguishing features of modern society is its scientific technology that has a profound impact on its educational system, not only in the economic and political life of India but also in the development of interests, values, and attitudes. Pedagogy is an effective way to develop knowledge, skills, and values as a teaching instructional process. This happens if teachers can select, plan, organize, and apply different teaching methods and strategies. Teachers need to read, learn, and explore in order to learn about different teaching methods and techniques and to develop the skills to use them. The materials they receive and the information they share with their colleagues is crucial. Besides that, this professional development is focused on preparing teachers for educational content.

Sterling (2010) advised paying particular attention to teaching strategies such as promoting a student-centred approach to teaching to achieve the required level of competency. They suggest changing the evaluation system to performance-based assessment. The quality of the curriculum, the desired results of the students, has been seen to develop and educate the staff for the new era (Sahlberg & Oldroyd, 2010). Moreover, teaching is experiencing several rapid changes, such as social, educational, and political change, which means that teachers require more and better continuous professional development to maintain change and become relevant to the teaching profession. Teacher quality is crucial, because the need for change places too much weight on teachers, such as meeting the challenges of large classes and students of different specialties. This has made teacher support more crucial than ever, so teachers need to advance professional development, which is often neglected in India (Jones & Iredale, 2010).

The curriculum has emerged as a continuous initiative to be included. There was a tendency to map the knowledge and skills gaps to define the core curriculum, update the curriculum, and provide guidance to programme developers of different organizations (Jones, 2013). Previous types of efforts include professional and interdisciplinary programmes that need to be recreated to address current challenges. Contrary to basic syllabus concepts, knowledge and skills tend to cross subject boundaries. Thus, the main goal of the curriculum is to allow students to gain the understanding they need to adapt optimally to different disciplines in order to tackle increasingly complex problems (Livingston, 2010).

The higher-education sector has evolved in the past few decades, and never before has there been such vigorous public debate about the university's place and its role in society. The number of part-time and distance-enrolled (online enrolled) students has increased significantly. Traditionally, in the higher-education settings, the students are enrolled between the age of 8–20 years; however, there has been dramatic growth in the number of students since the advent of the online education. We have seen a significant upsurge in the current pandemic where mature students are taking up the plunge to upgrade their skills using online methods. Another trend has contributed to the growth of online education—the demand from mature women who have free time in hand when children complete their education and start their career (López-Pastor et al., 2013).

Since the beginning of the century, this definite trend of supply has been shrinking with the emergence of new forms of content distribution based on the advancement of various information and communication technologies (ICTs). Then again, information and communication technology offers a variety of possibilities for determining, distributing, and storing data and resources, despite their format and type. Besides that, pictures, diagrams, and text, these include multimedia-based simulations of complex processes and educational practices from all regions easily accessible in real-time and in contexts, for example, biological and medical sciences, agriculture, and engineering (Burmeister et al., 2012). The flexibility of delivery has become a mantra for third-party students, and it is simultaneously utilizing new national and global opportunities. The essence of the future education is the innovation in pedagogy and curriculum by the process of discussing the programme's main concepts and objectives among the leaners and facilitators (Howlett et al., 2016). Further, the mechanism has to evolved along with the stakeholders to facilitate incremental learning of the cycle curriculum (Howlett et al., 2016).

Innovation in the curriculum for skill development

In the global environment, the demand for skilled and multi-skill candidates is increasing. The World Bank in 2012 predicted that 600 million jobs are going to be needed in the next 15 years to maintain current employment rates in the developing world, let alone increase them.

About 90 per cent of employment opportunities require vocational skills. Only 20 per cent of our graduates get employed. One of the primary reasons is that our institutions of higher education do not change their curriculum according to the market demand. It is a long and cumbersome process to upgrade or change the curriculum in higher-education institutions; therefore, students are forced to study the outdated curriculum. The main reason is that the teachers are not trained continuously to get the requisite know-how about the latest curriculum and changes around the world. It is a duty of the higher-education institutions to keep curriculum relevant, current and adequate training is provided to the teachers so that they can impart the curriculum to their students.

In conventional global higher-education institutions such as Stanford and Harvard, there have been sweeping changes in the last few years to make the curriculum for their existing programmes more relevant to the industry. Concepts such as Critical Thinking, Creativity, and Design approach have been introduced across the board in engineering, management, and so on. In India, many premier institutions such as IIT-Kanpur and IIM-Ahmedabad have taken steps in upgrading their curriculum. For example, these institutions now encourage students to take up entrepreneurial activities along with their regular classes, thus allowing them to acquire cross-sector skills during their university years.

Similarly, there is a continuous need to innovate the skill curriculum. Higher-education institutions need to have a framework where relevant skills are imparted to the students to make them more employable and market-ready.

Framework for innovative pedagogy for skill development in higher education

We are proposing the CASECAC (pronounced as case-cac) framework for higher-educational institutions in India for the implementation of the innovative pedagogical methodology.

- *Crossover Learning:* Crossover learning refers to the comprehensive bridging of formal and informal settings. In India, more focus is on formal classroom teaching methods. The reformed institutions shall adopt the mixed approach of bringing formal and informal methods into the classroom. The learners should be exposed to informal teaching environments such as visits to industrial sites, museums, or after-college activities. Formal teaching builds the foundation, and informal teaching deepens the experience of learning. The learner should draw experience from multiple settings, thus helping him/her for lifelong learning.
- *Adaptive Learning*: All learners are different, but all the material used by the institutions is the same for all learners. Therefore, the adaptability of the material is a challenge. Through adaptive teaching, instructors develop a personalized learning path for each learner based on his or her previous exposure and experience. Adaptive teaching works both

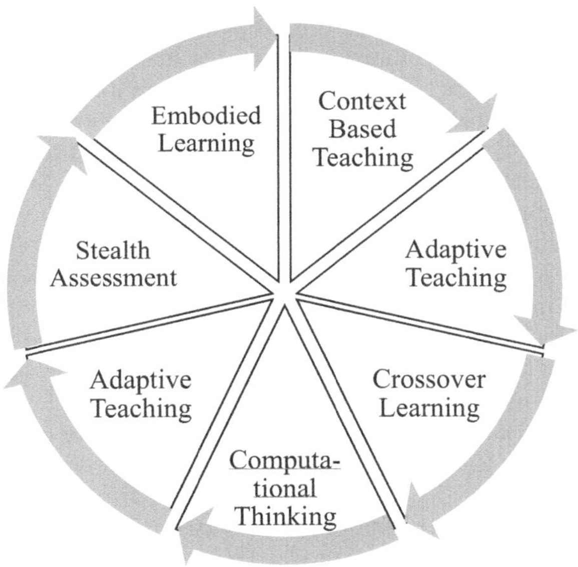

Figure 11.2 CASECAC framework for innovative pedagogy

Source: Authors' model and framework.

in classroom teaching and in the online environment where learners can choose their path. Given the focus on the implementation of digital methods, we propose a mixed approach where part of the curriculum is offered in the classroom, and the rest is offered in the online environment.

- *Stealth Assessment*: Stealth assessment is a continuous assessment of the performance of the student to assess his progress towards the targeted goal. Stealth assessment is all the more suitable for the fast-developing digital environment where the learner maybe learning at his own pace, and in the background, the automatic data is collected on how he used the content, participated in the discussions, responded to the queries, and appeared in the assessments. This data is useful in charting the individual learning path and making corrective changes as required.
- *Embodied Learning:* Embodied learning is a new pedagogy where alternative forms of learning/teaching can be accepted in the classroom. Though it is used in primary education to teach young children, now it is getting adopted mainly for adult learning; it would be especially useful for skill education. Embodied learning involves not just the intellectual part but using the whole body as a learning tool or in the more straightforward term 'learning with the object'—while the mind learns the concept, the body interacts with the object, thus immersing the learner into a different learning experience. New developments in wearable technologies and the introduction of digital tattoos, implanted technologies, and internal microchips are providing more information on how the body behaves in different situations, thus opening up newer avenues for learning. By examining the individual data, teachers can propose to train the individual in a particular skill where he or she is likely to succeed more.
- *Computational Thinking*: Computational thinking is solving the problem through a structured approach. It involves methods to solve the problems using techniques from computing. This is a powerful method where significant problems are broken down into smaller parts and looked at like an individual component and then the steps to solve the smaller problems are developed. Once all the sub-problems are solved, integrating them into the final solution is performed. Computational thinking is useful for problems in daily life, such as planning a holiday, writing a recipe for a favourite dish, and solving a difficult business challenge such as investing in the stock market.
- *Analytics of Emotions*: Students' emotional well-being is essential to creating a holistic learning environment. Analytics of emotions analyze the emotional state of the students, using tools that register eye movement and tools for facial recognition, to understand how students respond to the various concepts and methods. This is a new and promising way to judge whether the student is 'fit' to adopt the skill he is taught or not.
- *Context-based Teaching*: Traditionally, the Indian education system is entirely theoretical. In context-based teaching, the teachers are using

many cases and examples from Western organizations because there are not enough Indian cases that are documented. Hence, the problem of context is created. Students will be exposed to the context of the concept taught—how the concept can be helpful in real life or real business situations. Adequate audio/video tools can be used to demonstrate an example where the students can relate the particular concept to the local context.

The CASECAC framework is component-based, meaning that it can be used as a whole or in-parts according to the availability of the resources. Many of the ideas just proposed are futuristic, but Indian institutions are now ready to embrace these tools.

Conclusion

The CASECAC framework provides an opportunity to experiment with new ideas in the area of skill development in higher-education institutions. We all agree that continuous innovation in the curriculum is needed for the holistic development of the learners in order to train them in the skills for the future and make them more employable.

Indian higher education and skill development are riding on a roller coaster of technological changes. There is undoubtedly a great need to develop a learner-centric environment. There is a strong need and likelihood that digital technologies will be adopted seamlessly in higher-education delivery. The right confluence of formal and informal learning can pave the way for enriching the learning experience for the learner. The real challenge would be to design this integration of formal and informal for various courses and subjects across the degrees. Train the trainer programmes for faculty to orient them to tweak their curriculum to include both the elements will be needed. Faculty should be exposed to the newer methods and tools so that they can prepare the next-generation curriculum for the new India.

References

Burmeister, M., Rauch, F., & Elks, I. (2012). Education for sustainable development (ESD) and chemistry education. *Chemistry Education Research and Practice*, 13(2), 59–68.

Harman, K., & Bich, N. T. N. (2010). Reforming teaching and learning in Vietnam's higher education system. In G. Harman, M. Hayden, & P. T. Nghi (Eds.), *Reforming higher education in Vietnam: Challenges and priorities* (pp. 65–86). Dordrecht: Springer.

Howlett, C., Ferreira, J. A., & Blomfield, J. (2016). Teaching sustainable development in higher education: Building critical, reflective thinkers through an interdisciplinary approach. *International Journal of Sustainability in Higher Education*, 17(3), 305–321.

Jones, B., & Iredale, N. (2010). Enterprise education as pedagogy. *Education + Training*, 52(1), 7–19.
Jones, E. (2013). Internationalization and employability: The role of intercultural experiences in the development of transferable skills. *Public Money & Management*, 33(2), 95–104.
Klaus, S. (2016, January 14). The fourth industrial revolution: What it means, how to respond. *World Economic Forum*. www.weforum.org/agenda/2016/01/the-fourth-industrial-revolution-what-it-means-and-how-to-respond/.
Livingston, L. (2010). Teaching creativity in higher education. *Arts Education Policy Review*, 111(2), 59–62.
López-Pastor, V. M., Kirk, D., Lorente-Catalán, E., MacPhail, A., & Macdonald, D. (2013). Alternative assessment in physical education: A review of international literature. *Sport, Education, and Society*, 18(1), 57–76.
Sahlberg, P., & Oldroyd, D. (2010). Pedagogy for economic competitiveness and sustainable development. *European Journal of Education*, 45(2), 280–299.
Sterling, S. (Ed.). (2010). *Sustainability education: Perspectives and practice across higher education*. London: Taylor & Francis.

Chapter 12

Skilling India

Vocational orientation to higher education

Pankaj Mittal

India, the second largest higher-education system in the world, produces about 8 to 9 million graduates every year, out of which about 6 million are unemployed. In the case of the remaining graduates, there is a wide gap between the skills learnt by the students and the 'skill set' required by industry. Still worse is the fact declared by the McKinsey Report (2018) that 95 per cent of engineers in the country were not fit for software development jobs, and out of the remaining five percent, only 1.4 per cent could write functionally correct and efficient code. What is astonishing is that at exactly the same time when there is high graduate unemployment, there are also increasingly unfilled vacancies because people with the desired skill sets are lacking. The result is that our demographic dividend has slowly beginning to lose its sheen. There is an increasing pressure on the Indian higher-education system to equip students with not only traditional and theoretical knowledge but also with desired skills to enable them to play an effective role in the society. Of late, the thrust of education is shifting to employability, due to the paradigm shift from idealism to pragmatism. There is a shift from a specialized approach to a multidisciplinary approach with modular design to promote lifelong learning. The Higher Educational Institutes (HEIs) play a vital role in nurturing a quality culture in an organization by encompassing structural/managerial and cultural/psychological attributes to act in synergy (Bendermacher et al., 2016). These institutions need to be equipped with arrangements which can assure, support, develop, enhance, and monitor the quality of teaching and learning, thereby generating a skilled, competent, and employable workforce. The universities all around the globe need to reconsider their role in society and analyze their functioning with various constituencies, stakeholders, and communities (Jongbloed et al., 2008). Higher education's potential in contributing to economic well-being relates to understanding of the subject, acquiring vocational skills, and the possession of other value-added skills, qualities, and dispositions. Relevant disciplinary understanding along with skills and the soft or generic skills are key to employability. This chapter, while analyzing the need for vocationalization in higher education, offers a model for future-ready education based on technology and competence. It emphasizes on the need to move towards an ideal higher-education system through promotion of entrepreneurship and

DOI: 10.4324/9781003158349-15

skill enhancement. The international models for integrating vocationalization in higher education have been discussed, including the initiatives taken by India towards vocationalizing its higher education. Finally, a model has been suggested for India to revamp its higher education based on new occupational needs, practical orientation to traditional courses, on the job exposure, and a mixed approach consisting of teaching and field work.

Towards vocationalization in higher education

The present vocational education and training (VET) systems around the world adopt common trends like increasing the use of technology, increasing importance of information and communications systems, and changes to national demographics (Pilz, 2012). VET can be considered to be placed at the interface of education, training system, and employment. It contributes in meeting the transition from education to employment and providing the next-generation skilled force relevant to employment and economic scenario. There is a change in nature of vocationalization within the particular scope of higher education. Initially, it included a broader interpretation (education and training, health, standards of living) but over last few decades a narrower definition of vocationalization has come to prevail (Kelly, 2001) that emphasizes employability and economic returns to higher education.

There existed a balanced relationship between the vocational and higher-education systems, which has today moved towards the process of achieving a new dynamic equilibrium according to market demands. The vocationally oriented higher-education institutions in Japan are an example of this process (Maclean, 2010). Görke and Scholl (2006) analyzed the relationship between higher education, industry needs, and vocational education in terms of an 'autopoietic' system which is a self-organizing system for the society. According to this theory, needs of industry can be fulfilled through development of personal skills via university training (King & Thornhill, 2003). The theory further highlighted that the relations between the social communications systems and individual consciousness systems are structurally coupled.

Future-ready education

Over the last three decades under neo-liberalization and globalization, countries are focusing more on economic issues than on social issues. Pavlova and Maclean (2013) observed changes in the skill development model in the Asia-Pacific region. The study highlighted a change from an education-driven model to a functional-driven model in that particular region. Institutions like the World Economic Forum (WEF) classify national economic competitiveness and evaluate it to provide relative statistics for 'evidence-based' policy. The WEF classifies countries according to the stage of development: factor-driven economies (stage 1), efficiency-driven economies (stage 2), and innovation-driven economies (stage 3), with a transition phase between each stage. As a result, two dominant shifts that can be seen to impact future education are presented in the following two subsection.:

Increasing technology based self-learning

Presently, and more so in the near future, Artificial Intelligence, Internet of Things, Virtual and augmented Reality, Block Chain Technology, Robotics, Drones, Crypto Currency, Genomics, and so on will dominate the education space, with content more freely and readily available. Future education is supposed to be more of self-directed and self-paced learning which will be triggered by initiatives like problem-solving, innovation and creativity-driven education. The education will be collaborative where cross-institutional and cross-cultural educational opportunities, wherein learners play a key role as creators of knowledge, challenging the monopoly of teachers, will be important.

Increasingly competency-based

Education will have to be competency-based instead of merely information- or knowledge-based and demand-driven instead of supply-driven by incorporating skills capable of adapting themselves based on disruptive technologies. Education has to be flexible, modular, and lifelong, with equal emphasis on Emotional Quotient (EQ), Spiritual Quotient (SQ), and Intelligence Quotient (IQ). The new education will have to meet the need of Industry 4.0 and 5.0, enabling collaborative convergence of man and machines to explore new pedagogies. Education 5.0 will have to maximize the power of digital technologies, MOOCs, animated laboratories, and personalized data from the interconnected world.

Attaining an ideal higher-education system

Ideally, the higher-education system of the country should complement sustainable lifestyle education with successful professional life skills. Life skills will include the skills acquired by individuals in classroom learning or through life experience which can help them to eventually deal with problems they are expected to face in their lifetime or career. Acquiring life skills is the key factor for a rewarding professional and personal life. By learning these skills, they shall be able to inculcate the capacity for critical and creative thinking, be able to cooperate rather than to compete with fellow beings, and learn to be above the biases of gender, age, caste, religion, or nationality to become empowered graduates. The goal is to not just empower the graduates by instilling in them the vital skills essential for global employment but to enable them to realize their responsibilities and become socially responsive and humane citizens.

Life skills, consisting of effective communication, social skills, time management, problem-solving ability, decision making capacity, teamwork, leadership ability, and integrity, play a crucial role in boosting the employability of graduates. These skills empower them to be active participants in a democratic society. Life skills empower graduates with requisite self-confidence which will enable them to offer constructive, out-of-the-box yet sustainable solutions to the problems they face in their professional as well as personal life. This self-confidence equips them to apply learnt knowledge in unaccustomed and advanced circumstances with right attitudes while displaying human values like respect for fellow humans, the environment, and so on. In addition to 'knowing' and 'doing' aspects, there is the need to develop work ethics and inculcation of moral values in the students.

The document 'The four pillars of education' from UNESCO, which is elaborated by Delors (1996), rejects the mere instrumental and productivity-linked view of education; it states that the education of human beings must be organized according to four fundamental types of learning: learning to learn, learning to do, learning to live together, and learning to be (Olaniran, 2016). According to Werthein (2003), who is UNESCO's representative in Brazil, 'These four pillars must be found in the education quality improvement policy, since they cover human beings as a whole, from the cognitive to the ethical, from the aesthetical to the technical, from the immediate to the transcendent.'

Promoting entrepreneurship education and training for skill enhancement

'Entrepreneurship' is gaining increasing importance among higher-education institutions as well as students. The Government of India's focus on 'Start-up India', among other initiatives, has raised the aspirations and capability of innovation and creativity among enlightened youth. However, for a majority of our students, an entrepreneurial career still remains a remote priority. Despite the desire to establish an enterprise, most are inhibited by 'fear of failure', lack of awareness, guidance, finances, courage, willpower, and credible skill education in the discipline. A special report on 'Global Perspective on Entrepreneurship Education and Training' by Global Entrepreneurship Monitor (GEM) in 2008 enumerates the key ingredients of entrepreneurship education as building entrepreneurship knowledge and skills through a recognized programme. According to the GEM India Survey, India ranked 13th out of 54 economies in 'School Entrepreneurship Education'; however, it ranked 23rd out of 54 economies in higher education. It is, therefore, important to reinforce entrepreneurship education at all levels so as to harness the untapped entrepreneurial potential of youth.

A study conducted by Sunil Shukla (1998) suggested that 'curriculum of Entrepreneurship programme should have a mix of skill building trainings, knowledge acquisition courses and capability building for entrepreneurial attitude'. The programme delivery in entrepreneurship courses should be more applied but suitably coupled with theoretical nuances of management and behavioural sciences. The key focus of entrepreneurship programme should be on (1) Risk Propensity and Soft-Skills of Entrepreneurs; (2) Identification and Evaluation of Business Opportunities; (3) Detailed Project Report or Business Plan of an Enterprise; and (4) Support System Institutions and Implementation Strategy. Through these focused attempts, an entrepreneurship programme could prepare an individual to pursue an entrepreneurial career. The World Economic Forum's report (2009) on 'Educating the Next Wave of Entrepreneurs: Unlocking Entrepreneurial Capabilities to Meet the Global Challenges of the 21st Century' highlights key areas for maximizing the learning about entrepreneurship by the participants in terms of What, How, Where, and Who to teach entrepreneurship, which is reproduced next (Wilson et al., 2009)

a What

- Increasing entrepreneurial behaviour and building mindsets
- Confidence building, improving self-efficacy, and inculcating leadership
- Building creative and innovative thinking
- Mindset for problem solving
- Ability to manage risk, unpredictable outcome, and complexity
- Understanding business and financial issues
- Understanding on opportunity sensing
- Ability to build business, manage finance, and growth of ventures
- Building social networks

b How

- Pedagogy that involves interactive learning approach
- Course should have multidisciplinary learnings and programmes
- The teaching should have live projects, case studies, simulations
- Appropriate use of digital tools during course delivery
- Hands-on learning should be the focus
- Experiential learning approach to be followed
- Start-up internships is right way to enable students
- In-house business mentors would help coaching and counselling students

c Who

- Participants, emerging entrepreneurs and students
- Resource persons and faculty members
- Professors, instructors, trainers
- Business leaders and entrepreneurs
- Mentors, coaches, counsellors, advisors

d Where

- Academic institutions
- Across all academic disciplines
- Compulsory and elective courses

- Training and capacity building institutions
- Workplace-based training programmes
- Continuous and lifelong learning

International models

Integrate vocationalization in higher education

Some of the well-accepted and renowned international models for higher education are listed as follows.

Australia: The VET system is nationally regulated to conform to a national quality framework. The system offers a tertiary education pathway designed for acquiring workplace-specific skills. Training may take place in a classroom, online, or workplace which may be full-time or part-time.

Germany: Follows a dual VET system with theory and training combined in a real work setting. In-company training and support to the trainees by the trade unions ensures a skilled labour force. It is mandatory for industry to employ only a skilled workforce.

Korea: VET is provided across schools, colleges, and polytechnics (2–3 years) by the Ministry of Education. Further, the Ministry of Employment and Labour offers formal and informal training to unemployed and on-the-job training to existing employees. The Academic Credit Bank System, a central agency, recognizes diverse learning experiences via degrees gained at school and aggregates them. Robust National Competency Standards ensures that the VET system provides updated skills to meet the labour market needs.

China: Vocational education is introduced at junior secondary school (12–14 years of age). A test called the Zhongkao test is conducted at the school-leaving stage, and the scores obtained in that test determine entry in mainstream education or vocational streams. Training for students includes apprenticeships, on-the-job training, entrepreneurship training, and pre-job training. There are several training providers and options open to students such as vocational junior secondary schools, senior secondary vocational schools, and secondary specialized schools offering five-year advanced VET, and so on. Teachers at VET schools are provided with vocational certificates in relevant trades apart from the requisite degrees and are required to undergo one month of industry training every year. China also runs Luban Workshops, a project launched by the Tianjin government to provide state-of-the-art technical and vocational training, promote modern vocational education reforms, and enhance collaboration among vocational schools around the world. The Luban Workshops have been established in many countries, including in India (at Chennai) to impart vocational skills.

Switzerland: A three-layer system of government, vocational school, and industry support the vocational education system. Small and large companies support apprentices 15–19 years of age who learn all aspects of the trade required for a career. Like China, students take an early decision in their life between general and vocational education, and there is an entire supporting architecture for both.

Initiatives towards higher-education vocationalization in India

The two apex-level regulatory authorities of general academic and professional technical education have initiated schemes to incorporate elements to skill delivery under the new NVEQF. The Scheme of Career Orientation to Education/Career Oriented Programme/Career Oriented Courses in Universities and Colleges were started with the aim to provide knowledge, skills, and aptitude for gainful employment in the wage sector in general, and self-employment in particular, to undergraduates. The intention was also to reduce the pressure on institutions of higher learning for master's degree programmes and research. The courses under these schemes have been expanded and redesigned to include more credits for practical training. These courses run parallel to the conventional BA, B.Com, and B.Sc degrees and are interdisciplinary in nature. The students thus are being given the freedom to diversify into various fields, not necessarily related with their core discipline. For example, a science student could side by side pursue a course in event management, and a student with an arts background could have the option of pursuing a course in science journalism (UGC Annual report 2012–2013). During the XII Plan (2012–2017), 793 courses were approved for the next five years at 522 institutions (516 colleges + 6 universities) for the introduction of Career Oriented Courses (Khare, 2016).

The scheme of community colleges and B.Voc. as well as KAUSHAL KENDRAS (Skill Centres) too were launched by UGC/AICTE with the goal of developing a synergistic relationship between the community, community colleges (CC) and the job market. UGC and AICTE approved the scheme of community colleges to provide:

> low cost, high quality education encompassing the components of both traditional skill development as well as academic coursework, to provide an option to the learners to either move directly to employment sector or to higher education sector. It thus offers a flexible and open education system which also caters to community based lifelong learning needs.
>
> (University Grants Commission [UGC])

The target group here were the students currently pursuing higher education but actually interested in entering the workforce at the earliest opportunity. In order to ensure a local connection, under the scheme, universities/colleges were preferred to host CC if they had proximity to local industry partners. A similar attempt has been made by AICTE too for opening CC offering engineering/technical courses in engineering colleges.

UGC also established as many as 100 'Deen Dayal Upadhyay Centres for Knowledge Acquisition and Upgradation of Skilled Human Abilities and Livelihood (KAUSHAL) during the XII Plan period. The centres were designed to allow for vocational education in a pyramidical structure starting from a minimum of diploma to advanced diploma, B.Voc., and further studies at Post Graduate and research level. The purpose was to provide threefold services focusing on skills for employability, developing entrepreneurship traits, and acting as a centre of excellence through critical innovative research for skill development in specialized areas.

These centres also act as inter-university, inter-sectoral university-industry, higher-education system, and industrial-sector coordination facilitators.

Under both these schemes, the purpose was to enable students to pursue a bachelor's degree (Bachelor of Vocational Studies, B.Voc.) as part of college/university education, allowing for multiple exits such as diploma/advanced diploma under the NSQF along with broad-based general education. The course were designed to also incorporate specific job roles and their National Occupational Standards (NOSs). The course curriculum had a larger component of skill-based vocational education (60 per cent) and a smaller (40 per cent) component of general education in a credit-based semester system. The institutions were provided complete autonomy in identifying the courses to be offered, but some indicative courses were proposed by UGC by way of common guidelines (see Box 12.1).

Box 12.1 B.Voc. indicative courses (stream-wise)

Science Stream: Information and Computer technology, Refrigeration, Biotechnology, Hospital waste Disposal Management and Sericulture, and so on.

Social Sciences and Humanities Streams: The courses could be of interdisciplinary nature, namely, applied Sociology, Applied Psychology, Tourism, Fashion Designing, Translation Proficiency, Television, and Video Production.

Commerce Stream: Insurance, Banking, e-Commerce, World Trade, Foreign Exchange Trade, Retailing, and so on.

Source: Khare (2016).

Suggested model for India

A major problem in India relates to the lack of connection between higher education and the life roles for which students have to prepare themselves as earners, citizens, and parents for bringing up the future generations. The curricula in many of our HEIs consists of knowledge which is obsolete, and the teaching pedagogy imparts theoretical knowledge with no scope for application. This issue becomes very grave when we consider the fact that 88 per cent of our students in social sciences, humanities, basic sciences, and commerce will terminate their education at the bachelor's degree, and only about 10 per cent will enrol for the master's degree. Suggestions for revamping the model of higher education in India may be classified on four bases:

(1) *Understanding New Occupational Needs:* Modern education in India was founded on the need for administrators by the British. While the context of our needs has changed tremendously in the direction of requiring personnel for the sectors of rural development, agriculture, industry, health, education, information technology, emerging technologies, commerce, communication, and so on, the emphasis in many of our universities and colleges is still on preparing the graduates for clerical work, besides the nascent growth of commerce in the private sector.

(2) *Practical Orientation to Traditional Courses:* We require a reorientation of all our syllabi so that a graduate can find a niche in our business, industry, or rural environment. For instance, physics, chemistry, botany, biology, zoology, and so on all have applied components. Industrial chemistry and food processing technology are examples. We could have applied components to science subjects such as electronics, instrumentation, marine biology, biochemistry, and so on.

In the rural context, zoology, botany, and biology can have application in agro-industries, animal husbandry, poultry, pisciculture, sericulture, forestry, floriculture, and horticulture. Applications can be considered in the social sciences where, for example, sociology students can be trained for working in cooperatives or other development programmes. Political science students can be placed with urban local government and Panchayati Raj Institutions for practice experience, parallel to their courses. Psychology students can be placed in schools, colleges, or industrial organizations.

While commerce courses teach subjects which have applications, no practical experience is provided through placement in a business environment such as in banking, insurance, import-export, small-scale industries, and so on. Humanities students can also have real work-life experiences. For example, language students may intern in translation/interpretation jobs especially for business organizations; publishing, editing, and proofreading companies; and in the entire field of mass communication and in electronic and print media. The communications field needs social scientists for research and scriptwriting for their programmes.

(3) *On the Job Exposure:* Not only, therefore, do courses need to change but students need to have direct field experience through placements in organizations either in the form of internships or apprenticeships. Numerous field opportunities would have to be identified.
(4) *Mixed Approach:* The teaching part of the courses may be organized on four days of the week and the field work on remaining two days. Generally, students may pay the costs of travel and out-of-pocket expenses. Teachers may be reimbursed for travel. Since the courses should be relevant to the area/region of institutional location, the placements should be local and thus should not lead to an increase in the cost of vocationalization.

The advantages are numerous, because we do not need to create an infrastructure which already exists in the community. In an era when obsolescence of equipment occurs in a short span of time, universities and colleges necessarily need to utilize the infrastructure in the community in alternative ways and means. Moreover, potential employers/organizations may become partners and themselves tend to absorb the trainees in their organization after graduation or even during their vacation. Hence, such parallel field work placement is likely to be cost-effective, increase interaction of the field with the university and college, and bring the teaching community close to the field.

Such a model already exists in the country for certain disciplines such as social work, personnel management/industrial relations/labour, welfare, and so on. It needs to be replicated widely in other subjects through a reorganization of the existing curriculum to make it more applied and through the placement of students in organizations throughout the academic year (not only summer placements, which could be additional).

Conclusion

It can be concluded that a well-laid institutional and regulatory architecture for vocational education exists in almost all countries, and a similar structure is required in India, with its vast student community where youth with varied abilities can opt for suitable vocations, without forcible entry into the general stream. In the Indian context, much is taught about theory or knowledge aspects of the curriculum but not the applied aspects; not much material is available to the educators about instructional strategies and evaluation techniques in the practical area of skill development or skill learning.

Nowadays, a career for a lifetime is no longer an option. Most people hold jobs with a number of employers and move across different employment sectors during their working life. Therefore, they need to be flexible in their skills and be prepared to change jobs and/or sectors if there are better opportunities elsewhere. In order to be flexible, they need a set of 'transferable skills'—skills that are not specific to one particular job but are generic across all employment sectors. Employers are often looking for skills that go beyond qualifications and experience. They need the skills to apply knowledge that one has learnt in every sphere of life.

Educators today have to keep in mind that the 21st century learner needs to be handled differently. They have to use those technologies in the near future that haven't been invented yet. They have to undertake jobs that don't exist today. They have to get engaged in multiple tasks; be digitally literate, and have strong visual and spatial skills. They have to remain networked globally, learn things that matter, and look for challenging jobs. Thus, for the learner-driven education system of today, a new orientation towards skill development is required. Working with hands and thinking with brain will have to go together for holistic development of intellectual and manual skills. A number of personal and social skills popularly known as soft skills are essential for enhancing employability and self-employment, for which the higher-education sector has to proactively work together with the employer segment and reorient as well as revamp itself accordingly.

References

Bendermacher, G. W. G., Oude Egbrink, M. G. A., Wolfhagen, I. H. A. P., & Dolmans, D. H. J. M. (2016). Unravelling quality culture in higher education: A realist review. *Higher Education*, 73(1), 39–60. https://doi.org/10.1007/s10734-015-9979-2.

Delors, J. (1996). Learning: The treasure within. Report to UNESCO of the International Commission on Education for the Twenty-first Century.

Görke, A., & Scholl, A. (2006). Niklas Luhmann's theory of social systems and journalism research. *Journalism Studies*, 7(4), 644–655. https://doi.org/10.1080/14616700600758066.

Jongbloed, B., Enders, J., & Salerno, C. (2008). Higher education and its communities: Interconnections, interdependencies and a research agenda. *Higher Education*, 56, 303–324. https://doi.org/10.1007/s10734-008-9128-2.

Kelly, D. J. (2001). *Dual perceptions of HRD: Issues for policy: SME's, other constituencies, and the contested definitions of human resource development.* Paper presented to ninth annual meeting of PECC-HRD Pacific Economic Cooperation Council Human Resource Development Task Force PECC, Hualien.

Khare, M. (2016). Taking the skills March forward in India: Transitioning to the world of work. In M. Pilz (Ed.), *India: Preparation for the world of work-education system and school to work transition.* Wiesbaden: Springer.

King, M., & Thornhill, C. (2003). Luhmann's social theory. In *Niklas Luhmann's theory of politics and law* (pp. 1–34). London: Palgrave Macmillan. https://doi.org/10.1057/9780230503588_1.

Maclean, R. (2010). *Vocationalization of higher education: Issues and challenges.* Proceedings of the 1st UPI International Conference on Technical and Vocational Education and Training, November 10–11, 11–18, Bandung, Indonesia.

Olaniran, S. O. (2016). *Revisiting UNESCO four pillars of education and its implications for the 21st century teaching and learning.* Proceedings of 1st International Conference on Teaching and Learning Conference, Richards Bay, South Africa.

Pavlova, M., & Maclean, R. (2013). Vocationalisation of secondary and tertiary education: Challenges and possible future directions. In R. Maclean, S. Jagannathan, & J. Sarvi (Eds.), *Skills development for inclusive and sustainable growth in developing Asia-pacific* (Vol. 19, pp. 43–66). Dordrecht: Springer. https://doi.org/10.1007/978-94-007-5937-4_3.

Pilz, M. (2012). *The future of vocational education and training in a changing world.* https://doi.org/10.1007/978-3-531-18757-0.

Shukla, S. (1998). *Curriculum of entrepreneurship in institutions of higher learning: A critical analysis.* Biennial Conference (3rd): National Seminar on Current Trends in Entrepreneurship Research (March 18–20), EDII, Ahmedabad.

UGC, UGC GUIDELINES FOR COMMUNITY COLLEGESt UNIVERSITY GRANTS COMMISSION SCHEME OF COMMUNITY COLLEGES FOR UNIVERSITIES AND COLLEGES (2012-2017) https://www.ugc.ac.in/skill/pdf/Community%20Colleges%20XII%20Plan.pdf.

Werthein, J. (2003). *Education: The challenge of quality.* www.unesco.org.br/noticias/opiniao/artigow/artigow_qual/mostra_documento.

Wilson, K. E., Vyakarnam, S., Volkmann, C., Mariotti, S., & Rabuzzi, D. (2009). Educating the next wave of entrepreneurs: Unlocking entrepreneurial capabilities to meet the global challenges of the 21st century. *World Economic Forum: A Report of the Global Education Initiative.* https://ssrn.com/abstract=1396704 or http://dx.doi.org/10.2139/ssrn.1396704.

Chapter 13

Skill universities in India

S.K. Shukla and Komal Raghav

Higher education in India is offered through universities, colleges, and institutions of higher education. The universities consist of central universities, state universities, deemed universities, and private universities. Most universities, in general, are multi-faculty, and they offer study programmes in various disciplines. India also established single-discipline specialized universities to promote specific areas of specialization. For example, specialized universities have been established to promote agriculture, veterinary sciences, medical sciences, journalism, women's studies, technology, music, law, and sports. Similar examples are also found in the cases of Gujarat Forensic Science University; Sardar Patel University of Police, Security and Criminal Justice in Jodhpur; Railway University in Vadodara Rajiv; and Gandhi National Aviation University in Amethi, Uttar Pradesh. The idea of skill university also emanates from this very same idea of specialized universities. The focus of skill universities is promoting skill formation through university education and is very closely related to vocationalization of higher education.

This chapter takes a look at the evolution of skill integration in Indian universities that finally culminated into the formation of specific-skill universities. It provides an overview of skill universities in India by closely examining the study programmes offered and fees levied along with trends in enrolment and placements of students. The empirical basis of the chapter is based on both primary and secondary sources. The primary data was collected through a survey in selected skill universities and traditional universities. Out of five skill universities, Shri Vishwakarma Skill University, Palwal, was visited in order to have first-hand information about skill universities. From other skill universities, such as Bhartiya Skill Development University, Jaipur, and Seacom Skills University, West Bengal, the information was collected through personal communication. The secondary data was collected from information given on various skill universities' websites, annual reports of All India Survey on Higher Education (AISHE), annual reports of University Grants Commission (UGC), reports of Planning Commission, reports of the Ministry of Skill Development and Entrepreneurship and Union Budget 2020–2021, and so on. A survey was done from students enrolled in B.Voc. courses from colleges and universities in order to know their awareness about skill universities.

DOI: 10.4324/9781003158349-16

Growth of skill education in India

The UGC implemented the scheme of community colleges from 2013–2014 in a pilot mode on the initiative of the MHRD. With a view to enhance employability of the graduates and meet industry requirements, the UGC launched the B.Voc. degree programme to expand the scope of vocational education and also to provide vertical mobility to the students admitted into community colleges. Under the B.Voc. programme, the students also have the option to exit with a certificate, diploma, or advanced diploma after acquiring the requisite number of credits. To give further push to vocational education 'Deen Dayal Upadhyay (DDU) Centres for Knowledge Acquisition and Upgradation of Skilled Human Abilities and Livelihood (KAUSHAL)' were promoted.

As of 2019, there were 531 colleges/universities specializing in the area of skill development. Out of this number, 275 were B.Voc. colleges, 188 community colleges and 68 DDU Kaushal Kendra Colleges (PIB, 2019). The enrolment in B.Voc. programmes in various universities and colleges in India increased from 472 in 2011–2012 to 33,263 in 2018–2019 (see Table 13.1). In fact, the growth in enrolment was slow till the skill-based higher-education scheme was introduced by UGC in 2014. The enrolment growth picked up after 2014. Even then, the increase in enrolment was limited because of low acceptability and credibility of certification from these institutions by employers. This realization led to the need for university-based educational systems to provide credibility to the skills ecosystem in the country.

On the recommendation of a proposal given by a working group in Parliament in 2015, the skill universities in India were established. According to the proposal, the courses and programmes of skill universities will be skill-based courses, and their major focus will be on practical training rather than classroom study. The skills universities will offer sector-specific certificate, diploma, and degree programmes directly related to the job roles in demand. Everything will be planned according to market demand of specific sector jobs, such as designing the course curriculum, skill assessments, student and faculty training, apprenticeship, job training, placements, joint research projects, and so on. It was visualized that these programmes should be different from the conventional degree courses offered by academic institutions such as B.Sc. Electronics, B.Sc. Computers, and

Table 13.1 Total number of students enrolled under B.Voc. programmes in universities and colleges in India from 2011–2012 to 2018–2019

Year	*2011–2012*	*2012–2013*	*2013–2014*	*2014–2015*	*2015–2016*	*2016–2017*	*2017–2018*	*2018–2019*
Total Students Enrolled	472	411	544	3527	10205	17820	23891	33263

Source: http://aishe.nic.in/aishe/reports, 2011–2012 to 2018–2019.

Table 13.2 List of skill universities in India

S. No.	*Name of university/institute*	*Year of establishment*	*Place*	*State*	*Ownership*
1	Institute of Leadership Development (ILD)	1992	Jaipur	Rajasthan	Public
2	Teamlease Skills University (TLSU)	2013	Vadodara	Gujarat	Private
3	Seacom Skills University (SSU)	2014	Shantiniketan	West Bengal	Private
4	Shri Vishwakarma Skills University (SVSU)	2016	Palwal	Haryana	Public
5	Symbiosis Skills and Open University (SSOU)	2017	Pune	Maharashtra	Private
6	Bhartiya Skills Development University (BSDU)	2017	Jaipur	Rajasthan	Private

Source: Compiled from various sources. www.ugc.ac.in/oldpdf/Consolidated%20list%20of%20All%20 Universities.pdf.

so on.(Sneha, 2018). The first skill university was established in Palwal, Haryana, namely Shri Vishwakarma Skill University. This was followed by establishment of skill universities by various states (see Table 13.2). The Association of Indian Skills Universities (AISU) was formed in 2017. The establishment of skill universities signals transformation of Indian higher education with a strong bias towards skills education to enhance the employability of university graduates through better facilitation of industry–academia cooperation.

The universities shown in Table 13.2 have been opened in both the public and private domain, along with PPP mode. Some universities have only local area jurisdiction while others have centres across different towns. For example, the Institute of Leadership Development (ILD) is providing skill-based short-term training programmes at various Skill Development Centres (SDC) in Jaipur, Jaisalmer, and Ajmer. Apart from these, Assam Government is going to establish Skill University at Darrang district, and other states are also trying to establish skill universities in near future. Some private universities are also being established by business organizations. In September 2019, a partnership of Sony India Company with National Skill Development Corporation and Kedman Skilling Private Ltd has also been established for the provision of job opportunities to students.

Courses in skill universities in India

In the skill universities listed in Table 13.2, various skill courses are running (see Table 13.3); the detail of their seats and fee structures is given in the table.

From Table 13.3, it is clear that B.Voc. and M.Voc. programmes are running only in two universities, Shri Vishwakarma Skill University, a public university,

Table 13.3 Courses and fee structure of skill universities in India

Shri Vishwakarma Skill University			*Bhartiya Skill Development University*			*Seacom Skills University*		*Teamlease Skills University*			*Symbiosis Skill and Open University*	
Course	Seats	Total Fees (in Rs.)	Course	Seats	Total Fees (in Rs.)	Course	Total Fees (in Rs.)	Course	Seats	Total Fees (in Rs.)	Course	Total Fees (in Rs.)
Diploma	20–60	6,000–18,000	B.Voc.	30–60	1.80 Lacs to 4.5 Lacs	Certificate	45,000	DMLT	60	30,000	B.Arch	9 Lacs
D.Voc.	20–60	24,000	B.Tech	30	10 Lacs	B.Tech	2.95 Lacs	B.Com	60	60,000	B.Tech	9.80 Lacs
B.Voc.	30–60	26,000–33,000	M.Voc.	10	2 Lacs	BCA, B.B.A.	1.60 Lacs	B.Sc.	60	1.50 Lacs	B.Sc.	5.25 Lacs
M.Voc.	20	20,000–27,000	Ph.D.			B.Com., B.Sc.	95,000–2.50 Lacs	B.C.A.	60	1.50 Lacs	B.B.A.	6.90 Lacs
P.G. Diploma	20–30	11,000–15,000				B.Pharm	3.75 Lacs	B.B.A.	60	1.50 Lacs	P.G. Diploma	75,000–1.85 Lacs
						M.Com, M.Sc.	65,000–1.10 Lacs	Associate Degree	60	1 Lacs		
						M.C.A., M.B.A.	1.90 Lacs					
						M.Tech., P.G. Diploma,	1.55 Lacs					
						Ph.D.	3.10 Lacs					

Source: Compiled from various sources.

and Bhartiya Skill Development University, a private university. Seacom Skills University also started a B.Voc. programme but in session 2018–2019, it did not admit students in this course. These universities are following UGC Instructions for Vocational Programmes, National Skills Qualifications Framework (NSQF), AICTE Instruction for Vocational Programmes, NSQF RPL (Recognition of Previous Learning) Guidelines, Guidelines of respective Sector Skill Councils (SSC), National Occupational Standards (NOS), and Skills Qualification Packs.

Other skill universities like Teamlease Skills University, Symbiosis Skill and Open University are running courses with different nomenclature which are not considered under skill universities' programmes. The Ph.D. in skill-based programmes such as electrical and manufacturing are only provided by Bhartiya Skill Development University. Seacom Skills University is also providing the Ph.D. programme in various disciplines but not in skill courses. Thus, can be seen that although by nomenclature these are skill universities. The majority of skill universities are typically not offering exclusively skill courses but general courses like business application (B.B.A.), computer application (B.C.A.), pharmacy, architecture, and so on.

Course content in skill universities

The guidelines of the National Skills Qualifications Framework (NSQF) and the credit system are followed by skill universities. Under NSQF, levels 1 to 10 are given to school education and higher education for skill development among students. Levels 1–4 pertain to school level education; levels 5–7 for diploma, advanced diploma; graduation; and levels 8–10 are for honours at the undergraduate level, master's and doctoral. For each course, some credits are given by UGC, such as 60 credits for diploma, 120 credits for advanced diploma, and 180 credits for the B.Voc. degree. These credits are mandatory for all the universities. All skill universities are providing education in 60:40 ratios, meaning that the universities offer 60 per cent vocational education and 40 per cent general education through the Industry Integrated Dual Education Model (IIDEM) programme. The major focus of skill universities is on 'Learning by Doing' and 'Earn While Learn' by doing 'On the Job Training (OJT) at partners' industries in a year under the contractual employment or apprentice models like National Apprenticeship Promotion Scheme (NAPS)/National Employment Enhancement Mission (NEEM) programmes launched by Government of India. During this training period, stipendiary for 6–8 months will be given to the students as a trainee.

Enrolment of students in skill universities

In various courses, student enrolment is very low in these skill universities. Teamlease Skills University, established in 2013, has given a total of 29 degrees for undergraduate courses and 56 diplomas to students through 2019. Student numbers are high in government universities when compared to private universities because of the government's low fee structure. Shri Vishwakarma Skill University is a public university, established in 2016, which has admitted 224 students in undergraduate and 24 students in postgraduate courses in 2018–2019, while Bhartiya Skill Development University, a private university, had 257 students in undergraduate programme and 9 students in postgraduate courses in the same year. A fall in student enrolment can be seen in year 2019–2020, with 204 students in undergraduate and three students in postgraduate courses in this university.

Skills universities, like other traditional universities, must perform teaching and research activities. Out of surveyed students from selected skill universities, 65 per cent of students responded that the main emphasis of skill universities is on teaching only. The research activities are not being promoted properly. Only a few universities have facilities for Ph.D. No university is running M.Phil. programme. In academic session 2019–2020, Bhartiya Skill Development University has conducted five Ph.D. entrance tests in the summer and winter sessions through which a total of 29 students were enrolled in various subjects like electrical, electronics, English, entrepreneurship, IT and networking, library and information science, management, mechanical, and psychology, and so on. In Seacom Skills University, 30 students in 2016, 200 students in 2017, 86 students in 2018, and 45 students in 2019 were enrolled for Ph.D. in various disciplines such as Bengali, education, English, management, environmental science, geography, history, mathematics, Sanskrit, social sciences, physics, bioscience and zoology, but there was no admission for Ph.D. in skill-related subjects.

Absence of proper research facilities, dedicated research centres and shortage of research guides were identified as major issues. In terms of research, skills universities tried to accommodate scholars who could study new methods of pedagogies, evaluate existing programmes, suggest policy interventions, and so on. An alternative model of first incubating a smaller centre for vocational education and gradually expanding it to form a university can also be explored to achieve scalability in a cost-effective and sustainable manner.

Faculty in skill universities

According to the data available on official websites of skill universities, the total number of faculty in various skill universities in India is not sufficient. In Teamlease Skills University, there are only two professors, one associate professor and four assistant professors for teaching in various diploma and degree courses. The faculty strength in Seacom Skills University is three professors and 24 assistant professors, which is comparatively better than Teamlease Skills University.

In Bhartiya Skill Development University, there are 11 professors, four associate professors and 23 assistant professors. This staff strength is much better than that in other universities. In Shri Vishwakarma Skill University, there is only one professor and five assistant professors who are teaching in various D.Voc., B.Voc, and M.Voc. programmes.

Among these faculty members, very few have a doctorate and other UGC prescribed qualifications. Most faculty members have a technical background and do not having skill-based degrees. There is a shortage of good-quality trained teachers with any industrial experience or exposure because after completion of courses, most of the successful students wish to work in the industrial sector rather than continue in academics. Thus, the universities face difficulties in attracting the best faculty. These universities also avail themselves of professionals from different industries and other business concerns as visiting faculty. However, these are very limited in number, and the scope of strengthening the integration is low. It is important that to teach in these universities, industrial experts of related subjects should be appointed so that they can give practical exposure to students from their experience. A skill university must be allowed to deviate from hiring professors and assistant professors in the conventional hierarchical structure with set qualifications. Instead, sector-specific norms that focus on domain knowledge rather than academic qualifications must become the yardstick of choosing instructors either on a permanent or contractual basis.

Placement of students

Placement is a very important parameter for the success of any university. These universities are in a nascent stage. The B.Voc. programme in Shri Vishwakarma Skill University and Bhartiya Skill Development University started in 2017. Degrees in undergraduates and postgraduates programmes have not yet given by skill universities. Hence, the placement data on degree courses is still not available. Only the placement of certificate and diplomas students has been done in their various academic partners. The students of Bhartiya Skill Development University have been placed in RS India, Adani Group, Daikin, Adecco, Mahindra Rise, Rufil, Ruj Elecon Pvt. Ltd., Genus, Autopal, Sandhar, A & D International Pvt. Ltd., Motherson Techno Tools Ltd., Honda, Perto, Ceratizit, Nirmal Glasstech Industries, and so on.

Academic and industrial partners of skill universities

Skill universities in India have set up liaison with various business organizations for academic and other purposes. Shri Vishwakarma Skill University has an academic and industrial partnership with East West Automation Tech. Pvt. Ltd. for D.Voc. (industrial electronics), Roop Auto for D.Voc. (mechanical-manufacturing), BFDS for Diploma (footwear production), and so on. For B.Voc. programmes, it has an industrial partnership with Shivam Dairy/GNG Group for B.Voc. (agriculture), Dia Vikas Capital Pvt. Ltd. for B.Voc. (management-financial services), Concentrix for B.Voc. (management-BPM and analytics), Anand Group for B.Voc. (mechanical-manufacturing), and so on.

Seacom Skills University has signed MOU with Scotland's Colleges International (SCI) for academic collaboration in all engineering and technological spheres in the areas of pedagogy, learner-centric skill development and faculty and students exchange programmes, and so on. International collaboration with Bourneville College, Birmingham, UK, in the areas of pedagogy, skill development and faculty and students exchange programmes, and so on. It has also been chosen by global IT giant IBM, and a memorandum of understanding has been signed with IBM entitled 'Career Education in IBM Software (CEIS)'.

Teamlease Skills University has a Tie-Up with Model Career Centre, JBS, Erasmus+ UKIERI, Muni Seva Ashram, and so on.

The industry partners of Symbiosis Skill and Open University are ICICI Bank, SS, Enrich Salons, SKF, Daikin Air Conditioning, LSC, JNPT, and B&W SSC.

NAAC accreditation and ranking

To rank institutions of higher education in India, a National Institutional Ranking Framework (NIRF) method was approved by the Ministry of Human Resource Development on 29 September 2015, which consists of five parameters: Teaching, Learning & Resources (TLR), Research and Professional Practice (RP), Graduation Outcomes (GO), Outreach and Inclusivity (OI), and Peer Perception. This ranking is one of the key decision criteria for the students to take admission in various institutes. Through the NIRF ranking, students can choose the best university for admission. In the NIRF ranking list for universities and colleges, the Indian Institute of Science, Bengaluru, and Miranda House College, Delhi, were on 1st rank in 2019. But these skill universities are never listed in its ranking list, because these universities are not fulfilling the eligibility criteria for listing in NIRF ranking. It makes students not to choose these skill universities for education. To enhance student enrolment in skill universities, it is necessary for the universities to maintain the five parameters of NIRF ranking.

For higher education, none of the skill universities is accredited by the National Assessment and Accreditation Council (NAAC), whose accreditation is also necessary for the development of the institution. Skill universities should try to improve their academic as well as overall performance to get accreditation from NAAC.

Degrees/programmes in skill and traditional universities

It has been the experience of specialized universities that they do not run courses related to only the specialized areas for which they have been established. To attract students for enrolment, educational institutes are offering various courses. They are running courses with different nomenclature. As per table no. 13.3, out of five skills universities, B.Voc. and M.Voc. courses are being run in Bhartiya Skill Development University and Shri Vishwakarma Skill University. In Seacom Skill

University, there is no admission for B.Voc. courses in 2018–2019. Symbiosis Skills and Open University runs B.Tech., B.B.A., B.Arch., and B.Sc., and so on. Teamlease Skills University runs B.Com., B.B.A., B.C.A., and B.Sc., and so on. Institute of Leadership Development does not have any degree programme but is organizing an employment-linked skill training programme. As far as departments are concerned, these are also different in different universities. The sanctioned seats are fixed in a few universities.

The skills university is a specialized university established for promoting courses related to skills. Its courses should be different from other universities. If a skill university also runs B.B.A. and M.B.A., and so on, then it will be forfeiting its main objective of providing course in B.Voc./M.Voc. Also, the curriculum will include management, accounts, and economics-based subjects. Universities may open departments of these subjects only to provide requisite credit for B.Voc./M. Voc. degrees, but universities should not start main degrees in these subjects.

For skills universities, it was proposed that they should run B.Skill. and M.Skill. courses, but since these nomenclatures do not exist in UGC list, the universities are running B.Voc. and M.Voc. courses. After inclusion of the nomenclature in UGC list, the skills universities should run B.Skill. and M.Skill. with major skill orientation and skill-specific pedagogy.

Challenges faced by skill universities

Lack of competent faculty and infrastructure

As per data available on various skill universities' websites, there is a lack of competent and highly qualified faculties to teach in various skill-based undergraduate and postgraduate programmes.

Out of the surveyed students, 75 per cent from selected skill and traditional universities responded that there are a limited number of skill universities in India to provide skill training, which is a big hurdle in the skill development programme of government.

Even the infrastructure of existing universities wants priority attention. The basic infrastructure of Shri Vishwakarma Skill University is still not ready. They are running courses in rented buildings. Fifty per cent of students of selected skill universities reported that the problem of using hostels for outside students also raises major hurdles. Due to the lack of infrastructural facilities, students are not willing to attend certain skill universities.

Comparison between B.Voc. courses in skill and traditional universities

The enrolment of students is higher in B.Voc. programmes of traditional universities and colleges as compared to skill universities in India. Students prefer to transfer from traditional courses to skill-based courses in the same university due to ease of doing so and also because these universities have existed for a long time, which facilitates use of local resources of traditional universities for delivering skill courses. Lack of awareness in students regarding the existence of skill universities is also an important reason behind less admissions in these skill universities. Few students know of these universities, which is the basic reason for the shortage in student enrolment. Due to the lack of knowledge, only students of nearby places are enrolling in them. Admissions of students from other regions of the country are negligible. For the future, these courses in traditional universities may be transferred to skill universities. Some traditional universities and colleges are listed by the University Grants Commission for providing education in B.Voc. programmes, but in these universities and colleges, there is no individual department for B.Voc. courses. There should be separate departments for B.Voc. programmes in universities and colleges listed by UGC.

A skills university can follow the work-integrated training model, the institutional model, or a combination of both depending on factors like seed capital, available land, objectives of the university, and so on. While an institutional model would mirror a conventional university in many ways, a work-integrated training model would involve the university working largely as a facilitator, assessor, and certifier.

Conclusion

On the basis of appraisal of various skill universities in India, it has been concluded that skill universities are still at a very nascent stage. If the identified problems faced by them are not corrected in a timely fashion, there is little likelihood that they will succeed in achieving their objectives. The main objective behind their establishment was to develop work skills in youth by providing them skill-based education. For this, degree-level courses B.Voc. and M.Voc. were proposed, but it is observed that such courses are running in few skill universities. Most skill universities are providing education using different nomenclature. There is an absence of B.Skill. and M.Skill. courses, as this nomenclature is still not approved. The skill universities are functioning more on a regional level than a national level.

To facilitate skill universities, the UGC must allow them to follow a distinctive organizational and governance structure. A regulatory body was proposed for these skills universities with the name 'National Council for Vocational Education and Training'. This body should be established at the earliest opportunity. Skill universities have a bright future. To achieve their objectives, there is an urgent need to have more coordination between the University Grants Commission (UGC) and the National Skill Development Corporation (NSDC). This will help in promotion of skill universities exclusively running skill-based courses. The universities should have proper infrastructure and qualified faculty members having specialization in skill-based programmes.

References

https://economictimes.indiatimes.com/industry/services/education/budget-2020-online-degree-courses-to-students-from-weaker-sections-new-edu-policy-soon/articleshow/73835980.cms?from=mdr.

Ministry of Skill Development and Entrepreneurship (2018). Announcement on guidelines for skills universities in India. Government of India, New Delhi. www.msde.gov.in › announcements.

PIB (2019, July 15). *Skill development in primary and secondary education.* Press Information Bureau, Ministry of Skill Development and Entrepreneurship, New Delhi. https://pib.gov.in/PressReleasePage.aspx?PRID=1578773.

Sneha, S. (2018, September 26). Skills universities: The government of India's initiative towards a skilled India. *Franchise India Education.* www.franchiseindia.com/education/skills-universities-the-government-of-indias-initiative-towards-a-skilled-india.11808.

Union Budget 2020–21 (2020). Budget 2020: Online degree courses to students from weaker sections: New education policy soon. *The Economic Times.*

Chapter 14

Informal modes of skill formation

Vineeta Sirohi

In an era of globalization, technological evolution, migration, and ever-changing market dynamics with universal competition, the 21st century provides a big challenge for the educationists and the think tanks that are attempting to make youth ready for tomorrow—for their career growth and life ahead. Needless to say, the overall development of the critical skills and core competencies enables an individual to overcome the enormous challenges faced from time to time. Although India is enjoying the biggest demographic dividend with over 50 per cent of its people falling under the working-age group, 93 per cent of its workforce is in the unorganized sector. Thus, making Indian youth adept with essential requisite skill sets throws the biggest challenge due to predominance of the informal sector in both the job and skills-training markets.

There is a dearth of information about informal modes of skill formation, and the subject has not received much attention from researchers or policymakers. This chapter examines the concept of informal modes of skill formation by tracing its historical evolution and theoretical premise and by looking at the prevalent major forms of informal skill formation. Attempts have been made to map some interesting cases in India to understand their contributions to this domain of skill formation. The skills formed through informal modes do not have much value in the job market due to lack of certification. A later section of the chapter argues for the cause of recognition and validation of skills formed through informal modes and presents a few initiatives taken up in India, drawing lessons for policy formulation and effective programmes.

Informal sector and skills shortage—a global phenomenon

> The lack of jobs in the formal sector of the economy as the lack of skills in a large part of the labour force has resulted in the growth of a substantial informal sector in which most workers are in low-paid employment under unregulated and poor working conditions.
>
> (World Employment Report 1998–1999, ILO)

DOI: 10.4324/9781003158349-17

The literature suggests that limited and restricted access to formal education in terms of the years spent in education (Fluitman, 1989; Lautier, 2000) results in low levels of training among people who work in the informal sector. Compared to the formal sector, the time spent in terms of number of years in informal training, informal sector workers in some North and West African countries were found to have spent much more number of years in informal training. Moreover, due to the limited employment opportunities in the formal sector in some countries, a trend of increasing numbers of graduates joining the informal sector has been observed. In Senegal, for instance, the state provides some financial incentives for informal sector workers that attract recent graduates (Lautier, 2000). In another study in Kenya on the educational levels of micro-entrepreneurs in the informal sector, King and Abuodha (1995) observe a new phenomenon of scarcity of highly educated persons in the informal sector. Over and above a trend of increasing levels of education among the workers in the informal sector was observed, which is expected to continue due to weakening employment prospects in the formal sector, the lack of jobs, falling real wages, as well as poor career development and advancement prospects. However, in recent years, informal sector activities are getting acknowledged and have gained more popularity than ever before (Naik, 2009). In fact, some informal economy prospects may even attract flourishing and well educated people away from their secure jobs in the formal sector.

Most informal-sector workers who possess skills have acquired them through non-formal or informal modes. Informal training and learning-by-doing often play the most significant role in providing workers of the informal sector with skills (Overwien, 1997). In Latin America, informal sector workers acquire most of their competencies through practical, informal work. The region is characterised by unequal social stratification due to inequality in income and disparities in the attainment of skills; hence, the significance of formal and non-formal education varies with region, and do not often reach the same level of significance as learning-by-doing (Overwien, 1997). However, the King and Abuodha (1995) study of 100 Kenyan micro-entrepreneurs in the informal sector indicates the effectiveness of a combination of informal and formal sector training, as formal sector training alone cannot meet the requirement of acquisition of skills for the informal sector. Along similar lines, Singh (2000) points out that a consensus has emerged from the implementation of training projects and programmes in the informal economy that non-formal and informal training seem to best respond to the needs of informal sector workers.

Historical background

The concept of informal skill formation dates back to years before the industrial revolution. It precedes the peak of the industrial revolution during the 19th century in the form of guild support for traditional apprenticeships. It is also observed to be ubiquitous in the knowledge-based economy of the 21st century in the form of cognitive apprenticeship (Collins & Kapur, 2014). If the historical trajectory is considered, the end of the 20th century witnessed ebbing away of faith in formal education. Employers began complaining about the skills possessed by the university graduates, as they could not successfully meet the industry demand for soft skills. It was felt that if they were to thrive, they had to bring to the workplace experiential learning. Some secondary school and university graduates turned to service jobs and to manual labour, and some became apprentices to experts. Workers, such as fibre-optic technicians, transportation workers, medical and dental technicians, electricians, plumbers, and repairmen for power and communication lines, grew much in demand in the modern economy. Individuals who possessed basic literacy skills of reading and simple arithmetic calculations could acquire skills informally by undergoing short-term training combined with formal instruction.

Most of the skills acquisition took place 'on the job'. On the other hand, for those who could access technology, digital media became the key mode of voluntary skill formation. Thus, informal modes of skill formation surfaced alongside the formal modes, wherein the expertise of the young seemed to progress independently of authorities and curricula or any kind of external assessment. Long-standing expectations for transmission of skills and knowledge from expert to novice dominated. However, the nations with established state systems of schooling and compulsory education continued to lay key emphasis on formal learning. They left informal or any mode of learning that would take place beyond the classroom to ad hoc forces and agencies. Science and art learning in social entrepreneurial ventures were amalgamated by the persistent efforts of the community organizations. By doing this, the youth got the opportunity for apprenticeships and earning. Hence, community organizations became the visible epitome of informal skill formation, freely sought and delivered, across a wide range of activities beneficial to society. Employers in cutting-edge software development supported the exploratory creative skill-learning of young people. In some regions, learning laboratories were set up in conjunction with science or art museums. Besides offering opportunities for independent exploration of technologies, the ideas were conceived and tested with experts from professional fields, thereby creating software programmes and futuristic ideas for hardware development. In many modern economies, corporations such as Intel sponsored science fairs that enabled them to identify highly creative young people who evidenced a commitment to self-directed learning. Thus, several such informal systems developed in a formal fashion.

Informal mode of skill formation: theoretical perspective

Informal skill formation draws from the theory of experiential learning propounded by John Dewey (1938). The theory focuses on learning through the individual's experiences, lifelong learning, and the role of reflective thought in education. A strong supporter of progressive education, Dewey firmly believed in the importance of the human element in vocational education and strongly advocated developing skills in order to live and contribute as a productive member of society.

Informal learning research took longer to evolve, not emerging until the 1980s (Marsick & Watkins, 1990). Experiential, informal, and community-based learning finally became legitimate sources and settings for those engaged in work-based learning and the development of generic and transferable skills, multidisciplinary, multiliteracies, and transcoding (Edwards & Usher, 2001).

Experiential learning as viewed by Dewey is a dynamic and holistic process of learning from experience. Informal skill formation takes place through self-directed or experiential learning and is based on participation in a learning environment without any set curriculum or set establishment; the environment is often spontaneous and encourages creativity. Thus, experiential learning contributes to the theory and practice of informal skill formation. It is a process through which a learner constructs knowledge, skills, and values from direct experiences in an informal learning environment (Jacobs, 1999, as cited in Gross & Rutland, 2017). Dewey analyzed the importance of experience in the learning process and put forth that experiential learning would provide opportunities for students to be actively engaged in acquiring skills and knowledge. Students can thus move away from being just recipients of information to being active engagers and learners. He also referred to an 'experiential continuum' through which one's experience generates another experience (Dewey, 1963 [1938], as cited in Gross & Rutland, 2017).

Informal modes of skill formation

Informal education refers to the unexpected and less structured learning that individuals have with a variety of environmental influences and day-to-day experiences (La Belle, 1982, p. 163). It is not organized or structured in terms of objectives, time, or learning support. Similarly, informal skill formation is not formally structured and is usually learner-initiated, so it does not lead to a formal qualification. Informal skill formation takes place during our engagement in various daily activities such as in family, work, or leisure. It is generally acquired through communicating and interacting with or observing more knowledgeable or skilled individuals (including artists, musicians, actors) either at work or in the community. Therefore, it is often unintentional and contingent on interactions and relationships with people. In the informal mode of skill formation, the learners decide the content of learning and then formulate their own learning objectives. In addition, the learners also determine when they should acquire the skills and select the design and modality that best meet their needs. In other words, the learners are responsible for organizing and managing their own skill-formation activities.

In the competitive world of work, organizations often initiate special arrangements for ensuring skill formation through informal modes in the work context. Methods like job-redesign and job rotation, coaching and mentoring, quality circles, and learning partnerships are popular modes that enable individuals to engage in informal skill formation in the workplace. Informal modes of skill formation can facilitate both occupational as well as soft skill formation. While occupational skills formation activities may be carried out through methods like training programmes, mentoring, and coaching, soft skills formation can be cultivated through community based interactions in the workplace and at the local and regional level. Other modes of informal skill formation may also include skills acquired independently through reading books, newspapers, journals, online articles or entries, trial-and-error strategies, and extended practice. Some major forms of informal skill formation are discussed next.

Informal apprenticeship

Informal apprenticeship is broadly defined as an informal system of skills transfer that takes place between a master craftsperson (MC) to a young apprentice, who acquires skills through observation, imitation, and repetition while working with the MC. This transfer of knowledge and skills is based on an agreement (written and verbal) between the MC and the apprentice, in line with the local community norms and practices. Apprentices are usually referred to as 'helper' or 'assistant' and a verbal conformity between MC and apprentice seals the bond. Training through apprenticeships is not regulated by any legislation, and apprenticeship characteristics also vary from one country context to another and across regions. The use of the terminology may also vary depending on the context, such as informal apprentice, traditional apprentice, or apprenticeship in the formal economy. Despite variations, informal apprenticeship is the most prominent means to acquire skills by young people, especially in the developing countries, and particularly in economies that thrive on a large informal sector.

The emergence of vast informal sectors as major employers in developing countries has drawn immense attention to the potential of informal learning, resulting in the recognition of the value of informal apprenticeship. As part of education and training, informal apprenticeships transmit skills of trade to young people in small or microenterprises in the informal economies. This reduces the number of youths trapped in a never-ending cycle of poverty, low skills, low productivity, and low income (Association for the Development of Education in Africa, 2015). For instance, informal apprenticeship has been observed as a do-able alternative for building youth employment skills and is regarded as the source of power for developing economies in Africa and Asia, accounting for nearly 95 per cent of new jobs in these continents (Association for the Development of Education in Africa, 2015).

On-the-job training

On-the-job training, also known as OJT, is a hands-on method of cultivating skills, knowledge, and competencies required by employees to perform a particular task within the workplace. This method of skill formation takes place as an individual carries out assigned tasks related to his or her occupation under the supervision of a manager, coach, or mentor. The aim of on-the-job training is to broaden the employee's skill set and to increase their productivity by using the existing environment, tools, and skills available in the workplace. Therefore, the context of on-the-job training has special importance since this mode utilizes the existing workplace tools, machines, documents, equipment, and knowledge to train and help the employees to form skills required to perform their jobs effectively.

On-the-job training takes place within the employee's regular job setting and may transpire as one executes his or her actual work. It may also take place in specialized settings elsewhere within the workplace using training rooms, workstations, or equipment. Through on-the-job training methods, the human resources staff, managers, or co-workers educate the employees about interpersonal skills, company policies and requirements, leadership training, and the like that are, requisite for efficient performance and functioning at the workplace. OJT may be provided in-house by managers and experienced co-workers or by external experts. In the case of specialized skills and training needs, an external expert may occasionally provide OJT for specialized equipment or systems training. There are several companies in India which provide on-the-job training; for example, the Indian Railways Institute of Financial Management (IRIFM) imparts professional training to its officers in the skills of management of finance and accounts during difficult times and maintaining the financial strength of the organization. Another big company in the financial sector is ICICI Bank, who through the ICICI Manipal Academy imparts on-the-job training to newly recruited junior managers of the bank for a period of three months. In the area of information technology, Infosys' Global Education Centre in Mysore, imparts skills to the newly recruited engineers for 14.5 weeks as Initial Learning Programme. Infosys is the world's largest corporate training firm. Similarly, the Grand Hyatt Mumbai provides on-the-job training in hospitality.

Internship

Internship is an opportunity for structured work experience for students or fresh graduates, offered by firms/institutions/organizations for a fixed duration and designed to enhance their academic and personal development. Supervised by a professional in the relevant field, internship helps in forming new skills and gaining experience and knowledge of the workplace. The period of internship usually varies from one month to three months. The central purpose of internship for fresh graduates is to provide them the requisite exposure to the world of work and to give them opportunities to learn, under close supervision, skills and knowledge that will help them devise their career goals for life.

Academic internships are integrated in the courses for exploring career avenues and professional development by way of credit scores. Firms and companies offer summer and winter internships to students, providing them a window of opportunity to practice what they learn, gain industry knowledge, and learn new skills, and abilities while at the same time also helping the firms in their various areas of work. For example, according to AICTE Internship Guidelines (All India Council for Technical Education, 2018), a minimum of 14–20 credits of internship are counted towards B.Tech. degree programmes, and 10–14 credits are given for a three-year diploma programme. Here, one credit equals to a minimum of 40–45 hours of work. Thus, a full-time intern is expected to work 40–45 hours per week. Full-time internship is done during summer break, while part-time internship is done during academic sessions. Engineering students are required to do three internships mandatorily during their course. Likewise, medical institutions offer internship programmes to their students. Such opportunities help the students or fresh graduates to apply their knowledge by bridging the gap between classroom learning of theories and experience of professional settings.

Internships are usually offered by industry and organizations, NGOs, government organizations, micro/small/medium enterprises, and so on to help young students form skills required for the particular jobs and make them ready for the employment in the respective organization. Internship—working in real-world settings—is a vital opportunity for potential candidates to gauge themselves (their knowledge and aspirations) before making a final decision about a job offer. Internship, therefore, helps the young graduates in determining when and where to apply for future jobs. As the interns understand and gain experience of the workplace, they are empowered to make more focused future career decisions.

Mentoring

Mentoring is a developmental relationship between a more experienced individual, a mentor, and a less experienced partner, a mentee. It is an employee-training method wherein an experienced individual is assigned to act as an advisor or counsellor for a relatively less experienced junior employee. The mentor is charged with guiding the professional development of the mentee. Through regular interactions, the mentee relies on the mentor's guidance to gain skills, knowledge, and experience. A mentor is usually a person specialized and an expert in the chosen field who possesses wide knowledge and experience of the job at hand. Therefore, the mentor has a vital role to play in creating an efficient and skilled workforce through enrichment, growth, and development of relevant skills in the mentee. Mentoring can be carried out through various forms (University of Auckland, 2013):

Peer Mentoring refers to pairing of the mentees with other professionals in similar situations to share experiences and learn new skills, in order to achieve targeted learning outcomes.

Network Mentoring refers to the dynamic nature of the training needs to perform efficiently in the changing scenario of work, for which the individuals/mentees may seek inputs from a network of mentors with expertise and guidance for the situation.

Group or Team Mentoring is organized to meet and seek guidance from multiple senior advisors. They are either selected by the mentees or the employers who share common needs or goals.

E-Mentoring facilitates fruitful guidance and engagement between the mentees and the mentor online, thus eliminating the limitation of geographical distances. It allows the mentees to get mentored by people with varied expertise without confining themselves to one's own institution or country.

Reverse Mentoring is a type of mentoring where a junior employee is paired with a senior professional. The junior acts as the primary mentor as he is more knowledgeable and skilled in certain areas. This is usually done so that the seniors are kept informed of new methods or technological advances.

Coaching

Gerard (as cited in International Authority for Professional Coaching and Mentoring, 2019) defined 'Coaching is about performing your best through the individual and private assistance of someone who will guide you to keep growing'. To unlock a person's potential, to maximize and improve a person's performance—that is the role of a coach, who is required to help people learn rather than to teach them. Therefore, coaching is the art of facilitating the performance, learning, and development of another (Downey, 2003). The core concept of coaching is that the individual or team being coached already has the resources with them to move forward and that the coach's primary role is to help them access these resources. Coaching usually lasts for a short period and focuses on specific skills and goals. It is a professional partnership between a qualified coach and an individual or team that supports the achievement of extraordinary results, based on goals set by the individual or the team itself. Coaching is directly concerned with the immediate improvement of performance and development of skills by a form of tutoring or instruction. When done well, through constant feedback, coaching not only reinforces what learners learn through training but also opens the door to improvement that might not otherwise appear and remain latent.

Study circles

Study circles in higher education are created by a group of individuals who share common interests. The target audience/clientele varies from students within the same institution to the ones coming from other universities. They facilitate the students to further their understanding and share information on certain topics and interests, which are otherwise ignored and often neglected due to classroom curriculum. Issues like history, culture, politics, community problems, or topics that are of national or global interest are discussed. A study circle is a combination of students belonging to different levels and doesn't confine students to class/peer mates. It not only enhances deeper understanding of the subject matter or topics discussed at hand but also gives an opportunity to break down complex topics into manageable parts. Single sessions can have productive outcomes. With the advancement in science and technology, the concept of virtual study circles have shaped up in discussing issues that are of global interest to people from different demographic areas/institutions sharing ideas and knowledge. It is a potential source of accumulating knowledge and accelerating the pace of learning. It also helps in developing soft skills among the participants of the study circles.

Communities of practice

> Communities of practice (CoP) are groups of people who share a concern or a passion for something they do and learn how to do it better as they interact regularly.
>
> (Wenger, 2014)

The basic premise of communities of practice with respect to skill formation is that we all learn in everyday life from the communities in which we locate ourselves. Communities of practice are omnipresent, and almost each one of us belongs to some community of practice, whether it is our working colleagues or friends, our profession or job, or our leisure interests. Further, Wenger-Trayner (2000) views communities of practice (CoP) as the conduct of shared participation among their members. Community of practice differs largely from community of interest or a geographical community. Communities of practice evolve naturally and terminate when the community's shared concerns and objectives are accomplished. Communities of practice are considered as potential manifestations of an informal mode of skill formation which is found to be developed spontaneously to address community issues and challenges. Community of practice exists outside formal educational institutions and is flexible in terms of channels to be used for interaction like face to face and virtual or online. The participants are not so much concerned about obtaining any formal educational qualification but seek for enhancing skills for better performance and dealing with everyday life challenges. To make informal knowledge transferable, CoPs build on existing formal content tools such as portal and learning management systems. Communities of practice enable organizations to add a new dimension—the informal organization. They provide an opportunity for members to not only refer to learning materials from the institution but also combine information with it and share among themselves.

National Institute of Information Technology (NIIT): a case in India

The National Institute of Information Technology was established in 1981 with franchising model in IT education and established its reputation in the software domain. It aims to meet the fast-changing skill-set requirements needed to stay relevant with each generation. With the rising menace of unemployment among the youth of the country, it is the need of the hour to address the problem of skill development in India. In striving towards skills development, initiatives taken up by NIIT include the following:

Initiatives of Cloud Campus: It offers a unique '*Anywhere Lab*' feature, allowing students to practice the application of concepts learnt in class anywhere. They can also chat with experts and seek answers to their queries. They receive hands-on practice exercises at NIIT centres, thus ensuring consistent, high-quality learning experiences. Interactions are not limited to the same classroom; they can communicate and collaborate with students from other locations. It offers training programmes in IT, banking, global finance management, management, digital and social media marketing. These courses can be undertaken by both, engineering and non-engineering graduates seeking career-oriented education and also those professionals who are aiming at career progression.

NIIT.tv: NIIT is a digital learning initiative to bring the skills from the NIIT classrooms to every digitally connected learner for free anytime and to any place of their choice. It delivers skill-based live online training course to the masses.

Stack Route Immersive (SRI): SRI is a full-time, three-month immersive programme aimed at giving working experience rather than imparting training modules in a classroom environment. A graduate has to develop, test, and release new systems that are cloud- and mobile-enabled, scalable, and with industry-standard performance levels to complete the programme. It is designed for small groups. As an outcome of Stack Route, Digi NXT, a series of programmes, was created so as to serve the need of fresh graduates. Programmes such as MEAN Stack, Internet of Things, artificial intelligence, machine learning, design thinking, robotics, and so on were created to bring about digital transformation to spur the growth of skilled manpower in India's IT industry. Skilling with these programmes is expected to take India to a more advanced level and thus meet the demand for a large number of newly trained digital professionals.

NIIT and National Skill Development Corporation (NSDC): NIIT and National Skill Development Corporation (NSDC) entered into a joint venture to enhance skills and employability for youth across India. Its emphasis is on offering job-oriented training in semi-urban and rural areas to mainly low- and middle-income households. NIIT Yuva Jyoti Skill Development Centres, under this joint venture, is a part of a movement to make the "Skill India" programme a success. The training is imparted in nine sectors—Retail, IT/ITeS, BFSI, Education and Training Services, Media and Entertainment, Healthcare, Telecom, Hospitality, and Informal Sector. The primary targets for this initiative are the SSLC pass students (interested and seeking careers in the service sector), marginalized communities and for women and the physically challenged. It will be an opportunity for the aspirants to build successful careers through quality training along with formal education. Internship is also facilitated for students to apply learning skills in real-life situations and thus develop a deeper understanding of the industry requirements. Each centre is localized to suit the local community and customized for the requirements of the industry being addressed.

Micro, Small, and Medium Enterprise (MSME): a case in India

The MSME (Ministry of Micro, Small and Medium Enterprises) in India was established initially as the Small Industries Development Organization (SIDO). It assisted the states in encouraging entrepreneurship, employment, and livelihood opportunities. The GoI supplements the efforts of the state with various initiatives. It seeks to facilitate (1) the adequate flow of credit from financial institutions/banks; (2) support for technological upgradation and modernization; (3) integrated infrastructural facilities; (4) modernization of testing facilities and quality certification; (5) access to modern management practices; (6) entrepreneurship development and skill upgradation through appropriate training facilities; (7) support for product development, design intervention, and packaging; (8) welfare of artisans and workers; (9) assistance and better access to domestic and export markets; and (10) cluster-wise measures to promote capacity building and empowerment of the units and their collectives.

One of the main components of MSME is entrepreneurship and skill development. To achieve its objectives, sets of skills are imparted through Micro Small and Medium Enterprises Development Institute Centres (MSME-DIs) and Technology Centres. It caters to the needs of aspiring entrepreneurs. The Enterprise Development Centres (EDCs) are established at the district level under the administrative control of MSME. EDCs are further divided into two verticals, namely, Enterprise Development Vertical and Skill Development Vertical. This is done so as to ensure that the needs of the youth are well addressed. To support those who want to be self-employed and create business enterprises, technical skills to assist the same is imparted. These EDCs are connected with the National Resource Centre set up in the office of DCMSME.

The skill development under its approved Scheme Act with the age of participants of 18 years and above is a product-cum-process oriented activity-based programme. This is six weeks activity aimed at conducting special entrepreneurship development programmes for livelihood creation and rural enterprise development. These trainings aim at upgrading skills and hands-on practice. Some of the courses conducted under this programme are agro-based products, herbal cosmetics, fashion garments, hosiery, food & fruit processing trainings, soap and detergents/household chemicals, leather/jute/Rexene, products/novelties, carpet weaving, mechanical engineering workshop/machine shop, heat treatment, electroplating, basic/advanced welding/fabrication/sheet metal work, basic/advanced carpentry, glass and ceramics, industrial and art wares, servicing/repairing of household electrical appliances and electronic gadgets, TV repairing, washing machine repair, stereo/sound system/speaker assembly and repair, gem cutting and polishing, engineering plastics, solar/non-conventional energy equipment installation/maintenance, plumber work, information technology, computer hardware maintenance, computerized accounting, DTP and screen printing, tour operator, mobile repairing, and so on.

The Regional Testing Centres, Field Testing Stations, and Autonomous bodies like Tool Rooms and Technology Development Centres (TDCs) of the ministry conduct long-term and short-term field-specific and industry-specific courses as well as vocational training programmes. These Centres include specialized programmes so that upon completion of the course the trainees can get absorbed by the industries immediately. Some of the tool rooms conduct M.Tech-level programmes in collaboration with universities/technical institutions. In recent times, institutions have taken up special modules of training for women, physically challenged persons, and weaker sections of the society for which sponsorships are received from the state government. Centres for trainings conducted through Tool Rooms and technology development are:

- Long-term diploma and certificate courses in tool engineering
- Specialized high-tech courses on tool engineering for engineering graduates, diploma and ITI certificate holders and related discipline
- Skilled enhancement courses for industry personnel
- Upgradation courses for trainers in training institutions and industries
- Customized training programmes for industries

Recognition and validation of informal skill formation in India

All of us most of the time are engaged in acquiring skills from somewhere somehow, not realizing that skill formation takes place at home, in the workplace, and in our friendly neighbourhood. This is especially true for those who are outside the mainstream education and training system who firmly believe that learning outside of school is more significant than the entire formal curriculum-based situational learning. However, informal learning was much ignored and not well understood, discernible, or valued until the OECD countries agreed to develop strategies for 'lifelong learning for all'. Consequently, the learning outcomes of formal, non-formal, and informal learning were emphasized and gained more importance (Werquin, 2010). Irrespective of the mode and source, lifelong learning values all kinds of learning experiences; hence, skill learning outcomes must be recognized and validated. Thus, recognition and validation assume great significance in the realm of lifelong learning and should be an integral mechanism for all kinds of skill formation (Ouane, 2011).

The European Council adopted common principles for the identification and validation of non-formal and informal learning (European Center for the Development of Vocational Training, CEDEFOP, 2009), while in India, the Recognition of Prior Learning (RPL) policy under NSQF (National Skills Qualifications Framework) aims to provide formal recognition to individuals who have acquired skills informally at the workplace, community, and/or voluntary activities.

The recognition of prior learning is the practice of establishing the visibility and acknowledgement of competences that people acquire in various learning environments. In developing support system to validate all non-formal and informal learning, countries are at different stages: some have established systems, while other countries are in the process of developing provisions.

In India, 80 per cent of the work force are in the informal or unorganized sector, where approximately 85 per cent acquire skills through informal or non-formal channels (Singh, 2016). Mapping the existing skills and future skilling requirements of this sector is a huge challenge. Given the scenario, the RPL process for assessment is increasingly being adopted in the informal-sector training. The RPL process includes a pre-assessment, skill gap training, and a final assessment leading to certification of existing skills in an individual. Any individual could be a candidate of RPL and could be either fit for partial or full certification depending on the competence based on the National Skills Qualifications Framework (NSQF), against which prior learning through formal/informal channels is assessed and certified by diplomas and degrees (Singh, 2016). The following are cases of RPL initiatives in India.

Modular employable skills (MES)

Modular Employable Skills is a competency-based training pathway set up by the Ministry of Labour and Employment to provide minimum skills required for gainful employment. It aims to provide training and update skills for school-leavers, existing workers, child labours, and the unemployed. MES assesses industry skills demand and develops a matrix of courses and curricula. MES involves 5,200 vocational training providers, 22 assessing bodies, 48 sectors, and 1,109 modules. The modules take anywhere from 60 to 600 hours to complete. In addition to testing and certification of skills acquired on completion of a training course, skills acquired informally are also recognized. To ensure impartial testing, independent testing bodies not involved in delivering training conduct the tests for skills acquired by trainees (Singh, 2017b).

LabourNet

LabourNet is an NGO-based sector initiative of Movement for Alternatives and Youth Awareness, (MAYA) Bangalore, for evaluation of masons, carpenters, plumbers, and painters. LabourNet identifies skill gaps and provides appropriate skill-set training. As an institutional design for support, LabourNet has identified several parameters through RPL for identifying skills, documenting existing skills, and providing feedback to the learners. It adopts industry-based occupational standards to enable employment of workers after training (Singh, 2016).

National Institute of Open Schooling (NIOS)

The National Institute of Open Schooling (NIOS) in its policy framework for the Recognition of Prior Learning (RPL) recognizes prior learning or qualifications acquired both within and beyond formal learning. NIOS has created alternative pathways through open and flexible education and training to meets diverse learning needs at several levels, such as:

- Open Basic Education (OBE) at primary and upper-primary level education through alternate means for those unable to attend formal schools or who have left school without attaining a school-leaving certificate.
- For Adult Neo-literates (those who have completed a basic literacy programme) in cooperation with the National Literacy Mission Authority (NLMA).
- Secondary and Senior Secondary Levels (provide flexible choice of subjects/courses, accelerated learning, and transfer of credits) to enable learners' continuation of education.
- Vocational Education to provide prospects for the learners to become young entrepreneurs. As a way forward, NIOS is continually aligning its VET courses to meet the requirements of National Skills Qualifications Framework (NSQF) level descriptors.

(Singh, 2015)

Community colleges

Community colleges were established to serve as a bridge between vocational education and training and higher education to formalize skills through certification under the National Skills Qualifications Framework (NSQF). Community colleges award two-year advanced diplomas or associate degrees and also facilitate transfer to an undergraduate college, thereby enabling direct entry into an occupation or trade. The curricula in community colleges are periodically monitored, evaluated, and updated, making the courses industry-friendly through consultation with stakeholders such as the All India Council for Technical Education (AICTE) acts jointly with Bharat Sanchar Nigam Limited (BSNL) and the National Institute of Electronics and Information Technology (NIELIT) under the Department of Information and Technology. Community colleges and NIOS often collaborate to offer training programmes and courses that are 'modular, credit-based, career-oriented and relevant for local employers' (Singh, 2014).

Texila Educational Management and Services

Texila Educational Management and Services, based in Coimbatore, Tamil Nadu, under Recognition of Prior Learning, helps to formally recognize skills, knowledge, and competencies acquired through formal and informal training and education, work experience, and life experience. Here, RPL follows three stages, namely, pre-screening process, facilitation process to create and submit a portfolio within six months, and finally an assessment process in the form of an interview. On successful completion of the RPL assessment, students can undergo university academic learning of different durations, depending upon their prior learning and the qualification they want to achieve (Singh, 2017a).

New Education Policy (NEP) 2020 and skills

So far skill formation has been largely taking place through informal modes in India, but the recent government initiative through NEP 2020 policy provides enough scope for skill formation through formal modes also. The policy envisages integration of vocational education in all institutions throughout school and higher education. Integrating vocational education with general education is the most promising way to provide for holistic development of the students, equipping them with knowledge, skills, and competencies which will prepare them for life and work. The integration process will necessitate coordination between the Ministry of Education (MOE) and the Ministry of Skill Development and Entrepreneurship (MSDE) at the central level, and of the state Skill Development Missions and the state Education Departments at the state level. In order to impart vocational education/skills in a meaningful way, the institutions of higher education need to collaborate with industry in their vicinity and develop internship/apprenticeship programmes to expose students to the work environment and get the experience of hands-on practice. In higher education, to increase the exposure to vocational education/skills in higher education, in addition to the B.Voc. courses, elective vocational subjects/courses in all disciplines/programmes may be offered at the undergraduate and postgraduate level, and short-term certificate courses may be introduced. Moreover, the introduction of the credit-based system will facilitate smooth mobility of students between courses and programmes.

Conclusion

The informal modes of skill formation offer the advantage of individual liberty to choose the process of acquiring skills in terms of what, when, where, with whom, and how to acquire them. There are no deadlines or rigid structures for acquiring new skills, and learning proceeds by one's own free will. Engaging in this form of skill formation provides an expansive approach to workforce skill development which helps the individuals in acquiring social skills and formal qualifications, enhancing their competitiveness in the vast labour market. The key to retaining learning that occurs in informal, non-formal, and formal contexts is through recognition pathways. In the context of an economy with high levels of informality, and acknowledging the fact that there are many people who form skills through informal modes, the recognition of prior learning becomes important. Such learning enhances horizontal and vertical mobility and widens opportunity for formal employment. It calls for commitment of all stakeholders and practitioners at the national, state, and local levels. Recognizing the worth of validation and certification, with the present NSQF in place, the process of recognition and validation should contribute to value addition to skills formed informally to enable people to earn higher wages in the job market and also provide pathways to enter into the formal system of education and training. Moreover, it requires intensive research for informed policy decisions.

References

All India Council for Technical Education (2018). *Internship policy: Guidelines & procedures*. AICTE, New Delhi.

Association for the Development of Education in Africa (2015). *Informal apprenticeship: A viable alternative to building youth employment skills*. Policy Brief. www.adeanet.org/en/system/files/policy_briefs/policy_brief_informal_apprenticeship.pdf.

Collins, A., & Kapur, M. (2014). Cognitive apprenticeship. In R. K. Sawyer (Ed.), *The learning sciences* (2nd ed., pp. 109–126). New York: Cambridge University Press.

Dewey, J. (1963 [1938]). *Experience and education* (2nd ed.). New York: Collier Books.

Downey, M. (2003). *Effective coaching: Lessons from the coaches' coach* (2nd ed.). New York: Texere.

Edwards, R., & Usher, R. (2001). Lifelong learning: A postmodern condition of education? *Adult Education Quarterly*, 51(4), 273–287.

European Center for the Development of Vocational Training, CEDEFOP (2009). *European guidelines for validating non-formal and informal learning*. Luxembourg: Office for Official Publications of the European Communities.

Fluitman, F. (1989). *Training for work in the informal sector; an agenda item for the 1990's*. Discussion Paper 16. Geneva: Vocational Training Branch, International Labour Office.

Gross, Z., & Rutland, S. D. (2017). Experiential learning in informal educational settings. *International Review Education*, 63, 1–8. https://doi.org/10.1007/s11159-017-9625-6.

International Authority for Professional Coaching and Mentoring (2019). *My definition of coaching*. https://coach-accreditation.services/my-definition-of-coaching-gerard-odonovan-ceo-noble-mahattan-coaching/.

King, K., & Abuodha, C. (1995). Education, training and technological development in the informal sector of Kenya. *Science, Technology & Development*, 13(2), 175–202.

La Belle, T. J. (1982). Formal, nonformal and informal education: A holistic perspective on lifelong learning. *International Review of Education*, 28(2), 159–175.

Lautier, B. (2000). Received and debatable ideas on the informal sector. *Dossier*. Europa.eu.int/comm/development/publicat/courier/courier-178/en/en-053-ni.pdf.

Marsick, V., & Watkins, K. (1990). *Informal and incidental learning in the workplace*. New York: Routledge and Kegan Paul.

Naik, A. K. (2009). *Informal sector and informal workers in India*. Paper Prepared for the Special IARIW-SAIM Conference on Measuring the Informal Economy in Developing Countries. www.iariw.org/papers/2009/5a%20naik.pdf.

Ouane, A. (2011). Evolution of and perspectives on lifelong learning. In J. Yang & R. Valdés-Cotera (Eds.), *Conceptual evolution and policy developments in lifelong learning* (pp. 24–39). Germany: UNESCO Institute for Lifelong Learning.

Overwien, B. (1997). Employment-oriented non-formal training for young people in the informal sector in Latin America. *Education*, 55(56), 146–157. Tubingen: Institute for Scientific Cooperation.

Singh, M. (2000). Combining work and learning in the informal economy: Implications for education, training and skills development. *International Review of Education*, 46(6), 599–620.

Singh, M. (2014). *India RVA case study in education: RVA in community colleges*. UNESCO Institute for Lifelong Learning, Germany. https://uil.unesco.org/case-study/rva/india-rva-case-study-education-0.

Singh, M. (2015, March 10). *India RVA case study in education*. National Institute of Open Schooling (NIOS). UIL. (Accessed May 4, 2020, 05:59 CEST).

Singh, M. (2016). *India RVA case study in training and the world of work: RPL for the informal sector in India*. UNESCO Institute for Lifelong Learning, Germany. https://uil.unesco.org/case-study/rva/india-rva-case-study-training-and-world-work-0.

Singh, M. (2017a). *India RVA case study in education: RPL in the context of texila educational management and services in India*. UNESCO Institute for Lifelong Learning, Germany. https://uil.unesco.org/case-study/rva/india-rva-case-study-education.

Singh, M. (2017b). *India RVA case study in training and the world of work: Modular employable skills (MES)*. UNESCO Institute for Lifelong Learning, Germany. https://uil.unesco.org/case-study/rva/india-rva-case-study-training-and-world-work-1.

University of Auckland (2013). *A guide to mentoring*. New Zealand: The University of Auckland. https://cdn.auckland.ac.nz/assets/auckland/business/current-students/PDFs/mentoring-guide-final.pdf.

Wenger, E. (2014). *Communities of practice: A brief introduction*. https://wenger-trayner.com/wp-content/uploads/2013/10/06-Brief-introduction-to-communities-of-practice.pdf.

Wenger-Trayner, E. (2000). Communities of practice and social learning systems. *Organization*, 7, 225–246.

Werquin, P. (2010). *Recognition non-formal and informal learning: Outcomes, policies and practice*. Paris: OECD.

World Employment Report 1998–99 (1998). *Employability in the global economy: How training matters*. Geneva: International Labour Office.

Part IV

Education–industry relationship

Chapter 15

Industry–academia linkages in India's technical education sector

Raj Agrawal and Anuja Pandey

Introduction

State of technical higher education in India

India has one of the largest education systems in the world. According to the AISHE Survey (2019), there are 993 universities, 39,931 colleges and 10,725 stand-alone institutions. In addition, 298 universities are affiliated with colleges. 385 universities are privately managed, 394 universities are located in rural areas, and 16 universities are exclusively for women.

In addition to one central open university, 14 state open universities, and one state private open university, there are 110 dual mode universities which offer education through distance mode also. Thirteen of them are located in Tamil Nadu.

There are 548 general, 142 technical, 63 agriculture and allied, 58 medical, 23 law, 13 Sanskrit and nine language universities, and 106 remaining universities belonging to other categories.

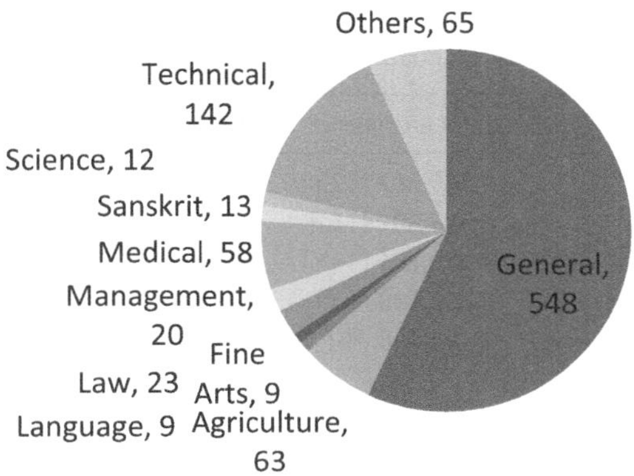

Figure 15.1 Specialization of universities

Source: AISHE Survey (2019).

DOI: 10.4324/9781003158349-19

Total enrolment in higher education has been estimated to be 37.4 million, with 19.2 million male and 18.2 million female students. Females constitute 48.6 per cent of the total enrolment. Gross Enrolment Ratio (GER) in higher education in India is 26.3 per cent. GER for the male population is 26.3 per cent and for females is 26.4 per cent. The Ministry of HRD in the 12th plan document is targeting a GER of 30 per cent for higher education by 2020, in order to support the requirements of industry of more than 250 million additional skilled workers by 2025.

Trend in programme-wise enrolment at various levels

The total enrolment at undergraduate level in major discipline/subject (see Table 15.1) shows that the highest number of students are enrolled in arts courses. The total number of students enrolled in arts courses are 93.49 lakh out of which 46.96 per cent are male and 53.03 per cent are female. Science is the second major stream, with 47.13 lakh student out of which 49 per cent are male and 51 per cent are female. Commerce is the third major stream, with 40.3 lakh students enrolled. The share of male students enrolled in commerce is 51.2 per cent, whereas female enrolment is 48.8 per cent. Engineering and technology is the fourth major stream with 38.52 lakh student enrolment. The share of male students enrolled in engineering and technology is 71.1 per cent, where female enrolment is 28.9 per cent. The medical science stream shows a different picture, with a higher number of female students, where out of total 11.96 lakh students, 7.25 lakh students are female, that is 60.65 per cent females and 39 per cent males.

Management stream has 6.5 lakh students with 4.05 lakh (62.3 per cent) male students. The students enrolled in the law stream are 3.98 lakh out of which 2.64 lakh (66 per cent) are males.

Table 15.1 Enrolment at undergraduate level in major disciplines/subjects (%)

Discipline	*Total enrolments*	*Male*	*Female*
Arts	9,349,287 (32%)	46.96	53.04
Science	4,713,301 (16.4)	49.00	51.00
Commerce	4,030,886 (14%)	51.21	48.79
Engineering (all branches)	3,852,188 (13%)	71.12	28.88
Medical Sciences (including Pharmacy)	1,196,758 (4.1%)	39.35	60.65
Management	6,50,498 (2.2%)	62.34	37.66
Law	3,98,584 (1.3%)	66.42	33.58
Graduates in all disciples	28,596,751	51.30 (14,671,231)	48.70 (13,925,520)

Source: Adapted from *Table 12: Enrolment at Undergraduate Level in Major Disciplines/Subjects (based on actual response)*, AISHE Survey report 2018–2019.

Industries predominantly employ a technical workforce equipped with the requisite technical qualifications to support their activities. Technical education which is a part of higher education includes engineering, technology, architecture, town planning, management, pharmacy, applied arts and crafts, hotel management, and catering technology, and so on at different levels. The total number of students in undergraduate programmes in India is 28,596,751. Moreover, only 19.9 per cent are enrolled in technical programmes.

Since the major enrolment of students in India, are arts, science, and humanities streams, the scope of industry linkages are limited. Significant industry–academia linkages worldwide are in technical and professional education. The major industry–academia linkages are based generally on time-sensitive problem solving with predefined results and tend to be articulated through contract research, consulting, and licensing, which may be difficult in arts and humanities streams.

Significance of industry–academia linkage

The collaboration between universities and industry globally is increasingly perceived as a vehicle to enhance economic growth for introducing innovations in industry. Such innovations should be transferred to industry and society through knowledge exchange.

One of the factors significant for current higher education is the 'linkages' between industry and academia. To operationalize and sustain for the future, there is a need that most institutions should be in sync with industry expectations. Industry today expects graduates to not only have conceptual understanding of the subjects but also possess the skills of problem solving, decision making, and execution. Industry also expects graduates to possess good 'soft skills' (including interpersonal skills that include communication skills). In other words, industry is looking for graduates who can start doing the job from day one.

Collaboration between academia and industry is critical for skills and competency formation as well as the generation, acquisition, adoption, dissemination of innovation and technology transfer. Currently this has also been closely linked with the promotion of entrepreneurship, both start-ups and spin-offs.

These collaborations can also facilitate and coordinate R&D agendas and avoid duplications, stimulate additional private R&D investment (additionally effect), and exploit synergies and complementarities of scientific and technological capabilities.

Academia-industry linkages may further effectively utilize the research carried out in public institutions and foster the commercialization of public R&D outcomes. University-industry collaboration substantially increased the propensity of firms to introduce new products and to patent (Marotta et al., 2007).

The benefits of the industry–academia linkages are far-reaching, as they can help in developing a curriculum which matches the future skill and meets the competency requirement of the industry. They stimulate R&D at the university/ institute level, which can complement and synergize the R&D initiatives of the industry and increase the mobility of human resources between industry and academia, thereby helping faculty and students to get industry exposure and giving industry a platform on which to share experiences.

It is essential for a university/institute teacher today to frequently visit industrial organizations/corporations to look at working conditions in the industrial sector so that he or she can deeply understand how to best prepare their students to work confidently in the corporation/industry on completion of their education.

In light of these benefits and relevance, it is crucial to ensure successful management of industry–academia linkages to realize the advantages on both sides. However, conceptualization, operationalization, and sustaining industry–academia linkages are challenging.

The reasons cited for low employability in India are primarily the mismatch between industry requirements and academic content, which is predominantly due to a lack of proper industry–academia linkages.

Unfortunately, universities/institutions have failed to deliver their promise of providing graduates who add value to the organizations. This case is more severe in the case of management and engineering education, which are considered as professional education. These courses are aimed to prepare students who act as vehicles for organizational transformation.

Practices and focus areas in creating industry-academia linkages

Industry–academia linkages have a long tradition in several countries worldwide (Ankrah & AL-Tabbaa, 2015). Today, universities/institutions play a crucial role in achieving economic growth in today's knowledge-based societies (Pinheiro et al., 2015). There are studies focusing on developing academia and industry linkages that aim to enhance innovation and economic competitiveness at institutional levels (e.g. countries and sectors) through knowledge exchange between academic and commercial domains (Perkmann et al., 2013).

The published literature on academia and industry linkage is primarily based on four key aspects. These are: proposing a typology for industry and academia linkages (Dess & Shaw, 2001), identifying firm/university characteristics as involved in university and industry linkages (Agrawal, 2001), addressing university and industry linkages antecedences and consequences (Perkmann et al., 2013), industry and academia linkages in general and not only on 'contract research', and commercialization of technology (Meyer-Krahmer & Schmoch, 1998). Moreover, commercialization of technology has an equal focus on both universities and industry perspectives on research and ways of technology exchange between academia and industry.

Over the last few years, the fourth industrial revolution has attracted more and more attention to the importance of industry–academia linkages all around the world. As Industry 4.0 gains ground, the world is witnessing the development of a few parallel trends, including the rapid emergence of ecological constraints, the advent of an increasingly multipolar international order, and rising inequality, ushering in a new era of globalization. Against this backdrop, the business environment is increasingly characterized by continuous change and growing complexity. The challenges for companies arise not only from the need for flexible technical solutions but also from managing complex socio-technical systems and contributing tangibly to the sustainable development of the economy and the environment.

This circumstance requires engineering researchers and graduates with the ability to understand complex technological processes in the context of social, environmental, economic, and global concerns. They will play a critical role and will be increasingly sought after in the emerging industrial and business worlds.

There is increasing need to analyze such collaborative ventures and propose a research agenda. Doing this can begin by considering the current research activities (e.g. main research directions, applied standards, employed software, and hardware) and indicating existing deficiencies and potential research directions. However, this body of knowledge is still evolving for efficient comprehensive view. Most of academia-industry links have been assessed by taking a modular approach with a defined set of parameters. However, there are different institutional arrangements (see Table 15.2). These arrangements have been highlighted by Perkmannand Walsh (2007) (see Table 15.3).

Table 15.2 A typology of industry–academia links, from higher to lower intensity

High (Relationships)	Research partnerships	Inter-organizational arrangements for pursuing collaborative R&D, including research consortia and joint projects.
	Research services	Research-related activities commissioned to universities by industrial clients, including contract research, consulting, quality control, testing, certification, and prototype development.
	Shared infrastructure	Use of university labs and equipment by firms, business incubators, and technology parks located within universities.
Medium (Mobility)	Academic entrepreneurship	Development and commercial exploitation of technologies pursued by academic inventors through a company they (partly) own (spin-off companies).
	Human resource training and transfer	Training of industry employees, internship programmes, postgraduate training in industry, adjunct faculty of industry participants, and case writings.
Low (Transfer)	Commercialization of intellectual property	Transfer of university-generated IP (such as patents) to firms (e.g. via licensing).
	Scientific publications	Use of codified scientific knowledge within industry.
	Informal interaction	Formation of social relationships (e.g. conferences, meetings, social networks).

Source: Adapted from (Perkmann & Walsh, 2007), Tables 15.1 and 15.2. "University-Industry Relationships and Open Innovation: Towards a Research Agenda." *International Journal of Management Reviews* 9 (4): 259–80, https://spiral.imperial.ac.uk/bitstream/10044/1/1396/1/Perkmann%20Walsh%202007.pdf.

Table 15.3 Priorities for university-industry partnerships at different stages of economic development along the three missions of universities

Type of partnership	*Focus of partnership*
Teaching university/ institutes	• Private participation in graduate programmes • Joint supervision of PhD students • Curricula development to improve undergraduate and graduate studies • Student internships
Research university/ institutes	• Research consortia and long-term research partnerships to conduct frontier research • Building absorptive capacity to adopt and diffuse already existing technologies • Focus on appropriate technologies to respond to local needs
Entrepreneurial university/ institutes	• Spin-off companies, patent licensing • Entrepreneurship education • Business incubation services • Entrepreneurship education

Source: Adapted from (Perkmann & Walsh, 2007), Tables 15.1 and 15.2.

Tables 15.3 and 15.2: National policies to attract R&D-intensive FDI in developing countries, World Bank, 2013.

These arrangements have different objectives and scope. Most of the collaborations also depend on the mission and vision of universities/institutes and companies, so the nature of collaborations vary from university/institutes to university/institutes. The collaboration may be more or less intense and may focus on training or research activities. Further, it could be specifically for a few activities and may be formal or informal. It has been seen that currently several types of collaboration—from formal equity partnerships, contracts, research projects, patent licensing, and so on, to human capital mobility, publications, and interactions in conferences and expert groups, among others (Hagedoorn et al., 2000)—are happening.

Three factors on the basis of which the industry–academia linkages may be classified are the intensity of relationship, the focus of partnership, and the duration of the collaborative activity.

Based on available literature, it can also be seen that the scope of academia and industry linkages are different in categories of university and institutes and also relate to the state of the economy. The type of university/institution is further classified as teaching universities/institutes, research university/institutes and entrepreneurial university/institutes in order to highlight the differences in their focus in terms of developing linkages with industry. Table 15.3 summaries the priorities for university-industry partnerships for these categories.

It has also been seen specifically in India that there are short-term and long-term collaborations. These depend on the nature of education and its supply of graduates to industry. The supply of technical graduates in industry is greater in large-scale formal industries than in liberal arts and other disciplines. There are several factors responsible for such collaborations.

Universities and institutes of technical education have long-term collaborations. In these universities and institutes, it has been observed that these collaborations are associated with joint projects and public-private partnerships. They have also established private-funded university institutes or chairs, joint university-industry research centres, and research consortia often allowing firms to contract for a core set of services and to periodically re-contract for specific deliverables in a flexible manner. Longer-term collaborations are more strategic and open-ended, providing a multifaceted platform where firms can develop a stronger innovative capacity in the long run, building upon the capabilities, methods, and tools of universities (Koschatzky & Stahlecker, 2010).

Firms and universities are increasingly finding it mutually beneficial to collaborate. On one hand, private firms are progressively adopting open innovation strategies to better access and integrate external sources of knowledge, leading to a stronger interest in collaboration with universities. On the other hand, since the 1990s, the strategic mission of universities has moved beyond the tradition of teaching and research toward a 'third mission' related to better addressing the needs of industry and contributing directly to economic growth and development.

The three university missions have given rise to the distinct concepts of teaching university, Research University, and entrepreneurial university. University-industry collaboration may take place under all of these university regimes, although it will have a distinct focus on training in the teaching university, on R&D in the research university, and on technology commercialization in entrepreneurial university. Some of the recent industry–academia linkages initiated by IITs and IIMs are listed in Table 15.4.

Table 15.4 Recent industry–academia linkages initiated by IITs and IIMs

SNo.	*Industry*	*Academia*	*Type of Collaboration*
1	WIPRO	IISc, Bengaluru	The Indian Institute of Science (IISc), Bengaluru, joined hands with global IT major Wipro in order to develop autonomous systems, robotics, 5G, and indigenous Metal 3D printing (additive manufacturing) machines. The main focus of this collaboration is to carry out the research and development of emerging technologies like artificial intelligence, IoT, machine learning, visual computing, and other such.
2	WIPRO	IIT Kharagpur	IIT Kharagpur signed a Memorandum of Understanding (MOU) with one of the leading global IT companies, Wipro. The aim behind this collaboration is to create industry-focused applied research in the areas of 5G and AI. Both the organizations will focus on AI research applicable in healthcare, education, and retail sectors as well as in domains such as climate change and cybersecurity.

(*Continued*)

Table 15.4 (Continued)

SNo.	*Industry*	*Academia*	*Type of Collaboration*
3	SAMSUNG	IIT Guwahati IIT Hyderabad, IIT Kanpur, IIT Delhi, IIT Kharagpur, and IIT Roorkee	Samsung India recently inaugurated a digital academy at IIT Guwahati. The academy plans to train more than 300 people in the next three years on cutting-edge technologies like artificial intelligence, machine learning, IoT, among others.
4	STERLITE ESPNcricinfo CII	IIT Madras	Recently, the data network organization Sterlite 5 Technologies joined hands with IIT Madras to conduct research and development in 5G. The company will sponsor a Chair Professorship in 5G technology at the institute, who will work towards accelerating the advancements in 5G by unifying IIT Madras' research and domain knowledge with STL's industry expertise in 5G. The institute collaborated with the sports news website ESPNcricinfo and launched a tool called Superstats. This tool is a combination of statistics metrics which use data science to provide context to every event. It will help in analyzing cricket statistics with the help of data science. Also, the institute has joined up with the Confederation of Indian Industry (CII) to nurture and promote innovative green start-ups across the country. The collaboration will facilitate brainstorming sessions between academia and industry to create deep-tech and disruptive research ideas and help start-ups gain industry access for pilot demonstrations of their cleantech ideas.
5	Japanese institutions of National Research Institute for Earth Science and Disaster Resilience	IIT Hyderabad	Recently, IIT Hyderabad signed Memoranda of Understanding with four Japanese institutions of the National Research Institute for Earth Science and Disaster Resilience in order to research in areas, including earthquake engineering, with a focus on numerical simulation. They will undertake a number of programmes such as joint research activities, faculty exchange, joint seminars, internship opportunities, and other such academic activities.
6	Mahindra Group	IIT Kanpur	In June 2019, IIT Kanpur signed an MoU with Mahindra Group, the Indian multinational subsidiary of the Mahindra Group, Tech Mahindra. The aim behind the collaboration is to conduct joint research in the domain of cybersecurity. According to reports, through this partnership, Tech Mahindra will bring real-world industry exposure to students of IIT Kanpur and work closely with the institute on research projects to develop and foster an environment to deal with automation in cybersecurity and to enhance digital resilience of critical national infrastructure.

SNo.	Industry	Academia	Type of Collaboration
7	Indian Space Research Organisation (ISRO)	IIT Delhi	In collaboration with the Indian Space Research Organisation (ISRO), IIT Delhi is going to set up a space technology centre at the institute premises. The aim behind the collaboration is to contribute to space technology research.
8	Apollo Tubes & Microsoft	IIT Roorkee	IIT Roorkee recently signed an MoU with APL Apollo Tubes Limited (APL Apollo), for research, training, and placement. And Microsoft to augment learning on quantum computing by means of conducting lectures on quantum computing for a full semester.
9	Tata Motors	IIT Bombay	A few months ago, a team of IIT Bombay students collaborated with Tata Motors to develop an electric race car called the 'EVoK'.

Source: Compiled by the authors from various sources.

In light of these benefits and relevance, it is crucial to ensure successful management of industry–academia linkages to realize the advantages on both sides. However, conceptualizing, operationalizing, and sustaining industry–academia linkages are challenging.

Critical factors in industry–academia collaboration

Technical education has been transforming significantly in India in the past two decades, initially witnessing a meteoric rise in the supply of technical graduates and postgraduates specifically in engineering and management. This period also saw a progressively widening gap between the industry requirements and the capability of engineering graduates, indicating an increasing gap between industry and academia and the siloed functioning of these two important stakeholders. Some such critical factors in making the IALs function effectively are discussed in the following sections.

Manpower planning

Technology and globalization have turned countries into knowledge-driven economies. They are radically accelerating the pace of change in the world and raising long-term risks. Success in a knowledge-driven and innovation-driven world order depends largely on the capabilities of the people, and higher education, especially engineering education, is the key to building those requisite capabilities.

Current challenges in technical education in India revolve around the failure to forecast the demand for future skills in a reasonably accurate fashion. There is high degree of focus on infrastructure. The institutions displayed their infrastructural approvals prominently to attract potential students. In a booming economy, this approach worked because corporations wanted to recruit manpower in larger numbers at different levels and hence visited or recruited from different management schools with a good infrastructural base. However, the decline in the economy led to corporations recasting their manpower plan, which affected the placement in almost all institutes (barring, perhaps, the top 30 to 40 institutes). Even the top institutes felt the heat of decline in numbers and had to explore new sectors and reach out to start-up firms. The smaller and marginal schools had no enrolments in the subsequent years and today many of them have closed down their operations.

There is no match with the forecast of managerial manpower and accordingly under-utilization of capacity.

Current (2017–2018) capacity utilization in the undergraduate and the postgraduate level is as low as 49.8 per cent (capacity vs enrolment). Creating any further capacity is a big drain on investments, since at the very basic level it involves the creation of physical infrastructure like buildings and lab infrastructure. The supply is greater than the demand. The excessive supply is also a factor for unemployment and underemployment.

There is need for developing a prospective plan for technical education that matches supply with demand and also provides for effective demand forecasting. The involvement of industry in preparing a prospective plan of technical manpower is also significant. It should be an ongoing exercise. Against the backdrop of a rapidly changing technology environment, technical education needs continuous monitoring.

Bringing curricula in sync with industry expectations

As institutions got approved by regulatory bodies like AICTE and UGC, almost all of them started offering the same programmes of technical, managerial, architecture, and other subjects. Even the nomenclature of the degree was the same. Each institution claimed to be using experiential pedagogy in their programme delivery. But it is not clear whether many of them understood the concept of experiential learning and the pedagogies involved.

One of the factors responsible for the current scenario is the 'disconnect' between industry and technical universities/institutions. The curriculum in most technical institutions is not in sync with industry expectations. Industry also expects technical graduates to possess good 'soft skills' (including interpersonal skills that encompass communication skills). In other words, industry is looking for technical graduates who can start working from day one.

Some changes were brought about by offering electives in emerging areas like e-commerce, retail, insurance, and so on. Some even introduced courses which were new to the discipline of technical education. Many of these changes faded with the passage of time, as there was no substantive body of either literature or placement opportunities. Hence, technical programmes became almost a vanilla product.

Technical education should be prepared and finalized according to the needs of the organizations which use their output—students. To achieve this goal, the board of studies should include qualified and experienced personnel from the industry as members for preparing and modifying the curriculum to make it more industry-oriented.

Addressing inadequate competencies of the faculty

The 'disconnect' with industry has also occurred because of the inadequate competencies of the faculty. In most cases, the faculty members either did not have the relevant experience. Even the visiting faculty from industry in most cases failed to deliver because of the limitation of their experience. Another source of disconnect was that although the faculty were good academic scholars, they had no industry exposure. While such faculty served well in pure disciplines of science, humanities, and social sciences, they failed to deliver in professional programmes like management and engineering, which presuppose a practical orientation. Lack of research, especially applied research, has further contributed to this disconnect.

Any amount of theoretical knowledge without practical experience can never make a student of technology capable of taking up his or her profession with confidence. Theory must be tested against existing practices in order to make theoretical knowledge purposeful and useful. Properly planned and effectively executed field work for a reasonably long period alone can ensure rich dividends from technical and managerial education. This could be achieved by simultaneously enhancing the capability of faculty members.

To accomplish the goal of increasing the capability of faculty members, it is important that all industry–academia partnerships go beyond placements. It is pertinent that industry participates in the boards of academic institutions and vice versa, increases activities to facilitate regular interactions between faculty and industry to provide inputs on curriculum, teaches proactively, explores potential joint research projects, and creates more start-ups that can complement and supplement industry needs. It is only when more interaction happens that collaborations will flower and flourish, and we can create an ecosystem of effective teaching by aware and experienced faculty.

Mismatch between research orientation of industry and academia

Most of the studies of Indian higher education have highlighted inherent mismatches between the research orientations of companies and academia. It has been observed that currently there is an excessive focus on fast commercial results in firms and on basic research in universities. Such collaboration generally works for short term with limited outcomes, while long-term collaboration involves high cost and the returns only accrue in the medium to long run. Most of the companies look for short-term results and clear contributions to current business lines. They are keenly interested in quick new patents or new products. But most of the time they seek to delay research publication in order to avoid disclosing information. Researchers from academia are more focused and motivated to publish research results to get academic credit.

Again, there is a mismatch between industry and academia with respect to expectations about intellectual property (IP) rights. To avoid this mismatch, agreements need to be established in a commercially timely manner that ensures the ability to commercialize with appropriate returns. Difficulties in negotiating a collaboration include lack of information, difficulties finding contact persons, and transaction costs of finding the right partner, among others.

Research on future trends in education indicates that student-centric learning needs to be given precedence. Students should be encouraged to focus on design thinking and practical approaches to learning. Students should also be made aware of real-life social problems for them to solve using their technology education.

In the case of research, it has been seen by global practice that the focus of collaboration should be on fostering appropriate long-term partnerships between academia and industry.

Inadequate adoption of disruptive technologies

Technology and globalization have turned countries into knowledge-driven economies. Technology is today defining the economic growth and influencing social changes. The All Management Association and PricewaterhouseCoopers (AIMA-PwC) report has highlighted "A sector that is getting impacted and also contributes to being a growth indicator is technical education". There is no doubt that the use of technology has changed the way training is delivered and consumed. It has created many new opportunities and avenues and also changed the learning process. The impact of technology is not just felt by students who are tech savvy but also by teachers whose initial uptake was gradual. However, disrupted technologies like AI and ML are still having very limited application in learning. Intensive research needs to be carried in area of adaptive learning, personalised learning alternative tools of learning like voice, video, animations, AI, and machine learning can improve the quality of teaching and raise vocational learning to larger extent. More researches need to be carried to convert mundane aggrading, personalised response to be accurately done using AI/ML.

Membership of governing body

Eminent educationalists/academicians should be nominated to the board of directors of industries, and the leaders in the industry should be nominated to the board of advisors' committee of educational institutions. This method of sharing expertise in techniques of management of institutions and industries will go a long way in helping institutionalize the IALs more efficiently. To some extent, it is already in practice because of regulatory norms, but it needs to be effectively implemented both for the benefit of academia and industry. This partnership should be based on long-term objectives and vision by identifying the relevant areas of collaboration.

Strategies to operationalize and sustain industry and academia linkages

Joint utilization of R&D results by industry

It is important to mention that research and industry linkages could also be seen in term of utilization of R&D results by industry (i.e. transfer of technology for manufacturing and production). It is also important to promote industry-funded research by R&D institutions in the areas relevant to the industry. We have witnessed that BITS Pilani has joint R&D programmes. These programmes are successfully conducted jointly by industry and institutes, and transfer of technology has taken place for the benefit of manufacturing and production. There is also adequate exchange of personnel at all levels. BITS is also successfully utilizing the research facilities of laboratories jointly created in collaboration with industry. There is also continuous use of specialized material as well as technologies used by industry in these laboratories. The trial and testing for product and technological development is also a continuous process. There is a need for identifying technical institutes and universities, where there is direct scope of applying the successful BITS Pilani model.

Use of disruptive technologies in academia and industry linkages

The way technology adoption has changed the conventional way of learning is something that we understand when we talk to millennials. Realizing this, educational institutions are using technological means to enrich content by incorporating animation, images, audio, and videos. Visualization has become a fundamental way of imparting key concepts. Riding the wave of mobility apps, educational institutions have deployed chatbots (an artificial teaching computer programme) as teaching assistants to troubleshoot and AI-driven engines to explain and answer student questions. Disruptive technologies such as mobile internet, cloud services, and automation through AI can certainly help reshape India's education sector Adoption of other disruptive technologies such as digital payments and KYC (Know Your Customer) will also enable transformation. While globally the passage to these techniques is at a fast pace, India is all set to reach the inflection point soon.

Leveraging technology, India could have about 24 million more high school and college-educated workers and 18 million–33 million more vocationally trained workers by 2025 due to the use of digital technologies in the education sector, with an estimated economic impact of $60–$90 billion per year by 2025 from the higher productivity of more skilled workers.

McKinsey, in a report titled 'Disruptive Technologies: Advances that will transform Life, Business and the Global Economy', has identified 12 potentially economically disruptive technologies for the future.

These are:

- Mobile Internet
- Automation of Knowledge Work
- The Internet of Things
- Cloud Technology
- Advanced Robotics
- Autonomous and Near-Autonomous Vehicles
- Next-Generation Genomics
- Fast, low-cost gene sequencing, advanced big data analytics, and synthetic biology ('writing' DNA)
- Energy Storage
- 3D Printing Additive manufacturing techniques to create objects by printing layers of material based on digital models
- Advanced Materials
- Advanced Oil and Gas Exploration & Recovery
- Exploration and recovery techniques that make extraction of unconventional oil and gas economical
- Renewable Energy

Some of these technologies which have a bearing on the future of technical education may be targeted well in advance.

Mobile phones (especially the smartphones) are the potential carriers of education and hence a catalyst of social change. Mobile internet is today a powerful tool to enhance connectivity with the learner community. It is also a tool by which one can reach out to markets beyond even the geographical boundaries. Mobile also today provides an opportunity to develop new products and solutions, including those that can be useful to students, faculty, and administrators.

Cloud technologies today provide opportunities to create new products and services and offer them in real time anywhere in the world. Many of today's learning software, like Blackboard, use cloud technology. This technology, combined with open software, will define a new world of knowledge creation which will be far more democratic in nature. It will also provide an opportunity to co-create new learning models. For example, it will not be uncommon in a virtual classroom situation for the learner and the faculty to jointly create a new body of knowledge on a particular subject. Virtual classrooms, therefore, will be an important element of the learning infrastructure.

Workforce skilling

We will be witnessing increased automation and diversity in the workplace. Automation will not just be in manufacturing but also services, including customer service. We are already witnessing these trends today. An increasing number of companies and organizations today use technology to reach out and serve the markets. The scope for human interaction over a period of time will be further minimized with the 'Internet of Things'(IoT) gaining momentum. As cities and towns become 'smart', workplaces will become more automated. Work from home, autonomous working, virtual teams, and 24 × 7 workplaces are already a reality today. Virtual communities are defining the workplace culture and the value system. The wave of technological change, which will also involve extensive use of advanced robotics, will only imply that some of the current jobs and skills will get eliminated and therefore will have a bearing on the placement scenario in management schools.

India's current workforce lacks skill and expertise in new technologies such as data analytics, additive manufacturing, and IoT. The government, industry, and academia need to collaborate to enable an Industry 4.0-ready workforce.

The availability of adequate talent—both at a strategic leadership level and on the factory floor—can prove to be a significant challenge for India Inc. on its way to Industrial revolution 4.0 maturity. Building leaders who can successfully navigate their organizations in the digital age and upskilling the workforce will require significant planning, investment, and collaboration from all stakeholders, including academia.

Further, in light of disruptive technologies, accelerated innovation, and complex business environment, the skills of the future are expected to change significantly. Effective linkages between academia and industry are required for imparting these skills in technical education.

Striking at employability gap

According to the 2016 National Employability Report for Engineers, by Aspiring Minds, which releases periodic reports based on an auditory mechanism for higher education, there is no significant improvement in the employability of engineering graduates in the preceding four years of the report.

The concept of '100 per cent placement' will perhaps have to make way for the importance of enhancing the employability of technical graduates. The skills of employability have been defined and identified by different institutions in their own context, but broadly speaking, the skills refer to the following:

- Understanding of the work and subjects. In other words, this refers to the cognitive and conceptualization skills.

- Skills that can be deployed to deliver results. For example, skills of problem solving, getting the work done, or getting to produce or sell to the customers. In other words, these are some of the skills of execution.
- Connecting with human beings and motivating them to achieve seemingly impossible goals is known as people skills.
- Belief in one's own self. This helps an individual to overcome the stresses in the workplace.
- Learning ability is about developing a mindset for lifelong learning.

A more holistic model of partnered teaching is the need of the hour. With the workplace changing and employment opportunity declining, the scope for entrepreneurship will grow. Management education will have to create new models which will help their graduates consider entrepreneurship as an alternative career.

With the job profiles changing rapidly, individuals will have to continuously learn, unlearn, and relearn.

Making industry internships more effective

In 2017, AICTE had made internships mandatory for all technical education students during summer vacations or regular semesters and signed several MoUs both with government agencies and start-ups to facilitate internships. AICTE has been appealing to industry to support its initiatives so that the graduating students learn to address the challenges of the future and enable industry to get well-honed graduates.

But, for example, the IT-ITES industry, which currently employs four million professionals and as a consequence should be enrolling at least 100,000 apprentices per annum, has so far enrolled just about 23,158 apprentices in 2019.

However, a look at the 2018 AICTE-CII Survey of Industry-linked Technical Institutes reveals the current state of industry–academia linkages in the country. Out of the 9,581 institutes, 70 per cent of the institutes are working with very few (<49) private-sector organizations. Much more can be accomplished in deepening the linkages between industry and technical institutes in the country. It is important that all industry–academia partnerships go beyond placements. It is pertinent that industry participates in the boards of academic institutions and vice versa. This is to facilitate regular interactions between faculty and industry to provide inputs on curriculum, proactively explore potential joint research projects, and create more start-ups that can complement and supplement the industry needs.

Conclusions and recommendations

The existence of high-quality institutes is highly dependent on a close as well as active interface with industry. The interface may be assessed by taking into consideration executive and management development programmes organized in close collaboration with industry for top- and middle-level executives; top industry professionals visiting the institutes; faculty members continuously engaged with industry in writing cases and conducting consultancy projects; and, most significantly, industry chairs instituted for distinguished professors. Two or three industries may come together to fund research projects of common interest. The problem of faculty shortage may be addressed by offering a bridge course to industry professionals by offering a transition programme (Industry to Academia).

The following critical factors are currently crucial in making academia and industry linkages successful but also operational and sustainable over a long period of time. The identified factors are as follows:

Academia

- Enhance quality of teachers and modernize learning infrastructure by interacting with industry by defining and creating and defining new roles for 4.0, which would be mostly managerial in nature
- Align course curricula in tandem with industry 4.0 requirements, with well-regulated and industry-relevant updated content
- Focus more on practical, results-oriented knowledge over theoretical content
- Promote a culture of research in upcoming areas like industry 4.0 and act as the test beds for innovation and new learning
- Participate actively in the development of MOOCs (Massive Open Online Courses)
- Provide reskilling opportunities by identifying a core set of industry-relevant skills and delivering them to employees with the active support of academia
- Collaborate with industry players in setting up academic labs, smart factories, support to MSME, internships, externships, industry lectures, and innovation and entrepreneurship cells
- Facilitate academia in developing and documenting cases of industry best practices
- Encourage deepening of industry–academia partnerships in applied research

Industry

- Provide reskilling opportunities by identifying a core set of industry-relevant skills and delivering them to employees
- Provide cross-function exposure to employees for them to learn outside their own disciplines
- Participate actively in PPP initiatives and collaborate in take up vocational training with the government

- Undertake and invest in R&D for disrupting and emerging technologies
- Create and define new roles for industry 4.0, which would be mostly managerial in nature

Role of government, AICTE, and the UGC

Business education is quite different from education in most other professions. It operates in a highly competitive, volatile, globalized, and innovative marketplace for industry. Therefore, there is a need to create effective linkages between academia and industry. Here, a slow-moving university system is poorly equipped to fight the necessary battles and win. Autonomy, agility, speed, and adaptability, and so on are the requirements for success in this field. And the market is an uncompromising and ruthless judge of the quality of a business school or its products.

Therefore, it is necessary for government, UGC, and the AICTE to reconsider some of the existing models of regulations and controls on the management schools system. Exactly as it used to happen during our 'license raj', shoddy goods and services can only exist in a protected system. Such goods and services cannot survive in a competitive situation. We need to produce graduates for industry; therefore, quality is paramount. The guarantee for quality is a discerning the high-quality graduates in a competitive market. One would not say all this about medical or science education, but business education is of a different kind, and it can and will perform better only in a competitive environment. Therefore, liberalization and globalization will only be effective if they are linked with business education, too. Then we would see the competitive capability of our business education system decisively contributing to the overall competitive capability of the country. Some identified areas where the role of AICTE and UGC are critical are as follows:

- Improve the quality of academic institutions and vocational training
- Upskill the whole country—government, industry, and academia.
- Create an integrated skill development platform with benchmarked technical education curriculum.
- Launch mass skilling initiatives like 'Skill India', which aims to skill about 40 crore Indians by 2022.
- Create proper infrastructure and develop innovation centres and test labs.
- Establish entrepreneurship as a minor elective for undergraduates.
- Tinkering labs similar to Atal Innovation Labs to be setup in every educational institution.
- Promote start-ups by having educational institutions set up incubation centres, mentoring clubs, and acceleration programmes.
- Provide supportive policies and adequate financing for skill development.
- Make apprenticeship mandatory on industry and also progressively mandatory on educational institutions (starting with 25 per cent moving to 100 per cent in five years).

References

AISHE (2019). *All India survey on higher education 2018–19.* Ministry of Human Resource Development, Department of Higher Education, Government of India, New Delhi.

Agrawal, A. K. (2001). University-to-industry knowledge transfer: Literature review and unanswered questions. *International Journal of Management Reviews*, 3(4), 285–302.

Ankrah, S. N., & AL-Tabbaa, O. (2015). Universities-industry collaboration: A systematic review. *Scandinavian Journal of Management*, 31(3), 387–408. www.sciencedirect.com/science/article/pii/S0956522115000238.

Dess, G. G., & Shaw, J. D. (2001). Voluntary turnover, social capital, and organizational performance. *Academy of Management Review*, 26(3), 446–456.

Hagedoorn, J., Link, A. N., & Vonortas, N. S. (2000). Research partnerships. *Research Policy*, 29(4–5), 567–586.

Koschatzky, K., & Stahlecker, T. (2010). New forms of strategic research collaboration between firms and universities in the German research system. *International Journal of Technology Transfer and Commercialization*, 9(1–2), 94–110.

Marotta, D., Mark, M., Blom, A., & Thorn, K. (2007). *Human capital and university-industry linkages' role in fostering firm innovation: An empirical study of Chile and Colombia.* Policy Research Working Paper No. 4443.World Bank, Washington, DC.

Meyer-Krahmer, F., & Schmoch, U. (1998). Science-based technologies: University-industry interactions in four fields. *Research Policy*, 27(8), 835–851.

Perkmann, M., Tartari, V., Mckelvey, M., Autio, E., Brostrom, A., D'este, P., et al. (2013). Academic engagement and commercialisation: A review of the literature on university-industry relations. *Research Policy*, 42(2), 423–442.

Perkmann, M., & Walsh, K. (2007). University-industry relationships and open innovation: Towards a research agenda. *International Journal of Management Reviews*, 9(4), 259–280.

Pinheiro, R., Wangenge-Ouma, G., Balbachevsky, E., & Cai, Y. (2015). The role of higher education in society and the changing institutionalized features in higher education. In *The Palgrave International Handbook of Higher Education Policy and Governance* (pp. 225–242). London: Palgrave Macmillan.

Chapter 16

Refuelling entrepreneurship education in India

A case study

Kavita Saxena

Rising unemployment continues to remain a matter of concern in India ever since it was recognized in the 1950s for the first time. According to the latest data compiled by the Centre for Monitoring Indian Economy (CMIE), the unemployment rate in India rose to 7.2 per cent in February 2019, whereas it was 5.9 per cent in February 2018 (Centre for Monitoring Indian Economy, 2018). Due to the dearth of formal employment opportunities, promoting entrepreneurship as a career option among youth seems to be an important way to contribute towards economic development (Fuentelsaz et al., 2015). Formal and structured entrepreneurship education from early school days can sensitize students towards entrepreneurship and prepare them better for the transition from school to work (Davey et al., 2016).

In recent years, India has witnessed a sea change in terms of people's attitudes towards entrepreneurs and entrepreneurship. Start-up entrepreneurs have started gaining respect in the community and are no longer looked down upon (Jain, 2016). Considering this wave of entrepreneurship in the country, this seems to be the right time to steer students and youth towards entrepreneurship education by developing programmes that are oriented towards informing, training, and educating them about the need to starting a new enterprise (Bechard & Toulouse, 1998). For effective interventions in the field of entrepreneurship education, one has to look at the wider landscape and bring together all the stakeholders of the entrepreneurship education ecosystem, namely, academicians, education leaders, universities, and policymakers, existing entrepreneurs, investors, incubation leaders, and bankers. Planned interventions can lead to increased understanding of entrepreneurship, thus infusing entrepreneurial skills, attitudes, and knowledge among the students and youth.

Entrepreneurship education can play an important role in inculcating a spirit of entrepreneurship among children and youth. This chapter highlights the growing importance of entrepreneurship education along with the role of higher-education institutions and government in supporting students in their entrepreneurial journey. In this chapter, readers will learn about the evolution of entrepreneurship education in our country and how this domain has emerged with various reforms introduced by the government from time to time. The chapter also presents a case

DOI: 10.4324/9781003158349-20

study on the Entrepreneurship Development Institute of India (EDII), Ahmedabad. The institute has a rich experience of working in the area of entrepreneurship education, research, training, and institution building since its establishment in 1983. The chapter concludes with recommendations in the form of interventions that are required at the primary, secondary, and higher-education level along with a collaborative working model where university-industry-government work together to create a culture of entrepreneurship in our country.

Role of higher-education institutions to support students towards entrepreneurship

Higher-education institutions, universities, and other autonomous academic institutions can play a vital role in driving country's entrepreneurial growth and innovation. University graduates, if given appropriate exposure and guidance, can develop innovative business ideas and also satisfy their thirst for entrepreneurship. However, the following are key issues that need immediate attention.

Aspiration not getting converted into action

With the government's rising emphasis on start-ups and entrepreneurship, many start-up enthusiasts are plunging into this domain to test their ideas. However, only few of them find scalable ways to capture the market despite having a solid knowledge base in their respective disciplines of study.

Box 16.1 Global Entrepreneurship Monitor

- Data from the Global Entrepreneurship Monitor (GEM) indicates the gap of 6.1% between intention and action for those aged 18–24 years, versus just 1.6% for those aged 25–34 years.
- This indicates that in most of the cases, their entrepreneurial potential remains underdeveloped, and aspirations are subdued under no action.

Source: Shukla et al. (2018).

Lack of appropriate support to start a new venture

Lack of guidance, encouragement and mentoring support affect the entrepreneurial intentions of students to a great extent. Universities can play a vital role as partners in the commercialization of university knowledge (Politis et al., 2018). Specific university support mechanisms that offer research lab facilities to aspiring student entrepreneurs and incubation centres to provide them with necessary technical, financial, mentoring, and networking support (Mian, 1997); (Torrance et al., 2013) can play a crucial role is strengthening entrepreneurship in our country. Report on the Gujarat Start-up saga by EDII Ahmedabad (EDII, 2019) indicates the lack of appropriate support to university graduates in starting new ventures. The theme is mentioned in Box 16.2.

Box 16.2 Entrepreneurship Development Institute of India

Reference

- Most of the university graduates lack adequate skills, knowledge, and experience to start a business.
- There is dearth of experienced mentors who can guide and support university graduates in identifying viable business opportunities and pursuing them.
- Graduates' mindsets are not attuned to taking the risk of starting a new venture compared to getting a stable job in the corporate world.
- Hence, start-up rates among graduates remain low primarily because of lack of support from their universities.

Source: Entrepreneurship Development Institute of India (2019a), Gujarat start-up saga, Ahmedabad, EDII.

Universities not geared up for the start-up wave

The success of entrepreneurship-led education should largely depend on its ability to create and develop new entrepreneurs. Universities and autonomous institutions must provide a culture where young and aspiring student entrepreneurs learn to overcome the fear of failure. This process of learning includes networking with mentors and experts as well as engaging in the process of acquiring knowledge and information seeking. Though modern universities have lots of resources like incubators, funding, and mentoring support, alumni network, and research and innovation facilities, they fail to move beyond their traditional roles and step up their game to turn the Indian Start-up ecosystem into a world leader. This is one of the main reasons for lack of good student start-up success stories at the regional and national level. In fact, universities must strive to nurture some of the small, local entrepreneurs and share their success stories with others and make them role models for the rest of the population.

Stimulating innovation using triple helix model

India's entrepreneurship ecosystem has grown at a phenomenal pace. With more than 1,000 new start-ups in 2017, the country is becoming an attractive hub for start-ups globally and also contributing to the growth and development of the economy through innovation and job creation (NASSCOM, 2017). One of the main reasons for this growth is a collaborative approach for research and innovation between academia, industry, and governments, to foster economic and social development. The last few years have seen a change wherein the focus has shifted from a single innovation source to the interaction among academia-government-industry as the source of innovation and social interactions. For example, the focus of innovation was earlier confined to a single institution, like policymaking in government and the creation and dissemination of knowledge was restricted to academia and product development in industry. But now all these players have started working together to create a synergistic effect on the ecosystem (Entrepreneurship Development Institute of India, 2019a).

All the three participants in the model (university, government, and industry) are interdependent in that they rely on one another for their effective functioning (as given in Table 16.1).

Table 16.1 Interdependence of university, government, and industry in the triple helix model

University	*Government*	*Industry*
Source of new knowledge and innovation	*Source of contractual relations*	*Locus of production*
• The role of the university has changed in last decade. • It no longer just supports innovation by providing trained human resources, research results, and knowledge to the industry but is also increasingly involved in creation of new technologies and innovation as an outcome of academic research. • Diffusion of knowledge to industries and professionals by engaging in cutting-edge research. • Working on live industry problems can give a boost to university research and make it more impact-making rather than having just high academic/theoretical value. • Commercialization of academic research can lead to important contributions in economic growth and development.	• Government plays a lead role in driving industry as well as academia. • By removing bureaucracy and announcing encouraging incentives for academia and industry, can foster collaboration among the players of the model. • In the Triple Helix Model, government sponsors start-up initiatives and funds science-based projects from academia and/or industry and thus acts as an enabler of innovation. • It also supports setting up of incubators, science parks, and technology and intellectual property markets.	• There is a shift in the industry working mechanism, too, whereby industries are not only building in-house laboratories and funding academic research but also boost mobility of researchers between academia and industry. • Industry has to have confidence that university research can create significant value. • It needs to provide relevant inputs to academia and support research progress and provide direction. • Also provide access to students, access to intellectual property and co-funded research projects to create a win-win situation for all the members of the model.

(*Continued*)

Table 16.1 (Continued)

University	*Government*	*Industry*
Source of new knowledge and innovation	*Source of contractual relations*	*Locus of production*
• For effective implementation, universities need dynamic faculty that has an ability to understand industry pain points and provide relevant solutions. • A supportive environment in terms of necessary infrastructure and allocation of time for industry-based research can result in a substantial contribution from universities.	• For effective implementation, government has to establish standards in such a way that it builds confidence in the industry. • Also, it has to understand that the results of such a collaborative model may not be immediate and may require a subjective evaluation process.	

Source: Compiled by the author.

Growing importance of entrepreneurial education

There has been a worldwide trend of exponential growth in entrepreneurial education across higher-education institutions (Kuratko, 2005). The most common reasons for this growth as cited by Kuratko are:

- Job creation
- Contribution in economic development of the nation
- Empowering people and organizations to create social value and impact
- Increased creativity and satisfaction
- Addressing societal challenges

Table 16.2 highlights the importance of entrepreneurial education at individual, organisational, and societal level.

Education can play a vital role in influencing the mindset of youth. Students can be sensitized towards entrepreneurship from an early stage by proper exposure, training, and education. According to a 2012 study (Shukla & Awasthi, 2012), lack of self-confidence and disapproval from the key decision-maker in the family are the two most important entry barriers faced by students who want to pursue their entrepreneurial journey and start their own enterprise. Coupled with lack of knowledge about viable business opportunities and inadequate information about procedures and formalities to start and manage an enterprise, such family opposition leads to hesitation in taking the risk of starting a new enterprise. Adequate mentoring and guidance on viable business opportunities and procedures and regulations to be followed to start an enterprise can encourage

Table 16.2 Importance of entrepreneurial education

	Individual level	*Organizational level*	*Societal level*
Commonly stated reasons for entrepreneurial education, but less effective in schools and for embedded approaches			
Creation of Jobs	There is a need to have a pool of individuals that are keen and competent to create jobs	Organizations in the growth stage can create more jobs	Job creation and subsequent growth can come through entrepreneurship and innovation
Economic success	Individuals can achieve economic success through entrepreneurship	Organizational renewal is fundamental to every firm's long-term success	Renewal processes are fundamental to the vitality of economies
Globalization, innovation, and renewal	Globalization, innovation, and renewal	Globalization, innovation, and renewal	Globalization, innovation, and renewal
Rarely stated reasons for entrepreneurial education but promising for schools and embedded approaches			
Joy, engagement, creativity	Creation/value creation/creativity is a main source of joy and pride for people	Employee creativity and joy is essential for the performance of new and existing organizations	Economic wealth of nations correlates with happiness of its citizens
Societal challenges	People can be the biggest contributors in bringing the change in the society	Corporations can collaborate with small social entrepreneurship initiatives to create social value	Many societal challenges and problems can be solved by social entrepreneurs and can bring a change in people's lives

Source: Lackéus, 2015.

youth to pursue entrepreneurship as a career choice. This clearly indicates that if entrepreneurship is embedded in the course curriculum at all levels in the education system, it can orient and prepare students by providing relevant inputs related to pre-start-up, start-up, and post-start-up phases and thereby encourage students to consider starting their own venture rather than looking for a job opportunity.

Researchers (Basu, 2014; Anand & Singh, 2013; Roy & Mukherkee, 2017; and (Sarathy & Silambarasan, 2011) have cited various objectives that can encourage entrepreneurship education among students and youth. A 2004 study (Alberti et al., 2004) highlighted the importance of entrepreneurship education, citing following benefits:

- Acquiring knowledge and skills relevant to entrepreneurship
- Identifying and stimulating entrepreneurial drive and competencies

- Gaining skills to undo the risk-averse behaviour
- Learning finer aspects of opportunity sensing and business plan preparation
- Stimulating the affective socialization element to get the support from the community and network and thereby encourage start-ups

Figure 16.1 shows the key aspects of educating emerging entrepreneurs.

If done well, with relevant and timely interventions, in the long run entrepreneurship education can result in changing the mindset of people, encourage and develop a culture of enterprise risk-taking, creating a strong support system where business failures are celebrated and treated as a milestone towards success rather than a taboo. If India aspires to attain sustainable economic development and societal progress, the country has to create a breed of dynamic global leaders and strong education systems that can create and nurture entrepreneurs, educators, industry practitioners, and individuals through

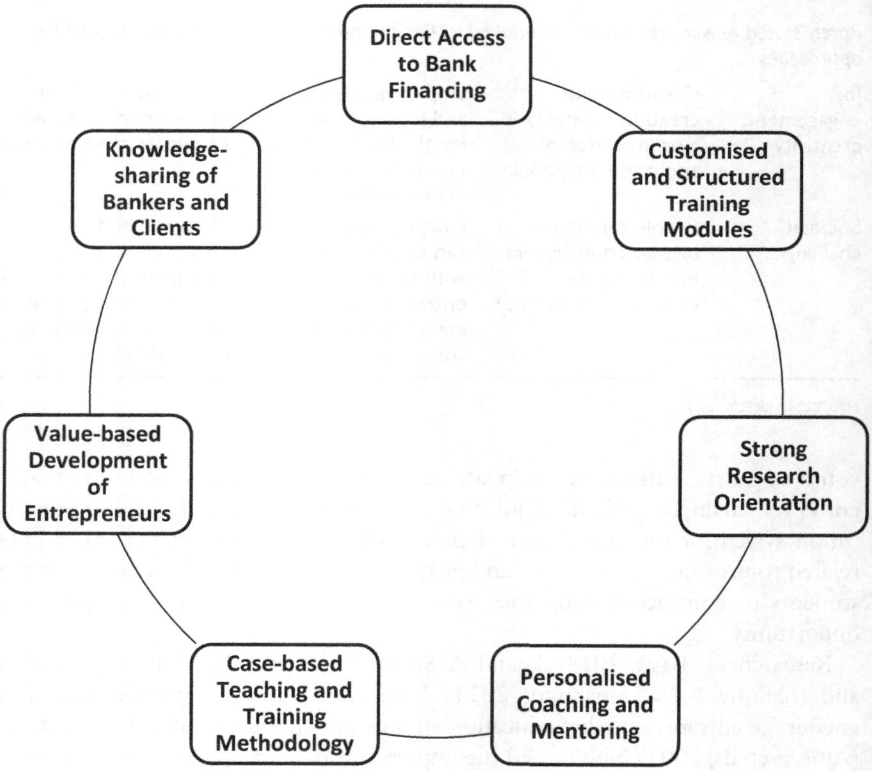

Figure 16.1 Key aspects of educating emerging entrepreneurs

Source: Compiled by the author.

multi-stakeholder partnership approach leading to renewed economic growth and human welfare.

Evolution of entrepreneurship education in India

The first and the biggest hurdle in the journey to build an entrepreneurial society is changing the mindset of people. For creating an entrepreneurial society where innovation, creativity, and risk-taking are the ways of life and considered normal, all the stakeholders of the ecosystem, namely, government, private sector, universities, and other academic institutions, non-profit sectors, and so on, have to be the facilitators of change that encourages new enterprise creation. This calls for rebooting the entire education system so that it can cultivate a vibrant learning environment and an entrepreneurial culture that would develop necessary skills, attitudes, and behaviour among students at all levels of primary, secondary, and higher education.

Entrepreneurship education started gaining popularity in the form of training programmes being conducted for MSMEs during the 1960s and 1970s. Later in the 1990s, liberalization of the economy further encouraged entrepreneurship activities in the country, resulting in the setting up of institutions for creating a pool of entrepreneurial talent. Figure 16.2 shows the evolution of entrepreneurship education in India.

In recent years various networking/training platforms other than education institutions have emerged and are playing an active role in strengthening

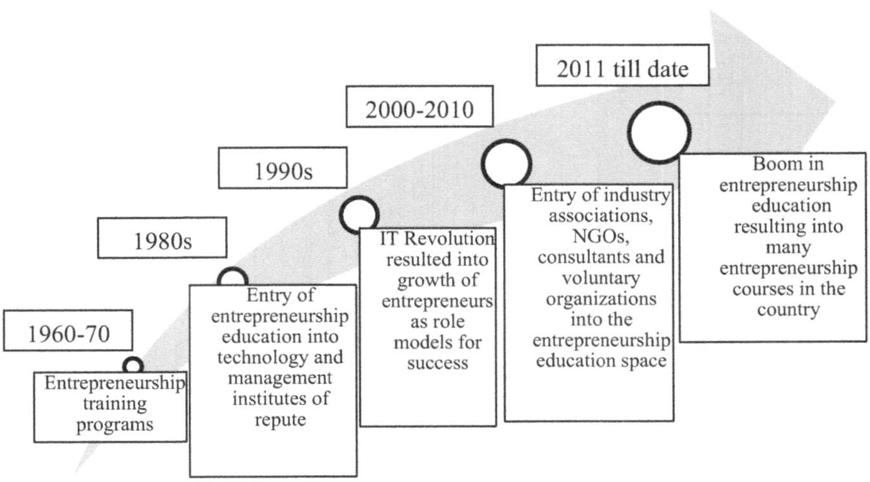

Figure 16.2 Evolution of entrepreneurship education in India

Source: Compiled by the author.

the entrepreneurship ecosystem in the country. Some of the prominent examples are:

- TiE (The IndUS Entrepreneurs) and e-Chai: Start-up networking platforms (visit tie.org and echai.in for more details)
- Entrepreneurship Development Cells established in technical institutions by The National Science & Technology Entrepreneurship Development Board (NSTEDB), The All India Council of Technical Education (AICTE) and University Grants Commission (UGC)
- Technology Business Incubators in various educational institutions, engineering colleges and management schools

Figure 16.3 shows the mentoring pool for entrepreneurship education available in our country.

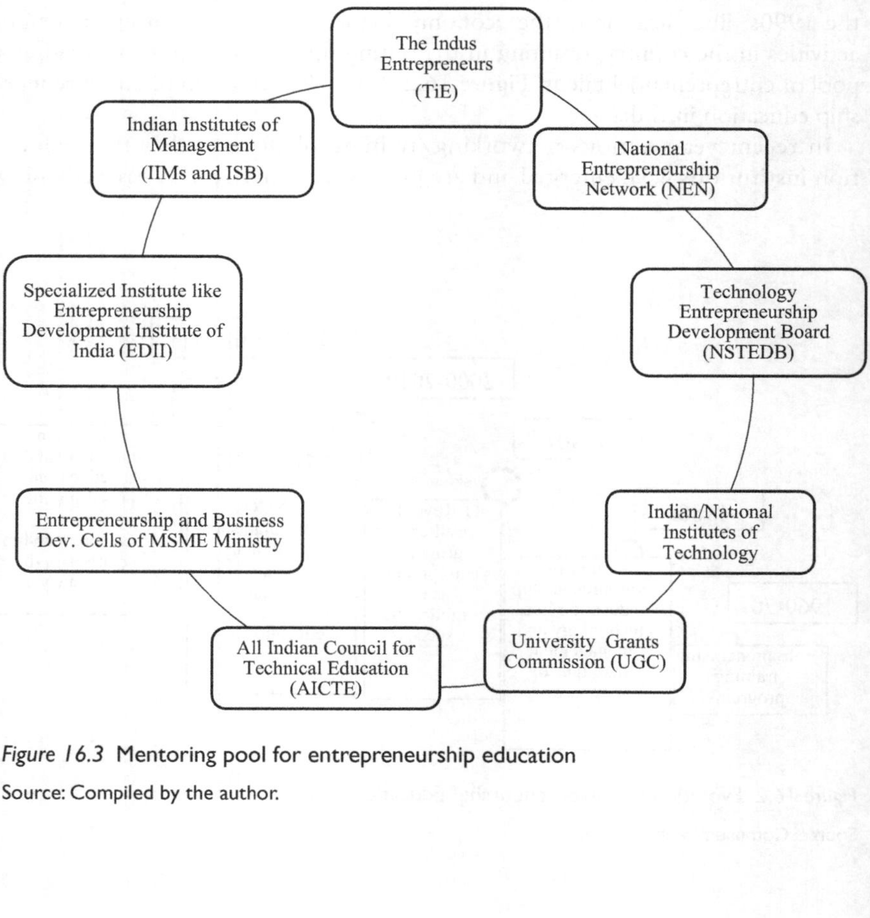

Figure 16.3 Mentoring pool for entrepreneurship education

Source: Compiled by the author.

Current status of entrepreneurship education in India

Over the last few years, there has been a significant change in the attitude and mindset of people towards entrepreneurship. The country is experiencing a pool of entrepreneurial talent and innovative business ideas across different sectors. The availability of seasoned mentors, growth stage investors, venture capitalists, and private equity players has infused lots of energy and positivity into the system (GradesFixer, 2019). Various initiatives in academic institutions, especially engineering colleges and management institutes, are taken to sensitize students towards entrepreneurship and triggering their interest and desire for setting up their own ventures. Today the trend is such that instead of looking for high-paying corporate jobs, a section of management graduates are opting out of campus placements and leveraging their management training at B-schools to pursue their dream of starting and running an enterprise. List of top-ten B-schools in India offering entrepreneurship programmes is given in Table 16.3.

Table 16.3 List of top-ten B-schools offering entrepreneurship programmes in India

No.	*Institute*	*Course*	*Duration*
1	Entrepreneurship Development Institute of India (EDII), Ahmedabad	PGDM-Entrepreneurship	2 years
2	SIBM, Pune	MBA in Innovation and Entrepreneurship	2 years
3	NMIMS, Mumbai	MBA in Entrepreneurship and Family Business	2 years
4	XLRI, Jamshedpur	Certificate in Entrepreneurship Management (PGP-CEM)	6 months
5	S P Jain Institute of Mgt. and Research, Mumbai	Start Your Business and Grow Your Business Certification Programme	9–12 weeks
6	Jain University, Bangalore	Entrepreneurship + Postgraduate Diploma in Enterprise Mgt.	2 years
7	IIM, Bangalore	Mgt. Programme for Women Entrepreneurs & Mgt. Program for Entrepreneurs & Family Business	1 year
8	Amity Business School, Noida	MBA in Family Business & Entrepreneurship	2 years
9	Nirma Institute of Management, Ahmedabad	MBA in Family Business and Entrepreneurship	2 years
10	National Institute of Entrepreneurship and Small Business Development	Various courses for budding entrepreneurs and small businesses	Short duration programmes

Source: Compiled from various online sources.

In spite of the growing popularity of entrepreneurship courses in the country, universities are still not geared up for the start-up wave. This is one of the main reasons for lack of good student start-up success stories at the regional and national level. A 2014 study (Trivedi, 2014) stated that various universities across the world are conducting courses on entrepreneurship and sensitizing students to consider this field as a career option. Most of these courses use classroom lectures, business simulations, case studies, and business plan preparation. One of the research studies (Hills, 1988) tried to evaluate the effectiveness of entrepreneurship teaching pedagogy and stated that business plan preparation and interaction with entrepreneurs and role models are more effective than case study discussions, classroom lectures, and assigned readings.

Table 16.4 highlights major aspects covered in entrepreneurship education to impart hard business skills and soft inter/intrapersonal skills to the potential entrepreneurs:

The strength of entrepreneurship curriculum (see Figure 16.4) also depends upon factors like:

- *Course duration and structure:* Hours of classroom teaching and other ways of student engagement, internship, and 'on-field engagement' and exposure visits to relevant business units, and so on.
- *Course syllabus:* Type of modules covering business and management electives, special modules on entrepreneurial competencies and skill development, and so on.
- *Faculty:* Number of entrepreneurship trained faculty, involvement of industry practitioners as subject/domain experts, guest sessions by entrepreneurs, and so on.

Table 16.4 Hard and soft skills of entrepreneurship education

Hard Skills	*Soft Skills*
Understanding entrepreneurship	Entrepreneurial competencies
Business opportunity identification	Innovation and creativity
Generating business ideas	Communication
Feasibility of a business idea in terms of technical/market/financial feasibility	Art of presentation
Business plan preparation	Marketing and selling skills
Legal forms of enterprise	Negotiation
Sources of finance and government schemes	Leadership and team building
Using accounting and financial statements	Goal setting
Managing sales and intermediaries	Problem solving
Using technology in business	Risk taking
Exploring global markets	Networking

Source: Compiled by the author.

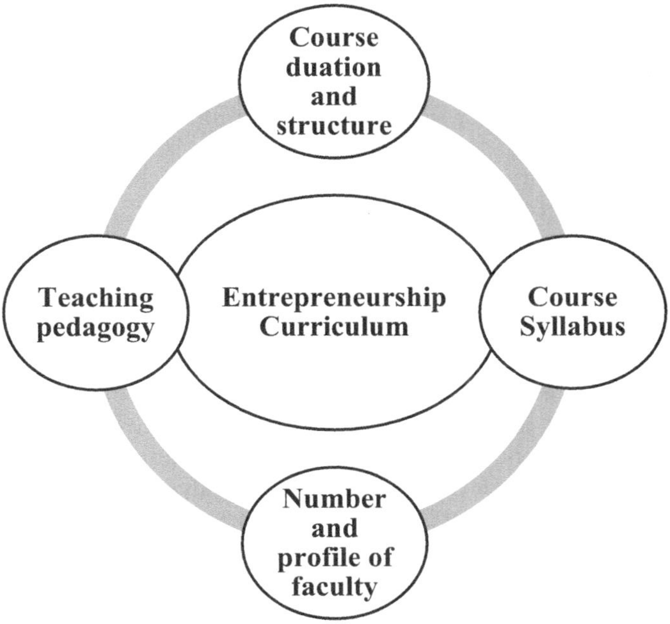

Figure 16.4 Key aspects of entrepreneurship curriculum

Source: Compiled by the author.

- *Teaching pedagogy:* Classroom teaching, projects, business plan preparation, market research, talks with investors and VC firms/angel investors, interaction with alumni network for support, guidance and mentorship, study visits to organizations, business units, foreign visits, participation in seminars/workshops to enhance knowledge and skills, business simulations, participation in business plan competitions, pitch deck sessions, fundraising contests, on-campus facilities like start-up launchpad, business incubation, and so on.

Thus, it is very important to understand that entrepreneurship education must focus on learning and development. In the first phase, it has to bring out a sea change in the mindset of students and inspire them to explore or pursue entrepreneurship as a career option. Hence, the curriculum planning of entrepreneurship should be carefully thought out and developed with the involvement of the leading entrepreneurship development institutions/organizations/government/entrepreneurs and all the other stakeholders that contribute to the creation of a robust entrepreneurial ecosystem in the country.

Role of government in promoting entrepreneurship education

Government initiatives

- India is renowned for its high level of information technology competency and large talent pool. This is due to greater emphasis on imparting quality education in science and technology. India has a large number of technology institutes with some, such as the Indian Institutes of Technology (IITs) and Indian Institute of Science, being globally acclaimed for their high standard of education. Top academic institutions like IITs and IIMs have incorporated incubation programmes to assist and mentor student start-ups and budding entrepreneurs.
- Department of Science and Technology (DST), GoI, is also playing a very important role in setting up an innovation-driven ecosystem in the country. The National Science & Technology Entrepreneurship Development Board, under the DST, also facilitates knowledge-driven and innovation-oriented start-ups in the country.
- Setting up of Technology Based Incubators and Research Parks, funding support to Student start-ups under programmes like Start-up NIDHI, encouraging and inculcating the spirit of innovation and entrepreneurship among students by setting up New Generation Innovation and Entrepreneurship Development Centres in technical institutions are some of the noteworthy contribution of DST in creating an enabling start-up ecosystem and entrepreneurship culture in the country. All this has made India a home for large pool of talent for start-up development.
- Government of India has initiated a SWAYAM programme by introducing Massive Open Online Courses (MOOCs) for students who are deprived of mainstream education. The digital platform offers various electives including a course on entrepreneurship. The course focuses on practical aspects of entrepreneurship to help students to explore innovative and creative opportunities in markets.

State initiatives

- In various states across the country, the academic institutes with the help of local government have started organizing innovation challenge through ED Cells. They also provide challenge grant to the selected innovators to support their ideas. Such activities create a culture of entrepreneurship on the campus.

- Government of Gujarat has announced Student Start-up and Innovation Policy 2017–2021 to support student innovations. The policy aims to benefit 1.4 million students of the state, support 1000 innovations per year, build pre-incubation support capacity for every university and at least 200 educational institutes over a period of five years, and harness at least 500 Student start-ups in the next five years. Government has already created a Student Innovation Fund (SIF) of Rs. 200 Cr for a period of five years to support the innovative Student start-ups in the state.
- Recently, Delhi Government has announced to include Entrepreneurship Curriculum in the state run schools from the forthcoming year for standards 9 to 12 with the objective to cultivate an entrepreneurial mindset among students from an early age.

Entrepreneurship Development Institute of India (EDII)—a case study

The Entrepreneurship Development Institute of India (EDII) has a rich experience of working in the area of entrepreneurship education, research, training, and institution building since its establishment in 1983. The institute's contribution in the field of entrepreneurship education is noteworthy. The PGDM-E (Entrepreneurship) is a two-year, full-time residential programme at the EDII. The programme has been designed specifically for entrepreneurs and entrepreneurial managers to encourage critical and lateral thinking, nurture their ambitions, and enable new ventures through an academically rigorous, directly relevant, and highly practical learning experience. Table 16.5 highlights unique aspects of EDII's PGDM-B. Under this course, the institute also offers a specialization in development studies and thereby grooms graduates, employees, and NGO nominees as 'change agents' in the development sector. The institute also offers an Open Learning Programme in Entrepreneurship (OLPE) through correspondence and personal counselling. The programme aims to equip the learners with the ability to function dynamically and acquire the requisite knowledge and skills to plan and successfully launch their own dream ventures. Through all these efforts, the institute has channelized unemployed youths towards self-employment and has also led to the creation of gainful employment opportunities.

To address the gap in the availability of trained educators, researchers, and resource persons in entrepreneurship at higher learning institutions across the country, EDII launched a Fellow Programme in Management (FPM) in 2014 with an emphasis on entrepreneurship. The programme aims at grooming the potential scholars in various facets of entrepreneurship.

Table 16.5 Unique aspects of EDII's PGDM-BE

Milestone-based learning	*Incubation support*	*Specialization*
• List of milestones to achieve the stepping stones in their entrepreneurial journey. • Seed funding to successful milestone bonus point achievers for setting up new ventures.	• Launchpad is a co-working space for student start-ups and is a part of pre-incubation activity. • It helps students to work individually or in teams towards their business ideas.	• The programme offers specialization in New Enterprise Creation, Family Business Management, and Social Entrepreneurship. • Start-up, Business Analytics & Information Systems, and Social Enterprise Mgt. are some of the new electives offered.

Source: Compiled by the author.

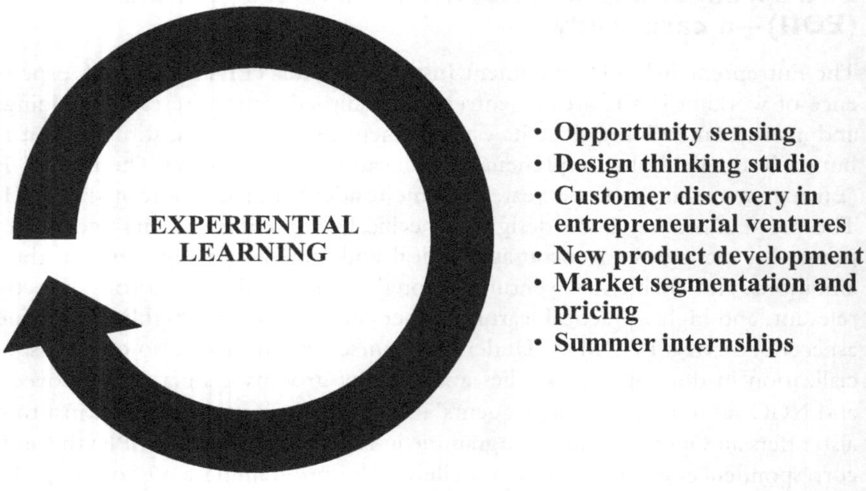

Figure 16.5 Experiential learning as a part of PGDM-E

Source: Compiled by the author.

The PGDM-BE programme focuses a lot on experiential learning; key aspects of the same are given in Figure 16.5.

The institute offers industry verticals in various upcoming sectors like health and wellness, agri and food processing, tourism and hospitality, pharma and biotech, to name a few. These verticals help the students to explore business opportunities in various emerging business areas. The overall teaching pedagogy followed at EDII is summed up in Figure 16.6:

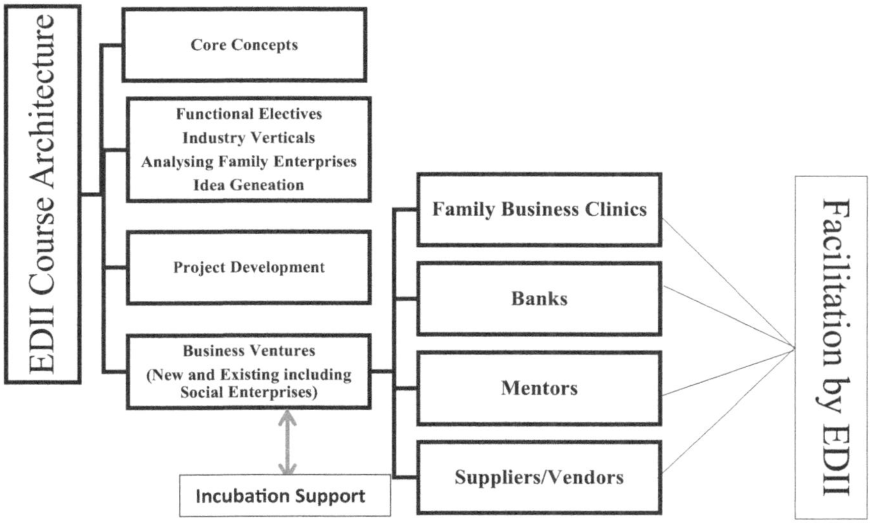

Figure 16.6 Teaching pedagogy at EDII

Source: Compiled by the author.

* Note: Entrepreneurship Development Institute of India (2019b). See www.ediindia.org for complete course details.

Major career trends and stories of EDII alumni—the newgen entrepreneurs

Youths are the torchbearers of the future and form the cornerstone on which the country stands. EDII endorses this and seeks to give direction to their entrepreneurial inspirations. The following are some of the highlights of EDII's alumni accomplishments:

- EDII alumni are rich in diversity and represent 27 states of India, with a total alumni base of 1,600 graduates.
- EDII alumni are also present in countries such as Iraq, Nepal, Sri Lanka, Uganda, and Cambodia.
- A recent survey conducted on EDII's alumni revealed that 78 per cent of EDII alumni have chosen entrepreneurial careers, out of which 54 per cent have joined family businesses and have successfully taken them on the growth path; 23 per cent have created new business ventures; and 1 per cent have set up social enterprises.
- Out of 78 per cent of alumni who have chosen an entrepreneurial career, 32 per cent are in the manufacturing sector, 37 per cent in the service sector, and 31 per cent are in trading businesses.

- Out of the total new business ventures created, a quarter are technology-based start-ups.
- Most of the alumni found the course personally, professionally, and financially rewarding.

As per the EDII alumni survey report 2017, the key programme takeaways are highlighted in Figure 16.7.

- Other programme benefits cited are:
    - Preparation of detailed project report
    - Community based projects
    - Seminar courses
    - Entrepreneurial laboratory
- Many of them are working at top positions in the industry. With their intrapreneurial skills, the alumni have reached senior positions in reputed organizations like Standard Chartered Bank, AC Nielson, Kotak Securities, Patni Computers, to name a few.
- Many of them have alone created jobs recruiting 100–1500 employees per enterprise, with an annual turnover ranging between Rs. 1 crore to more than Rs. 100 crore.

Alumni of the EDII PG programmes surveyed in this report find their education to be rewarding personally, professionally, and financially. Handling crises

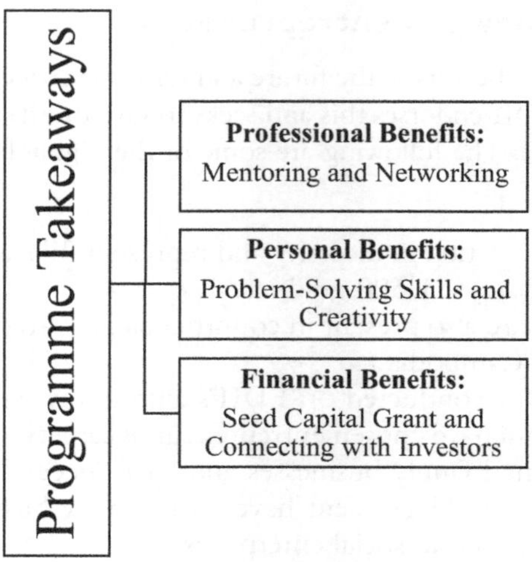

Figure 16.7 Key programme takeaways for alumni

Source: Malodia et al. (2017), EDII alumni survey report Ahmedabad.

and overcoming challenges of family businesses are considered to be important learning derived from the course for most of them. Studying and analyzing several project reports as a part of the course curriculum turned out to be extremely helpful for all those who were planning the expansion of their family businesses. These inputs helped them to set clear long-term business goals and achieve them with a focused approach and perseverance. Achieving their goals has led to many of them scaling up their family businesses to new heights.

The alumni opting for new enterprise creation also found the course very appropriate and insightful. The continuous support and mentoring from EDII faculty helped most of them to identify commercially viable and profitable business opportunities. The opportunity to interact with other start-up founders and network with existing entrepreneurs and other players of the ecosystem is very well appreciated by the students. The institute's network has helped many students to make business partnerships and get funding support.

Note: Visit www.ediindia.org/SuccessStories.aspx to learn more about the success stories of EDII students and catch a glimpse of their out-of-the-box thinking, innovative mindset, and perseverance.

Recommendations to strengthen entrepreneurship education in India

Since awareness and education play a vital role in instilling entrepreneurial intentions and mindsets, interventions through entrepreneurship development programmes and training are being highly recommended. Entrepreneurship needs to be promoted more through education to the masses and through committed implementation of programmes launched so that any capable person with entrepreneurial intent can take benefit from it. Entrepreneurship education must be included in the curriculum at all levels of education, from primary to higher education. Entrepreneurship training programmes, sensitisation workshops, phase-wise training programme for pre-start-up, start-up, and post-start-up can be organised for aspiring and existing young entrepreneurs.

A collaborative working model, wherein university-industry-government work together to promote innovative business ventures by investing in research and development, can help in transfer of research from laboratory to market by commercializing it as a new business opportunity.

Interventions at primary school level

- Various soft interventions can be planned at this stage to sensitize students towards entrepreneurship at an early age.
- Sharing the success stories and entrepreneurship journey of leading entrepreneurs can inspire the young minds and inculcate a sense of achievement in them.

- Business simulations can encourage them to be inquisitive and may lead to nurturing of problem-solving attitude.
- Training programmes for teachers of primary education can also be instrumental in imparting entrepreneurship-related skills and knowledge to the students.
- Short duration 'Camps on Entrepreneurship' during summer and winter vacations can expose children to creativity, innovation, excellence, and achievement.

Interventions at secondary school level

- The basic orientation received during primary school can further be strengthened by making entrepreneurship a compulsory subject at the secondary level in all the schools and not just a vocational course. The government of Gujarat has already introduced such a course in its vocational stream with the help of EDII.
- Summer camps on entrepreneurial simulation can be organized for school children and college students. Since 1992, EDII is organizing National Summer Camps for Children and Youths to instil the 'spirit of enterprise' at a young age so as to inspire children and youths to select an independent, innovative career option and excel in it. Through these camps, to date, the institute has trained around 4,032 children and youths across the country.
- Government must announce teachers' training programmes in entrepreneurship and also support in the development of teaching material, textbooks, and reference material that can be available for students for reading and reference.
- B-Plan competitions, idea-scouting contests, and field visits to relevant business units can also create an impetus among students towards entrepreneurship.

Interventions in higher education

- Revamping the education system with a basic course on entrepreneurship as a part of the curriculum from the early stage in higher education can play an important role in giving momentum to the start-up movement.
- This can be done by making entrepreneurship an integral part of higher education and introducing it as a mandatory full-credit course in all the faculties.
- The evaluation of students should not be simply based on their performance in the examination but on identification of a viable business opportunity and preparing a sound, bankable business plan at the end of the course.
- Efforts must be made to reach out to the school/college dropouts. Such candidates should be given an option to pursue entrepreneurship

education in a distance-learning mode and thereby facilitate their taking up entrepreneurship as a career option.

- The University Grants Commission must allocate higher grants and funding support to institutions that successfully motivate and support students who set up their own ventures.
- The emergence of tech start-ups and their growing contribution in developing the entrepreneurial ecosystem in the country necessitates the setting up of incubation centres and ED Cells in the higher-education institutions of the country. With support from NSTEDB, DST, and GoI, EDII has established a Technology Based Incubator—the 'Centre for Advancing & Launching Enterprises (CrAdLE). Both the entities, EDII and CrAdLE, are working in synergy to provide pre-start-up, start-up, and post-start-up support to the early stage start-ups and businesses. They are also contributing towards nurturing start-ups in achieving scalable and sustainable growth. (See https://cradle-edii.in/ for details about CrAdLE.)
- Capacity-building programmes like FDPs (Faculty Development Programmes) in entrepreneurship must be made mandatory for all teachers who are going to teach entrepreneurship courses in their respective institutions.
- The Ministry of MSME is creating and setting up EDCs (Entrepreneurship Development Courses) in science and technology institutions. Faculty and support staff at these EDCs must be well trained to provide hand-holding support to students and thus facilitate setting up of new ventures by them.
- There should be special training programmes for college students on topics like business opportunity identification, pitching, B-plan preparation, fund and talent management, managing growth, scaling up, and so on.
- A knowledge-base-like manual or handbook of business opportunities should be created for easy access to young aspiring entrepreneurs.
- There is a strong need to bring in consistency in innovation in existing institution/systems to improve the quality of education. The educational institutions should develop pedagogy, curricula, learning methods, case studies, and so on to encourage critical and lateral thinking and greater linkage between theory and practice. From early school days onward, students should be sensitized towards entrepreneurship as a career option. Government should frame regulatory setup in order to bring harmony between school education and entrepreneurship education. The national policy on education needs to be overhauled to create enough room for creativity, innovation, and critical thinking right from school level to higher education and beyond.
- Government must fund the development of new courses on innovation based on specific problems, including those that fulfil social needs.

Courses on interdisciplinary subjects can be helpful to improve understanding of market needs while generating ideas.

- There is a need to revise HR policies and UGC and AICTE rules to incentivize faculty engagement in innovation and entrepreneurship. Academicians and researchers should work in collaboration with industrial and commercial stakeholders that can convert research outcomes into practical applications. Government must declare commercialization of new technologies as a priority activity and incentivize it just like other priority activities.
- If India has to emerge as a global economic leader, all the key stakeholders in the ecosystem, namely, corporations, start-ups, educational institutions, funding agencies and venture capitalists, state and central governments, academic/research institutions and universities, have to work in collaboration with one another to empower India and lead to systematic economic transformation.

References

Alberti, F., Sciascia, S., & Poli, A. (2004). *Entrepreneurship education: Notes on an ongoing debate.* Proceedings of the 14th Annual International Entrepreneurship Conference, University of Napoli Federico II, Italy, 4(7).

Anand, N., & Singh, B. (2013). Redesigning entrepreneurship education in India. *Journal of Commerce and Management Explorer: A Quarterly International Journal of Social Science Research*, 3(2), 336–350.

Basu, R. (2014). Entrepreneurship education in India: A critical assessment and a proposed framework. *Technology Innovation Management Review*, 4(8).

Bechard, J. P., & Toulouse, J. M. (1998). Validation of a didactic model for the analysis of training objectives in entrepreneurship. *Journal of Business Venturing*, 13(4), 317–332.

Centre for Monitoring Indian Economy (2018). *Report on unemployment.* CMIE, Mumbai.

Davey, T., Hannon, P., & Penaluna, A. (2016). Entrepreneurship education and the role of universities in entrepreneurship: Introduction to the special issue. *Industry and Higher Education*, 30(3), 171–182.

Entrepreneurship Development Institute of India (2019a). *Gujarat startup saga.* EDII, Ahmedabad.

Entrepreneurship Development Institute of India (2019b, September 9). EDII, Ahmedabad. www.ediindia.org/academics/download-brochure.html.

Etzkowitz, H., & Leydesdorff, L. (1995). The triple helix-university-industry-government relations: A laboratory for knowledge based economic development. *EASST Review*, 14(1), 14–19.

Etzkowitz, H., Webster, A., Gebhardt, C., & Terra, B. R. C. (2000). The future of the university and the university of the future: Evolution of ivory tower to entrepreneurial paradigm. *Research Policy*, 29(3), 313–330.

Fuentelsaz, L., González, C., Maícas, J. P., & Montero, J. (2015). How different formal institutions affect opportunity and necessity entrepreneurship. *Business Research Quarterly*, 18(4), 246–258.

GradesFixer (2019, May 27). *Entrepreneurship in India: Evolution and transformation.* https://gradesfixer.com/free-essay-examples/entrepreneurship-in-india-evolution-and-transformation.
Hills, G. E. (1988). Variations in university entrepreneurship education: An empirical study of an evolving field. *Journal of Business Venturing*, 3(2), 109–122.
Jain, S. (2016). Growth of startup ecosystems in India. *International Journal of Applied Research*, 2(12), 152–154.
Kuratko, D. F. (2005). The emergence of entrepreneurship education: Development, trends, and challenges. *Entrepreneurship Theory and Practice*, 29(5), 577–597.
Lackéus, M. (2015). *Entrepreneurship in education: What, why, when, how.* Paris: OECD Publishing.
Malodia, S., Yagnik, J., & Acharya, S. R. (2017). *Planting thoughts, propelling ideas: EDII Alumni Survey Report 2017.* Ahmedabad: Entrepreneurship Development Institute of India.
Mian, S. A. (1997). Assessing and managing the university technology business incubator: An integrative framework. *Journal of Business Venturing*, 12(4), 251–285. https://doi.org/10.1016/S0883-9026(96)00063-8.
NASSCOM (2017). *Indian startup ecosystem: Traversing the maturity cycle.* NASSCOM, Mumbai.
Politis, D., Winborg, J., & Dahlstrand, Å. L. (2018). Exploring the resource logic of student entrepreneurs. *International Small Business Journal*, 30(6), 659–683.
Roy, A., & Mukherkee, K. (2017). Entrepreneurial education in India. *International Journal of Advanced Engineering and Management*, 2(1), 15–20.
Sarathy, T., & Silambarasan, C. (2011). Entrepreneurship education in India: Need for policy interventions. *Indian Journal of Applied Research*, 1(2), 23–25.
Shukla, S., & Awasthi, D. N. (2012). *Gen Y and entrepreneurship: The enablers, the killers, and the eco-systems.* Ahmedabad: Perfect Professionals, 20–23.
Shukla, S., Parray, M. I., Chatwal, N. S., Bharti, P., & Dwivedi, A. K. (2018). *Global entrepreneurship monitor India report 2017–2018.* Emerald Group Publishing (India) Private Limited, New Delhi.
Torrance, W., Rauch, J., Aulet, W., Blum, L., Burke, B., D'Ambrosio, T., . . . Jacquette, J. (2013, August 10). *Entrepreneurship education comes of age on campus: The challenges and rewards of bringing entrepreneurship to higher education.* https://papers.ssrn.com/sol3/papers.cfm?abstract_id=2307987.
Trivedi, R. H. (2014). Are we committed to teach entrepreneurship in business school?: An empirical analysis of lecturers in India, Singapore and Malaysia. *Journal of Enterprising Communities: People and Places in the Global Economy*, 8(1), 71–81.

Chapter 17

Executive education and career advancement

Sustainable employment

Neetu Jain and Ajay K. Jain

India is expected to become the second-largest economy by 2050, with the world's largest working-age population of nearly 962 million by 2035. In order to fulfil its commitments towards sustainable development and lifelong learning opportunities for all, it is imperative that India's working population should have an adequate skill set to address the challenges posed by the volatile, uncertain, complex, and ambiguous (VUCA) environment. Organizations today urgently require new managerial and executive capabilities to cope with an array of challenges. These include coping with narrowing profitability gaps; enabling continual innovation; increasing customer responsiveness; meeting regulatory requirements; contending with demand-side volatility and uncertainty; and managing increasingly complex new services and value chains. These challenges call for continuous upgrading of 'skills for work'.

Demand for executive and managerial talent is growing, driven in part by shortages of skills and capabilities in established economies and the growth of emerging economies. The competition for attracting and retaining the skill base has also intensified exponentially. Therefore, budget allocations of organizations towards training has also seen an increment over the years (Das, 2020). Global expansion of businesses and rising domestic as well as international competition have been major growth drivers for the increase in the executive education market. Executive education is offered within the institutes as well as through virtual means by all the private, public, and foreign business schools in India. Larger organizations and multinational corporations spend a significant amount of their overall expenditures on executive education programmes.

Significance of executive education for career planning

Career planning through which individuals can identify and implement steps to attain career goals is important for self and nation. The individual's career orientation reflects both the nature of his or her goals and the strategies used to attain them (Schein, 1978). Employees taking the view that career advancement will occur outside the current organization have goals different from those focusing

DOI: 10.4324/9781003158349-21

upon career within a firm and pursue different career strategies. It is labelled as 'careerism'. Robinson and Rousseau (1994) identified careerism as an important factor in determining a desired employment relationship. Individuals who are high on careerism scale perceive their current employer as an instrument and stepping stone to the inter-organizational career ladder and are likely to adopt a more 'transactional' employment relationship with their employer. This relationship is not intended to be long term, and what is exchanged has a short-term focus. What the employee values are the more immediate rewards of the relationship such as pay, training, and credentials to obtain a better job in another organization. In contrast, those low on the careerism scale have a more relational orientation. They believe their career path to be through a long-term relationship with their employer and value not only what they gain from their employer. Results show that employees who are high on competency scales have a strong, positive career orientation or careerism. This means these behavioural competencies may mobilize the employees to remain employable for a long time, maybe with different organizations.

It is thus critical for executives to turn their acquired knowledge into skills to make it truly useful for career advancement and sustainable employment. Executive education results in enhanced organizational performance, talent development, job satisfaction, and employee retention. Executive education is expected to have an enduring power in explaining the success of executives in sustaining their employment.

Executive education is meant for developing key talent in the organization. Skill development is the raison d'être of executive education programmes. The term 'executive education' refers to an academic programme at graduate-level business schools across the globe for executives, functional managers, and business leaders. Executive education programmes tend to focus on specific role or markets, or on developing specific leadership skills such as negotiation, communication, team building, and persuasion skills. Executive education programmes have also evolved from being just a tool for skill upgradation to a medium for developing strategic initiatives to streamline business goals. The VUCA-specific significance of the skills receives strong support from studies like IBM's Global Chief Executive Officer survey (Palmisano, 2010). The survey of 1,500 CEOs indicated that 'rapid escalation of complexity is the biggest challenge confronting the world's public- and private-sector leaders'. The study further found that more than half of those surveyed doubted their ability to manage the anticipated rise in the complexity of the chief executive's predicament. Another study revealed that only 15 per cent of North American companies believed they had enough qualified successors (Fernández-Aráoz et al., 2011). The rise of executive education or increased commitment to continuing education can be attributed to heightened competition for scarce managerial talent, especially at middle- and senior-management level; firms preferring to hiring a young Indian workforce and focusing more on 'on the job' training and disruptive technology led the transformation of virtually every business and sector of society. Executive education, thus, consists of integrating courses for first-time managers, specialized certifications, challenge projects, integrated work, learning packages, and so on. Modern executive education is no longer the preserve of senior executives alone but spans all managerial levels of organizations.

Current jobs are disappearing, prized skill sets are becoming obsolete at a record pace, and new 'jobs', titles, positions, and skills we had never heard of until a few years ago are becoming crucial to the continued success and even existence of many organizations. Some of the following reasons are why executives choose these executive education programmes at prestigious institutions: (1) to interact and gain knowledge from the highly qualified faculty in the top institutions; (2) to get certified from a top institution; (3) to develop a strong network of like-minded individuals; and (4) to be a part of the strong alumni base of these institutions. Executive education programmes are also seen as an important mechanism for employee retention, which has given a positive push for the development of Executive education market in India.

In this chapter, we study the executive education landscape in India. By undertaking training need analysis of the executives working at junior, middle, and senior levels, an attempt is made to identify the nature of distinctive competencies, to identify the challenges faced by the executives with regard to sustainable employment, and to measure the effectiveness of various pedagogical and learning tools used for executive education. An attempt is also made to understand the perception and experience of different participant groups such as organization-sponsored vs self-sponsored programmes and officials working in different types of organizations, namely, government and public and private sector. In order to assess the efficacy of such programmes, two institutions offering executive education have been selected as a case study. One institution is in the public domain and is for government officials (the Indian Institute of Public Administration, New Delhi), and the other is in the private domain and is for corporate executives (MDI Gurgaon, Gurugram). The assessment of their functioning and impact is done within the defined competency frame of the Government of India.

Role of competencies in executive education

Mintzberg's managerial role theory

Henry Mintzberg distinguishes ten key managerial roles that managers and executives fulfil. He recommends breaking down management roles and responsibilities and organizing the workplace to simplify complex concepts. This helps to organize companies into a more efficient culture, and it allows each member to develop their own skills. These managerial roles are divided up into three categories: (1) Interpersonal role: Interpersonal contact concerns the contact between the manager and the people in his environment. For example, subordinates, other managers, the board of directors, the works council, customers, and suppliers. This Mintzberg Managerial role incorporates Figurehead role, Leader role, and Liaison role; (2) Information processing role: According to Henry Mintzberg, the managerial role involves the processing of information, which means that they send, pass on, and analyze information. Managers are linking pins; they are expected to exchange flows of vertical information with their subordinates and horizontal flows of information with their fellow managers and the board of directors. This role incorporates Monitor role, Disseminator role, and Spokesman role; (3) Decision-making role: Managers are responsible for decision making and they can do this in different ways at different levels. The leadership style is important in decision making. An authoritarian leader is sooner inclined to make decisions independently than a democratic leader. This role incorporates Entrepreneur role, Disturbance handler, Resource allocator role, Negotiator role.

Competency-based management

Competencies have been defined by Boyatzis of Hay Group (1982) as 'underlying characteristics of an employee such as motive, trait, skill, aspects of one's social image, social role, or a body of knowledge, which can result in effective and/or superior performance in a job or role'. In order to meet the demands of a job, a person requires a unique combination of knowledge, skills, attitudes, and behaviours, commonly referred to as competencies. Hondeghem and Vandermeulen (2000) described competencies as 'all work related personal attributes, knowledge, experience and skills and values that a person draws on to perform his/her work effectively. Thus, a competency is any knowledge, skill, trait, motive, attitude, value, or other personal characteristic that is essential to perform a job (Threshold Competency) and differentiates typical from superior performers (Differentiating Competency).

The Department of Personnel and Training (DOPT) of the Government of India initiated the project titled 'Strengthening HRM of Civil Service' in 2011 in collaboration with the United Nations Development Programme (UNDP). The project was undertaken to support the Government of India in shifting from rule-based personnel administration towards a competency-based system of strategic human resource management for the Indian Civil Services. The goal was to also build an enabling environment for developing civil servants so who can perform in a more effective manner. A primary outcome of this initiative was the creation of a 'Competency Dictionary' (Government of India-UNDP, 2013). The competency dictionary was developed in consultation with a large number of civil servants in the centre and state governments. The overarching purpose for developing a competency dictionary was to foster more effective, efficient, and transparent and accountable public administration at the national and state levels. Towards this end, the Civil Services Competency Dictionary identified 25 core competencies across the various roles and positions of civil service employees.[1] The 25 core competencies were grouped in four sets: Ethos, Ethics, Equity, and Efficiency. Figure 17.1 depicts the competency framework for the Indian Civil Service.

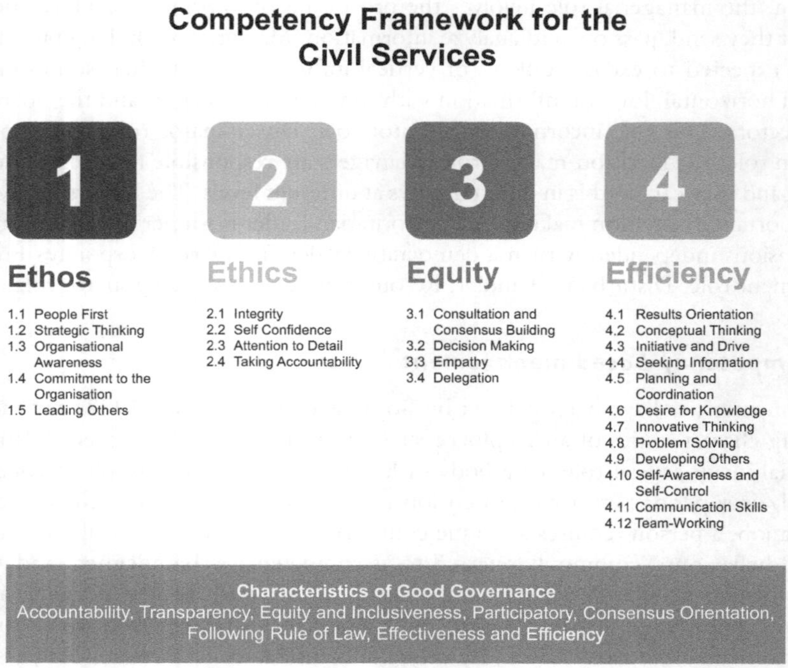

Figure 17.1 Competency framework for Indian civil service

Source: DoP&T Civil services competency dictionary, Government of India, https://dopt.gov.in/sites/default/files/Competency Dictionary for the Civil Services.pdf, p. 10.

Each of these competencies are further defined in detail (annexure)

The study presented in this chapter draws insights from the competency framework developed by DoP&T for the civil services officers. There are 25 competencies given in this framework, but three more competencies have been added in this study keeping in view their significance for executive development. The significance of three more competencies, that is Emotional Intelligence, Compassion, and Decisiveness was observed and experienced by the authors during conduct of training programmes for senior and middle level executives at their organizations, namely, Indian Institute of Public Administration, New Delhi and Management Development Institute, Gurugram.

Methodology

For this study, a mixed methodology was used. The study is both qualitative and quantitative in nature. For the purpose of data collection, a questionnaire was developed in five parts. The first part of the questionnaire entailed a demographic profile of the respondents. The second part incorporated all the competencies suggested by Department of Personnel and Training for the civil services officers in the competency framework given earlier in Figure 17.1 and three more competencies. Therefore, executives were asked to rate these 28 competencies on a five-point Likert scale ranging from 1 being least suitable to 5 being most suitable based on their significance for their career advancement or sustainable employment. The third part included questions on training pedagogy. The respondents were required to rate the learning or pedagogical tools which can help maximize learning in executive education programmes on a five-point Likert scale ranging from 1 being least suitable to 5 being most suitable. The fourth part included a scale on careerism, a five-item scale developed by Robinson and Rousseau (1994). The careerism/career orientation was measured using five questions (such as 'I have many jobs to choose besides this job,' 'The jobs I can find are much better than this job,' 'There are many career opportunities I expect to explore after I leave my present employer'). The respondents were asked to rate these statements on a five-point Likert scale from 1 being strongly disagree to 5 being strongly agree. Higher values on the items reflected a greater degree of careerism. The scale's Cronbach alpha was .74. The fifth part included a question on the extent to which they would attend a self-sponsored or organization-sponsored programme. One open-ended question was also asked about any other competency which is not covered by the authors and which they consider important for the career development of executives.

This questionnaire was then administered to various officers, and data were collected with an objective to evaluate the landscape of executive education from the career advancement perspective of those executives who had attended executive education programmes. Around 350 questionnaires were administered to the executives from government organizations, public sector and private sector. Of the 350, only 300 complete responses were received and were used for data analysis. Interviews with around 30 government officials were also conducted. Desk review of studies, documents, reports, and other printed/published documents related to executive education was also carried out. Primary data collection through focused group discussion and evidence-based observation and in-depth interviews helped in strengthening qualitative aspects of the data.

Executive education landscape in India

Executive education providers in India

There are various types of executive education programmes and providers in India. These may be broadly categorized into five providers, as follows:

Corporate Universities: Corporate universities, which provide skill-, self-, and team capability development programmes, are usually staffed by full-time coaches, trainers, teachers, and instructors. They can acquire, on to provide targeted, contextualized learning experiences to groups, teams, and individuals. Corporate universities differentiate themselves from other providers of executive education by offering highly contextualized learning experiences. They include content relevant to the organization, delivered in the context in which the skills must be applied, and they provide customized access to developmental experiences. Some of the examples of corporate universities are Shiv Nadar University of the HCL group, Infosys University of Infosys, NTPC School of Business of NTPC, G.L Bajaj University of Bajaj Group and others.

Business Schools' Executive MBA and Open Enrolment Programmes: Business schools mean the faculties of business administration or management at established universities. The business schools' Executive MBA (EMBA) and open enrolment programmes use both on-campus and mixed-mode (classroom and on-the-job projects) teaching, focusing on developing the participants' intellectual, personal, and social capital. They differentiate themselves from all the other education providers by their pedagogical tools and tropes. Academics at the business schools have learnt to turn the empirical data and theoretical frameworks associated with academic disciplines into frameworks and methods that help solve business problems.

Human Resource Consultancies: Human resource (HR) consultancies offer individual and team-level evaluation, selection, and coaching services to companies. In the process, they have developed the capabilities to identify the causes of executive problems, to discover competency gaps, and develop data-intensive portraits of leadership abilities through focus groups, surveys, and 360-degree performance evaluations. These specialized consultancies have complemented their diagnostic services with remedial coaching and therapeutic interventions at the individual and team levels for some time now. More recently, the HR firms have started offering individual and team-based executive development programmes aimed at remedying the leadership and relational challenges surfaced by clients. The programmes are flexible in terms of their duration, can be modified to meet the specific requirements of clients and participants, and are informed by the precise needs the HR consultants have identified. Some of the HR consultancies are Mercer Consulting, Optimum Talent, and Hay Group.

Strategic Consultancies: Strategic consultancies provide an array of executive development experiences for clients. They provide training as part of consulting engagements, with learning occurring as part of the interventions. In a recent development, the firms also offer training as a stand-alone offering—for example, the McKinsey Approach to Problem Solving—where the course is customized to tackle specific capability gaps or is offered to a variety of organizations trying to develop the same capability. The consultancy companies' offerings differ from competing products primarily because of their laser-like focus on the specific challenges facing an organization and the generalized problem-solving capabilities of the management consultancy. Some of the strategy consultancies are Accenture, BCG, Bain, Deloitte, Ernst & Young, KPMG, and McKinsey.

Remote and personalized learning platforms

Personal learning platforms draw on fourth-generation learning management systems and content from leading universities and think tanks. They provide private learning experiences (courses, classes, and modules). The personal learning platform can be used for cultivating a broad set of managerial abilities and competencies, largely grounded in algorithmic-functional-technical skills. They impart competencies whose acquisition can be measured using standard remote-testing processes. Some of the online learning platforms are Coursera, EdX, Lynda.com, Massive, open, online courses (MOOCs), Swayam course.

Training pedagogy and learning tools

Executives need different sets of skills to cope with the VUCA business landscape. There is a mismatch between executive development offerings and the skill sets executives need in a VUCA, Web 2.5-enabled economy. This 'executive skills gap' between the skills needed and the skills being imparted by executive development programmes is obvious and costly. Providers of executive development face an unprecedented set of opportunities to respond to the organizational capability and executive skills gaps posed by the VUCA economy. Business executives attending executive programmes are seeking not information or knowledge but skills (Schrage, 2014) of a kind and quality not presently being delivered by executive development programmes. An IBM survey of 1,500 chief executives (Palmisano, 2010) provides an example of not developing the right skills in individuals capable of applying them at the right time and in the right context: A majority of those surveyed worry about their own as well as executive team members' ability to manage complex predicaments in the competitive, regulatory, operational, and organizational environments in which they work. CEOs also report a scarcity of the trust, creativity, resiliency, fault-tolerance, and experimental zest and intensity that characterize high-performing organizations. Skills learnt in seminars, case discussions, classrooms, and laboratories are rarely applied in the contexts in which they would be most useful. The following training and learning tools are used for imparting executive education:

(1) Classroom-based Lectures: The lecture is an extensive presentation of material by the lecturer in a formal venue or through an online medium, but its general structure remains unchanged. The basic important feature of Lecture method is that it is generally a one-way communication; (2) Case Study Discussions: Case study method is a learning technique in

which a real-life situation or series of events together with the surrounding facts, opinions, and prejudices which influence decisions is presented to trainees for their analysis and consideration of possible solution of problems identified; (3) On-the-job training: On-the-job training refers to the training which is given to the employee at the workplace by his immediate supervisor. It is based on the principle of 'learning by doing'; (4) Coaching sessions: Coaching is the process of providing one-on-one guidance and instruction to improve the knowledge, skill, and work performance of the person being coached. The coach provides periodic feedback and opinion to the trainee or subject under training; (5) Management games: Management games are a learning exercise in which groups of trainees operate as management teams of imaginary companies in a carefully defined competitive market. Management games require trainees to actively gather information, analyze the information, and make decisions typically for the purpose of developing managerial skills; (6) Role Plays: The role play is an enactment (or simulation) of a scenario in which each participant is given a part to act out. Role plays provide more detailed descriptions of each character's attitudes, needs, opinions, and so on; role plays help in developing interpersonal skills. (7) E-learning: E-learning or online learning refers to instruction and delivery of training by computer online through the internet or the web. E-learning includes web-based training, distance learning, and virtual classrooms; it may involve a CD-ROM as well; (8) Demonstration: The word demonstration means to give demos or to perform the particular activity or concept. During the demonstration, clear language should be used so that trainees may understand concepts easily; (9) Simulation activities: Simulation activities refer to the imitation of real-world activities and processes in a safe environment. Simulations aim to provide an experience as close to the 'real thing' as possible. The simulation method is best known for imparting hands-on experiences to the participants; (10) Live project: Live project is learning practically, while working on a project. It is basically taking up a project in a company to get one's hands on some practical knowledge. (11) Movie clips and storytelling: One sure way to boost a presentation's value is through anecdotal examples, like scenes from TV shows or movies. Movie scenes help reinforce key messages by driving engagement, learning, and retention levels.

The market for corporate training has witnessed positive technological advances which have significantly altered the training methodology across organizations. E-learning has eased the conduct of training programmes for geographically diversified teams. Also, organizations have showed greater inclination towards blended modules when compared to traditional instructor-led classroom trainings only. Massively distributed online learning systems (Kroner, 2014) promise to deliver, as needed, context and setting-specific 'skills on demand' to managers and executives. Such offerings can be found in free as well as fee-based configurations and stand-alone and 'certificate bundle' formats, and they exhibit increasing degrees of intimacy and understanding of learners' needs.

The corporate training market in India is projected to rise exponentially by 2025. The market is getting bigger than ever before. It's growing faster than assumed as people are investing their money and time in it. As the higher-education industry becomes increasingly global and competitive, it is expected to see more universities from England and Australia, and from privately funded universities, become very active in Indian markets. According to the research report by Ken Research (Ken Research, 2015) titled 'India Executive Education Market Outlook to 2020: Preference for skill based MDPs and virtual education and virtual education to drive future', the executive education market will grow at a considerable CAGR rate, thus exceeding 10.9 billion Rs. by 2020 due to the increasing number of MDPs and enhancements in the role of virtual education.

According to this report, the Indian executive market is estimated to record revenues worth Rs.10.9 billion by 2020, which is an indicator of the size of the market executive education is about to capture. This growth is slated to be achieved via virtual programmes with a focus towards customized programmes. The revenue generated by executive education programmes is only expected to grow over the years. The executive education market in India has shown that enrolment has increased over the years, from FY 2010 to FY 2015, to reach 17.6 per cent of the CAGR. The demand for executive education has surged with the economic improvement and integration with world economies. With advances in technology and the widespread application of ICTs in the education sector, the online sector of executive education also saw an increase in value to around Rs.1 million during FY 2015.

According to the Executive education Market Research Reports (Ken Research, 2015) many key players are functioning in this market because they have captured a huge market share. These key players include reputed Indian universities, Management Development Institute Gurgaon, different Indian institutes of management, Indian School of Business, National Institute of Financial Management, Harvard Business School, National HRD Network, Indian Institute of Public Administration, and several other private organizations and institutions. These universities, organizations, and Institutes of Excellence offer various courses in executive programmes that perhaps would have more than 80 programmes (1-year duration) for a total intake of around 30,000 odd students.

The courses offered by these organizations generally include general management courses, advanced management programmes, senior management programmes, leadership development programmes, and some special skill-oriented programmes with course duration ranging from 2 to 12 weeks. These programmes are mainly designed for working professionals and for men and women in business who seek to adapt to the changes and advancements of the modern day businesses in their respective industries. These organizations are also offering customized learning programmes in order to meet the need for flexibility for employees. In-campus programmes and open MDPs are quite prevalent in the market. Advanced management programmes or leadership development programmes are also offered independently by several business schools, and these contribute significantly to the overall market revenue, followed by technical, managerial, and sales trainings.

Mumbai, Delhi, Gurgaon, Noida, Bangalore, Pune, Hyderabad, and Chennai have been the major cities catering to the growth of the training market in India. The northern region of India has contributed the highest revenues to the executive education market. Also, the volume of middle management and younger managers seeking training is also expected to rise significantly in the next 2–3 years. It is expected that the overall revenue of the executive education industry will further grow. The Indian executive education landscape is marked by a considerable demand for customized trainings. The institutes are also focusing upon strengthening their enrolments for executive education programmes. Therefore, they are trying to offer programmes that are customized according to the requirement of the executives.

Case study institutions

Indian Institute of Public Administration, New Delhi

The Indian Institute of Public Administration (IIPA), set up in March 1954, has been engaged in strengthening the capacity of senior executives of the Government of India and neighbouring countries by enhancing the leadership and managerial capacities of executives in government, public-sector enterprises, and other public organizations. Currently, IIPA is under the Department of Personnel & Training (DoPT), Government of India, with the Hon'ble Vice President of India as its president. Enhancing leadership and managerial qualities on the one hand and developing a service-orientation on the other are the focus areas of the Institute's education and training activities. Its faculty is involved with research work mainly to suggest policy changes to ensure improved delivery of public services. IIPA is engaged in addressing the critical areas of governance and management through training, research, and consultancy. The institute has to its credit over 2,000 research projects in niche areas of governance and has conducted over 7,000 training and executive development programmes both for national and international organizations and in the process trained over 530,000 personnel from across sectors.

Management Development Institute Gurgaon, Gurugram

Since its inception in 1973, Management Development Institute (MDI) has offered various full-time and part-time executive development programmes. Apart from running short-duration management development programmes (MDPs) such as certificate programmes running from two days to six months,

MDI offers highly specialized 18-month, full-time postgraduate diploma programmes: (1) National Management Programme; (2) Postgraduate Programme in Public Policy Management; and (3) Postgraduate programme in energy management. MDI also offers two part-time executive education programmes: (1) Executive Management Program (two years); and (2) Executive-Fellow Program in Management. Most of these programmes are being accredited by the All India Council for Technical Education (AICTE) and are also accredited by the United Kingdom-based Association of MBAs. MDI provides various forms of short- and long-duration programmes. All in all, MDI provides training to 3,500–4,000 executives every year in various functional areas (transformational leadership, change management, marketing and sales, digital marketing and communication, finance and accounts, supply-chain management, customer relationship management, data analytic tools and techniques, and project management).

Respondents profile

The details of respondents are presented in Table 17.1.

From Table 17.1 it is clear that the majority of the respondents fall in the age group of 51 to 60 years, 90 per cent of the respondents are male. Most of the respondents (i.e. 147) belong to the senior management cadre. Most of the respondents (i.e. 131) have professional degrees. A majority of the respondents (i.e. 98) are from organizations having mixed ownership (an organization having features of both private and public or government organization) followed by public-sector organizations. All the respondents carry different experience. A majority of the respondents (i.e. 122) have experience ranging from 7 to 12 years. Around half of the respondents (i.e. 152) work in large organization having more than 2,500 employees.

Table 17.2 indicates the importance of different competencies. The top-five competencies rated by the respondents are integrity, self-confidence, decision making, commitment to organization, and taking ownership. All the 28 competencies were rated high, as the lowest mean was 3.89 for the competency titled 'Empathy'. However, compassion, consultation and consensus building, delegation, and empathy were rated relatively lower than the other competencies.

Table 17.3 indicates the result of exploratory factor analysis (EFA) for 28 competencies. EFA was used to categorize these 28 competencies into a few meaningful categories. Principal component analysis with direct oblimin method has been used to explore the underlying dimensions. EFA has yielded three factors which are named as (1) Excellence-centric (2) Culture building; and (3) People development. In this study, we have found three factors while DOP&T has categorized competencies into four factors, namely, Ethos, Ethics, Equity, and Efficiency. Communication skills, and consultation and consensus building, had relatively low factor loading.

Table 17.1 Demographic profile of the respondents

Gender	Male	259
	Female	41
Age	21–30	49
	31–40	124
	41–50	103
	51–60	15
	Above 60	1
Education	Bachelor's	111
	Master's	59
	Professional degree (e.g. MBA, M. tech, BE, CSE)	131
Nature of education	Engineering	145
	Management	51
	Both	47
	Others	58
Management cadre	Junior management	61
	Junior middle management	71
	Senior management	147
	Top management	19
Marital status	Married	118
	Unmarried	143
	Others	3
Size of organization based on number of employments	Small organization (100–1,500)	125
	Medium (1,500–2,500)	19
	Large organization (more than 2,500)	152
Experience	0–6	77
	7–12	122
	13–18	31
	19–25	64
	>25	7
Type of organization	Government organization	35
	Public organization	62
	Private organization	54
	MNC	52
	Mixed ownership	98

Source: All tables in this chapter are by the authors.

Table 17.2 Mean score-wise ranking of competencies

No.	*Variables*	*Mean*	*Std. deviation*
8	Integrity	4.60	.788
9	Self-confidence	4.52	.815
13	Decision making	4.48	.764
11	Taking accountability	4.42	.815
7	Commitment to the organization	4.40	.936
3	Decisiveness	4.39	.892
27	Team-working	4.37	.876
26	Communication skills	4.33	.901
1	Leading others	4.31	.907
5	Strategic thinking	4.30	.899
25	Self-awareness and self-control	4.28	.872
18	Initiative and drive	4.25	.905
23	Problem solving	4.25	.907
16	Results orientation	4.24	.896
20	Planning and coordination	4.24	.918
24	Developing others	4.23	.928
10	Attention to detail	4.22	.890
6	Organizational awareness	4.20	.829
28	Emotional intelligence	4.19	.973
21	Desire for knowledge	4.17	.943
22	Innovative thinking	4.12	.937
19	Seeking information	4.09	.925
17	Conceptual thinking	4.08	.907
4	People first	4.00	1.010
2	Compassion	3.96	.991
12	Consultation and consensus building	3.95	.882
15	Delegation	3.93	.960
14	Empathy	3.89	.988

Table 17.3 Results of exploratory factor analysis of 28 competencies

Components	*1*	*2*	*3*
% of variance	52.218	6.370	3.873
Reliabilities	.94	.92	.84
No. of items	10	10	6
Factor naming	Excellence-centric (Efficiency)	Culture building (Ethos and ethics)	People development (Equity)
21. Desire of knowledge	.878		
17. Conceptual thinking	.767		

(*Continued*)

Table 17.3 (Continued)

Components	*1*	*2*	*3*
23. Problem solving	.765		
19. Seeking information	.738		
22. Innovative thinking	.726		
20. Planning and coordination	.721		
18. Initiative and drive	.720		
16. Results orientation	.682		
25. Self-awareness and self-control	.600		
15. Delegation	.407		
26. Communication skills	.37		
8. Integrity		.855	
7. Commitment to the organization		.773	
3. Decisiveness		.717	
9. Self-confidence		.689	
1. Leading others		.639	
11. Taking accountability		.637	
13. Decision making		.559	
6. Organizational awareness		.483	
10. Attention to detail		.469	
5. Strategic thinking		.455	
12. Consultation and consensus building		.35	
28. Emotional intelligence			.750
24. Developing others			.613
4. People first			.607
14. Empathy			.602
2. Compassion			.593
27. Team-working			.462

Respondents' perception on pedagogic tools

Table 17.4 shows the importance of different training pedagogy and learning tools. Live projects and on-the-job training got highest mean scores of 4.28 and 4.23, respectively.

E-learning and classroom-based lecture got lowest mean scores of 3.62 and 3.57, respectively. It clearly indicates the significance of using live projects over e-learning and classroom-based lectures.

Table 17.5 delineates the results of factor analysis for 11 training tools. As a result of it, training tools are categorized into two categories (1) Experiential learning tools and (2) Coaching tools.

Table 17.4 Mean scores of training pedagogy and learning tools

No.	*Training pedagogy & learning tools*	*Mean*	*Std. deviation*
10	Live projects	4.28	.916
3	On-the-job training	4.23	.901
9	Simulation activities	3.98	.944
2	Case-study discussions	3.97	.930
8	Demonstration	3.90	.962
11	Movie clips	3.82	1.069
6	Role plays	3.82	.952
4	Personal coaching sessions	3.78	.959
5	Management games	3.67	.961
7	E-learning	3.62	1.009
1	Classroom-based lectures	3.57	1.045

Table 17.5 Exploratory factor analysis for training pedagogy and learning tools

Components	*1*	*2*
% of variance	38.41	20.13
Reliabilities	.89	.71
No. of items	8	3
Factor naming	Experiential learning tools	Coaching tools
9. Simulation activities	.767	
8. Demonstration	.766	
10. Live projects	.747	
2. Case-study discussions	.721	
6. Role plays	.711	
3. On-the-job training	.664	
5. Management games	.663	
7. E-learning	.600	
4. Personal coaching sessions		.827
1. Classroom-based lectures		.744
11. Movie clips/ Storytelling		.640

Relationship between competencies and training pedagogy

Correlation was run between three categories of competencies, namely, Excellence-centric, Culture building, and People development; two categories of training pedagogy (i.e. Experiential learning tools and Coaching tools); and career orientation.

Table 17.6 indicates a positive association among the three categories of competencies and two categories of training pedagogy. Experiential learning tools

Table 17.6 Correlation among three dimensions of competencies, career orientation, and training pedagogy

Variables	*1*	*2*	*3*	*4*	*5*	*6*	*7*	*8*	*9*	*10*	*11*	*12*	*13*	*14*	*Mean*	*SD*
Age	1														2.24	0.88
Gender	−.25**	1													1.14	0.34
Education	0.03	−0.019	1												2.07	0.89
Nature of Education	0.03	0.093	0.093	1											2.06	1.18
Management Cadre	.509**	−.218**	0.07	−0.013	1										2.42	0.88
Marital Status	−0.063	0.063	0.1	−0.088	0.059	1									1.56	0.51
Organization Size	−.125*	0.006	0.068	−.119*	−.183**	−0.06	1								2.09	0.97
Organization Type	.753**	−.272**	0.069	−0.006	.564**	.251**	−.191**	1							3.39	1.41
Experience	−.139*	−0.018	0.007	−0.086	−.146*	0.029	−0.039	−0.063	1						2.34	1.14
Experiential Learning Tools	−.144*	0.103	0.018	−.155**	−0.086	0.008	−0.033	−0.091	0.02	1					3.93	0.71
Coaching tools	0.032	0.058	−0.013	−.126*	.147*	0.08	−.198**	.156**	−.138*	.600**	1				3.72	0.8
Excellence Centric	−.117*	.116*	−0.074	−0.063	0.008	−0.005	−0.051	−0.075	−0.002	.613**	.455**	1			4.16	0.72
Culture Building	0.021	0.08	0.013	−0.106	.137*	0.092	−.146*	.148*	0.001	.574**	.492**	.766**	1		4.38	0.65
People Development	−0.094	.125*	−0.065	−0.099	0.01	−0.036	−.147*	−0.02	0.007	.549**	.472**	.742**	.787**	1	4.1	0.75
Career Orientation	−.301**	−0.022	−0.038	−0.068	−.206**	−.178**	−.124*	−.329**	0.096	.284**	.231**	.247**	.129*	.204**	3.08	0.88

and coaching tools both have positive relationship with the Excellence-centric, Culture building, and People development competencies. The results also indicate a positive relationship between competencies categories and career orientation. The results mean that people with such behavioural competencies feel more empowered and competent enough to take up different jobs.

Table 17.7 demonstrates the results for Multiple Regression Analysis where competencies are treated as criterion variables, and training pedagogy and learning tools are taken as predictor variables. Results show that Excellence-centric competencies are positively predicted by lectures, case study, management games, e-learning, and demonstration. Moreover, these learning tools explain 35 per cent variances in Excellence-centric competencies. Culture-building competencies are positively predicted by lecture, on-the-job training, personal coaching sessions, and simulation activities. These learning tools explain 37 per cent variances in Culture-building competencies. Lastly, People-development competencies are positively predicted by lectures, role plays, and demonstration; and these learning tools explain 41 per cent variances in People-development competencies. Overall, lectures are found to be useful pedagogical tools to instil these behavioural competencies among the executives.

Table 17.7 Multiple regression analysis for competencies categories as criterion and training pedagogical tools as the predictors

Predictor Variables	*Criterion Variables*		
	Excellence-centric	*Culture building*	*People development*
Classroom-based lectures	.187**	.159**	.232**
Case-study discussions	.119*	.108	.076
On-the-job training	.002	.128*	.039
Personal coaching sessions	.077	.152**	.076
Management games	.130*	−.002	.012
Role plays	.019	−.006	.128*
E-learning	.152**	.109	.047
Demonstration	.204**	.117	.270**
Simulation activities	.039	−.013	−.061
Live projects	.074	.172*	.031
Movie clips	−.098	−.017	.008
F Value	F (11,280) = 15.27<.00	F (11,280) = 16.26<.00	F (11,280) = 19.10<.00
Adjusted R Square	.35	.37	.41

Moreover, we also conducted a regression analysis for the factors of learning tools: (1) experiential learning tool and (2) coaching tools as predictors of three sets of competencies: (a) excellence-centric, (b) culture builder, and (c) people development as the criterion. Results indicated that both the learning tools are found to be significant positive predictors of all three competency developments.

Demographic difference across three categories of competencies

T-test and ANOVA were conducted to assess the significant difference of mean across gender, age, nature of education, experience, marital status, management cadre, type and size of organization, and so on.

Gender: Female participants were found to be significantly higher on excellence-centric and people-development competencies. However, both were found not to be significantly different on culture-building competencies.

Age: No significant difference of mean was observed across various age groups.

Nature of Education: No significant difference of mean was observed across nature of education.

Management Cadre: No significant difference of mean was observed across various management cadres.

Marital Status: Unmarried people reported significantly higher importance of culture-building competency as compared to married and other people.

Organization Size: Respondents of small and large organizations had rated significantly higher importance of these competencies compared to medium-size organizations. However, respondents of small organizations have rated the importance of culture-building and people-development competencies higher than large organizations.

Organization Type: Results showed that respondents working in organizations with mixed ownership assign more importance to culture-building competencies over executives from private and public organizations.

Experience: Respondents with more than 25 years of experience have rated the higher importance of culture-building competencies over those who had less than 18 years of work experience.

Overall, culture-building competencies were rated significantly higher by unmarried people and more experienced executives. Culture-building competencies were also rated higher in small organizations and organizations with mixed ownership. These are universally significant competencies for all the executives regardless of their age and experience. This was the reason that the difference pertaining to the importance of these competencies across different demographic parameters was insignificant in most of the cases.

Government vs private-sector officials

Discussion with the executives during the interview brought out the issue that challenges for sustainable employment are less for a government official in comparison with an executive from the private sector. The underlying reason is that after getting through the civil service examination or entrance examination of a given Public Sector Enterprise (PSE), officers rarely switch over their jobs until they superannuate. While being in government service, they have the option to go on deputation to different departments and ministries which give them the exposure of different kinds of work and thereby help enrich their jobs. There is a well-defined career path for a PSE officer. An executive in a PSE moves to another PSE only if (1) There is no career growth available in the current organization; (2) There is a jump in designation or higher position available in another PSE; or (3) They are lured by the private sector to join at a much higher salary than the present salary which they are drawing.

Self-sponsored vs company-sponsored

Executives were asked about their desire to participate in organization-sponsored and self-sponsored executive training programmes. Most of the executives from government departments were of the view that they generally do not attend self-sponsored programme. They prefer to attend the programmes which are sponsored by their organizations. On the contrary, it was found that counterparts from the private sector spend their personal funds to attend self-sponsored programmes, as these executives have a deep desire for their career growth and development. If these executives from the private sector find any programme crucial for their growth and development, then they do not hesitate to attend self-sponsored programmes because of its direct bearing on sustainable employment.

Major takeaways

This piece of research validated the competency framework of DoP&T. The analysis indicates that all the discussed competencies are important for the purpose of executive education and career advancement of working executives at all the levels (i.e. junior, middle, and senior). All the competencies have a mean score of more than 3.5 on a five-point scale. Therefore, executive education providers and business schools should conduct programmes for executives in these areas only if the programmes would help in their career growth. This fact is also validated by high correlation between career orientation and three categories of competencies (i.e. excellence-centric, culture building, and people development competencies).

Indeed, identifying specific competency requirements of the executives prior to conducting executive education programmes is of utmost importance as this not only helps in identifying specific problem areas but also indicates the gap in desired and expected level of competencies of the executives. Competence assessment should be an ongoing process, as it provides valuable inputs on competences which need to be developed in the executives for their work effectiveness and development. Developing and implementing executive education programmes without properly assessing the competency requirement would run the risk of overdoing training, doing too little training, or missing the point completely. A random approach of conducting executive education programmes would not bear fruit; instead, a systematic approach to design and development of executive education based on the executives' specific requirements and needs would help zero in on their competency gaps.

Heads of organizations should allocate a significant chunk of money for executive education. Generally, the budget for executive education is trimmed in the absence of evidence pertaining to its contribution to the bottom line. If the top management executives or HR heads take a lead and are able to link executive education with the improvement of the performance on the job, then acceptability of the executive education programmes for the top management would be more widespread. Since executive education programmes are expensive in nature, they are usually looked upon as a nuisance rather than a contribution to the bottom line of the organization. This happens when champions of the executive education fail to develop a cost–benefit analysis for the programmes. If problem deficiencies or competency gaps can be identified correctly, then benefits of executive education can also be measured in quantitative terms. If HR heads are able to show how executive education would improve the performance of the executives on the job and contribute to the bottom line, then the budget for these programmes would not be trimmed.

There is a need for a paradigm shift in the way we impart executive education. Currently, the focus is more on imparting knowledge than developing soft skills such as interpersonal skills, decision-making skills, behavioural skills, and right attitudes. It has been said that 'one's attitude, not one's aptitude, determines one's altitude'. Although it is easy to find senior executives stating in different forums and platforms that the mindset of people is the biggest challenge faced by organizations in growth, expansion, acquisition, and merger of corporations and in implementing new technology initiatives, it is often just lip service being paid to this serious issue of changing the 'mindset' of people. People's attitude and mindset is the biggest hurdle in sustaining the profitability of the organization. However, not much attention is paid to changing the mindset of people. By and large, executive education programmes in government organizations fail to adopt innovative pedagogical tools such as experiential learning tools, simulation exercises, role plays, and management games while these were considered more important for developing different competencies when compared to traditional class room based lectures by the respondents. Public organizations are more bureaucratic than private organizations (Boyne, 2002). Public administrators tend to believe that they have less discretion in exercising leadership and do not have much latitude of action. This is the reason private organizations are more open to use innovative learning tools. Big business houses or multinational organizations are spending heavily on executive education and are open to new ways and means of developing skills of the people (Pathak, 2013). They invite the best trainers available in the market to deliver speeches to their executives and engage some of the popular executive education programme providers for skill development of their executives.

Industry players peg the size of India's executive education market at Rs 500 crore. Ken Research states that the executive-education market in India will generate revenues worth Rs. 10.9 billion by 2020. Judging by the demand, the executive-education market is set to escalate in India. With the advancements in the technology and extensive application of ICT in the education sector, the online executive-education sector has experienced an increase over the years. It is also predicted that virtual programmes and customizable MDPs will mark the future of Indian executive education. Mobile learning is still at a nascent stage in India and is rarely used as a training tool due to connectivity and bandwidth issues in the country. Instructor-led classroom trainings are still dominant among various modes of learning in the corporate structure. Some of the trainings were done through the blended module as well. Virtual classroom and mobile learning did not get much traction and would take some more time to pick up in India. Executive education and professional development is also fuelled by a DIY (Do It Yourself) movement enabled by Massive Open Online Courses (MOOCs) and online platforms such as EdX, Coursera, Swayam, and numerous others. Domestic organizations, in lieu of imitating the MNC culture, have been undertaking regular training programmes and deploying increased budgets for the same.

Policy implications

This piece of research has helped in uncovering the following important insights about executive-education programmes.

The challenges posed by VUCA markets and the organizational capability gaps demand a fundamental rethinking of the approach to developing the executives and high potential managers who will lead the organizations of the future. Undoubtedly, executive education is delivering predictable learning outcomes and measurable value in terms of enhanced productivity, performance, and leadership in executives. Industry 4.0 needs to be backed by Executive Education 4.0.

Needless to say, executive education builds and strengthens the employability skills and expands employment opportunities. However, organizations also need to facilitate positive employability support mechanisms which can help executives build trajectories towards sustainable employment. Executive-education programme providers must address two major current gaps: The gap between the skills required by executives and those provided by suppliers ('the skills gap'), and the gap that separates skill acquisition from skill application ('the skills transfer gap').

Organizations should deploy more budget for the executive-education programmes. One of the valuable inputs to policymakers and heads of organizations both in public and private organizations is to take concerted efforts to ensure and provide a significant chunk of budget for the executive education so that learning and development becomes a continuous process. The top-management executives and HR heads should take a lead in linking executive education with the improvement of their on-the-job performance.

The nature of the programmes proposed by management schools and institutions should be designed using advanced learning tools, adapted to the needs of each programme, with a focus on active participation of the executives. Programmes must be tailored to the needs of the executives and aim to improve their skills. Executive-education providers should use advanced pedagogical tools that are aligned to the skill requirement of the executives and should have an emphasis on active participation rather than passive assimilation of the learning in the programme.

Equal emphasis should be laid not only on imparting knowledge but on developing important behavioural competencies coupled with changing the mindset of executives. There is a need to bring revolutionary change in the way skill development happens, and organizations need to bring that change about through their practices. Focus should be given more on innovative techniques such as outbound or adventure learning, which entails fire walks, wall climbing, mountaineering, trust falls, river rafting, spider web, trekking, and so on, which helps to not only drive home the given concept but to develop the given behavioural competency. Other innovative pedagogical tools such as experiential learning tools, simulation exercises, role plays, management games, or In-basket exercises also play an important role in developing different competencies when compared to traditional classroom-based lectures. Therefore, executive-education programme providers must incorporate these experiential learning tools and simulation activities in the executive-development programmes. By weaving experiential learning into executive education, powerful experiences can be crafted which can deliver impactful learning outcomes.

Post-training initiatives or interventions should be adopted by the organizations to strengthen the learning for the executives. Post-training interventions are any learning activity which complements the primary classroom/physical workshop intervention. These could include any of the following: Email communications with the training content/deck/pdfs; Videos related to the content of the training; Application exercises (case-lets or scenarios) wherein learners can apply their learning; Webinars with experts in the subject; Use of WhatsApp/social platforms for interactions; Game-based content; Case Studies, and so on.

There is a need to revolutionize the way executives learn by focusing on informal learning and collaborative learning that is dynamic, social, and personal. The thrust needs to be on continuously blurring the lines between what is taught in classroom-based advanced management courses and the situations and challenges executives or managers confront in their jobs. Learning technologies such as self-authored video, online channels, virtual classroom learning, and MOOCs are becoming more promising over time. Hence, organizations should make an attempt to integrate new learning technologies in the existing mode of conducting executive-education programmes.

Note

1 https://darpg.gov.in/sites/default/files/5%20DARPG%20Guwahati%20-Final.pdf https://dopt.gov.in/tool-kit-competency-dictionary-civil-services-officers (accessed 23 April 2020).

References

Boyatzis, R. E. (1982). *The competent manager: A model for effective performance.* New York: John Wiley & Son.

Boyne, G. A. (2002). Public and private management: What's the difference? *Journal of Management Studies*, 39(1), 97–122. https://doi.org/10.1111/1467-6486.00284.

Das, G. (2020, February 1). Budget 2020: Govt proposes Rs. 3000 crore for skill development. *Business Today.* www.businesstoday.in/union-budget-2020/decoding-the-budget/budget-2020-govt-proposes-rs-3000-crore-for-skill-development/story/395227.html.

Fernández-Aráoz, C., Groysberg, B., & Nohria, N. (2011). How to hang on to your high potentials. *Harvard Business Review*, 89(10), 76–83.

Government of India-UNDP (2013). *Country programme action plan.* United Nations Development Programme, New Delhi.

Hondeghem, A., & Vandermeulen, F. (2000). Competency management in the Flemish and Dutch civil service. *The International Journal of Public Sector Management*, 13(4), 343.

Ken Research (2015). *India executive education market outlook to 2020-preference for skill based MDPs and virtual education to drive future.* www.kenresearch.com/education-and-recruitment/education/india-executive-education-market-research-report/675-99.html.

Kroner, G. (2014). Does your LMS do this? *Edutechnica.* http://edutechnica.com/2014/01/07/a-model-for-lms-evolution/. (Accessed September 2015).

Palmisano, S. J. (Ed.) (2010). *Capitalizing on complexity: Insights from the global chief executive officer survey.* New York, USA: IBM Insights Report. https://www.ibm.com/downloads/cas/1VZV5X8J.

Pathak, K. (2013, October 2). This slowdown, B-schools bet big on executive education. *Business Standard.* www.business-standard.com/article/management/this-slowdown-b-schools-bet-big-on-executive-education-113100200832_1.html.

Robinson, S. L., & Rousseau, D. M. (1994). Violating the psychological contract: Not the exception but the norm. *Journal of Organizational Behavior*, 15(3), 245–259. https://psycnet.apa.org/doi/10.1002/job.4030150306.

Schein, E. H. (1978). *Career dynamics: Matching individual and organizational needs.* Boston: Addison-Wesley Publishing Company.

Schrage, M. (2014). Big data's dangerous new era of discrimination. *Harvard Business Review* [Blog Network]. http://blogs.hbr.org/2014/01/big-datasdangerous-new-era-of-discrimination.

Annexure

Competency definitions

1. Ethos

Competency		Definition
1.1)	People First	Passion for serving people with special care for the marginalized and disadvantaged. Being approachable, welcoming, caring and rising above bias while interacting with people. Understands the needs of the people and constantly strives to improve the services.
1.2)	Strategic thinking	Ability to understand dynamic internal and external environment and its impact. Responds to the opportunities and challenges for the betterment of society.
1.3)	Organizational awareness	Understanding of the organization's mandate, structure, policies, processes, norms and its interface with other organizations. It also includes an understanding of the organization's informal structures, power dynamics and constraints.
1.4)	Commitment to the organization	Aligns behaviours and interests with the needs and goals of the organizations.
1.5)	Leading Others	Ability to engage, energise, and enable the team to excel.

2. Ethics

Competency		Definition
2.1)	Integrity	Consistently behaves in an open, fair and transparent manner, honours one's commitments and works to uphold the Public service values.
2.2)	Self-Confidence	Belief in own capability to accomplish a task and being able to express confidence in dealing with challenging circumstances without being arrogant or boastful.

Competency		Definition
2.3)	Attention to Detail	Having an underlying drive to being thorough and meticulous and to comply with procedures, rules, guidelines, and standards. Digs deeper and strives to reduce uncertainties and errors.
2.4)	Takes Accountability	Takes ownership for outcomes (successes or failures) while addressing performance issues fairly and promptly.

3. *Equity*

Competency		Definition
3.1)	Consultation and consensus Building	Ability to identify the stakeholders and influencers, seek their views and concerns through formal and informal channels. Build consensus through dialogue, persuasion, reconciliation of diverse views/interests and trusting relationships.
3.2)	Decision Making	Makes timely decisions that takes into account relevant facts, tasks, goals, constraints, risk and conflicting points of view.
3.3)	Empathy	Empathy is about being able to accurately hear out and understand the thoughts, feelings and concerns of others, even when these are not made explicit.
3.4)	Delegation	Delegates responsibility with the appropriate level of autonomy so that others are free to innovate and take the lead.

4. *Efficiency*

Competency		Definition
4.1)	Result Orientation	High drive for achieving targets and competing against a standard of excellence.
4.2)	Conceptual thinking	Understanding a situation or environment by putting the pieces together and identifying patterns that may not be obviously related. Connecting the dots while resisting stereotyping.
4.3)	Initiative and Drive	Contributing more than what is expected in the job. Refusing to give up when faced with challenges and finding or creating new opportunities.
4.4)	Seeking Information	An underlying curiosity to know more about things, people, or issue. This includes "digging" for exact information and keeping up-to-date with relevant knowledge.

(Continued)

Competency		Definition
4.5)	Planning and coordination	Ability to plan, organize and monitor work with effective utilization of resources such as time, money, and people.
4.6)	Desire for Knowledge	Keeps up-to-date with relevant knowledge and technology, share latest developments with others, and advocates the application of acquired knowledge.
4.7)	Innovative thinking	Open to change, approaches issues differently, offers alternate/out of box solutions and strives for efficiency by working smartly.
4.8)	Problem Solving	Understanding a situation by breaking it into small parts, organizing information systematically and setting priorities.
4.9)	Developing Others	Genuinely believes in others' capabilities to develop and take personal responsibility for their development. Creates a positive environment for learning and provides developmental opportunities for individual and team.
4.10)	Self-awareness and Self-control	Identifies one's own emotional triggers and controls one's emotional responses. Maintains sense of professionalism and emotional restraint when provoked, faced with hostility or working under increased stress. It includes resilience and stamina despite prolonged adversities.
4.11)	Communication Skills	Articulates information to others in language that is clear, concise, and easy to understand. It also includes the ability to listen and understand unspoken feelings and concerns of others.
4.12)	Team-Working	Working together as a unit for common goal, building teams through mutual trust, respect and cooperation.

Source: DoP&T Civil Services Competency Dictionary, Government of India.

Index

Page numbers in *italic* indicate a figure and page numbers in **bold** indicate a table on the corresponding page.

3D printing 28
4th industrial revolution 252; opportunities and challenges 197; skills needed in 197–198
11th Five Year Plan (2007-2012) 170
XII Plan period (2012-2017) 213, 214
'100 per cent placement' 263

'academic campus connect policy' 129
Academic Credit Bank System 212
academic excellence 115, 116, 121, 122, 145
academic factors 118, 120
academic interface programme 123
academic internships 235
acquired skills gap (ASG) 116–117
adaptability 115, 127, 140–142, 145
adaptive learning 203–204
Adult Education 192–193n8
Adult Schools 176
agriculture 2, 4, 69, 75, 97; households 46; workers 77
AICTE-CII Survey of Industry (2018) 264
AICTE Instruction for Vocational Programmes 223
AICTE Internship Guidelines 236
All India Council of Technical Education (AICTE) 171, 186, 190, 198–200, 213, 214, 243, 258, 264, 266, 276, 288, 301
All India Survey on Higher Education (AISHE) 134, 219, 249
All India Management Association and PricewaterhouseCoopers (AIMA-PwC) 260
analytics of emotions 204
Anand Group 225
Anglo-Saxon model 169, 183
Annual Employability survey 134
ANOVA 308
Apprentices Act (1961) 33
apprenticeships 149, 150, 152, 170, 176, 185, 216, 231, 232, 234
aptitude 12, 121, 125, 128, 148, 151
Article 19, Indian Constitution 53
artificial intelligence (AI) 28, 134, 139, 239, 260, 261
Aspiring Minds 139, 263
Assam Government 221
ASSOCHAM Education Committee (AEC) 135
Associated Chambers of Commerce and Industry of India (ASSOCHAM) 135
Association of Indian Skills Universities (AISU) 221
Australia 212
automation 3, 14, 28, 34, 35, 37, 77, 106, 127, 263
'autopoietic' system 208

bachelor of vocational studies (B. Voc.) programme 174, 186–188, 190–192, 200, 213, 214, 219–221, **220**, 223, 225–228, 244
bachelor of skill (B.Skill.) 200
Bangladesh 181, 182
Bangladesh National Skill Development Policy 2011 181
banking industry employers 119
'Bank Young Bankers' 124
BFDS for Diploma 225

Bharat Sanchar Nigam Limited (BSNL) 243
Bhartiya Skill Development University 219, 223–226
Bihar 10, 60
BITS Pilani 261
Blackboard 262
Board of Examination and Evaluation 188
Bourneville College 226
'bumping down' effect 153
Bureau of Manpower and Training (BMET) 181–182
business education 266
B&W SSC 226

Cabinet Committee on Skill Development 12
'Camps on Entrepreneurship' 286
campus engagement policy 123
campus facilities 122, 129
campus facilities index 121, 122
capital markets 30, 32
Career Education in IBM Software (CEIS) 226
'careerism' 291, 295
CARE Rating 14
CASECAC framework 203, *203*, 205
case study method 297–298
caste 90, 106; and education level 7, 7–8; *see also specific castes*
casual employment 94, 96
casual labour 8, 44, 46
Census Adjustment Multiplier (CAM) 69
Census Commissioner 60
Census of India 38, 44, 69, 157
Census Projected Population 69
Central Board of Secondary Education (CBSE) 172, 177
Central Staff Training and Research Institute (CSTARI) 177
Centre for Advancing & Launching Enterprises (CrAdLE) 287
Centre for Monitoring Indian Economy (CMIE) 14, 268
Centre for Policy Research in Higher Education (CPRHE) 15
chatbots 261
China 62, 173, 176, 180, 183, 212
Civil Services Competency Dictionary 293
classroom-based lectures 297, 304
cloud campus 239
cloud technologies 262
coaching 237, 298, 304
co-agglomerations 41
Code on Social Security (2019) 48
cognitive jobs 2, 3
cognitive skills 134
commercialization of technology 252
communication skills 114–116, 129, 140–143, 145
communities of practice (CoP) 238
community colleges (CC) 186, 213, 214, 243
Competency Based Curriculum (CBCs) 177, 178
competency dictionary 293
Compound Annual Growth Rate (CAGR) 299
Comptroller and Auditor General of India 192n6
computational statistics 28
computational thinking 204
computerization 28
computer skills 115, 129, 145
Concentrix 225
conceptualization skills 115, 116, 143, 145, 148
consumption expenditure 46
context-based teaching 204–205
Continuous Internal Evaluation (CIE) 150
contractualization 26
corporate social responsibility 124
corporate training market 299
Coursera 297, 311
COVID-19 pandemic 13, 14
credit-based modular programmes 186
credit-based semester system 175, 214
critical thinking 3, 140–142
crossover learning 203
culture-building competencies 308
Current Daily Status (CDS) 82
Current Weekly Status (CWS) 82
curriculum: industry-oriented 258–259; quality 201, 202

Daikin Air Conditioning 226
data mining 28
data science 134
decent employment 90, 106
Deen Dayal Upadhyay Knowledge Acquisition and Upgradation of Skilled Human Abilities and

Livelihood (KAUSHAL) Centres 186, 213, 214, 220
deindustrialization 28
Delhi 61
Delhi Government 281
demographic dividend/disaster 27–28, 34, 35
demonstration and simulation activities 298
Department of Information and Technology 243
Department of Personnel and Training (DOPT) 293–295, 300, 309
Department of School Education and Literacy 192n8
Department of Science and Technology (DST) 280, 287
dependent self-employment 48
design thinking 239
Dia Vikas Capital Pvt. Ltd. 225
Digi NXT 239
digitalization 4, 127
digital methods 204
digital payments 261
digital technologies 262
diploma graduates 92, 93, 105, *105*
Director-General of Employment and Training (DGET) 198
disguised employment 48
disheartened labour force **85**, 85–86
disruptive technologies 260–262
'Disruptive Technologies: Advances that will transform Life, Business and the Global Economy' 262
Dissimilarity Index (DI) 102
Do It Yourself (DIY) movement 311
domain knowledge 139, 141
domain specific skills 141–143, 151; general education graduates 142; professional education skills 143; technical education skills 142
domain-wise employment opportunities and employability *136*, 136–137, **138**, *138*
Draft Emigration Bill 2019 64

'Earn while you Learn' 152
East West Automation Tech. Pvt. Ltd. 225
e-Chai 276
economic growth 1–6, 13–17, 25, 27, 34, 38, 39, 68, 89, 106, 153, 260, 275
Economic Growth-Human Development (EG/HD) 4
economic reforms 37, 89, 102, 170, 183
economic returns 208
EDII's alumni accomplishments 283–285
educated entrepreneurs 44
educating emerging entrepreneurs 274, *274*
'Educating the Next Wave of Entrepreneurs: Unlocking Entrepreneurial Capabilities to Meet the Global Challenges of the 21st Century' 211
education: destination regions **58**, 59; and disheartened labour force 85, **85**; distribution of men and women **45**; and employment 62; female migration for 53; in household industry and non-household industry 42–43, *43*; inequalities 10; levels *157–158*, 157–159, 162; LFPR and age groups 71, 75; and manufacturing sector workers 77–79, **78**; migration for 57, 60–62; and non-manufacturing-sector workers **79**, 79–80; planning 170; policy 165; quality 52, 92, 96, 106, 280; and sector-wise labour force participation 70–71; and service sector workers 80–82, **81**, 99; systems 2, 12, 196; types 69; and unemployment 82, **83–84**; and workers in agriculture and allied sector 75, **76**, 77, 99; and WPRs 92–93, **99**
EdX 297, 311
efficiency-driven economies 208
e-learning 196, 298, 304
elementary occupations 155, 156
Eleventh Five-Year Plan document 31
embodied learning 204
e-mentoring 237
empirical method (EM) 154–155
employability 2, 10, 15, 52, 57, 59, 208, 217; gap 263–264; graduate 17, 118–125; lack of 153; skills 11–14, 112, 123, 128, 132, 135, 138–139, 143, 151
employability quotient (EyQ) 117–122, **118**, 129
employability skill development: and college/university experience of employees 148, **148**; initiatives by

general, technical, and professional education institutions 149–151
employee(s): campus experience 121–125, **122**; college/university experience and employability skill development 148, **148**; job preparedness 143, 145; from non-urban locations 119–120; perspective on skill importance 143, **144**, 145; self-rating of skills 145, **146**, 148
employer: and employee gap 126, *126*; perception on employability skills 138–139; and student interactions 129
employment 1–6, 13–17, 25–27, 28, 37, 38, 46, 69; in agriculture and allied sectors 75, **76**, 77, 97; and education 7–8, 62; industrial structure of **98**; in manufacturing sector 77–79, **78**, 97; in mining and quarrying **160**, 161; nature and structure of 94–96, *95*, *96*; in non-manufacturing sector **79**, 79–80; opportunities 64, 89, 90, 93, 97, 100, 106, 111, 231; patterns 69; quality 90, **95**, 96, 106; in service sector 80–82, **81**; structural shifts and social category 97–99, **98**, *98*
Enrich Salons 226
Enterprise Development Centres (EDCs) 240
Enterprise Development Vertical 240
entrepreneurial university 255
entrepreneurship 38, 39, 150, 151, 207, 240
Entrepreneurship Curriculum 281
Entrepreneurship Development Cells 276, 280, 287
Entrepreneurship Development Courses (EDCs) 287
Entrepreneurship Development Institute of India (EDII) 269, 270, 281–282, *283*, 287
entrepreneurship education 210–212, 268–288; B-schools offering **277**; curriculum 278–279, *279*; EDII 281–285; evolution *275*, 275–276; hard and soft skills **278**; higher-education institutions to support 269–270; importance of 272–275, **273**; mentoring pool for *276*; recommendations to strengthen 285–288; role of government in promoting 280–281; status 277–279; triple helix model 270–271, **271–272**
environmental education 13
equal opportunity employment policies 119, 120
Erasmus+UKIERI 226
establishments 37, 44, 48
ethnicity 90, 106
European Center for the Development of Vocational Training 242
European Council 242
executive education 290–313; for career planning 290–292; competence assessment 309–310; competencies and training pedagogy 305, **306**, 307–308; competency-based management 293–294; demographic difference and categories of competencies 308–309; Indian Institute of Public Administration (IIPA) 300; methodology 294–295; Mintzberg's managerial role theory 292–293; policy implications 311–313; providers 295–297; remote and personalized learning platforms 297; respondents' perception on pedagogic tools 304, **305**; respondents profile 301, **302–304**; training pedagogy and learning tools 297–300
Executive-Fellow Program in Management 301
Executive Management Program 301
Executive MBA (EMBA) 296
experiential learning 150, 177, 211, 232, 233, *282*, 304, 305, 308, 311
exploratory factor analysis (EFA) 301, **305**
extracurricular activities 123

factor-driven economies 208
faculty competencies 259
Faculty Development Programmes (FDPs) 287
family migration 52
Fellow Programme in Management (FPM) 281
feminisation of migration 53
Field Testing Stations 241
Focus Group Discussion (FGD) 116, 119, 122, 140
foreign language skills 114, 115, 148
formal classroom teaching methods 203

formal education 44, 154, 176, 231, 232, 238, 240
formal enterprises 39–44, 49n11, 183
formal learning 200, 205, 232
France 184
free-market approach 30
full-time internship 236
functional skills 128
'future labour power' 60
future-ready education 208–209; competency-based 209; technology based self-learning 209

gainers and losers, in education migration 60–62, **61**
Gandhi National Aviation University 219
GEM India Survey 210
gender 90, 106; bias 119; and education level 7; gap in WPRs 90–91, *91*, *93*
general education 133–134, 136, 143, 145, 148, 152, 164, 165, 172–175, 186, 188, 214, 244; graduates 132, 133, 137, 142, 145, 148; institutes 149–150
General Education Council (GEC) 13
generic skills 116, 117, 121, 128, 129, 142, 151, 207
Germanic model 169, 183
Germany 212
gig worker 48
G.L Bajaj University 296
Global Chief Executive Officer survey 291
Global Compact for Safe, Orderly and Regular Migration (*GCM*, 2020) 64
Global Entrepreneurship Monitor (GEM) 210, 269
globalization 151, 208, 253, 257, 260, 266
'Global Perspective on Entrepreneurship Education and Training' 210
Good and Services Tax (GST) 49n11
governmental intervention 28–31, 33–35
government-funded training institutions 178
Government of Gujarat 281
Government of India (GoI) 14, 26, 31, 33, 35, 46, 47, 133, 171, 178, 190, 210, 223, 240, 280, 287, 292, 293, 300
government *vs.* private-sector officials 309
graduate employability determinants 118–125; employee campus experience 121–125, **122**
graduate job seekers 132–133
Graduation Outcomes (GO) 226
Grand Hyatt Mumbai 235
Gross Domestic Product (GDP) 4, 14, 25–27, 32, 39–40, 48, 75, 155, 156, 159, *159*, 161, 163, *163*, 165, 169
gross enrolment ratios (GER) 10, 250
group/team mentoring 237
Gujarat 25
Gujarat Forensic Science University 219
Gujarat Start-up saga 270

Harrod-Domar model 27
Harvard Business School 299
Haryana 25
high-end jobs 2, 3, 128
higher education 2, 10, 196, 198, 205, 243, 251; attaining ideal 209–210; basic course on entrepreneurship 286–288; enrolment in 2, 10; expansion of 10–11; funding for 61–62; girls enrolment in 69; and labour market 111; model of 215–216; quality in 12; sector 128–129, 130, 201, 217; skill development in 196; system 198, 207, 208
Higher Educational Institutes (HEIs) 12, 13, 57, 112, 121–124, 126, 129, 140, 148, 149, 151, 152, 198, 202, 205, 207, 215, 269, 272
higher-education graduates 8, 11, 15, 111; employability challenges 112–113; recruitment *140*
Higher Education Policy Retreat 2018, The 134
higher-paid jobs 10
higher secondary education 8, 70–71, 75, 82, 159, 172, 174, 175
high-tech skills 129, 130
hiring patterns and employers 139–143; common skills 140–141, *141*; domain specific skills 141–143
horizontal and vertical mobility 174–176
horizontal mismatch 154
household (HH) capital 120
household industry 38–42, *40–42*, 48, 94, 96, *97*
Hub-and-Spokes model 187, 189
Hub Partner 187–189

human capital 106, 117, 120, 156; formation 96; theory 29, 30
human resource (HR) consultancies 296
Human Resource Development (HRD) Ministry 134, 250

IBM 226, 291
ICICI Bank 226, 235
ICICI Manipal Academy 235
identity-based discrimination 96, 120
IIM-Ahmedabad 202
IISc-Bangalore 61, **62**
IIT Bombay 61, **62**
IIT Delhi 61, **62**
IIT-Kanpur 202
IIT Madras 61, **62**
illiterate workers 77, 78, 80, 81, 100, **101**, **102**
incentives 30, 33
income inequality 2–4, 10, 89, 119, 153
India Higher-Education Report (IHER) 15
India International Skills Centres 200
India Labour Report 8
Indian Civil Services 293, *294*
Indian Institute of Public Administration (IIPA) 294, 299, 300
Indian Institute of Science 226, 280
Indian Institute of Technology (IIT) **255–257**, 280
Indian Institutes of Management (IIM) 135, **255–257**, 280
Indian-origin students *63*
Indian Railways Institute of Financial Management (IRIFM) 235
Indian School of Business 299
India Ratings and Research 14
India Skills Report 134–137
industrialization 26
industrial revolution 169, 231
industrial sector 15, 16, 18, 31, 99, 113, 115, 116, 123, 126, 128–130, 150, 151, 155, 161, 164, 166
Industrial Training Institute (ITI) 31, 33, 153, 169, 170, 171, 174, 175, 177, 181
Industry 4.0 14, 28, 126, 209, 252, 263, 311
Industry 5.0 126, 209
industry-academia linkages 18–19, 129, 130, 149, 221, 249–266, **253**, **255–257**; critical factors in 257–261; practices and focus areas 252–255, 257; significance 251–252; state of technical higher education 249–250; strategies to operationalize and sustain 261–264; trend in programme-wise enrolment **250**, 250–251
Industry Integrated Dual Education Model (IIDEM) 223
industry-oriented curriculum 151
informal education 233
informal employment 3, 4, 11, 26
informal enterprises 4, 38–44, 46, 106
informality 28, 37, 39, 40, 48
informal learning 18, 176, 196, 200, 205, 233, 242
informal-sector workers 231
informal skill formation 17–18, 230–245; coaching 237; communities of practice (CoP) 238; global phenomenon 230–232; historical background 231–232; informal apprenticeship 234; internship 235–236; mentoring 236–237; Micro, Small, and Medium Enterprise (MSME) 240–241; National Institute of Information Technology (NIIT) 238–240; on-the-job training 234–235; recognition and validation 241–244; study circles 237–238; theoretical perspective 232–233
informal teaching 203
informal training 18, 212, 231, 244
Information and Communications Technology (ICT) 134, 202, 299, 311
information asymmetry 32–34
information technology (IT) 31–32, 132, 264
Infosys 32
Infosys' Global Education Centre 235
Infosys University 296
Infrastructure Leasing and Finance Services (ILFS) 192n6
in-house training 171
Initial Learning Programme 235
in-migrant students 60
innovation 3, 29, 150, 202, 205
innovation-driven economies 208
input-based traditional education system 176–180
Institute of Leadership Development (ILD) 221, 227

institutional capital 117
institutional factors 118–120
institutional theory 39
intellectual property (IP) rights 260
internal migration 51–53, 57, 64
International Authority for Professional Coaching and Mentoring 237
International Labour Organization (ILO) 2, 3, 13, 182, 193n9
international migration 51–53, 62–64
international models for higher education 212–214; initiatives towards vocationalization 213–214; integrating vocationalization 212–213
International Monetary Fund (IMF) 14
Internet of Things (IoT) 239, 263
internships 14, 149, 150, 155, 185, 216, 235–236, 240, 264
interpersonal skills 141, 235
inter-state and intra-state migration 52, 56, 57, **57**, 59, **59–60**, 61
IT-enabled services (ITeS) 31, 32, 132, 264

Jan Shikshan Sansthan 192–193n8
Japan 208
JBS 226
Jharkhand 61
JNPT 226
job evaluation method 154
jobless growth 1, 2, 4–6, 11, 15, 25–35, 106; capacity building through government intervention 33–34; demographic dividend/disaster 27–28, 34, 35; growth and employment disconnect 26–27; overview 25–26; service sector 28–29; skill development 29; skills training 29–33
job-loss growth 15, 106

Karnataka 59, 61
Kedman Skilling Private Ltd 221
Kenya 231
knowledge-driven economies 257, 260
Know Your Customer (KYC) 261
Korea 212
Kuznets, S. 38

labour force 28, 102, 106
labour-force participation rate (LFPR) 6, 15, 44, 49n13, 68–86, *70*, **72–74**; data and methods 69; education and changing employment 75, 77–82; by sector and gender groups *70*; trends in 69–71, 75; unemployment and 82, 84–86
Labour Market Information System (LMIS) 34
labour markets 3, 6, 11, 26, 32, 37, 38, 69, 71, 89, 90, 92, 93, 96, 98, 105–107, 111–114, 125, 128, 142, 143, 151, 153, 155, 162, 165, 175, 176, 180, 182, 184, 213; awareness gap 113; and higher education 111
labour migration 51, 52
LabourNet 242–243
labour regulations 26, 27
language barrier 120
layoffs 14
learner-centric environment 200–205
learner-driven education system 217
learning-by-doing 231
life skills 209–210
live project 298, 304
lower-skilled jobs 2, 3, 10, 28, 35
LSC 226
Luban Workshops 212
Lynda.com 297

machine learning (ML) 28, 134, 139, 239, 260
Madhya Pradesh 10
Maharashtra 59–61
Mahatma Gandhi National Rural Employment Guarantee Act (MGNREGA) 29
'Make in India' initiative 27
male: LFPR 6, 69–71; unemployment 104; workers 8, 100; WPRs 90, 102
Management Development Institute (MDI) 294, 299–301
Management Development Programmes (MDPs) 299, 300, 311
management games 298
managerial skills 115–117, 128, 143, 148
manpower planning 257–258
manufacturing labourers **160**, **161**, **164**
market failure 29–32, 34, 35
Market Research Reports 299
Massive Open Online Course (MOOC) 149, 280, 297, 311, 312
master craftsperson (MC) 234

Master of Business Administration (MBA) 135, 137
Master of Computer Applications (M.C.A.) 135
Master of Vocation (M. Voc.) 221, 224, 226–228
McKinsey Report (2018) 207
mean-EM method 155
MEAN Stack 239
mechanization 69, 71, 75, 77
medium-skilled jobs 2, 3
Memorandum of Understanding (MoU) 152, 190, 226, 264
micro, small, and medium enterprises (MSMEs) 32, 240–241, 275
microenterprises 47
Microsoft Excel 151
Microsoft PowerPoint 151
migration 51, **55–56**; for education 57, 60–62; international student 62–63; policy framework 64; state level scenario of student 57, 59; trends 52–53; type of **54**
Mincer equations 155, 156
Ministry of Education (MOE) 212, 244
Ministry of Employment and Labour 212
Ministry of External Affairs (MEA) 64
Ministry of Finance 12, 33
Ministry of Human Resource Development (MHRD) 169–171, 178, 190, 192n8, 198, 220, 226
Ministry of Labour and Employment 33, 48, 170, 171, 190, 192n4, 198, 242
Ministry of Micro, Small, Medium Enterprises 171, 287
Ministry of Rural Development 171
Ministry of Skill Development 198, 200
Ministry of Skill Development and Entrepreneurship (MSDE) 11, 33, 177, 198, 219, 244
Mintzberg's managerial role theory 292–293
Miranda House College 226
mobile internet 262
mobile learning 311
mobile phones 262
Model Career Centre 226
modern education system 200, 215
modular employable skills (MES) 242
Monster India Wage Index Report 2018 119
motivation-related theories 39
Movement for Alternatives and Youth Awareness (MAYA) 242
movie clips and storytelling 298
MSME Development Institute Centres (MSME-DIs) 240
Mudra loans *see* Pradhan Mantri MUDRA Yojana (PMMY)
multinational IT company 123
multiparty employment 48
multiple regression analysis 307, **307**
multitasking skills 126, 128, 129
Muni Seva Ashram 226

National Apprenticeship Promotion Scheme (NAPS) 223
National Assessment and Accreditation Council (NAAC) accreditation and ranking 226
National Commission for Enterprises in the Unorganized Sector (NCEUS) 38
National Council for Skill Development (NSDC) 198
National Council for Vocational Education and Training (NCVET) 33, 228
National Council of Educational Research and Training (NCERT) 172
National Curriculum Framework (NCF) 172
National Education Policy 2020 (NEP, 2020) 13
National Employability Report for Engineers (2016) 263
National Employment Enhancement Mission (NEEM) 223
National Higher Education Qualification Framework (NHEQF) 12, 13
National HRD Network 299
National Institute of Educational Planning and Administration (NIEPA) 15
National Institute of Electronics and Information Technology (NIELIT) 243
National Institute of Financial Management 299
National Institute of Information Technology (NIIT) 238–240
National Institute of Open Schooling (NIOS) 243

National Institutes of Technical Teacher Training and Research (NITTTR) 177
National Institutional Ranking Framework (NIRF) 61, 226
National Instructional Media Institute (NIMI) 177
nationalized finance company 124
National Literacy Mission Authority (NLMA) 243
National Management Programme 301
National Occupational Standards (NOS) 33, 177, 179, 180, 183, 184, 191, 214, 223
National Policy of Skill Development and Entrepreneurship 33
National Policy on Education 1986 173
National Programme on Technology Enhanced Learning (NPTEL) 149
National Qualification Register 179
National Register for Professional Certifications (Repertoire National des Certifications Professionnelles/ RNCP) 184
National Resource Centre 240
National Sample Survey (NSS) 4, 5, 69, 155, 156, 157
National Sample Survey Office (NSSO) 1, 6, 8, 39, 44, 46, 90, 171
National Science & Technology Entrepreneurship Development Board (NSTEDB) 276, 280, 287
National Skill Development Agency (NSDA) 33
National Skill Development Corporation (NSDC) 33–34, 171, 173, 174, 177, 179, 192n6, 221, 228, 239–240
National Skill Development Mission (NSQF) 198
National Skill Development Policy 170, 192n4
National Skills Policy 2015 176
National Skills Qualifications Framework (NSQF) 12, 33, 170, 171–181, 184, 191, 200, 214, 223, 242, 243, 245; implementation of vocational qualifications frameworks 181–186; tertiary-level programmes of vocational education 186–190; TVET challenges and 172–181
National Statistical Office (NSO) 90
National Summer Camps for Children and Youth 286
National Technical and Vocational Qualifications Framework (NTVQF) 181, 182, 193n9
National Vocational Education Qualifications Framework (NVEQF) 11–12, 170, 171, 178, 192n2, 213
National Vocational Qualifications Framework (NVQF) 169, 170, 172, 178, 181, 182, 184
National Vocational University 190
Neither in Labour Force nor in Education and Training (NLET) 84, 86
neo-liberalization 208
network mentoring 236
New Education Policy (NEP, 2020) 244
New Generation Innovation and Entrepreneurship Development Centres 280
NIIT.tv 239
Nobel, Alfred 38
Nodal Institute for Vocational Training 198
non-banking financial company (NBFC) 119, 124
non-farm employment 68, 80, 82, 106
non-household industry/workers 41–42, *42*
non-standard employment 48
NOS Sub-committee 179
not in education, employment, or training (NEET) 6
Not in Labour force Education and Training (NLET) 6, 69
NSQF Recognition of Previous Learning (RPL) Guidelines 223
NTPC School of Business 296
numeric skills 143, 145

occupational pattern of graduate 100, **101**, **102**
occupational regulation 183
occupational skills 234
online assessment 196
online courses 13
online learning *see* e-learning
on-the-job training (OJT) 187, 188, 223, 234–235, 298, 304
open and distance learning system 174
Open Basic Education (OBE) 243
open enrolment programmes 296
Open Learning Programme in Entrepreneurship (OLPE) 281

open unemployment 82, *83*, **83**–84, 86
Open University 223, 226, 227
Organization for Economic Co-operation and Development (OECD) 62, 241
organization-sponsored *vs.* self-sponsored programmes 291, 309
Orissa 10
Other Backward Classes (OBCs) 8, 9, 90; employment in 95, 96, 100; unemployment rate 103–105; WPRs of 92, 93
Other Categories (OCs) 90; employment in 95, 96, 98, 100, 106; occupational dissimilarity 102; unemployment rate 103–105; WPRs of 92, 93
outbound learning 150
out-migrant students 60, 64
Outreach and Inclusivity (OI) 226
over-education 153–156, 159, **162**, 162–164, *163*, 165
Own Account Enterprises (OAE) 5, 37, 44, 47, 48
own-account workers 44

Pandit Sundarlal Sharma Central Institute of Vocational Education (PSSCIVE) 177
part-time employment 48
payroll taxes 33
pedagogical approach and skill development 200–205; framework 203–205; innovation 202
peer mentoring 236
Peer Perception 226
people-related skills 115
perception gap 114–116, **114–116**
Periodic Labour-Force Survey (PLFS) 37–39, 44, 46, 48, 69, 90, 171
personal and personality skills 114–117, 121, 128, 143, 145, 148, 208
Planning Commission 170, 192n5, 219
positive attitude 139, 141, 142
Post Graduate Diploma in Management-Business Entrepreneurship (PGDM-BE) 281–282, **282**, *282*
Postgraduate Programme in Energy Management 301
Postgraduate Programme in Public Policy Management 301
post-training initiatives/interventions 311
poverty 4, 29, 39, 46
Pradhan Mantri Kaushal Vikas Yojana (PMKVY) 11, 33, 34, 176, 192
Pradhan Mantri MUDRA Yojana (PMMY) 47
pre-labour market investments 106
primary education 77, 78, 81, 93, 170, 204
primary school 158, 162, 285–286
Prime Minister's Employment Generation Programme (PMEGP) 47
Prime Minister's Rozgar Yojana and Rural Employment Generation Programme 47
principal component analysis 301
private colleges 11
private-sector initiatives 31, 33
private training providers 34
private universities 10–11
professional course 11
professional education 113, 135, 136, 145, 148, 251; graduates 143, 145, 148; institutes 150–152; skills 143
professional language skills 120
profits and workers' wages *26*
property rights 32
public goods theory 29–30
public-private partnerships 255
Public Sector Enterprise (PSE) 309
Public Sector Undertakings (PSUs) 178

Qualification Frameworks (QF) 11–12, 183–185
Qualification Packs (QPs) 177, 179, 183, 184, 191
Qualification Registration Committee 179
Quality Review Committee (QRC) 179
quota system 33

Railway University 219
Recognition of Prior Learning (RPL) 34, 176, 242–245
recruitment process 120
'*Redistribution with Growth*' (Chenery et al.) 2
Regional Testing Centres 241
regular employment 94, 96
Research and Development (R&D) 251–252, 255, 261

Research and Professional Practice (RP) 226
research orientation of industry-academia 259–260
research university 255
resource allocation theory 39
reverse mentoring 237
robotic process automation (RPA) 139
robotics 239
Robust National Competency Standards 212
role plays 298
Roop Auto 225
rote learning 176–180
rural India 25, 46, 47, 70, 75, 90
rural-to-rural migration 53

Samagra Shiksha 174
Sardar Patel University of Police 219
Scheduled Castes (SCs) 7–9, 89, 90; employment in 95, 96, 98–100, 106; occupational dissimilarity 102; unemployment rate 103–105; WPRs of 92, 93
Scheduled Tribes (STs) 7–9, 89, 90; employment in 95, 96, 98–100, 106; occupational dissimilarity 102; unemployment rate 103, 104; WPRs of 92, 93
Scheme of Career Orientation 213
'school of education' 124
Scotland's Colleges International (SCI) 226
Seacom Skills University 219, 223, 224, 226
secondary education 1, 8, 77, 78, 80–82, 85, 92, 172–175, 286
Second Industrial Revolution 197
Sector Skill Councils (SSCs) 33, 35, 171, 175, 177, 179, 188, 223
sector-specific skills 115
Security and Criminal Justice 219
self-and-wage employment programmes 106
self-directed learning 209, 232
self-employment 5, 8, 11, 37–39, 46–48, 48n1, 94, 96, 106, 174, 184, 213, 217
self-learning 209
Senegal 231
senior secondary vocational schools 180–181
services-led economy 28, 34
Shivam Dairy/GNG Group 225
Shiv Nadar University 296
Shri Vishwakarma Skill University 219, 221, 224–227
single-worker firms *see* Own Account Enterprises (OAE)
SKF 226
Skill Acquisition and Knowledge Awareness for Livelihood Promotion Programme (SANKALP) 200
skill development 29, 30, 32–35, 153, 165, 196–200, *199*, 205, 208, 217, 240, 291; pedagogical approach towards 200–205; skill universities 200
Skill Development Centres (SDC) 221
Skill Development Vertical 240
skilled manpower 28–32
skill enhancement training 210–212
skill gaps 132, 133, 135, 154, 242, 297
Skill India Mission 33
"Skill India" programme 11, 239, 266
Skill Knowledge Partners (SKPs) 187–190
skill obsolescence 154
skill perception gap 145, **147**
skill shortages 154
skills mismatch 17, 111–130, 153–156, 165; determinants of graduate employability 118–125; with employer community 113–117; future vision of employers **125**, 125–128, *127*; graduate employability challenges 112–113; policy implications 128–130
Skills Qualification Packs 223
skills training 29–33, 35, 153; firm size 30–31; government failure in 31; information asymmetry 32–33; limited involvement of industry sectors 31–32; self-investment in 30
Skills Training Providers 188
skill types 165
skill universities 200, 219–228; academic and industrial partners of 225–226; courses and fee structure 221, **222**, 224; degrees/programmes in 226–227; faculty in 224–225; growth of skill education 220–221; lack of competent faculty and infrastructure 227; list of **221**;

NAAC accreditation and ranking 226; placement of students 225; students enrolment in 223–224; *vs.* traditional universities 227–228
Skill University, Darrang district 221
skill wage premium 32
Small and Medium Enterprises (SMEs) 171
Small Industries Development Organization (SIDO) 240
social capital 117, 120
social disparities 90
social networks 89, 96, 98, 99
social security 27, 28, 38, 39, 48, 89, 94, 106
social security schemes 48
socio-demographic factors 118
socio-economic development 68
socio-economic inequalities 89
soft skills 119, 124, 125, 128, 134, 151, 207, 217, 234, 258
Sony India Company 221
South Asia 52, 53
specialized skills training 128
SS 226
SSC Governing Council 179
Stack Route Immersive (SRI) 239
standard of living 68, 75
start-up entrepreneurs 268
Start-up India 210
Start-up NIDHI 280
State Boards 172, 177
stealth assessment 204
strategic consultancies 296–297
'Strengthening HRM of Civil Service' 293
structural transformation 26, 27, 68, 75, 77, 80
student-centred approach 201
student engagement programmes 123, 129
student-faculty-employer programmes 124
Student Innovation Fund (SIF) 281
student migration 52, 57, 59, **61**, 61–64
Student Start-up and Innovation Policy (2017-2021) 281
Study Webs of Active-Learning for Young Aspiring Minds (SWAYAM) 149, 280, 297, 311
subjective method 154
subsidies 30, 31, 33, 34
Sustainable Development Goals (SDGs) 2, 38, 51, 106
sustainable employment progression 128
Switzerland 213
Symbiosis Skills 223, 226, 227

Tamil Nadu 60, 61
Tata Consultancy Services (TCS) 32–33
Tata Institute of Social Sciences (TISS)-School of Vocational Education (SVE), VET programme at 186–190, 191; assessment 188–189; curriculum and pedagogy 188; model 187–188; quality monitoring 189; sustainable funding model 189–190
teacher education programmes 180
Teaching, Learning & Resources (TLR) 226
Teamlease Skills University 223, 224, 226, 227
Technical and Vocational Education and Training (TVET) 31, 34, 35, 169–172, 183, 185, 191, 192; challenges 172–181
technical education 93, 113, 134–136, 145, 148, 198, 251, 255, 257–260, 264; graduates 142, 145, 148; institutions 150–152, 170–171, 264
technical qualification 77–80, 82
technical skills 115–117, 121, 127, 128, 139, 142, 143, 145, 148, 165
technological progress 28, 151
technological revolution 127
Technological Revolution *see* Second Industrial Revolution
Technology Business Incubators 276
Technology Development Centres (TDCs) 241
temporary employment 48
Texila Educational Management and Services 244
The IndUS Entrepreneurs (TiE) 276
Tool Rooms 241
transferable skills 216
triple helix model 270–271, **271–272**
t-test 308

UGC Instructions for Vocational Programmes 223
under-education 154, 155, 159
underemployment 153
undergraduate degrees (UG) 125, 126
undergraduates 1, 213

unemployment 1–2, 6, 10, 38, 44, 46, 68, 69, 90, 102–105, 137, 153, 268; caste and gender-specific **103**; of educated 8–11, 89, 100, 103; and labour force 82, 84–86; rate among illiterate population 103; rates in social groups **9**; youth **104**, *104*, 107
uniformity, lack of and qualifications 172–173
unincorporated enterprises 37, 38, 44, 47, 48
Unincorporated Non-Agricultural Enterprises 49n11
Union Budget (2020-2021) 219
Union Cabinet 198
United Kingdom 169
United Nations (UN) 2, 51, 64, 106
United Nations Development Programme (UNDP) 293
United Nations Educational, Scientific and Cultural Organization (UNESCO) 181, 210
universities: corporate 295–296; curriculum reforms in 2; and industry partnerships 254, **254**, 255; offering technical and professional education 134, 135; specialized 219, 226, *249*; and start-up wave 270
University Grants Commission (UGC) 12, 177, 187, 188, 190, 191, 198, 213, 214, 219, 220, 225, 227, 228, 258, 266, 276, 287, 288
unorganized sector 38, 40, 242
unorganized workers 38–39, 48
unpaid family workers 44
urban India 25, 46, 47, 69–71, 75, 90
usual principal and subsidiary status (UPSS) 82, 90
Uttarakhand 60
Uttar Pradesh 10

value-based education 13
vertical mismatch 154
virtual classrooms 262, 298, 311, 312
virtual education 299
Vocational Aptitude Systems (VAS) 189
vocational education 13, 44, 46, 48, 75, 93, 153, 172–175, 180, 191, 212, 214, 233, 244; programmes 171; tertiary-level programmes of 186–190
Vocational Education and Training (VET) 170, 171, 173, 174, 178, 191, 208, 212, 243; at TISS-SVE 186–191
vocationalization in higher education 207–208, 213–214
vocational qualification 71, 77–80, 82
vocational qualifications frameworks 172, 181–186
vocational teachers and trainers 180–181
vocational training 34, 156–159, 161, 162, 164, 165
vocational training providers (VTPs) 171, 173, 174
volatile, uncertain, complex, and ambiguous (VUCA) environment 290, 291, 297, 311
Voluntary Agencies (VA) 192–193n8

wage distribution 158, *158*
wage employment 5, 8, 9, 46, 106, 174
West Bengal 60
Wheebox 135
Wipro 32
women: career 119, 120; educated 6, 9; education and 6, 250; graduate workers 101; LFPR 6, 15, 71, 86, 157; OBC 103, 104; OC 103, 104; SC and ST communities 95, 96, 103, 104; in self-employment 95; structure of employment 97–99; WPRs 90, 102
workforce participation rates (WPRs) 44, 49n13, *91*, **94**; changing contours of 90–93, *91*, *92*; extent of occupational segregation 102; gender and caste hierarchies in 90, 95; nature and structure of employment 94–96, *95*, *96*; occupational structure and social category 99–101, **100–101**; structural shifts in employment and social category 97–99, **98**, *98*; unemployment 102–105
workforce skilling 263
working-age population 71
Work Integrated Training Programme (WITP) 187
World Bank 2, 28, 171, 202
World Economic Forum (WEF) 14, 197, 208, 211
World Employment Programme (WEP) 2

Yuva Jyoti Skill Development Centres 239

Zhongkao test 212